D0886410

The Earl & the Fairy

Story & Art by Ayuko
Original Concept by Mizue Tani

From Cobalt Series *Hakushaku to Yosei Aitsu Wa Yuga Na Daiakuto* (The Earl and the Fairy: He Is an Elegant Scoundrel)

Last time in The Earl & the Fairy

Kidnapped...twice?!

→Edgar whisks Lydia away from Huxley, only to take her for himself!

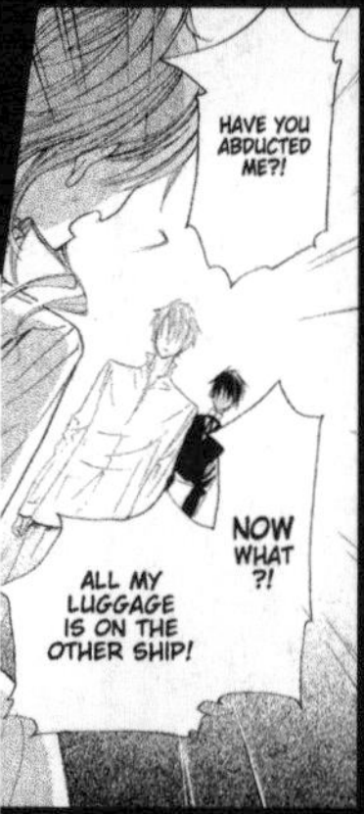
HAVE YOU ABDUCTED ME?!
NOW WHAT ?!
ALL MY LUGGAGE IS ON THE OTHER SHIP!

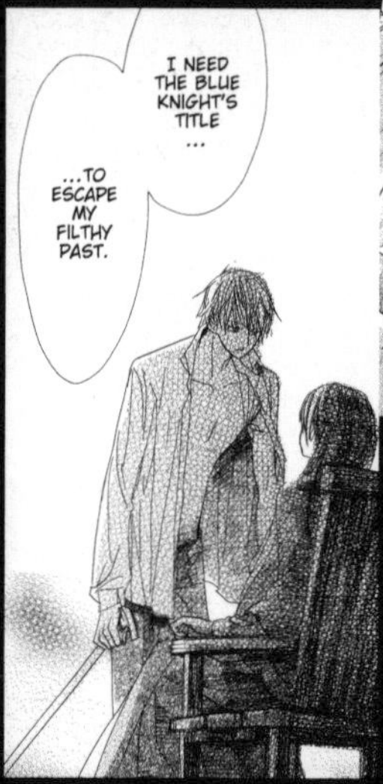
I NEED THE BLUE KNIGHT'S TITLE ...
...TO ESCAPE MY FILTHY PAST.

Nineteenth-century England, Lydia Carlton can see fairies, but she is otherwise a completely normal girl. She is on her way to spend a holiday with her father in London when a young man named Edgar drags her into a struggle over the Treasure Sword of the legendary Blue Knight Earl. Claiming to be the earl's descendant, Edgar employs Lydia to help him find the sword, but he turns out to be a fraud. And to make matters worse, he may be a thief and murderer!

What are Edgar's true motives?

←Does he want to be an earl so he can wash away his past?

The Earl and the Fairy Realm

Terms

The earl's official title is Lord Ibrazel. For generations, he who holds that title has also been a lord of the Fairy Realm. He is adored in legends and folktales and is an honorable and noble man.

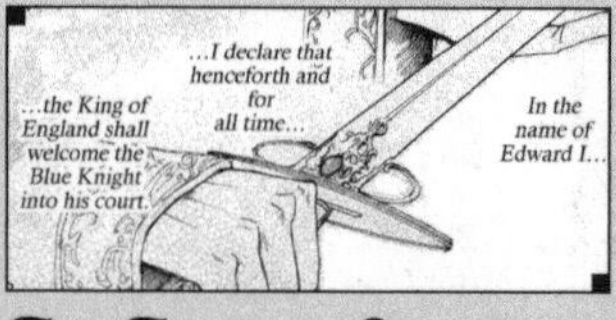
In the name of Edward I...
...I declare that henceforth and for all time...
...the King of England shall welcome the Blue Knight into his court.

The Treasure Sword and the Star Sapphire

The Treasure Sword proves the earl's right to his title. The Star Sapphire in the hilt is also called the Merrow Star.

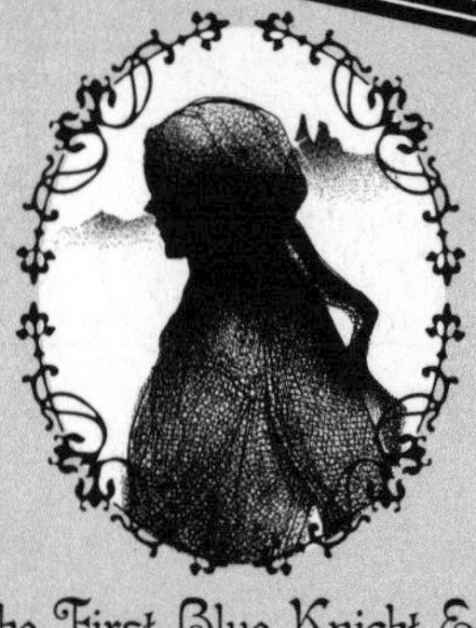

The First Blue Knight Earl

The founder of the Ashenbert family. He swore fealty to Edward I, who bestowed upon him his title and the Treasure Sword. According to legend, he led fairies in battle.

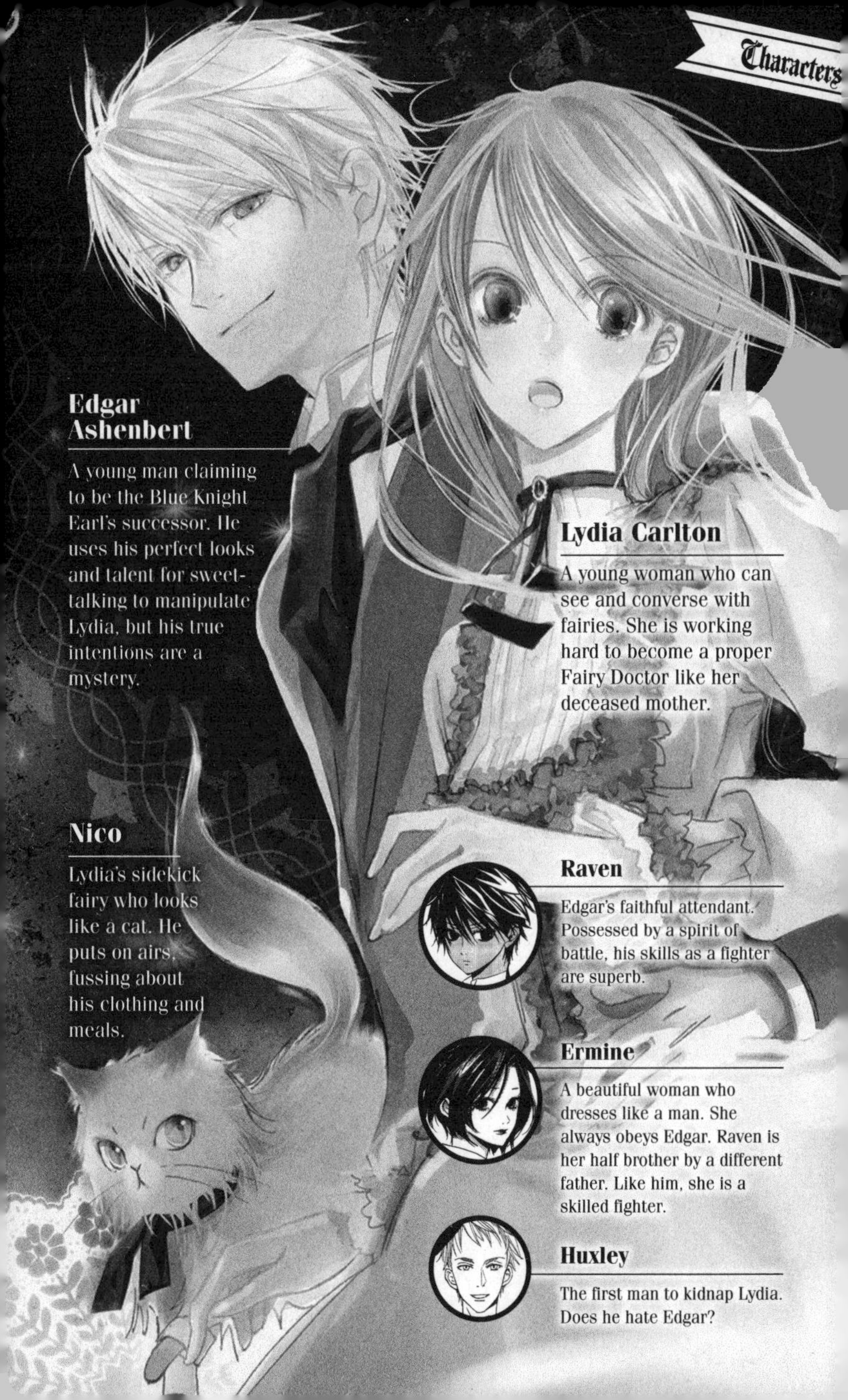

Characters

Edgar Ashenbert

A young man claiming to be the Blue Knight Earl's successor. He uses his perfect looks and talent for sweet-talking to manipulate Lydia, but his true intentions are a mystery.

Lydia Carlton

A young woman who can see and converse with fairies. She is working hard to become a proper Fairy Doctor like her deceased mother.

Nico

Lydia's sidekick fairy who looks like a cat. He puts on airs, fussing about his clothing and meals.

Raven

Edgar's faithful attendant. Possessed by a spirit of battle, his skills as a fighter are superb.

Ermine

A beautiful woman who dresses like a man. She always obeys Edgar. Raven is her half brother by a different father. Like him, she is a skilled fighter.

Huxley

The first man to kidnap Lydia. Does he hate Edgar?

The Earl & the Fairy

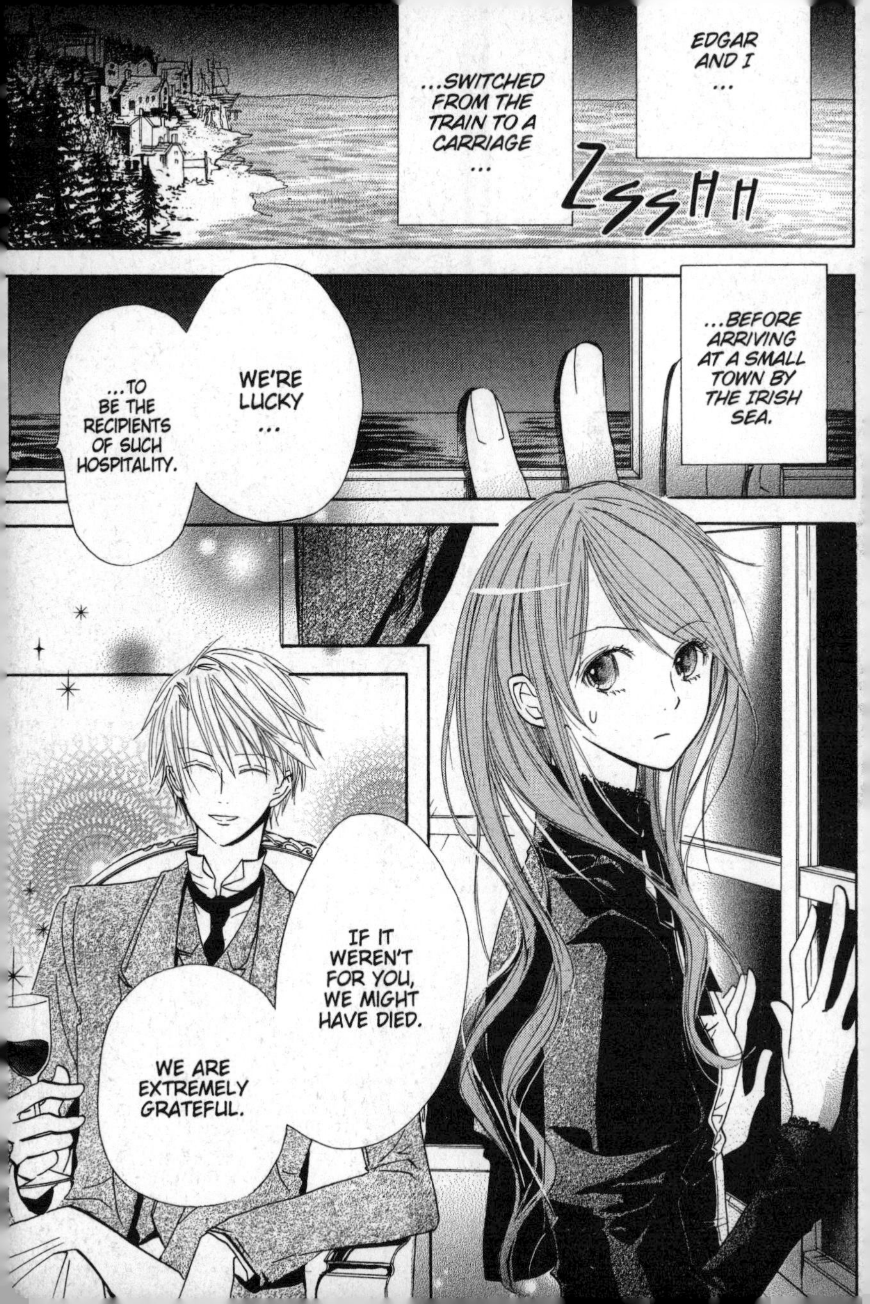
EDGAR AND I ...
...SWITCHED FROM THE TRAIN TO A CARRIAGE ...
ZSSHH
...BEFORE ARRIVING AT A SMALL TOWN BY THE IRISH SEA.
WE'RE LUCKY ...
...TO BE THE RECIPIENTS OF SUCH HOSPITALITY.
IF IT WEREN'T FOR YOU, WE MIGHT HAVE DIED.
WE ARE EXTREMELY GRATEFUL.

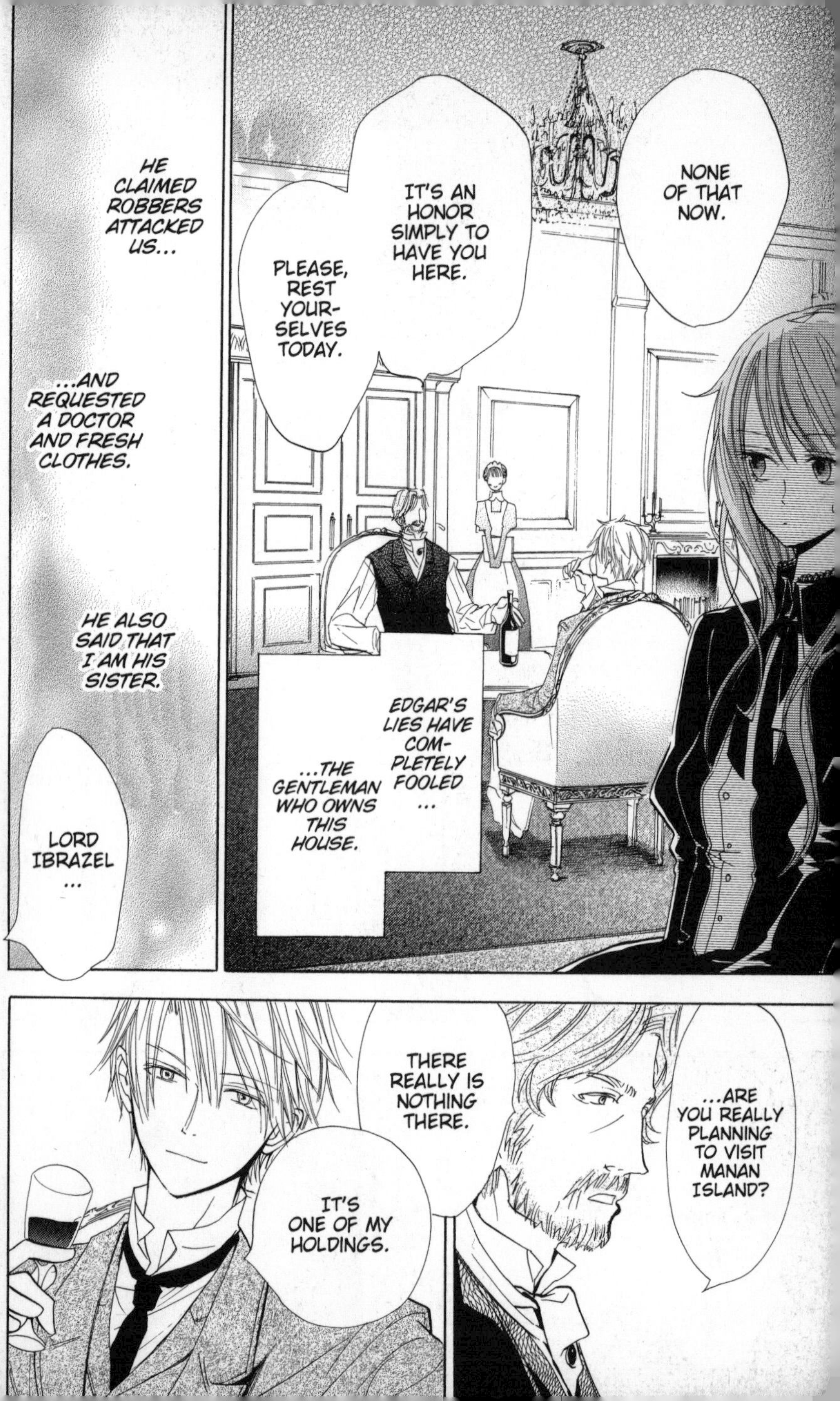
NONE OF THAT NOW.
IT'S AN HONOR SIMPLY TO HAVE YOU HERE.
PLEASE, REST YOUR-SELVES TODAY.
EDGAR'S LIES HAVE COM-PLETELY FOOLED ...
...THE GENTLEMAN WHO OWNS THIS HOUSE.
HE CLAIMED ROBBERS ATTACKED US...
...AND REQUESTED A DOCTOR AND FRESH CLOTHES.
HE ALSO SAID THAT I AM HIS SISTER.
LORD IBRAZEL ...
...ARE YOU REALLY PLANNING TO VISIT MANAN ISLAND?
THERE REALLY IS NOTHING THERE.
IT'S ONE OF MY HOLDINGS.

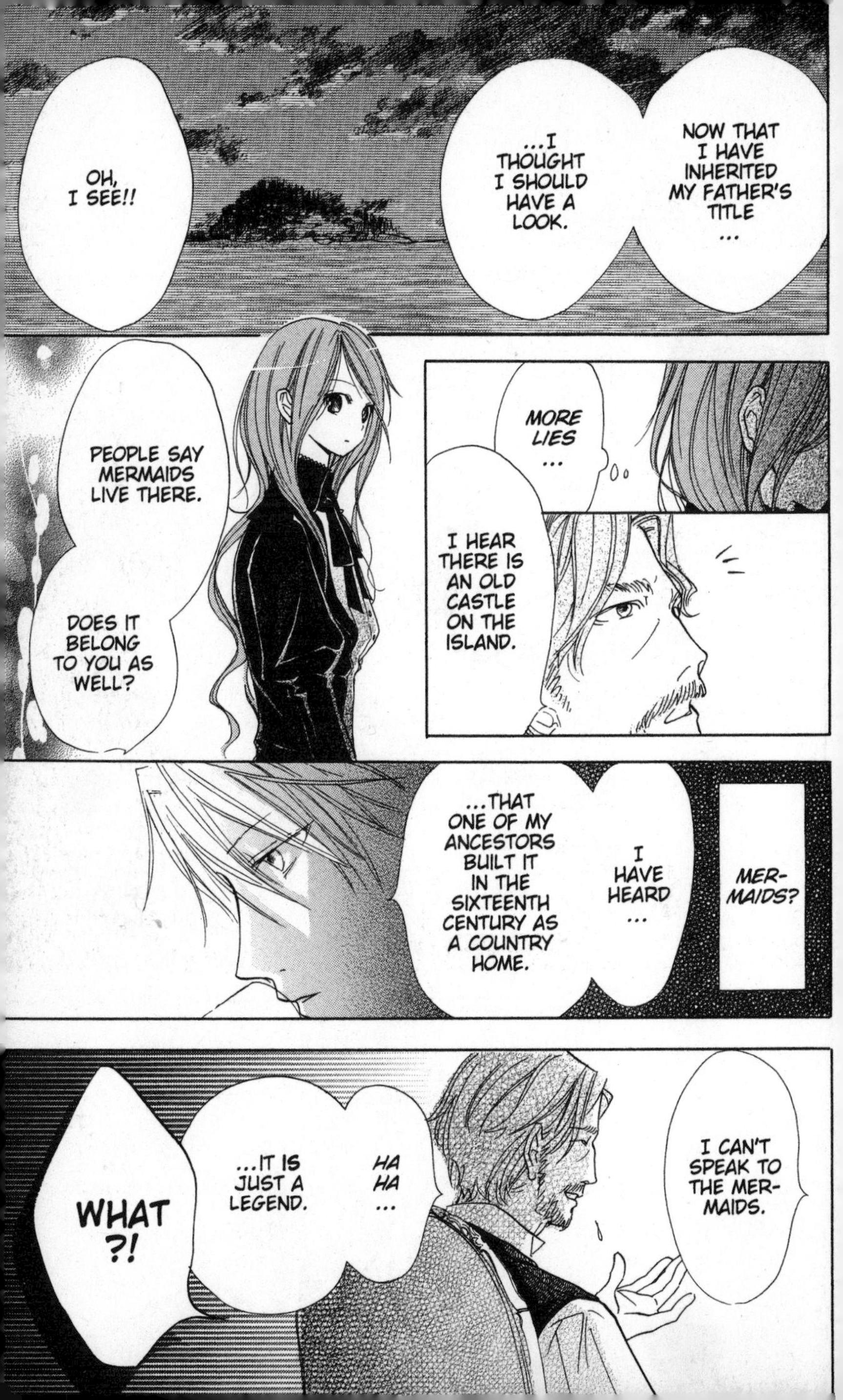
NOW THAT I HAVE INHERITED MY FATHER'S TITLE ...
...I THOUGHT I SHOULD HAVE A LOOK.
OH, I SEE!!
MORE LIES ...
I HEAR THERE IS AN OLD CASTLE ON THE ISLAND.
PEOPLE SAY MERMAIDS LIVE THERE.
DOES IT BELONG TO YOU AS WELL?
MER-MAIDS?
I HAVE HEARD ...
...THAT ONE OF MY ANCESTORS BUILT IT IN THE SIXTEENTH CENTURY AS A COUNTRY HOME.
I CAN'T SPEAK TO THE MER-MAIDS.
HA HA ...
...IT IS JUST A LEGEND.
WHAT ?!

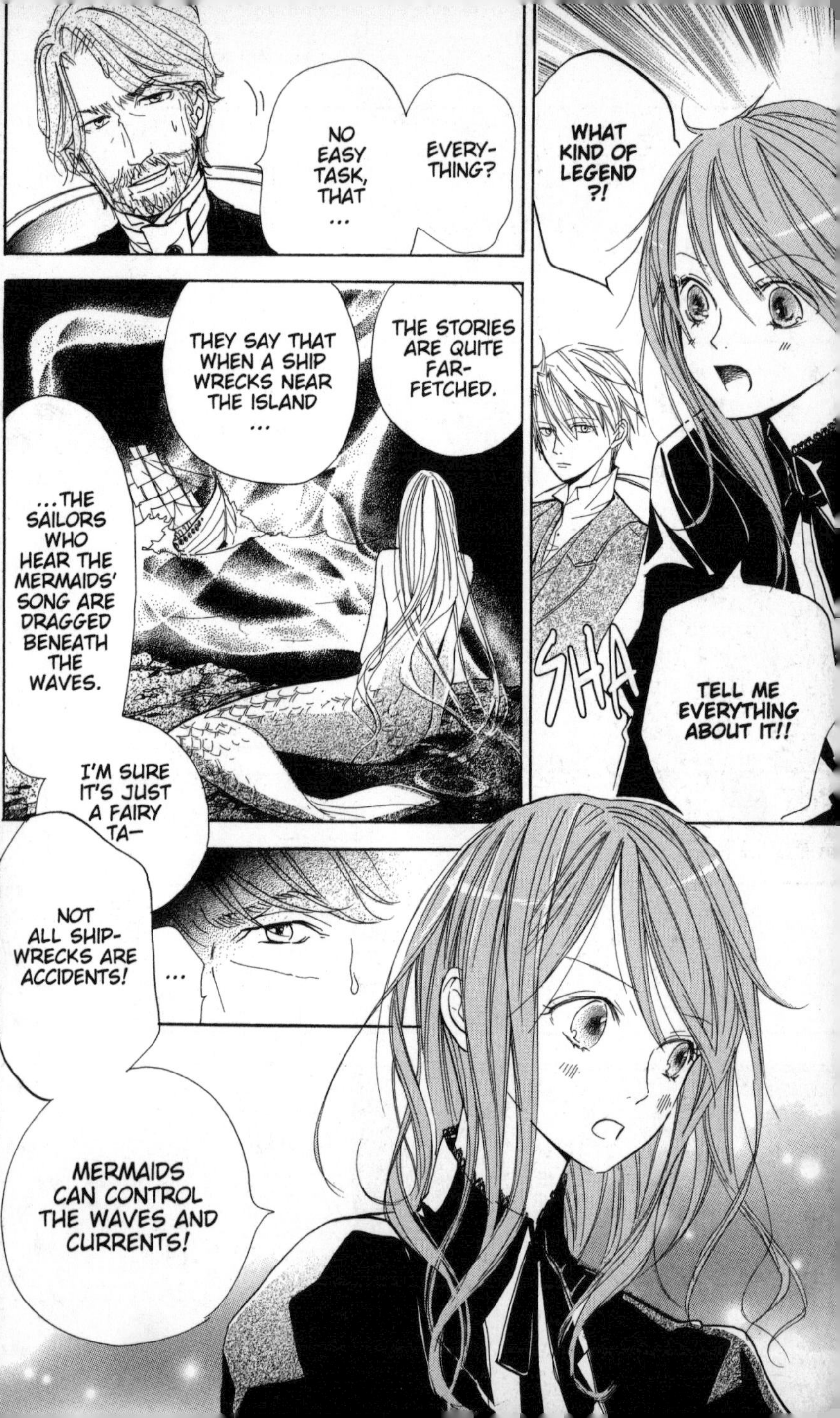
WHAT KIND OF LEGEND?!
SHA
TELL ME EVERYTHING ABOUT IT!!
EVERY-THING?
NO EASY TASK, THAT ...
THE STORIES ARE QUITE FAR-FETCHED.
THEY SAY THAT WHEN A SHIP WRECKS NEAR THE ISLAND ...
...THE SAILORS WHO HEAR THE MERMAIDS' SONG ARE DRAGGED BENEATH THE WAVES.
I'M SURE IT'S JUST A FAIRY TA—
...
NOT ALL SHIP-WRECKS ARE ACCIDENTS!
MERMAIDS CAN CONTROL THE WAVES AND CURRENTS!

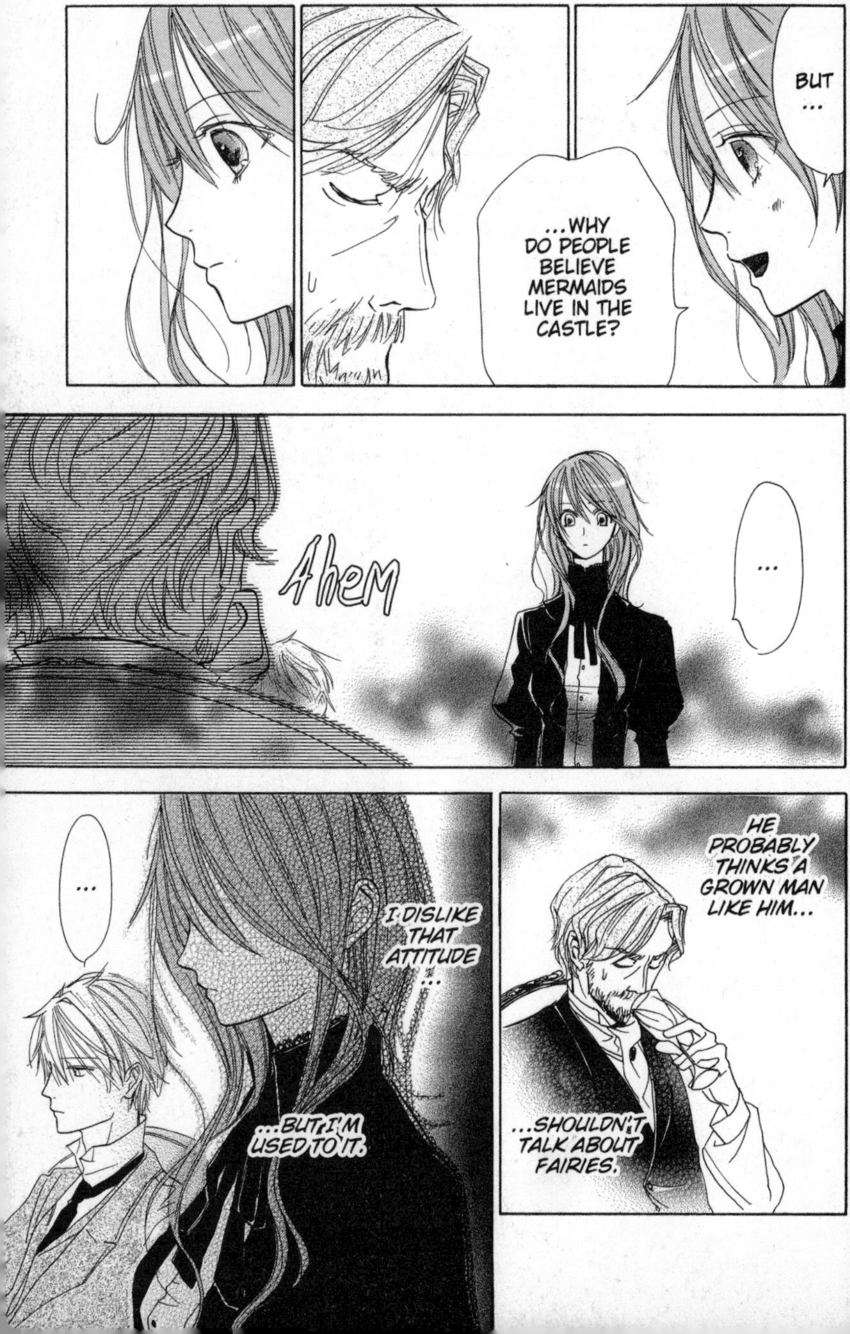

BUT ...
...WHY DO PEOPLE BELIEVE MERMAIDS LIVE IN THE CASTLE?
...
Ahem
HE PROBABLY THINKS A GROWN MAN LIKE HIM...
...SHOULDN'T TALK ABOUT FAIRIES.
I DISLIKE THAT ATTITUDE...
...BUT I'M USED TO IT.
...

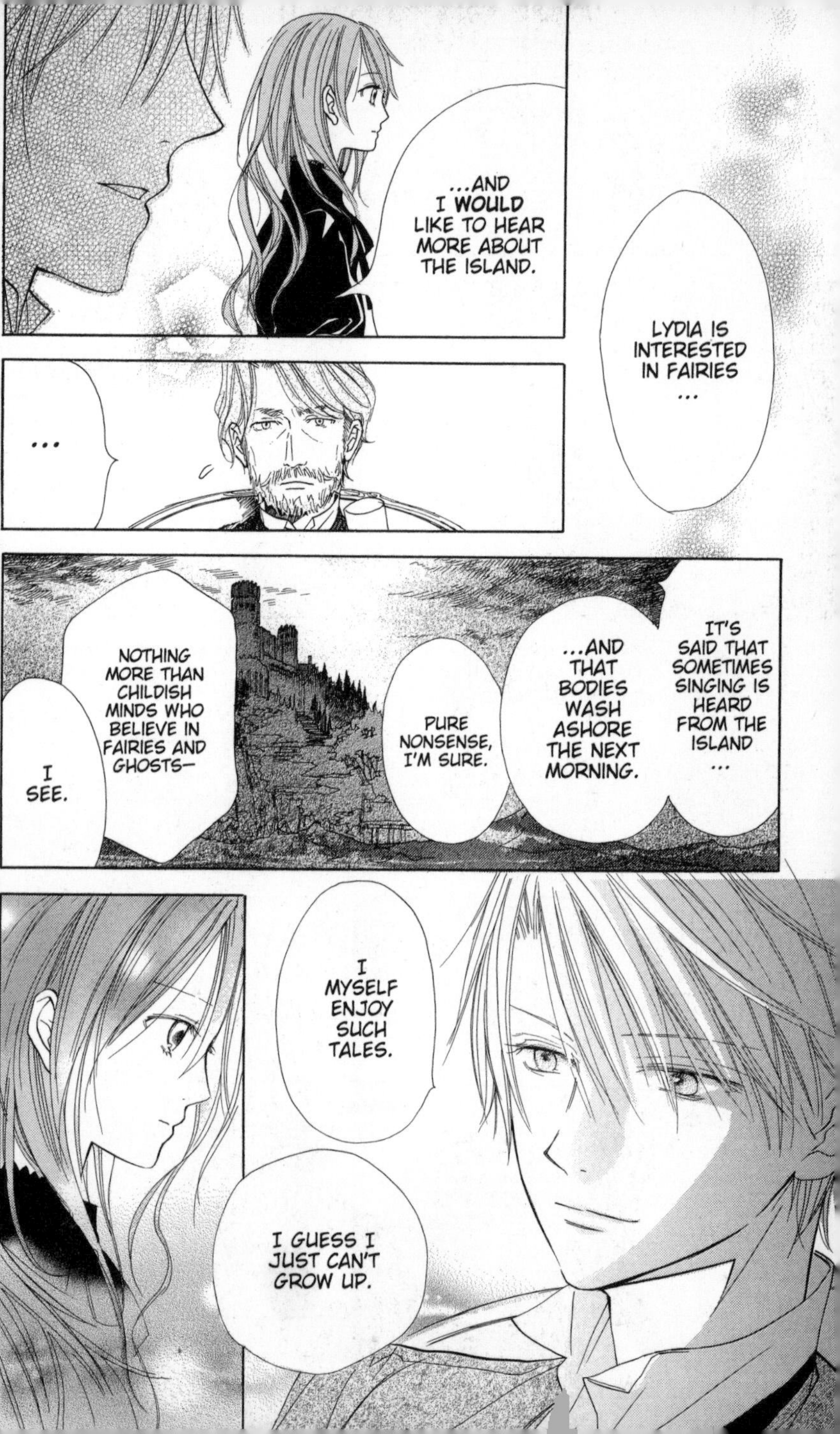
LYDIA IS INTERESTED IN FAIRIES ...
...AND I WOULD LIKE TO HEAR MORE ABOUT THE ISLAND.
...
IT'S SAID THAT SOMETIMES SINGING IS HEARD FROM THE ISLAND ...
...AND THAT BODIES WASH ASHORE THE NEXT MORNING.
PURE NONSENSE, I'M SURE.
NOTHING MORE THAN CHILDISH MINDS WHO BELIEVE IN FAIRIES AND GHOSTS—
I SEE.
I MYSELF ENJOY SUCH TALES.
I GUESS I JUST CAN'T GROW UP.

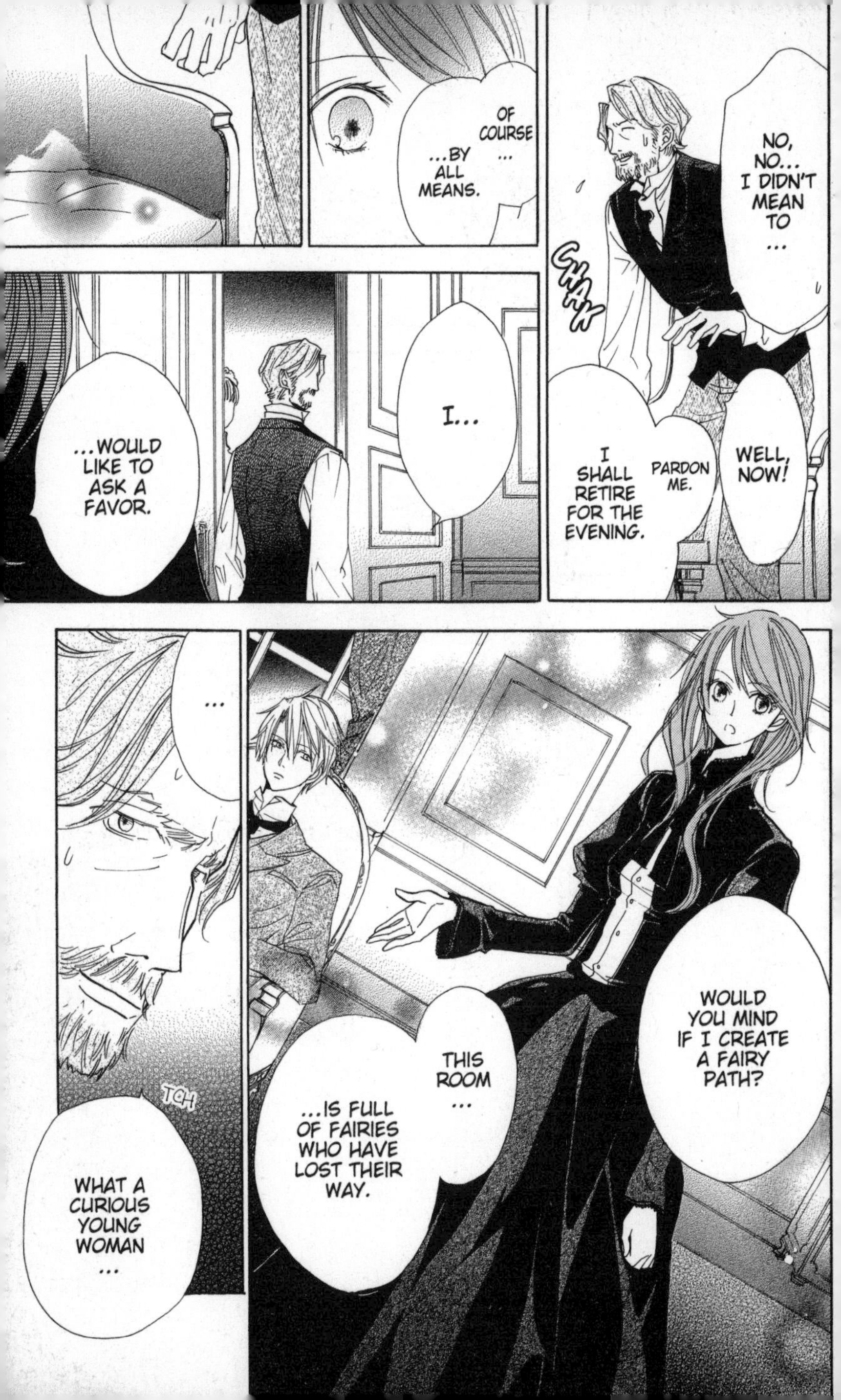

NO, NO... I DIDN'T MEAN TO ...
CHAK
WELL, NOW!
PARDON ME.
I SHALL RETIRE FOR THE EVENING.
OF COURSE ...
...BY ALL MEANS.
I...
...WOULD LIKE TO ASK A FAVOR.
WOULD YOU MIND IF I CREATE A FAIRY PATH?
THIS ROOM ...
...IS FULL OF FAIRIES WHO HAVE LOST THEIR WAY.
...
TCH
WHAT A CURIOUS YOUNG WOMAN ...

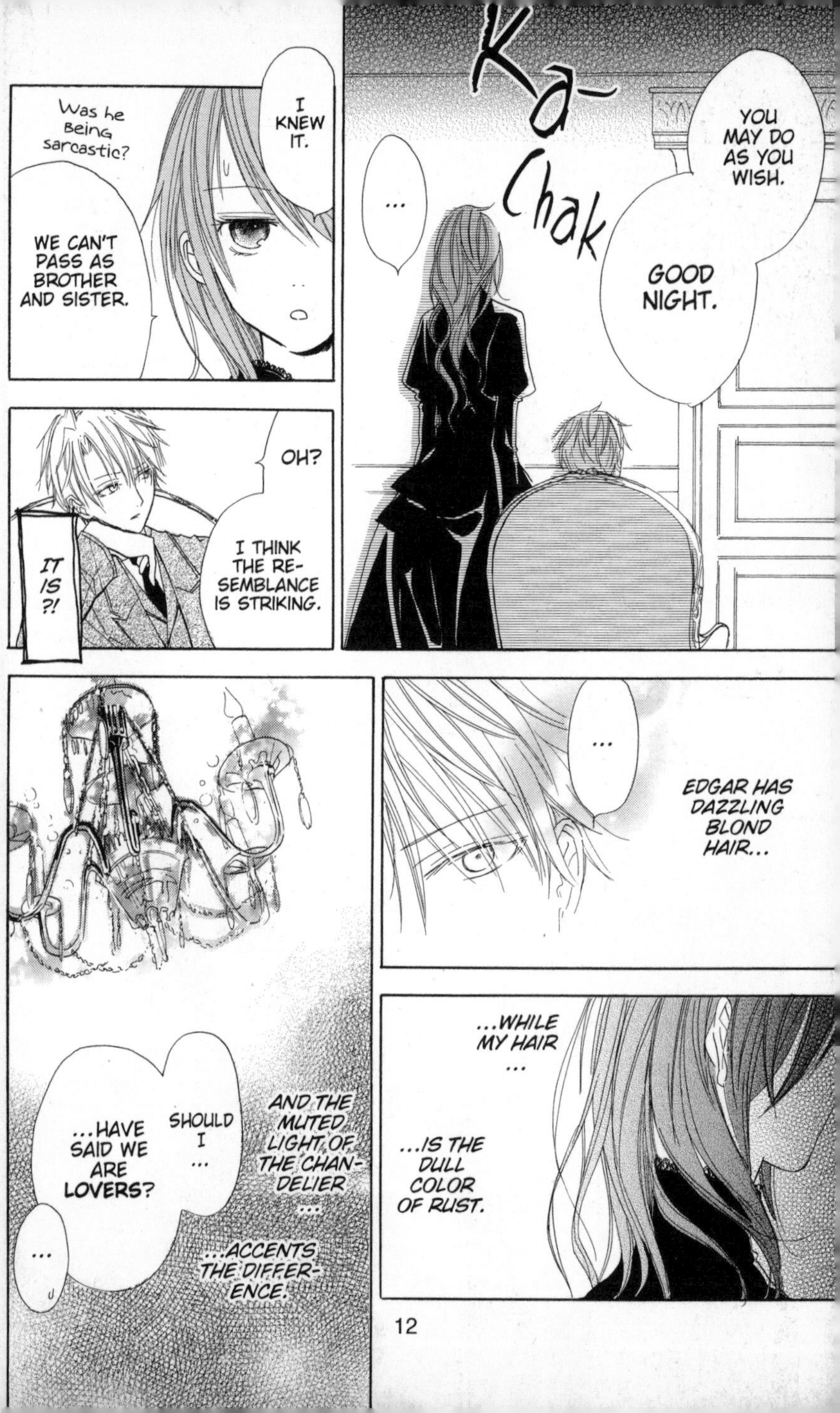
Ka-Chak
YOU MAY DO AS YOU WISH.
GOOD NIGHT.
...
I KNEW IT.
Was he Being sarcastic?
WE CAN'T PASS AS BROTHER AND SISTER.
OH?
I THINK THE RE-SEMBLANCE IS STRIKING.
IT IS ?!
...
EDGAR HAS DAZZLING BLOND HAIR...
...WHILE MY HAIR ...
...IS THE DULL COLOR OF RUST.
AND THE MUTED LIGHT OF THE CHAN-DELIER ...
...ACCENTS THE DIFFER-ENCE.
SHOULD I ...
...HAVE SAID WE ARE LOVERS?
...

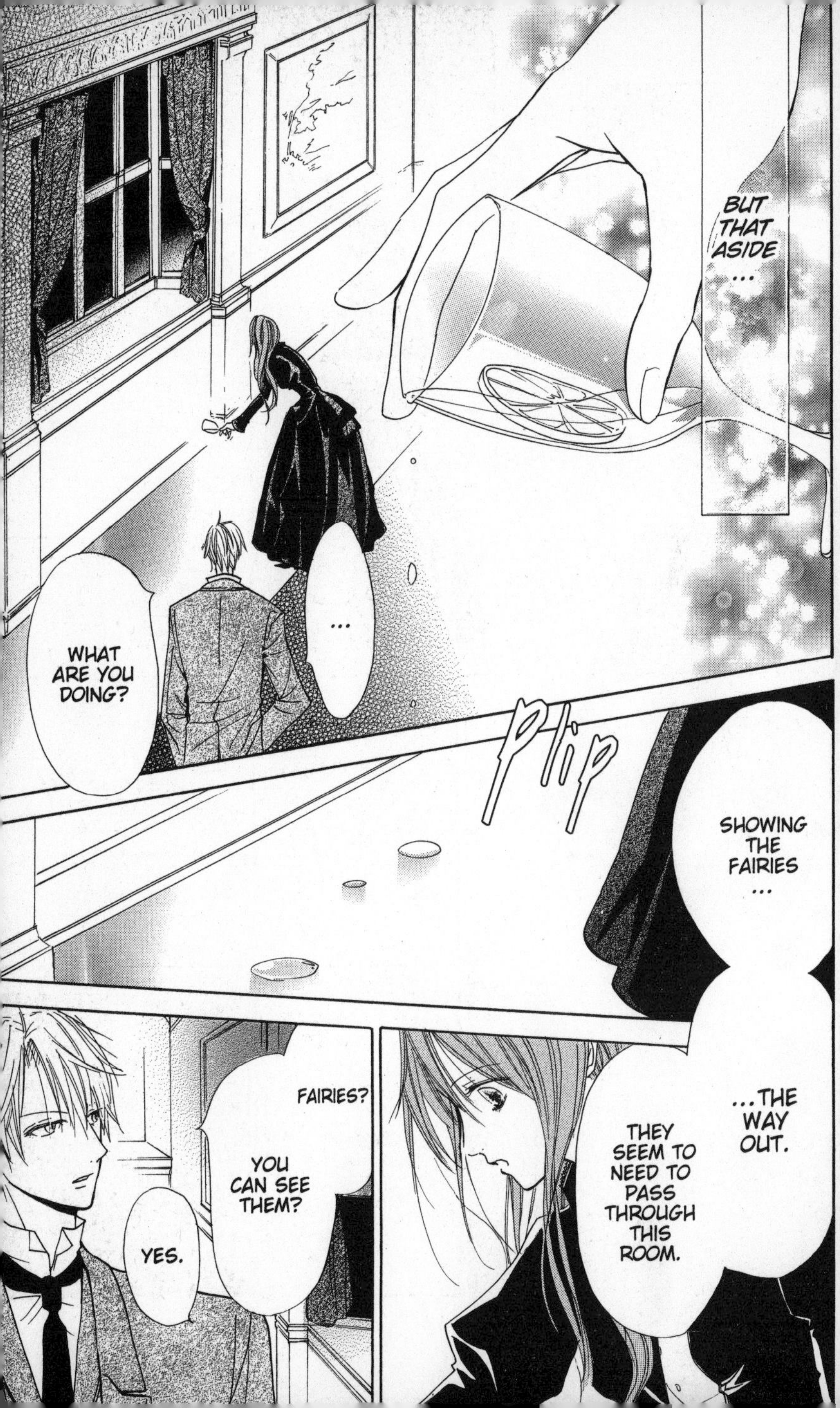
BUT THAT ASIDE...
...
WHAT ARE YOU DOING?
Plip
SHOWING THE FAIRIES...
...THE WAY OUT.
THEY SEEM TO NEED TO PASS THROUGH THIS ROOM.
FAIRIES?
YOU CAN SEE THEM?
YES.

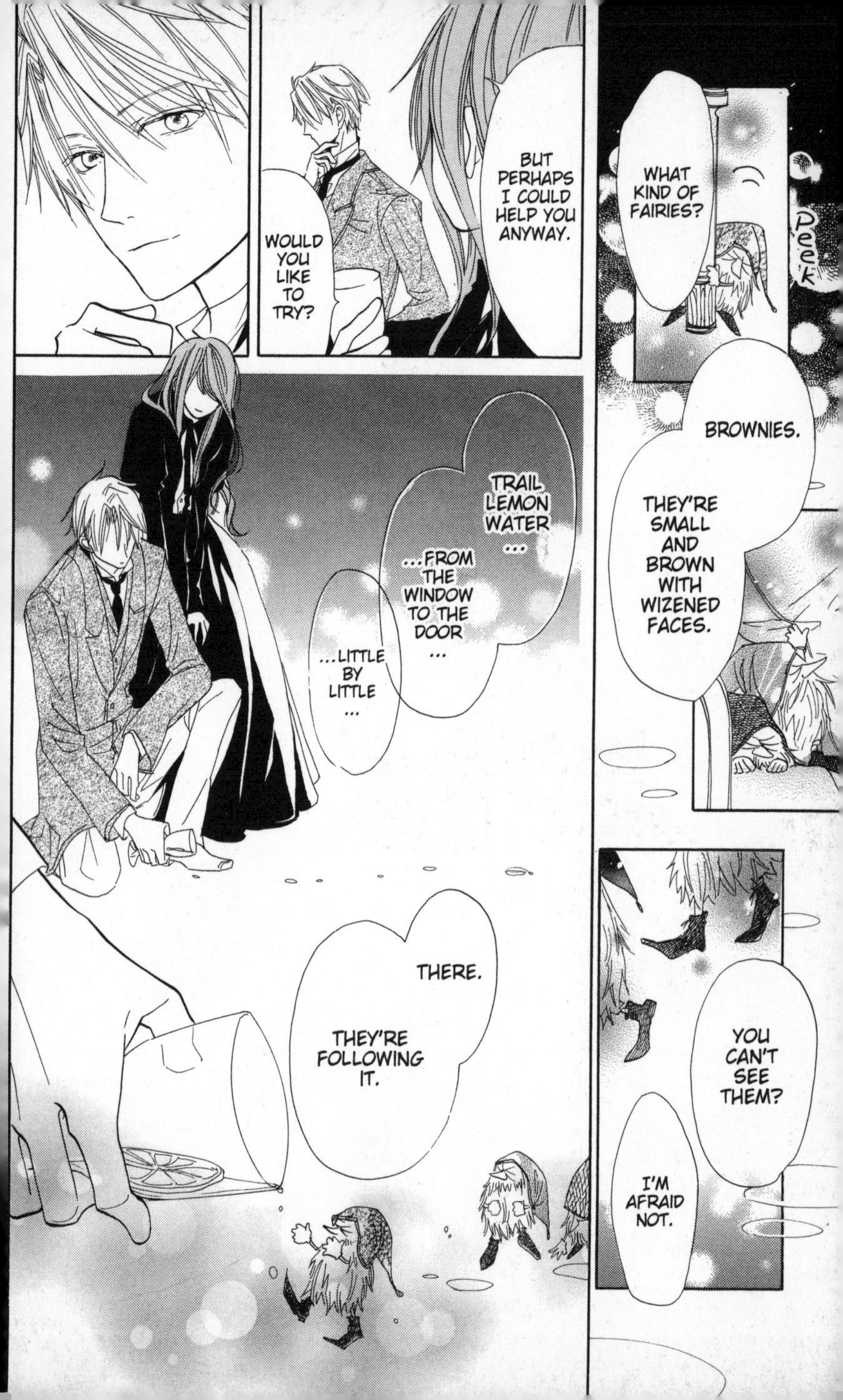

WHAT KIND OF FAIRIES?
PEEK
BROWNIES.
THEY'RE SMALL AND BROWN WITH WIZENED FACES.
YOU CAN'T SEE THEM?
I'M AFRAID NOT.
BUT PERHAPS I COULD HELP YOU ANYWAY.
WOULD YOU LIKE TO TRY?
TRAIL LEMON WATER...
...FROM THE WINDOW TO THE DOOR...
...LITTLE BY LITTLE...
THERE.
THEY'RE FOLLOWING IT.

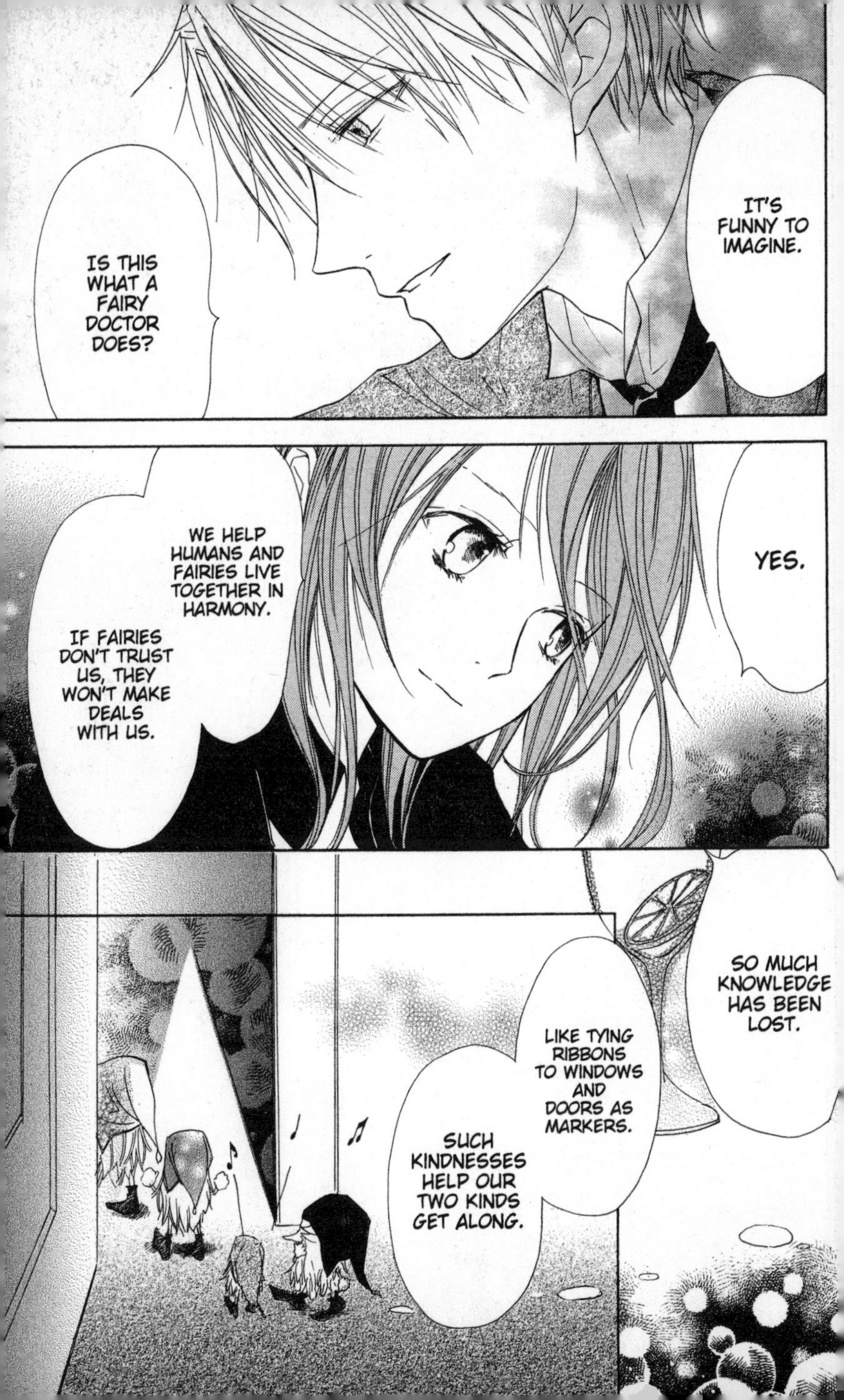
IT'S FUNNY TO IMAGINE.
IS THIS WHAT A FAIRY DOCTOR DOES?
YES.
WE HELP HUMANS AND FAIRIES LIVE TOGETHER IN HARMONY.
IF FAIRIES DON'T TRUST US, THEY WON'T MAKE DEALS WITH US.
SO MUCH KNOWLEDGE HAS BEEN LOST.
LIKE TYING RIBBONS TO WINDOWS AND DOORS AS MARKERS.
SUCH KINDNESSES HELP OUR TWO KINDS GET ALONG.

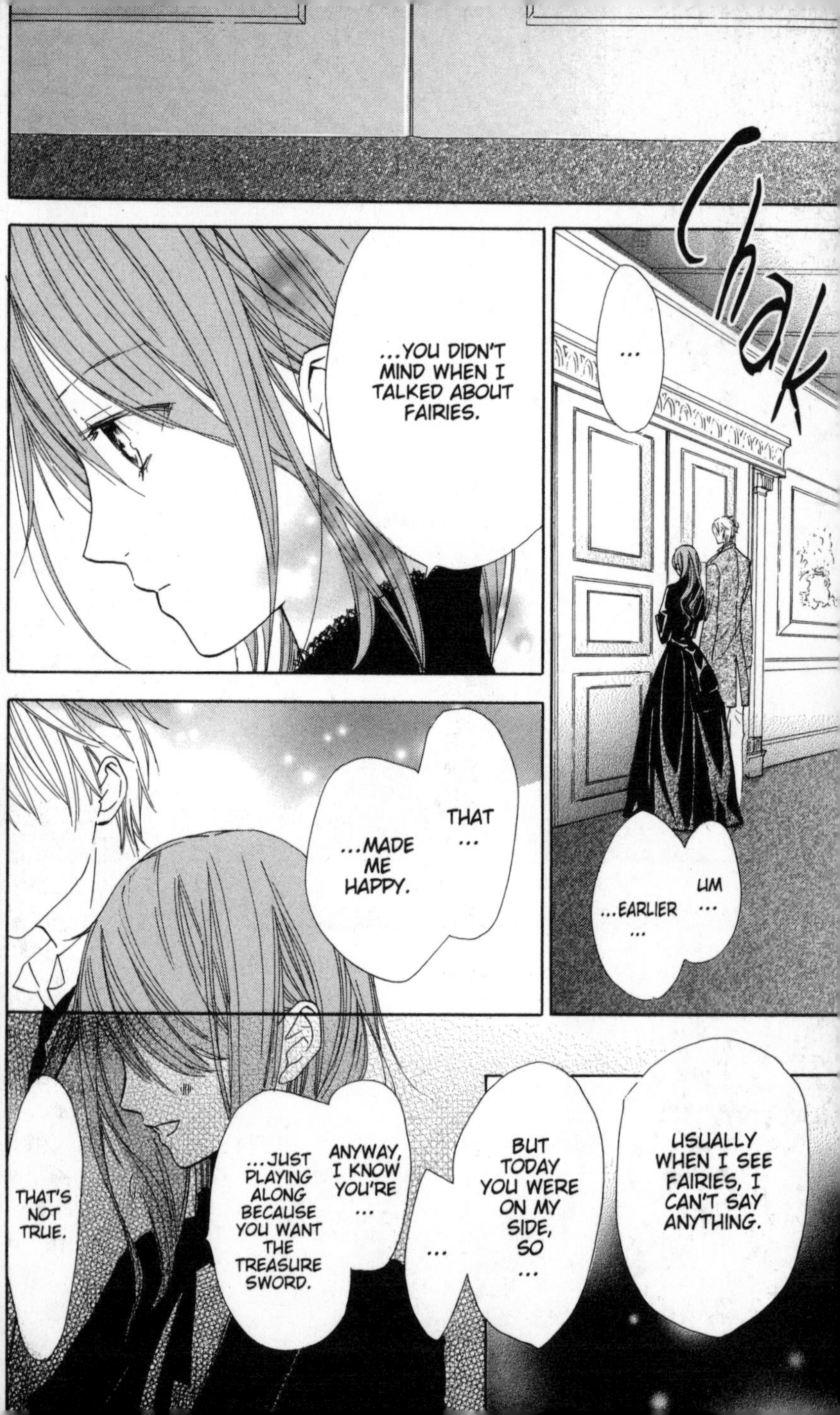
Chak
...
UM... ...EARLIER...
...YOU DIDN'T MIND WHEN I TALKED ABOUT FAIRIES.
THAT... ...MADE ME HAPPY.
USUALLY WHEN I SEE FAIRIES, I CAN'T SAY ANYTHING.
BUT TODAY YOU WERE ON MY SIDE, SO...
...
ANYWAY, I KNOW YOU'RE... ...JUST PLAYING ALONG BECAUSE YOU WANT THE TREASURE SWORD.
THAT'S NOT TRUE.

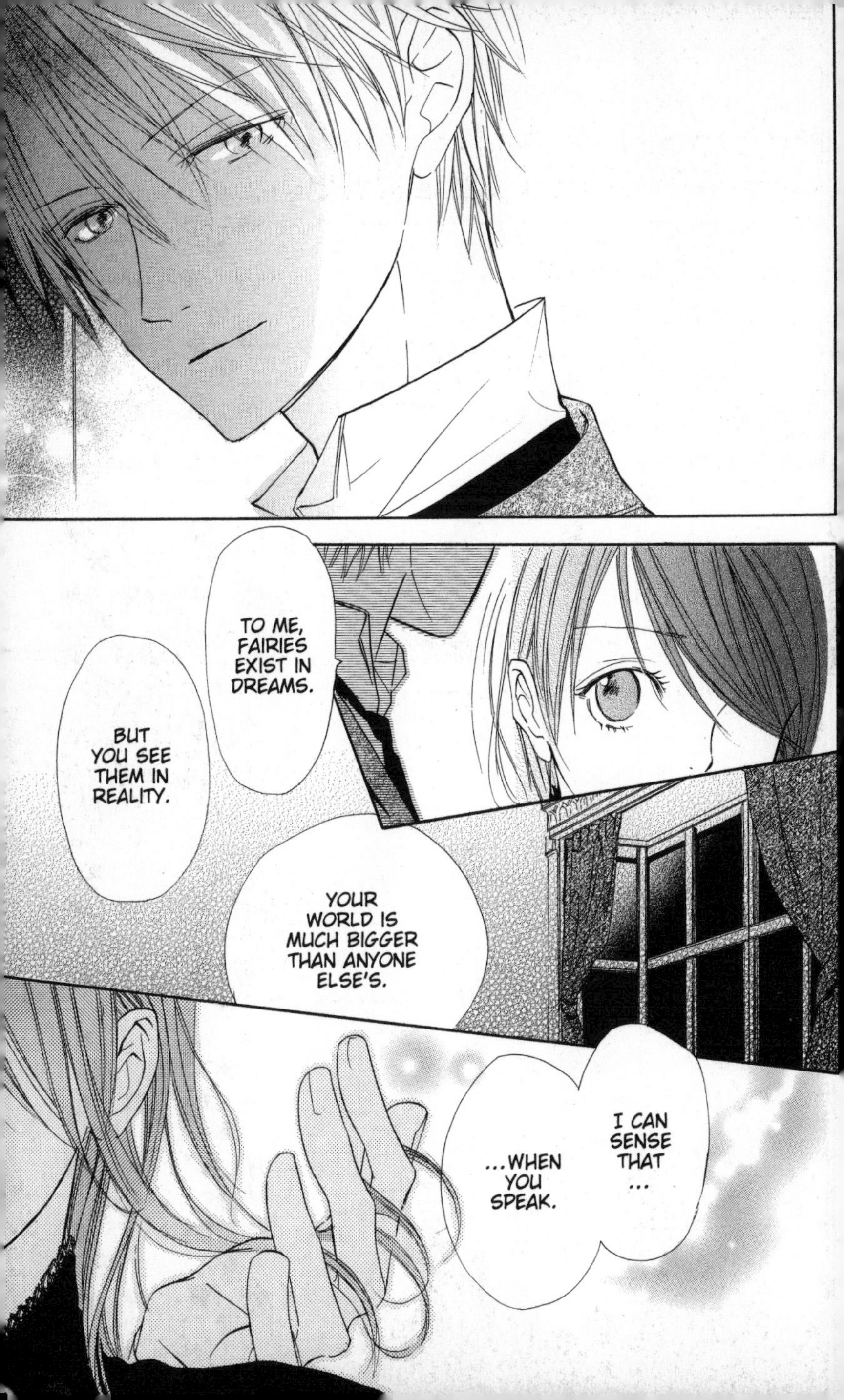
TO ME, FAIRIES EXIST IN DREAMS.
BUT YOU SEE THEM IN REALITY.
YOUR WORLD IS MUCH BIGGER THAN ANYONE ELSE'S.
I CAN SENSE THAT ...
...WHEN YOU SPEAK.

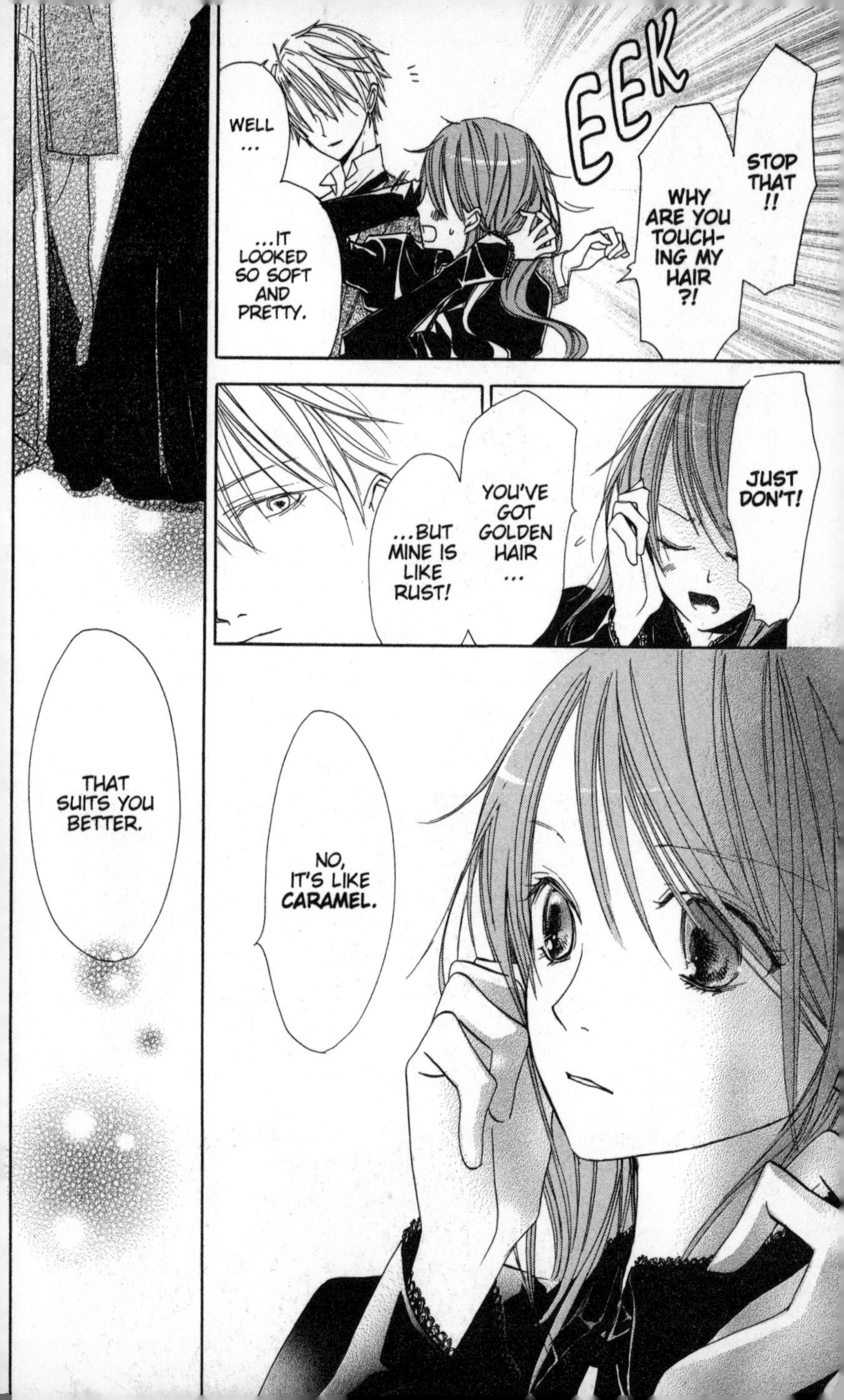
EEK
STOP THAT!!
WHY ARE YOU TOUCHING MY HAIR?!
WELL...
...IT LOOKED SO SOFT AND PRETTY.
JUST DON'T!
YOU'VE GOT GOLDEN HAIR...
...BUT MINE IS LIKE RUST!
NO, IT'S LIKE CARAMEL.
THAT SUITS YOU BETTER.

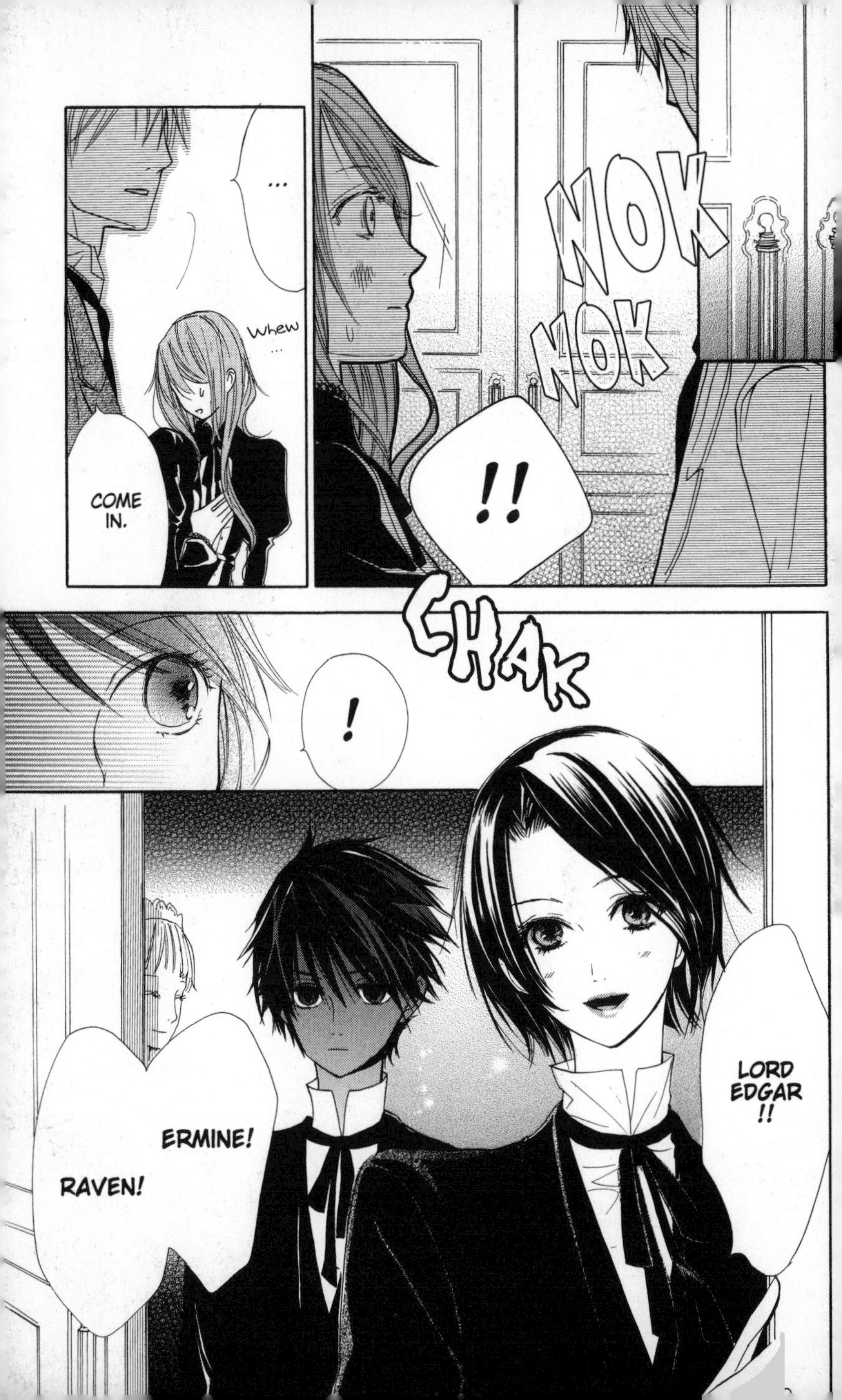
NOK
NOK
!!
...
Whew ...
COME IN.
CHAK
!
LORD EDGAR !!
ERMINE!
RAVEN!

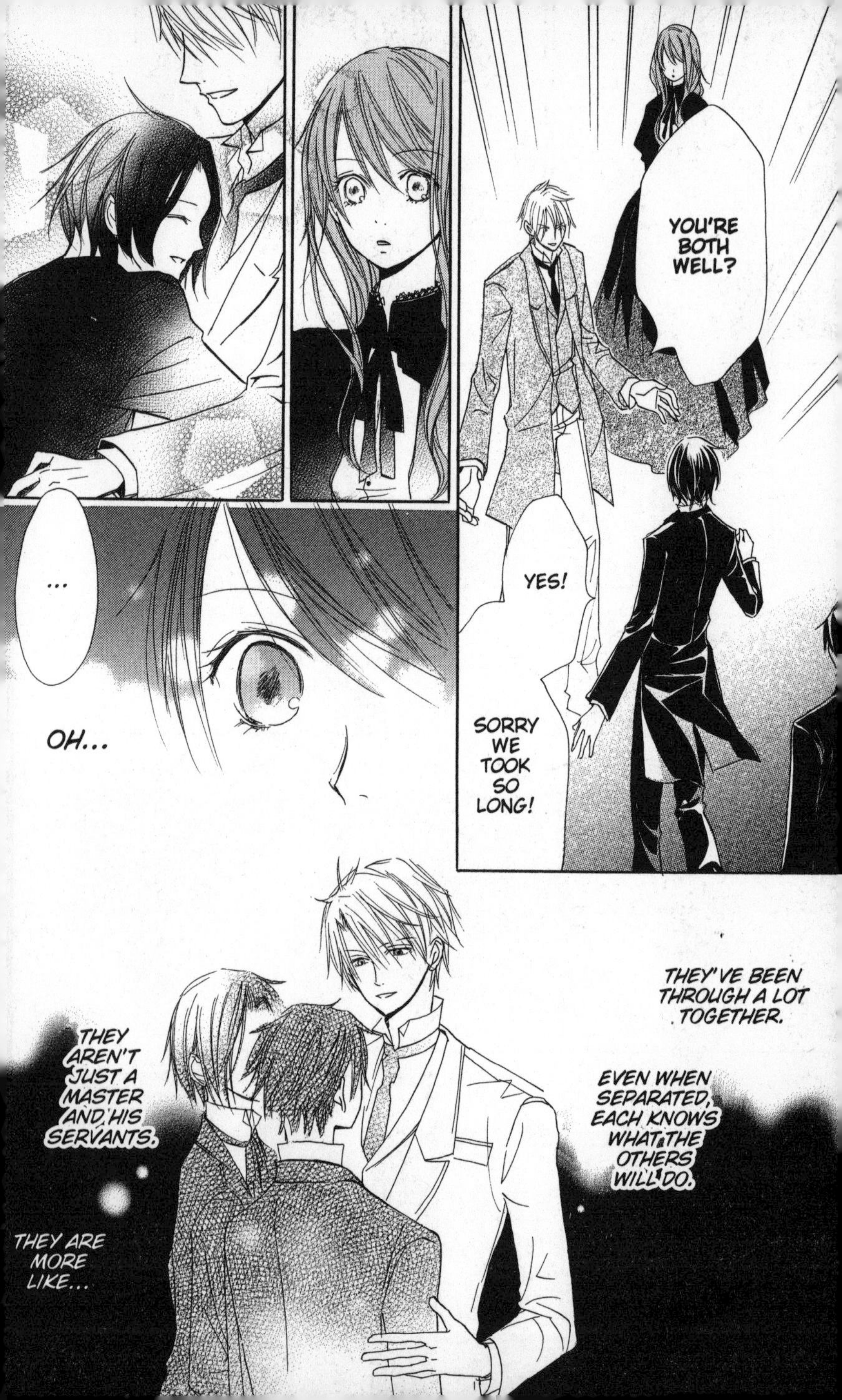
YOU'RE BOTH WELL?
YES!
SORRY WE TOOK SO LONG!
...
OH...
THEY'VE BEEN THROUGH A LOT TOGETHER.
EVEN WHEN SEPARATED, EACH KNOWS WHAT THE OTHERS WILL DO.
THEY AREN'T JUST A MASTER AND HIS SERVANTS.
THEY ARE MORE LIKE...

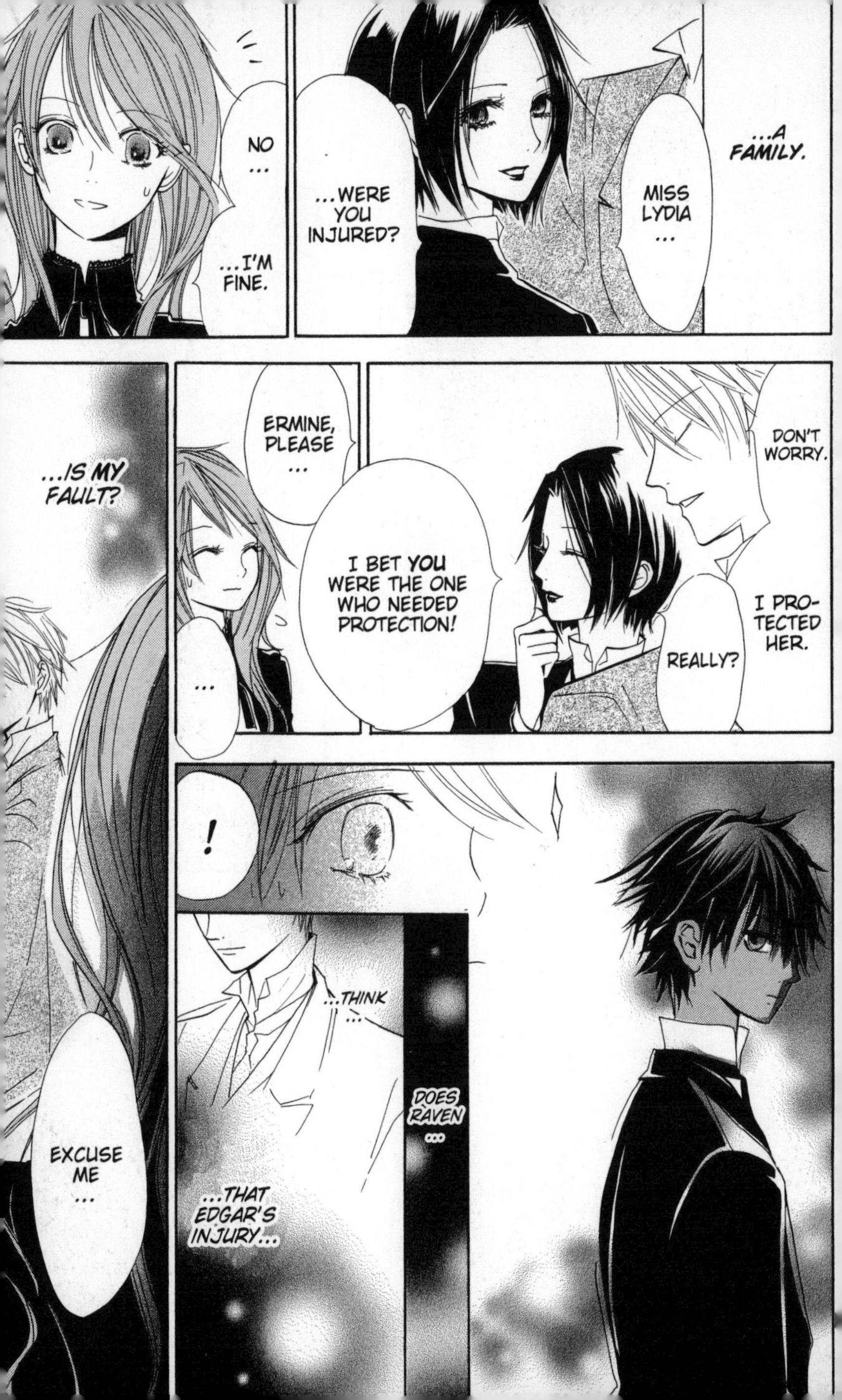
...A FAMILY.
MISS LYDIA ...
...WERE YOU INJURED?
NO ...
...I'M FINE.
DON'T WORRY.
I PROTECTED HER.
REALLY?
ERMINE, PLEASE ...
I BET YOU WERE THE ONE WHO NEEDED PROTECTION!
...
!
DOES RAVEN ...
...THINK ...
...THAT EDGAR'S INJURY...
...IS MY FAULT?
EXCUSE ME ...

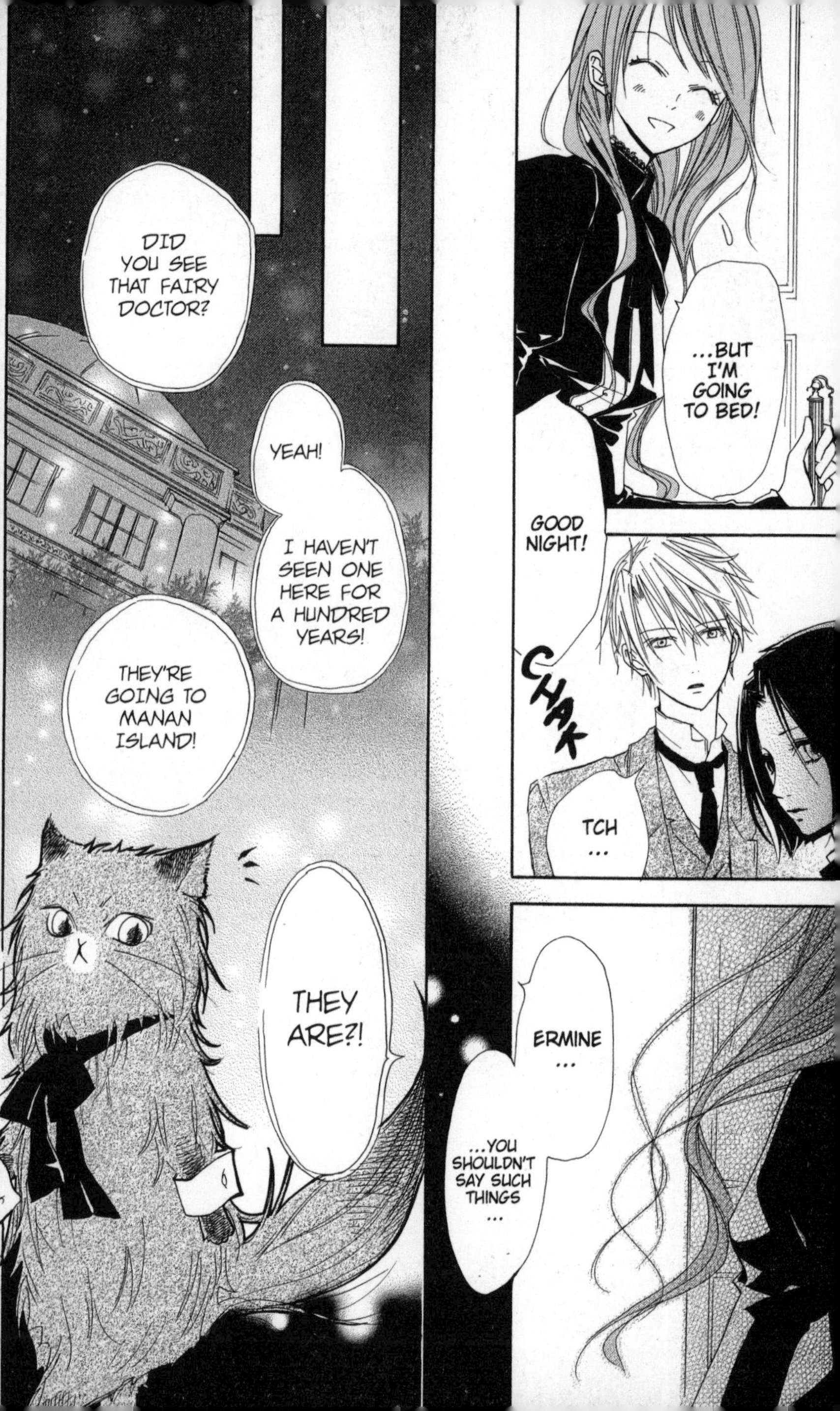
...BUT I'M GOING TO BED!
GOOD NIGHT!
CHAK
TCH ...
ERMINE ...
...YOU SHOULDN'T SAY SUCH THINGS ...
DID YOU SEE THAT FAIRY DOCTOR?
YEAH!
I HAVEN'T SEEN ONE HERE FOR A HUNDRED YEARS!
THEY'RE GOING TO MANAN ISLAND!
THEY ARE?!

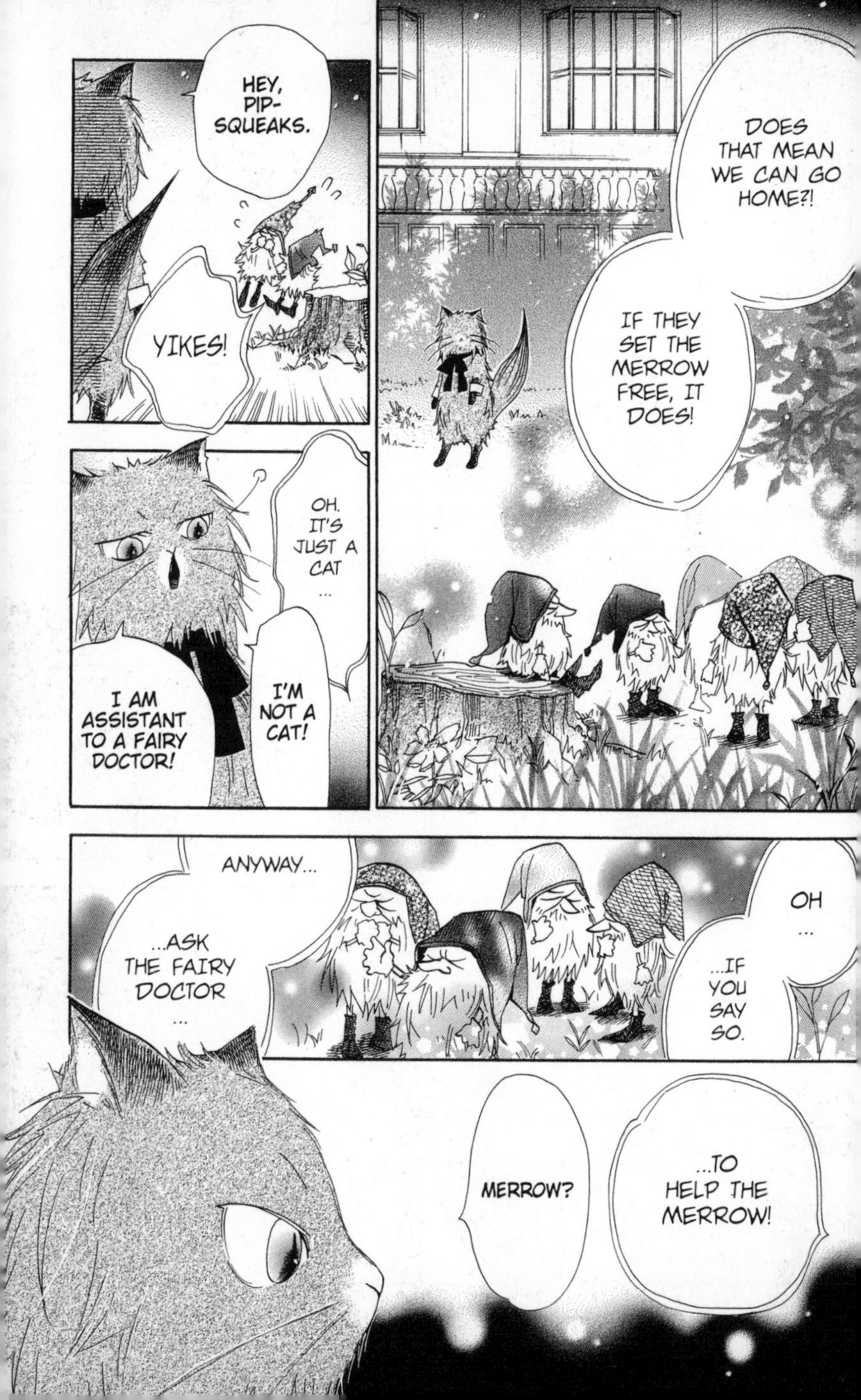
DOES THAT MEAN WE CAN GO HOME?!
IF THEY SET THE MERROW FREE, IT DOES!
HEY, PIP-SQUEAKS.
YIKES!
OH. IT'S JUST A CAT ...
I'M NOT A CAT!
I AM ASSISTANT TO A FAIRY DOCTOR!
OH ...
...IF YOU SAY SO.
ANYWAY...
...ASK THE FAIRY DOCTOR ...
...TO HELP THE MERROW!
MERROW?

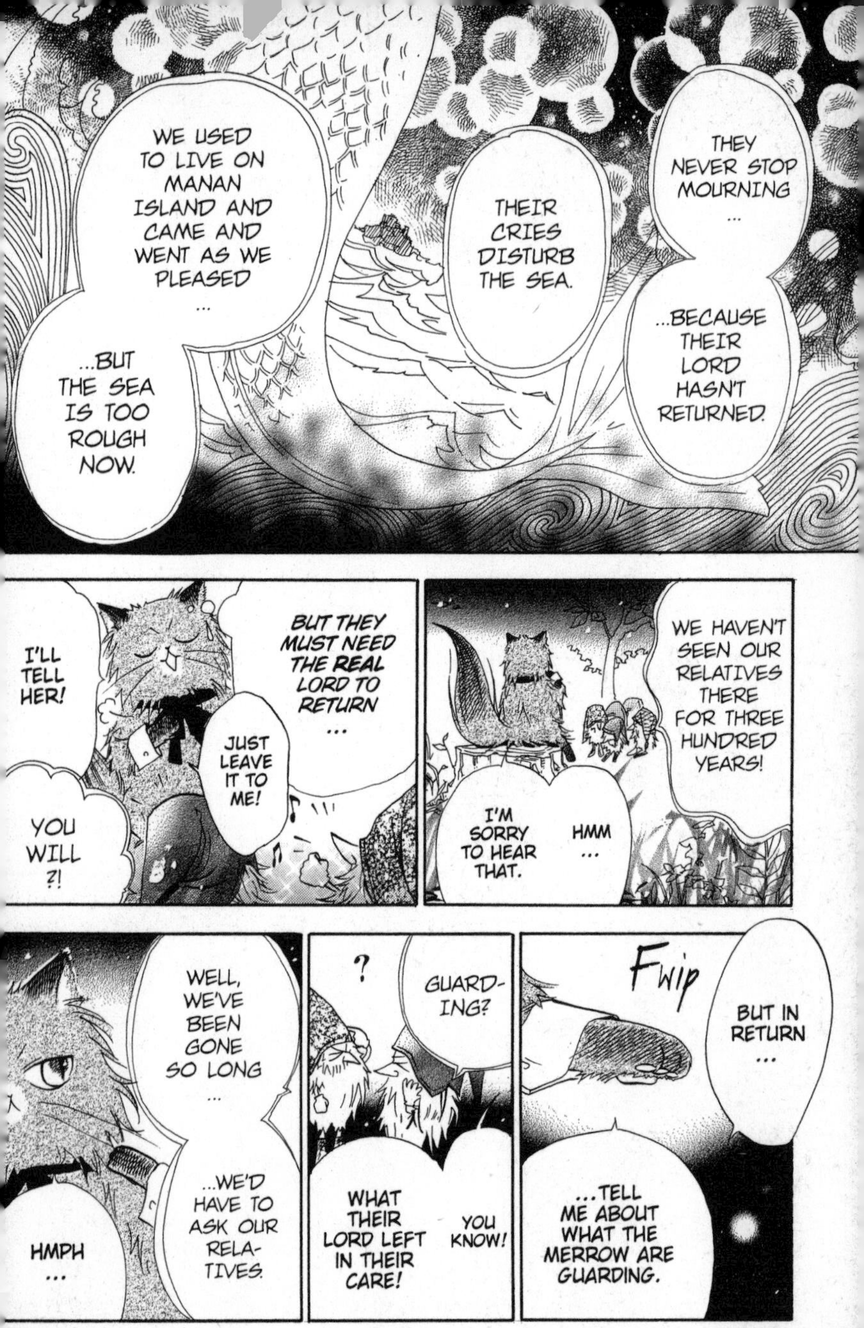
THEY NEVER STOP MOURNING ...
...BECAUSE THEIR LORD HASN'T RETURNED.
THEIR CRIES DISTURB THE SEA.
WE USED TO LIVE ON MANAN ISLAND AND CAME AND WENT AS WE PLEASED ...
...BUT THE SEA IS TOO ROUGH NOW.
WE HAVEN'T SEEN OUR RELATIVES THERE FOR THREE HUNDRED YEARS!
HMM ...
I'M SORRY TO HEAR THAT.
BUT THEY MUST NEED THE REAL LORD TO RETURN ...
I'LL TELL HER!
JUST LEAVE IT TO ME!
YOU WILL ?!
Fwip
BUT IN RETURN ...
...TELL ME ABOUT WHAT THE MERROW ARE GUARDING.
GUARD-ING?
?
YOU KNOW!
WHAT THEIR LORD LEFT IN THEIR CARE!
WELL, WE'VE BEEN GONE SO LONG ...
...WE'D HAVE TO ASK OUR RELA-TIVES.
HMPH ...

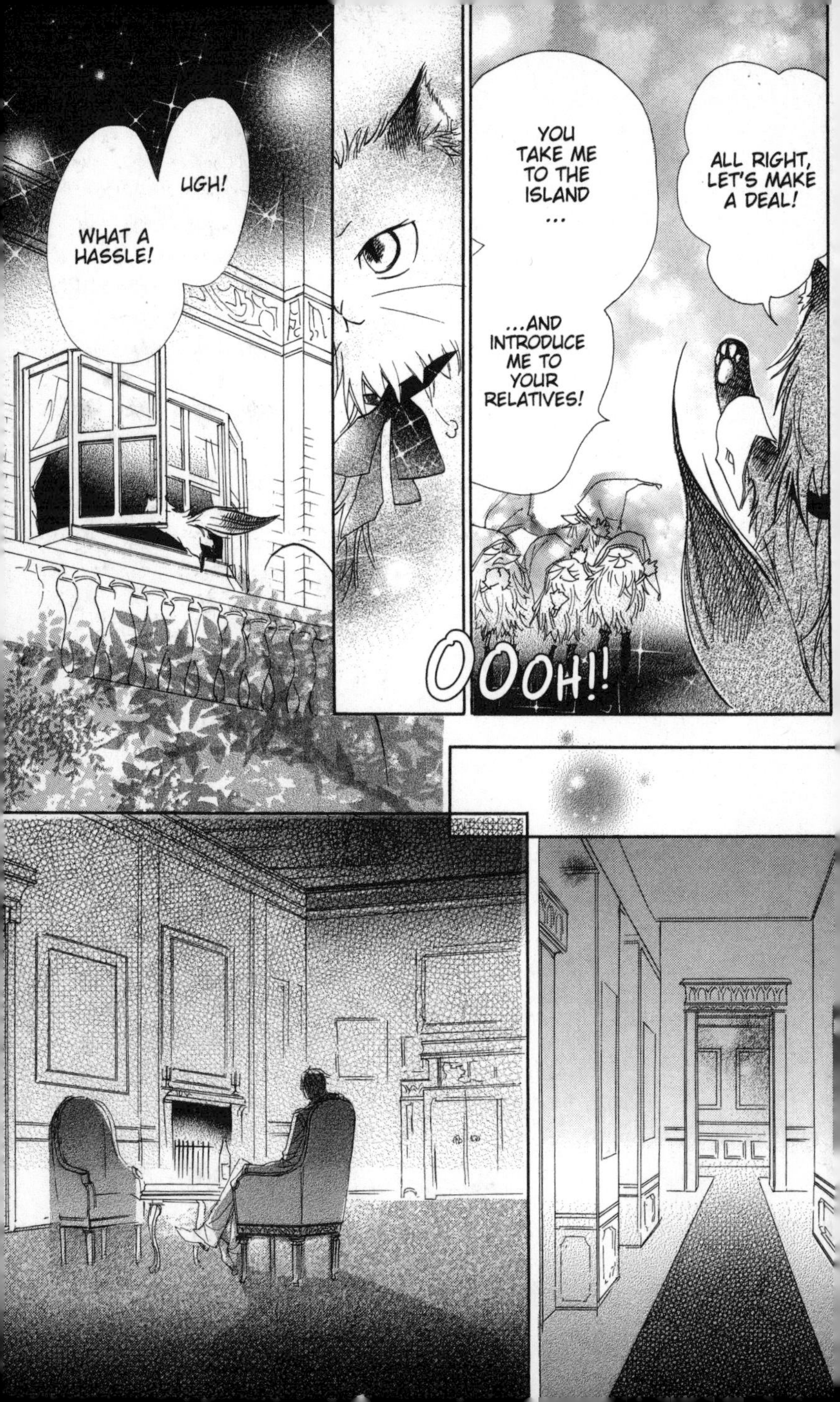
ALL RIGHT, LET'S MAKE A DEAL!
YOU TAKE ME TO THE ISLAND ...
...AND INTRODUCE ME TO YOUR RELATIVES!
OOOH!!
UGH!
WHAT A HASSLE!

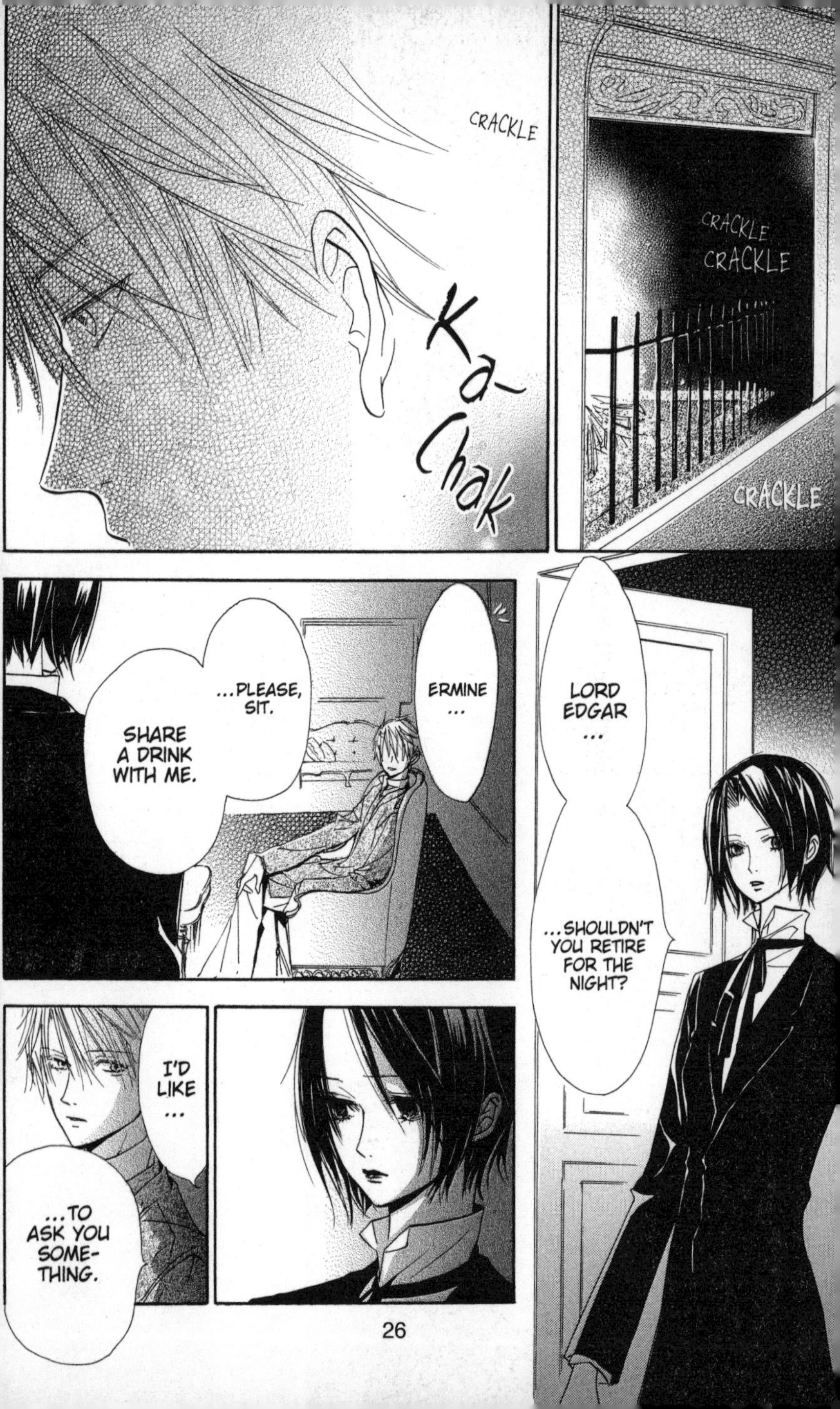
CRACKLE
CRACKLE
CRACKLE
CRACKLE
Ka-Chak
LORD EDGAR ...
...SHOULDN'T YOU RETIRE FOR THE NIGHT?
ERMINE ...
...PLEASE, SIT.
SHARE A DRINK WITH ME.
I'D LIKE ...
...TO ASK YOU SOME-THING.

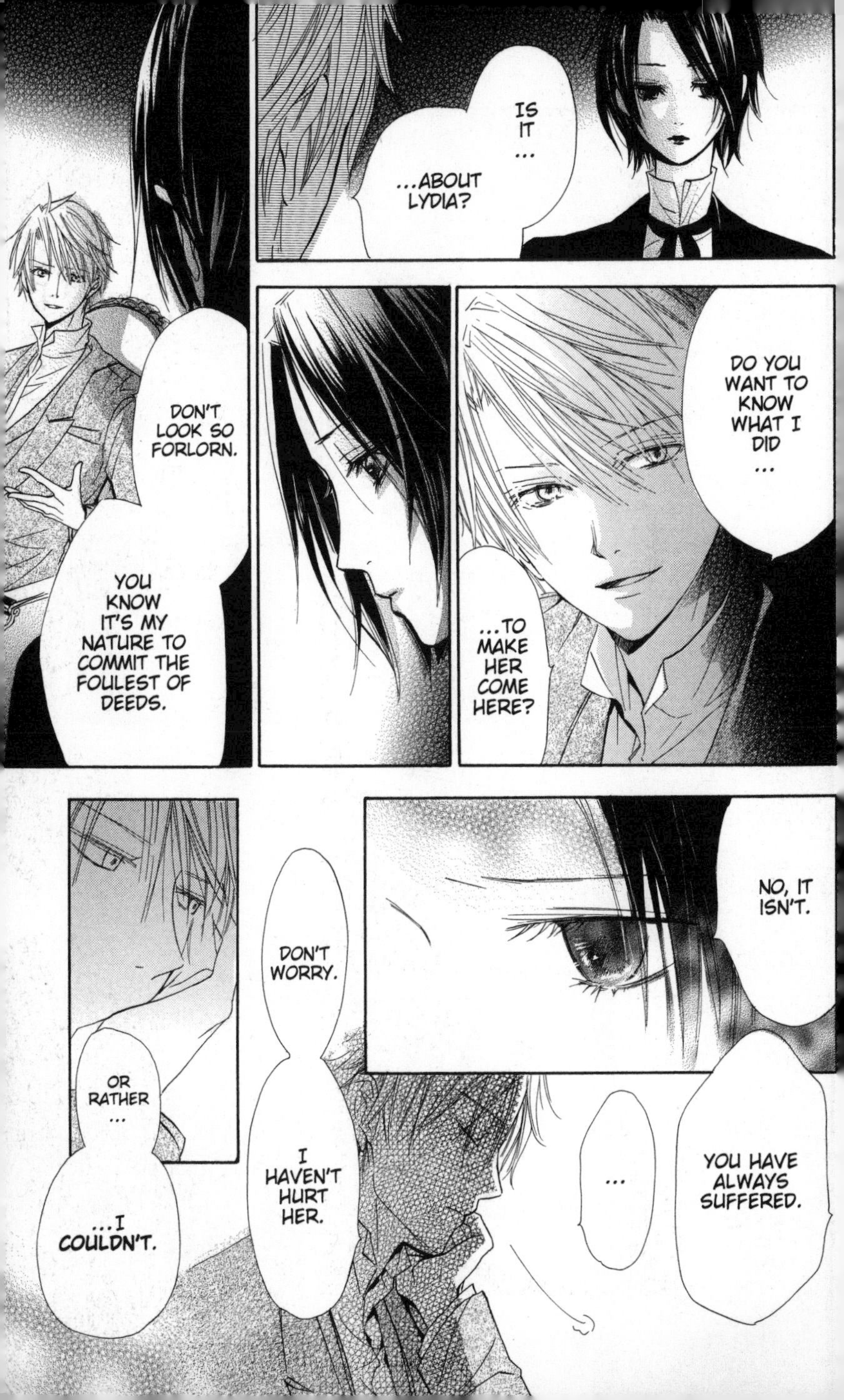
IS IT ...
...ABOUT LYDIA?
DO YOU WANT TO KNOW WHAT I DID ...
...TO MAKE HER COME HERE?
DON'T LOOK SO FORLORN.
YOU KNOW IT'S MY NATURE TO COMMIT THE FOULEST OF DEEDS.
NO, IT ISN'T.
YOU HAVE ALWAYS SUFFERED.
...
DON'T WORRY.
I HAVEN'T HURT HER.
OR RATHER ...
...I COULDN'T.

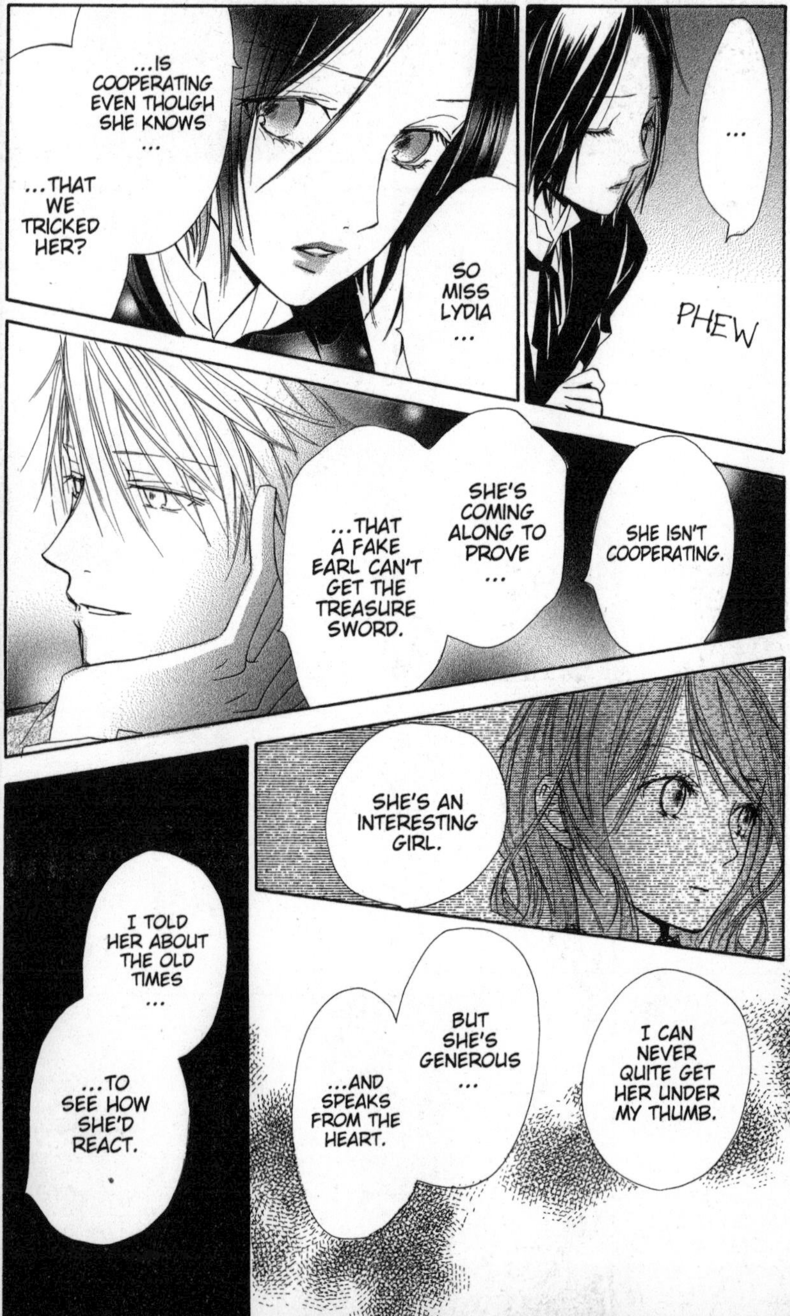
...
PHEW
SO MISS LYDIA ...
...IS COOPERATING EVEN THOUGH SHE KNOWS ...
...THAT WE TRICKED HER?
SHE ISN'T COOPERATING.
SHE'S COMING ALONG TO PROVE ...
...THAT A FAKE EARL CAN'T GET THE TREASURE SWORD.
SHE'S AN INTERESTING GIRL.
I CAN NEVER QUITE GET HER UNDER MY THUMB.
BUT SHE'S GENEROUS ...
...AND SPEAKS FROM THE HEART.
I TOLD HER ABOUT THE OLD TIMES ...
...TO SEE HOW SHE'D REACT.

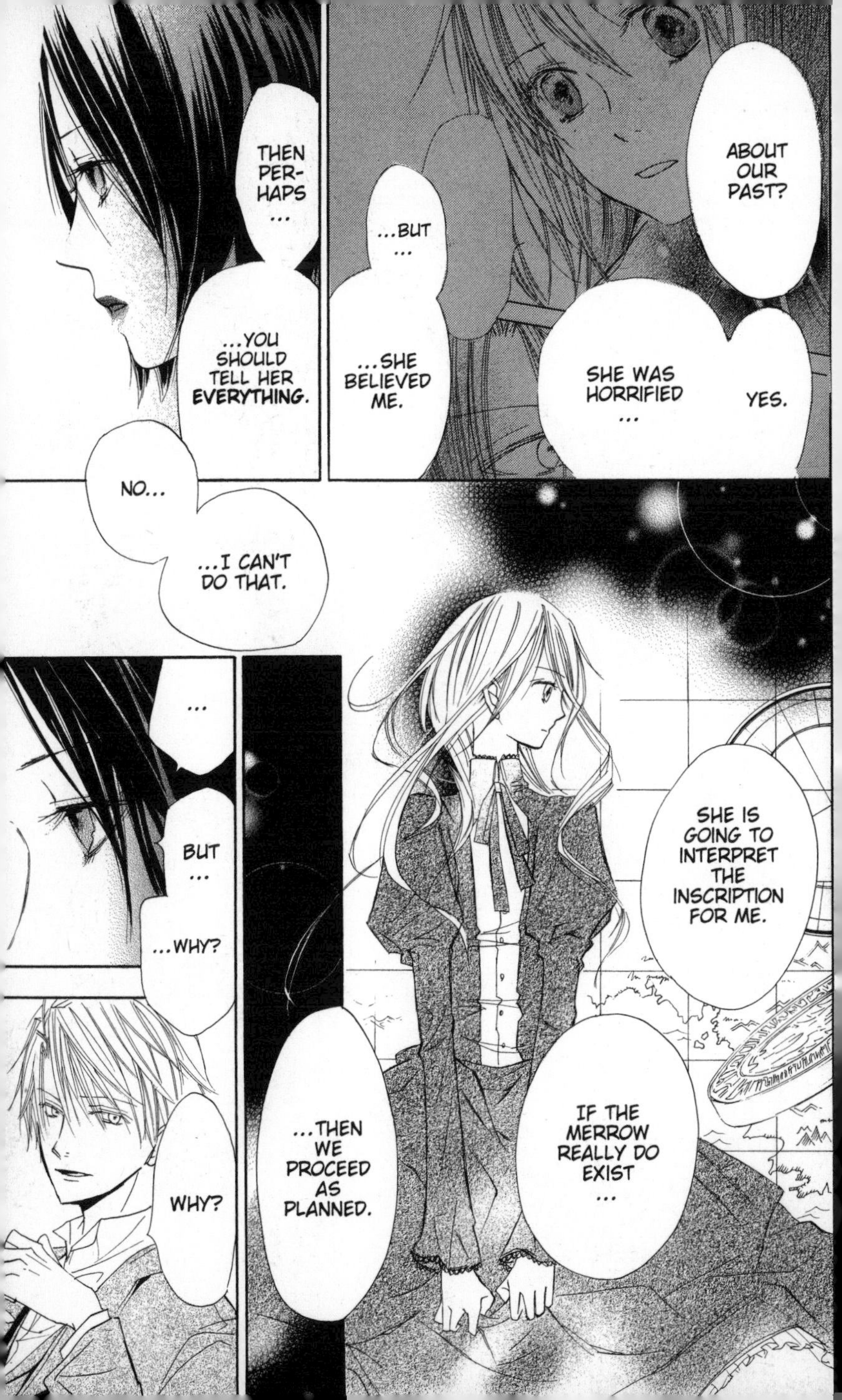
ABOUT OUR PAST?
YES.
SHE WAS HORRIFIED ...
...BUT ...
...SHE BELIEVED ME.
THEN PER-HAPS ...
...YOU SHOULD TELL HER EVERYTHING.
NO...
...I CAN'T DO THAT.
SHE IS GOING TO INTERPRET THE INSCRIPTION FOR ME.
IF THE MERROW REALLY DO EXIST ...
...THEN WE PROCEED AS PLANNED.
...
BUT ...
...WHY?
WHY?

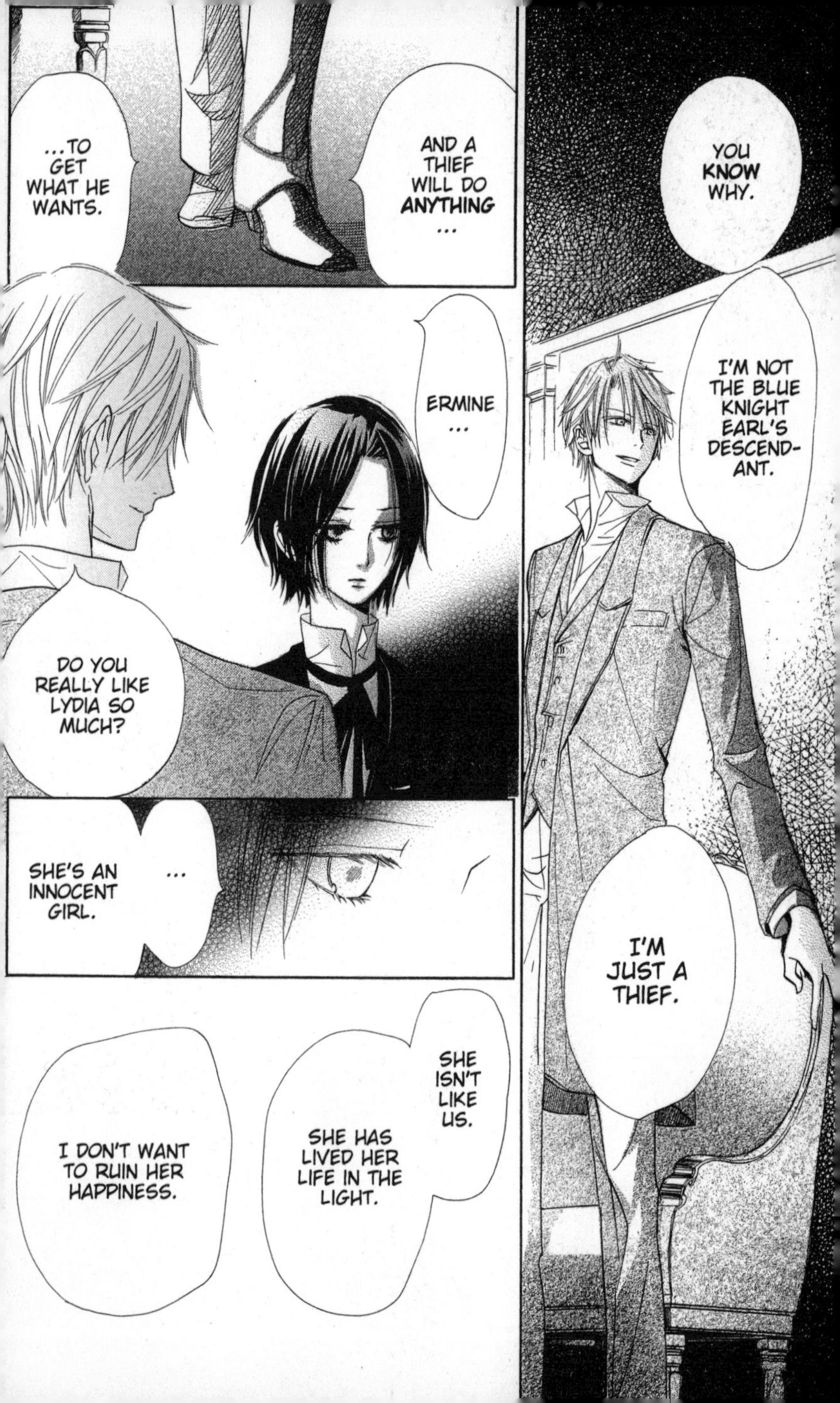
YOU KNOW WHY.
I'M NOT THE BLUE KNIGHT EARL'S DESCEND-ANT.
I'M JUST A THIEF.
AND A THIEF WILL DO **ANYTHING**...
...TO GET WHAT HE WANTS.
ERMINE...
DO YOU REALLY LIKE LYDIA SO MUCH?
...
SHE'S AN INNOCENT GIRL.
SHE ISN'T LIKE US.
SHE HAS LIVED HER LIFE IN THE LIGHT.
I DON'T WANT TO RUIN HER HAPPINESS.

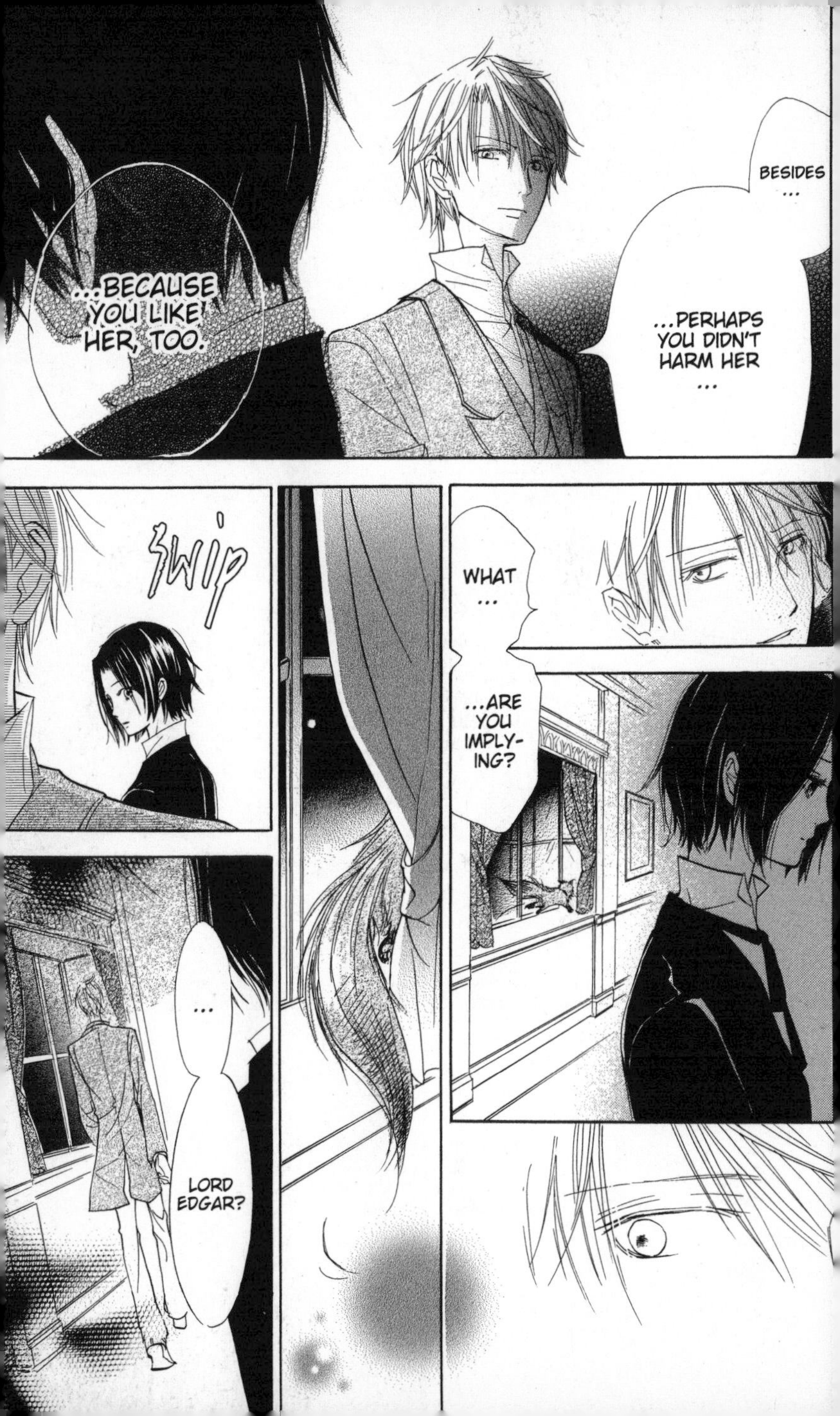
BESIDES ...
...PERHAPS YOU DIDN'T HARM HER ...
...BECAUSE YOU LIKE HER, TOO.
WHAT ...
...ARE YOU IMPLYING?
swip
...
LORD EDGAR?

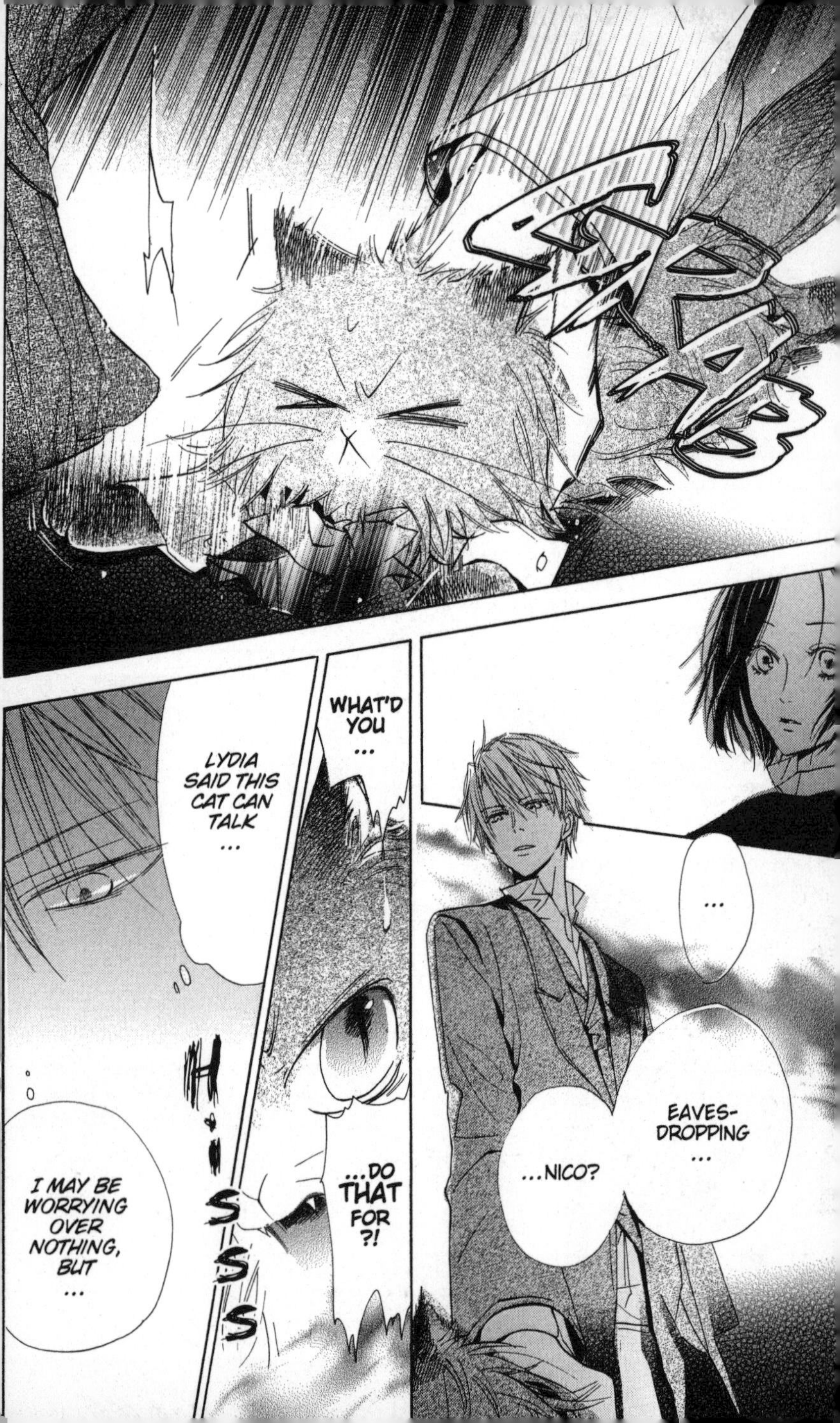
GRAB
...
EAVES-DROPPING ...
...NICO?
WHAT'D YOU ...
HISSS
...DO THAT FOR?!
LYDIA SAID THIS CAT CAN TALK ...
I MAY BE WORRYING OVER NOTHING, BUT ...

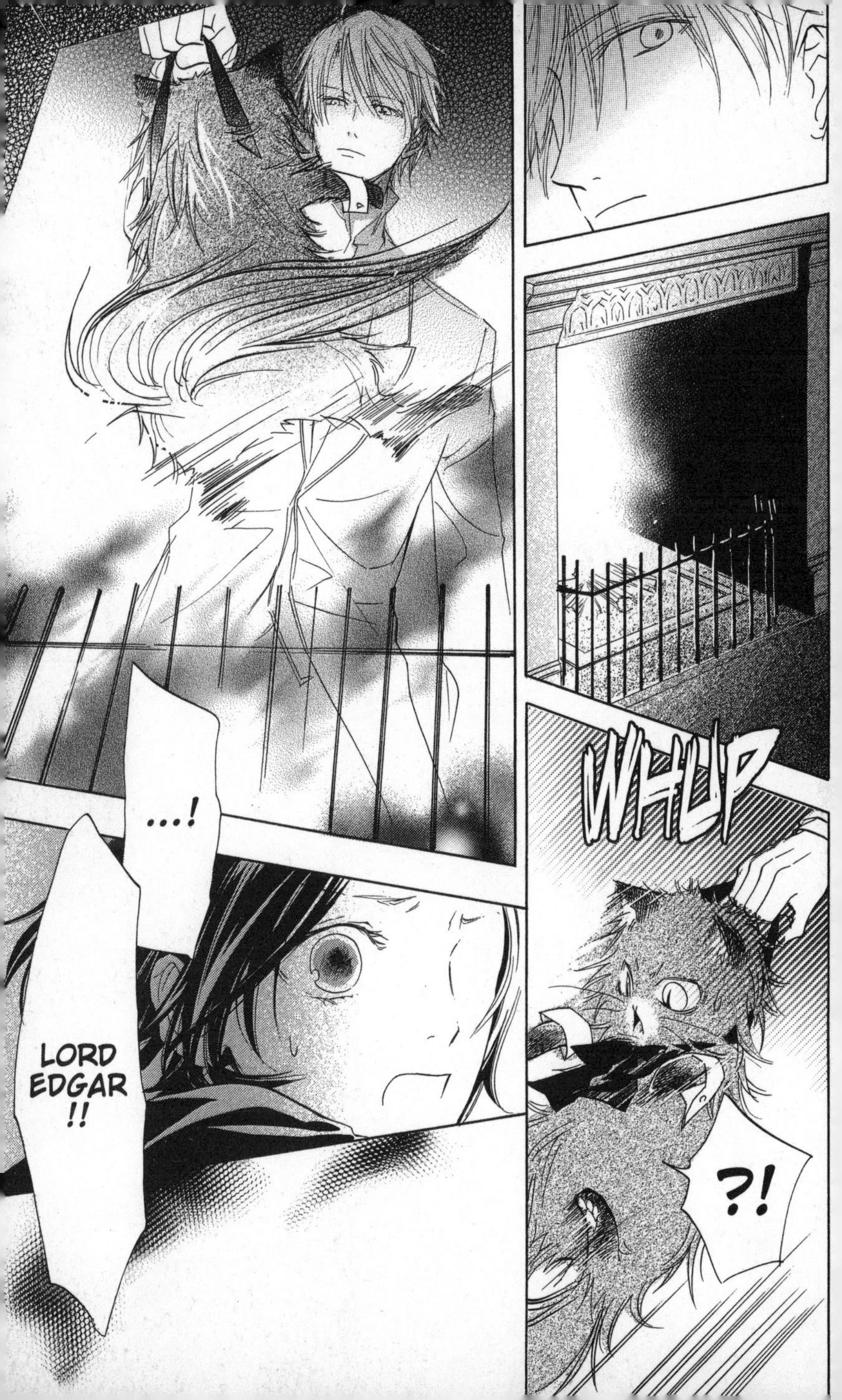
WHUP
?!
...!
LORD EDGAR !!

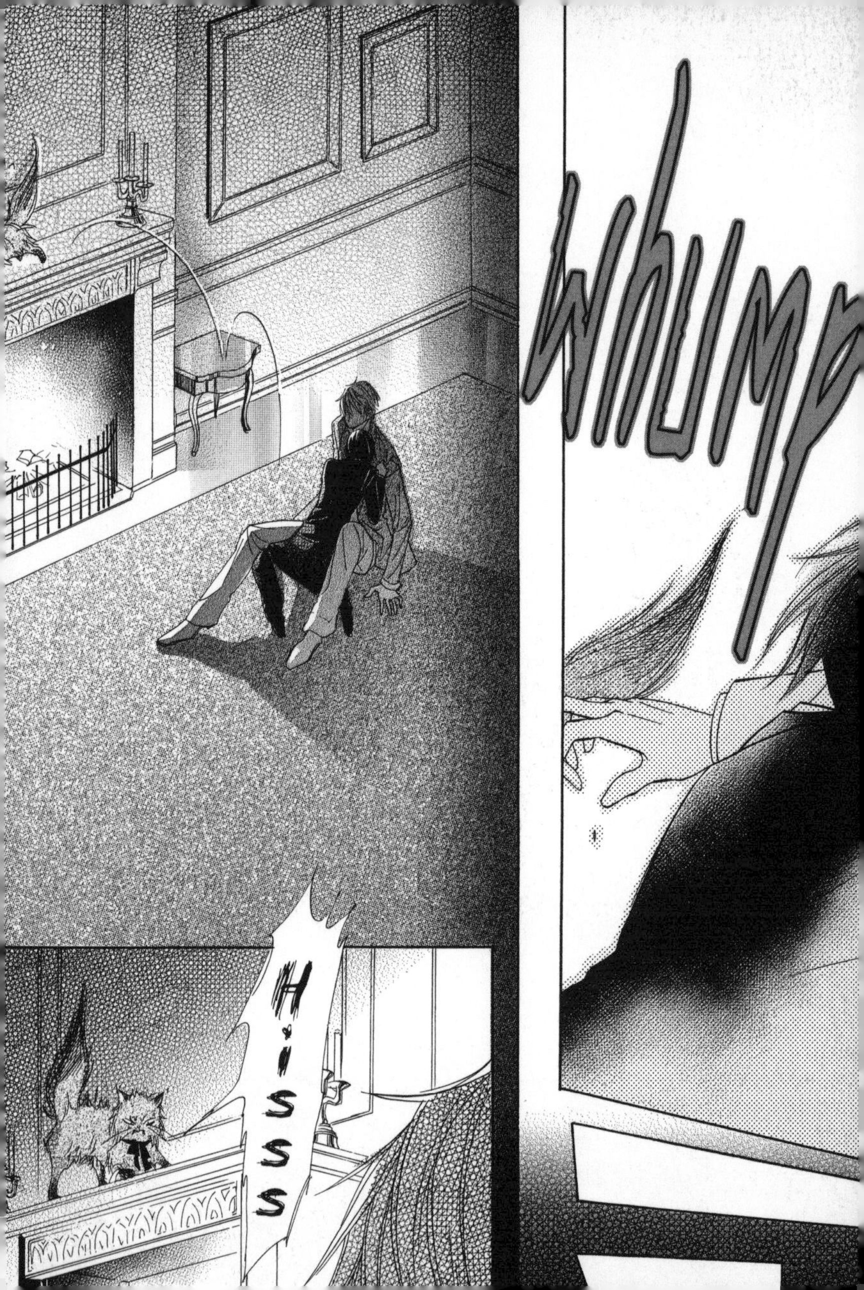
Whump
HISSS

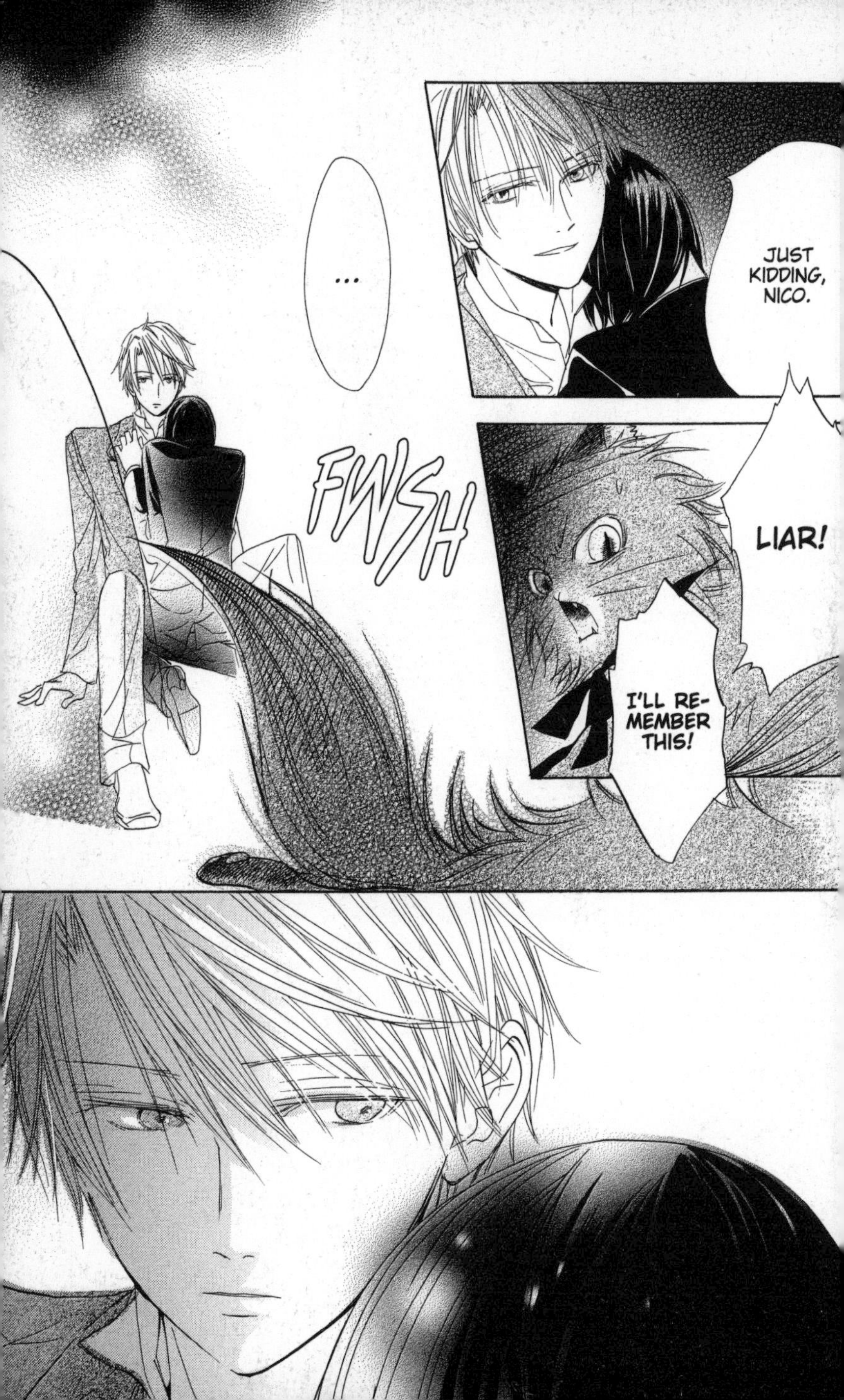
JUST KIDDING, NICO.
LIAR!
I'LL RE-MEMBER THIS!
...
FWSH

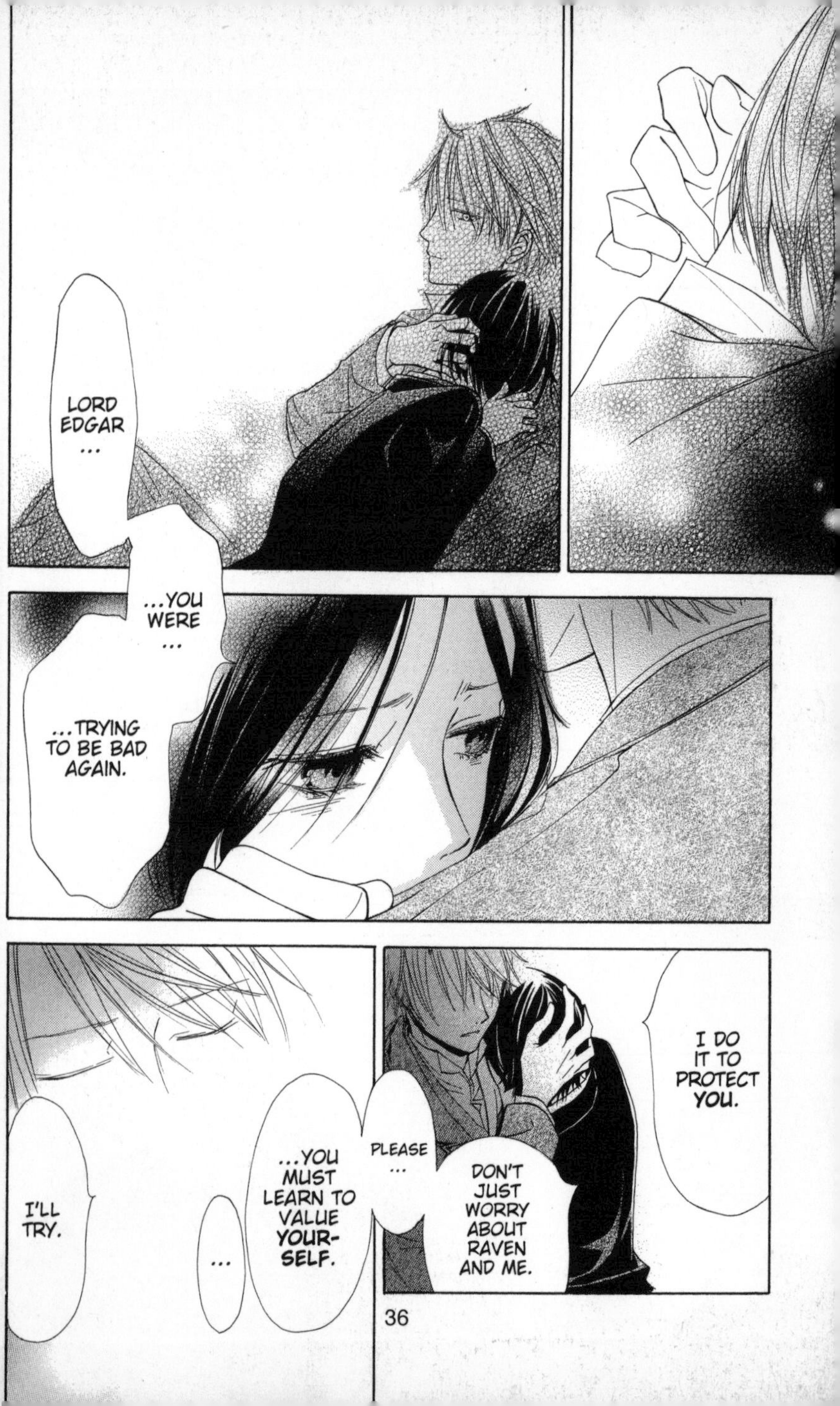
LORD EDGAR ...
...YOU WERE ...
...TRYING TO BE BAD AGAIN.
I DO IT TO PROTECT YOU.
DON'T JUST WORRY ABOUT RAVEN AND ME.
PLEASE ...
...YOU MUST LEARN TO VALUE YOURSELF.
...
I'LL TRY.

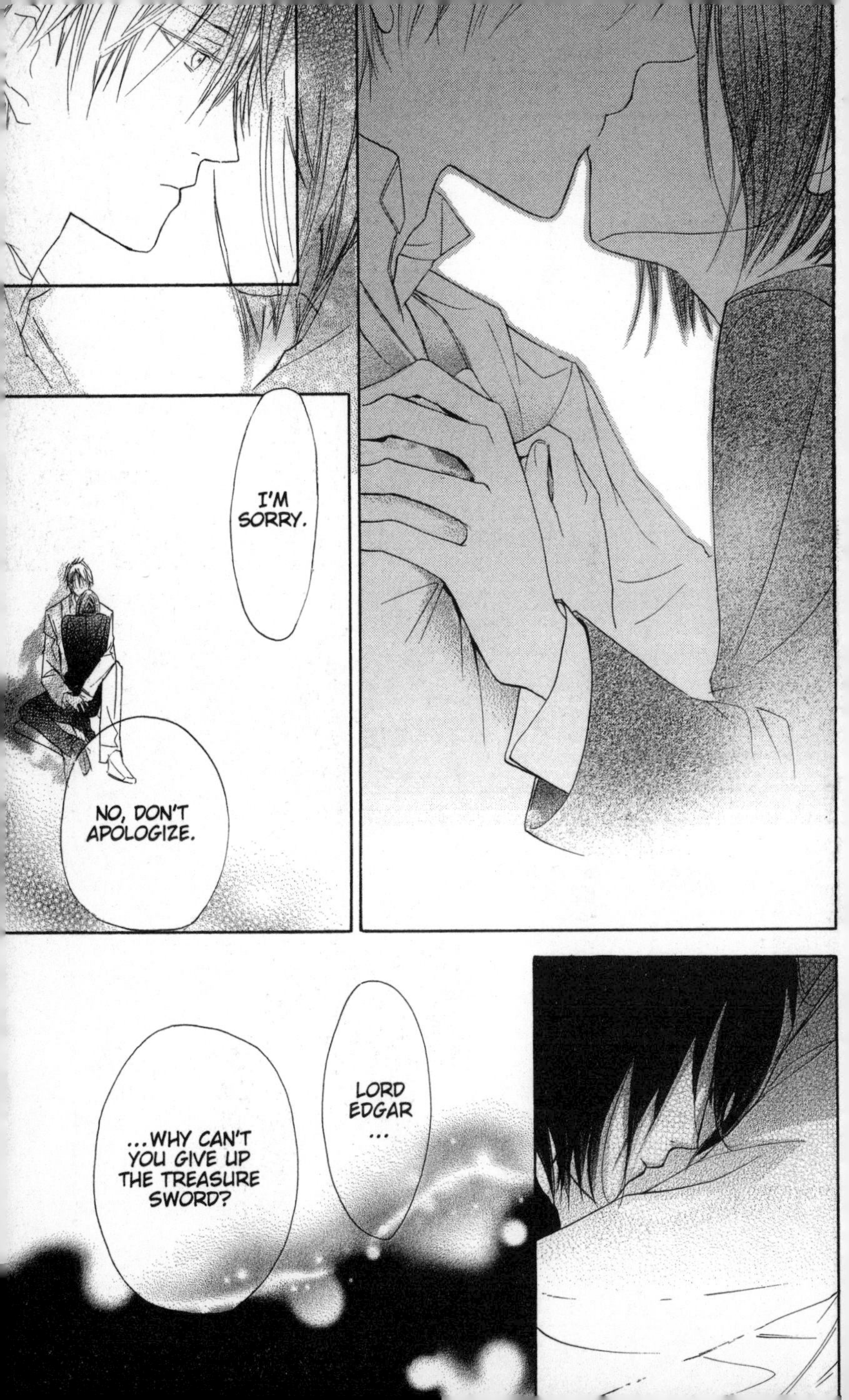
I'M SORRY.
NO, DON'T APOLOGIZE.
LORD EDGAR ...
...WHY CAN'T YOU GIVE UP THE TREASURE SWORD?

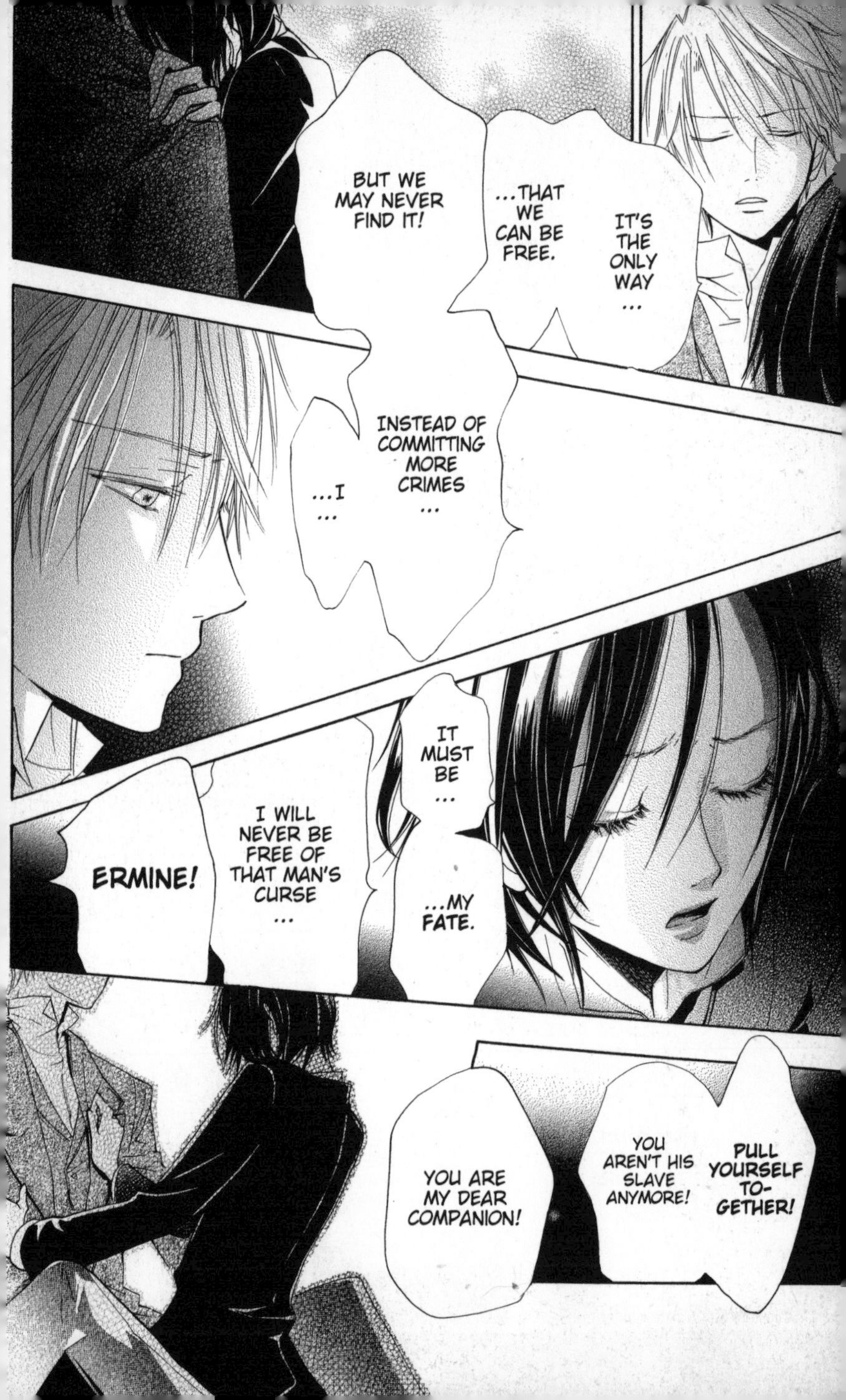
IT'S THE ONLY WAY ...
...THAT WE CAN BE FREE.
BUT WE MAY NEVER FIND IT!
INSTEAD OF COMMITTING MORE CRIMES ...
...I ...
IT MUST BE ...
...MY FATE.
I WILL NEVER BE FREE OF THAT MAN'S CURSE ...
ERMINE!
PULL YOURSELF TO-GETHER!
YOU AREN'T HIS SLAVE ANYMORE!
YOU ARE MY DEAR COMPANION!

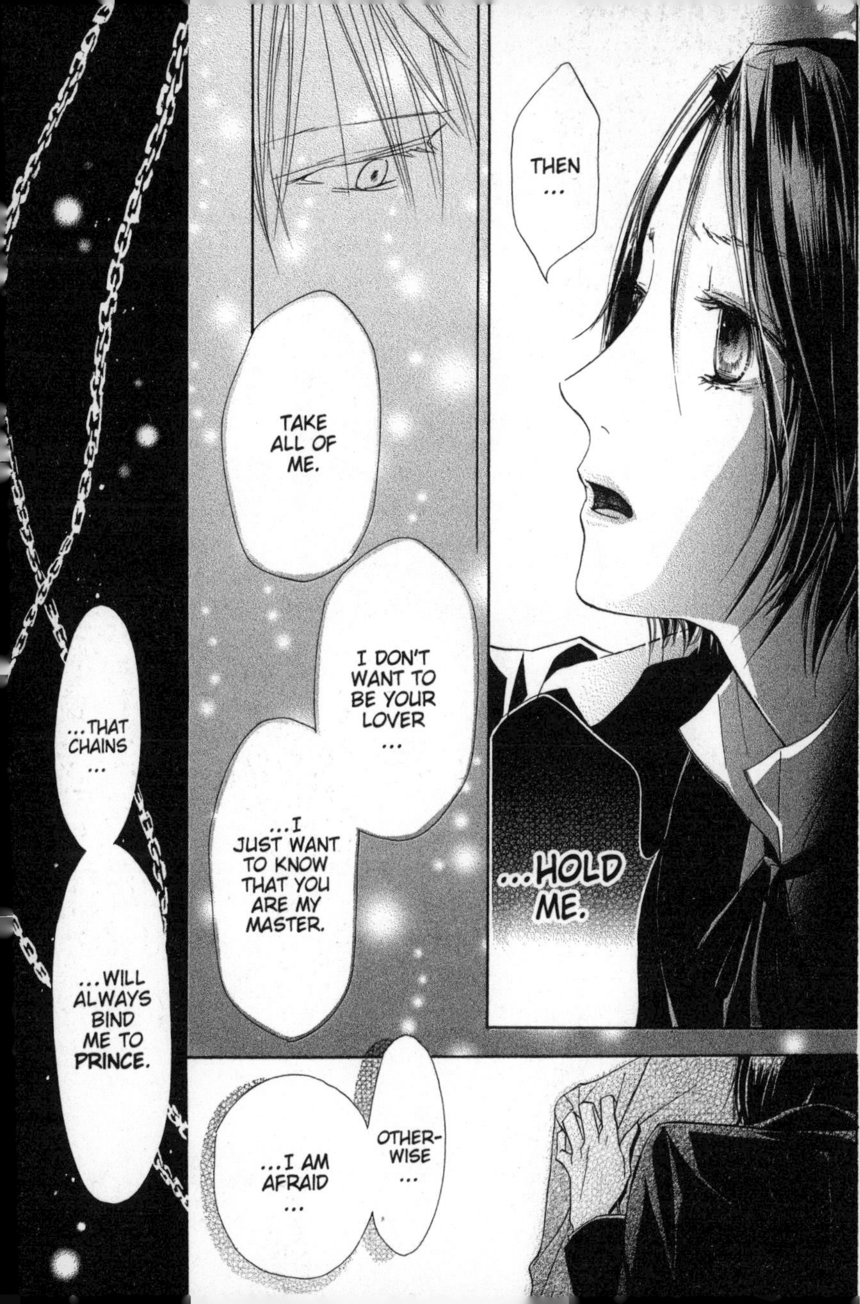
THEN ...
...HOLD ME.
TAKE ALL OF ME.
I DON'T WANT TO BE YOUR LOVER ...
...I JUST WANT TO KNOW THAT YOU ARE MY MASTER.
OTHER-WISE ...
...I AM AFRAID ...
...THAT CHAINS ...
...WILL ALWAYS BIND ME TO PRINCE.

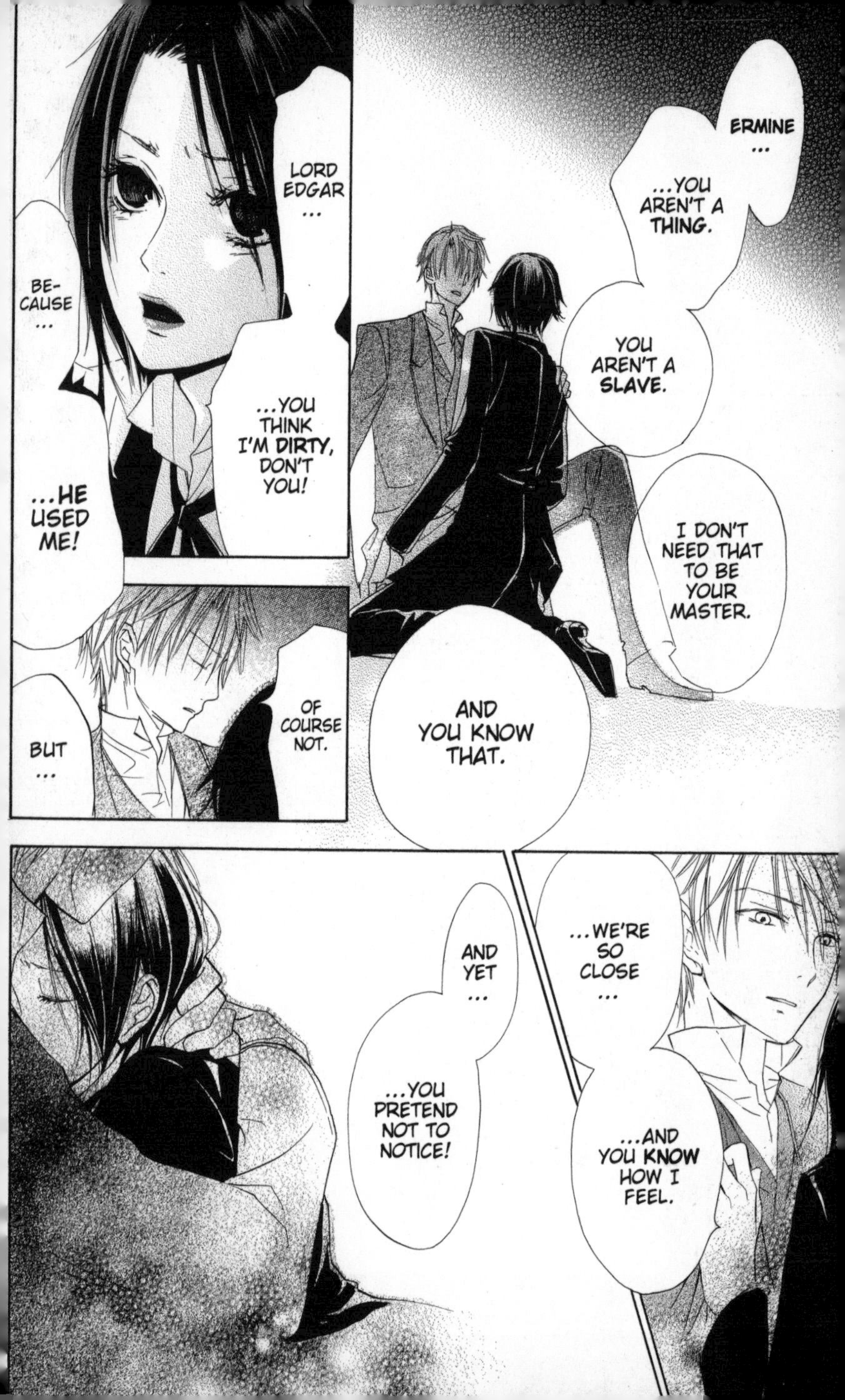

ERMINE ...
...YOU AREN'T A THING.
YOU AREN'T A SLAVE.
I DON'T NEED THAT TO BE YOUR MASTER.
AND YOU KNOW THAT.
LORD EDGAR ...
...YOU THINK I'M DIRTY, DON'T YOU!
BE-CAUSE ...
...HE USED ME!
OF COURSE NOT.
BUT ...
...WE'RE SO CLOSE ...
...AND YOU KNOW HOW I FEEL.
AND YET ...
...YOU PRETEND NOT TO NOTICE!

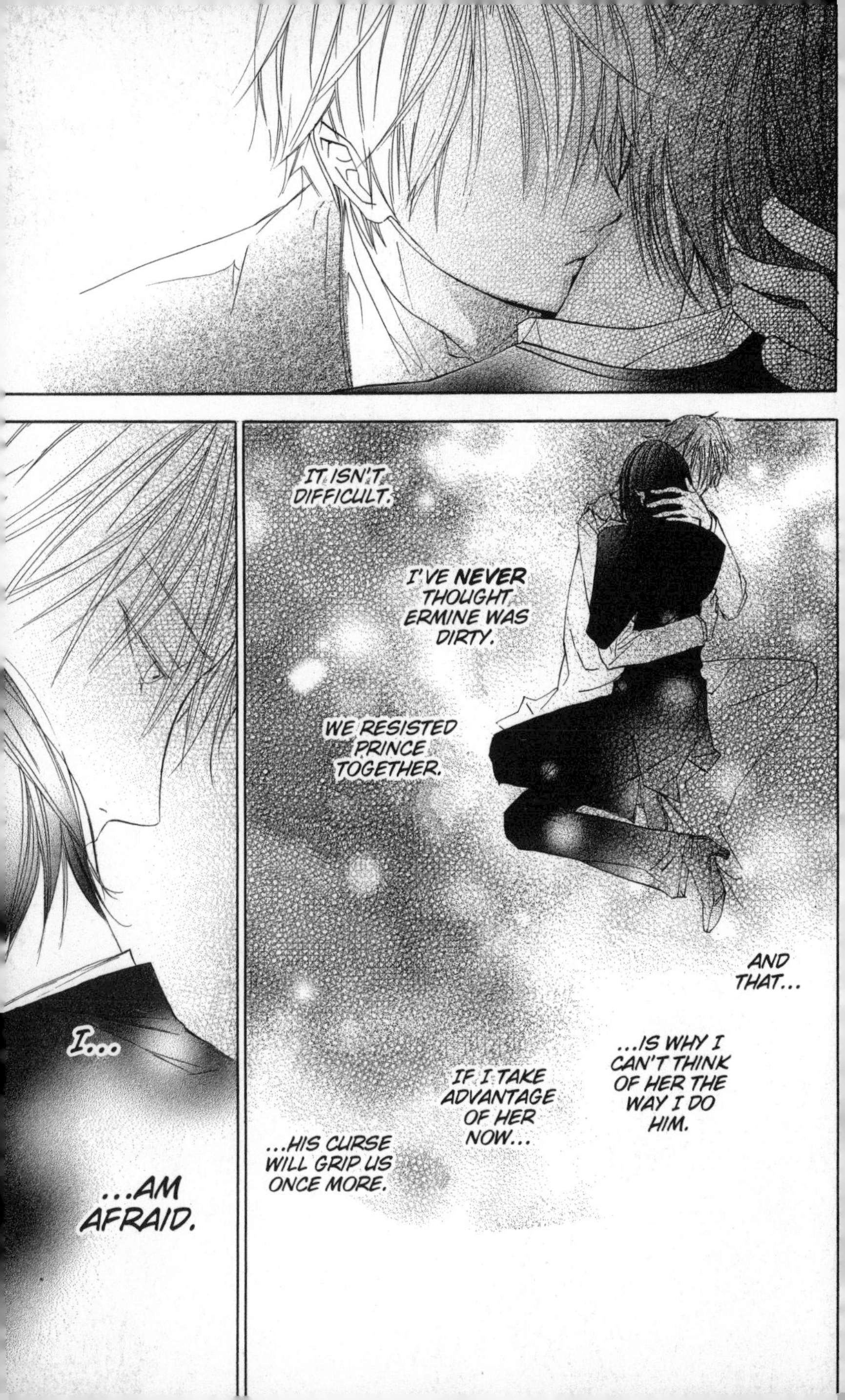
IT ISN'T DIFFICULT.
I'VE **NEVER** THOUGHT ERMINE WAS DIRTY.
WE RESISTED PRINCE TOGETHER.
AND THAT...
...IS WHY I CAN'T THINK OF HER THE WAY I DO HIM.
IF I TAKE ADVANTAGE OF HER NOW...
...HIS CURSE WILL GRIP US ONCE MORE.
I...
...AM AFRAID.

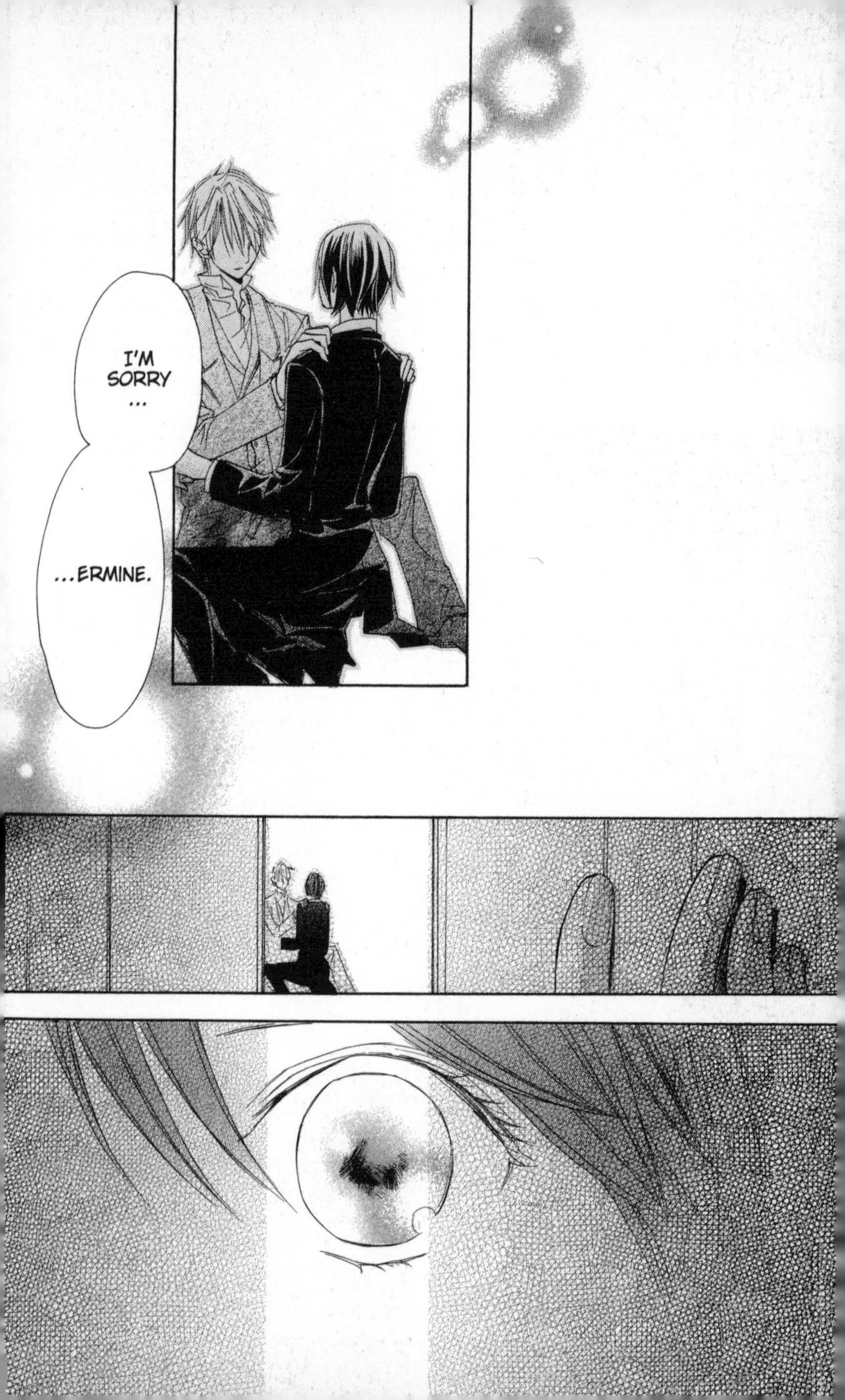
I'M SORRY ...
...ERMINE.

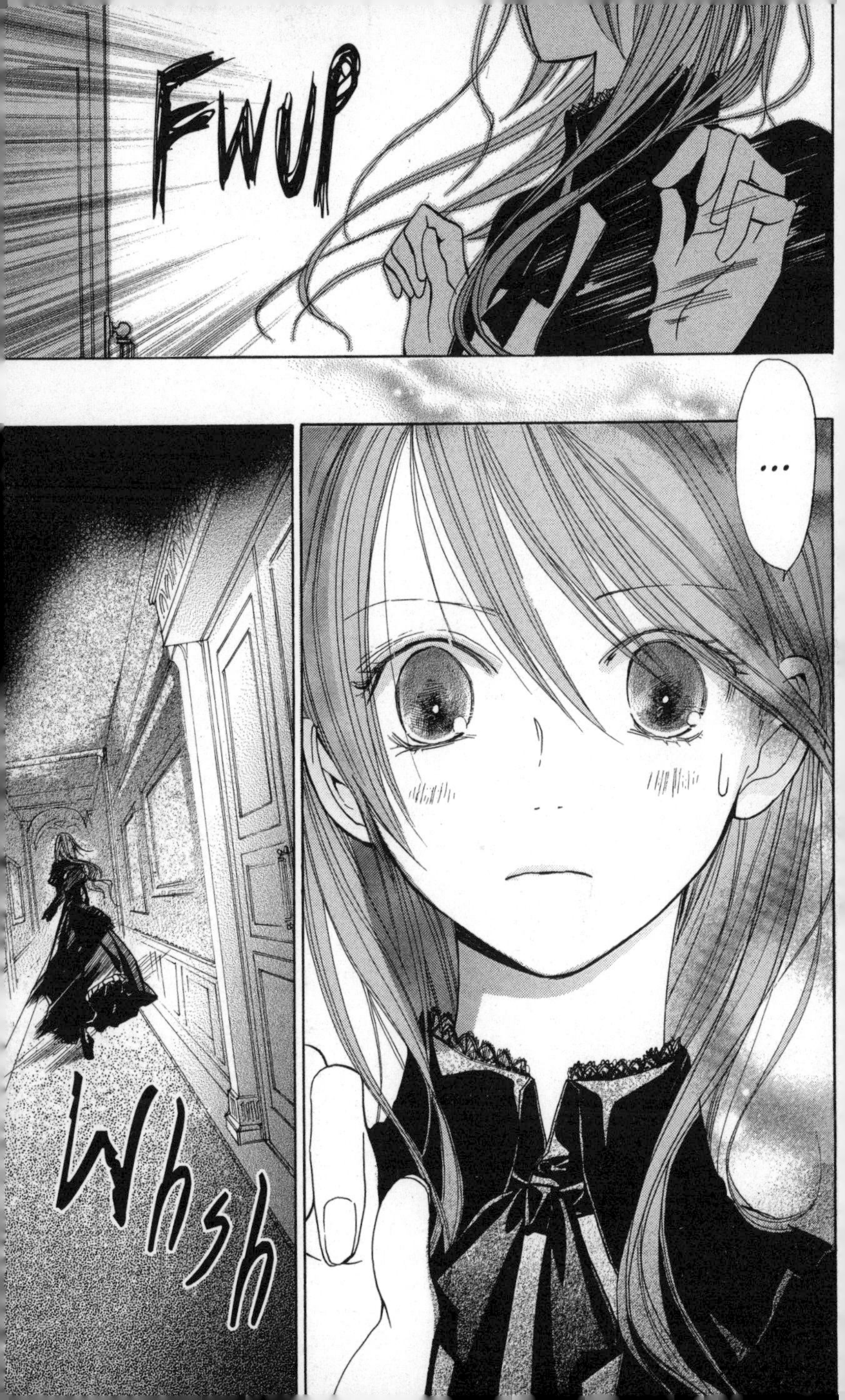
FWUP
...
Whsh

The Earl & the Fairy

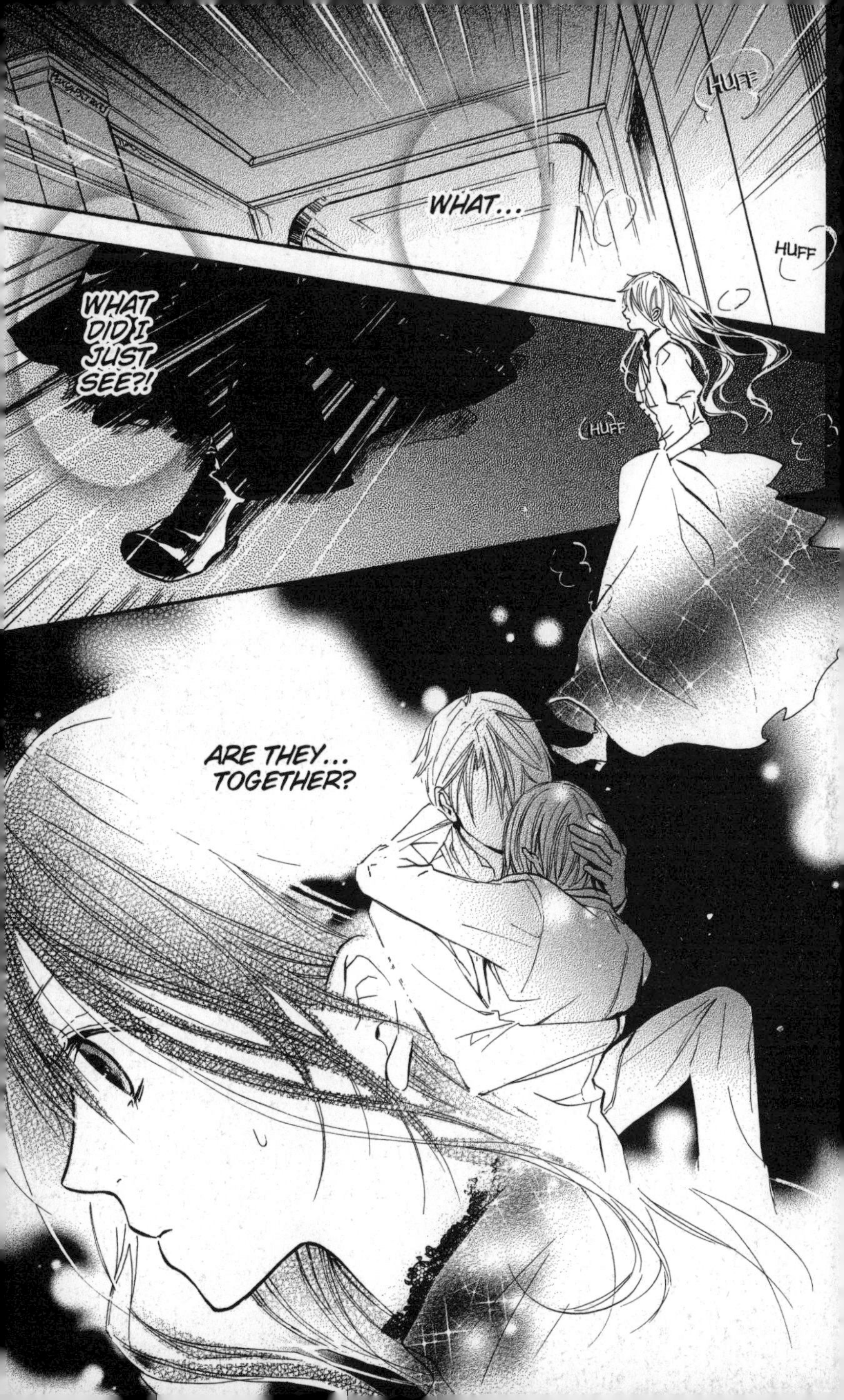
HUFF
WHAT...
HUFF
WHAT DID I JUST SEE?!
HUFF
ARE THEY... TOGETHER?

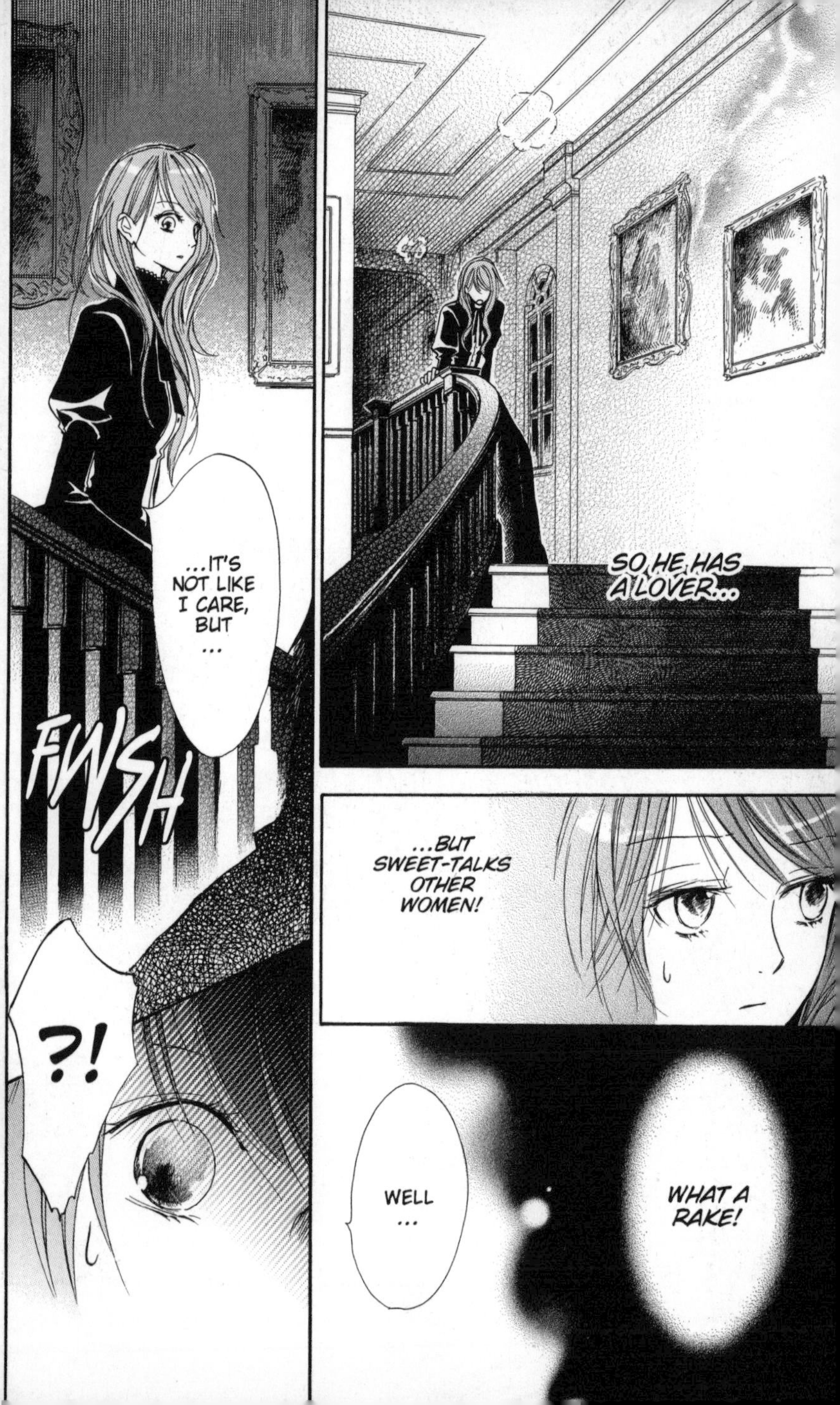
SO HE HAS A LOVER...
...BUT SWEET-TALKS OTHER WOMEN!
WHAT A RAKE!
WELL ...
...IT'S NOT LIKE I CARE, BUT ...
FWSH
?!

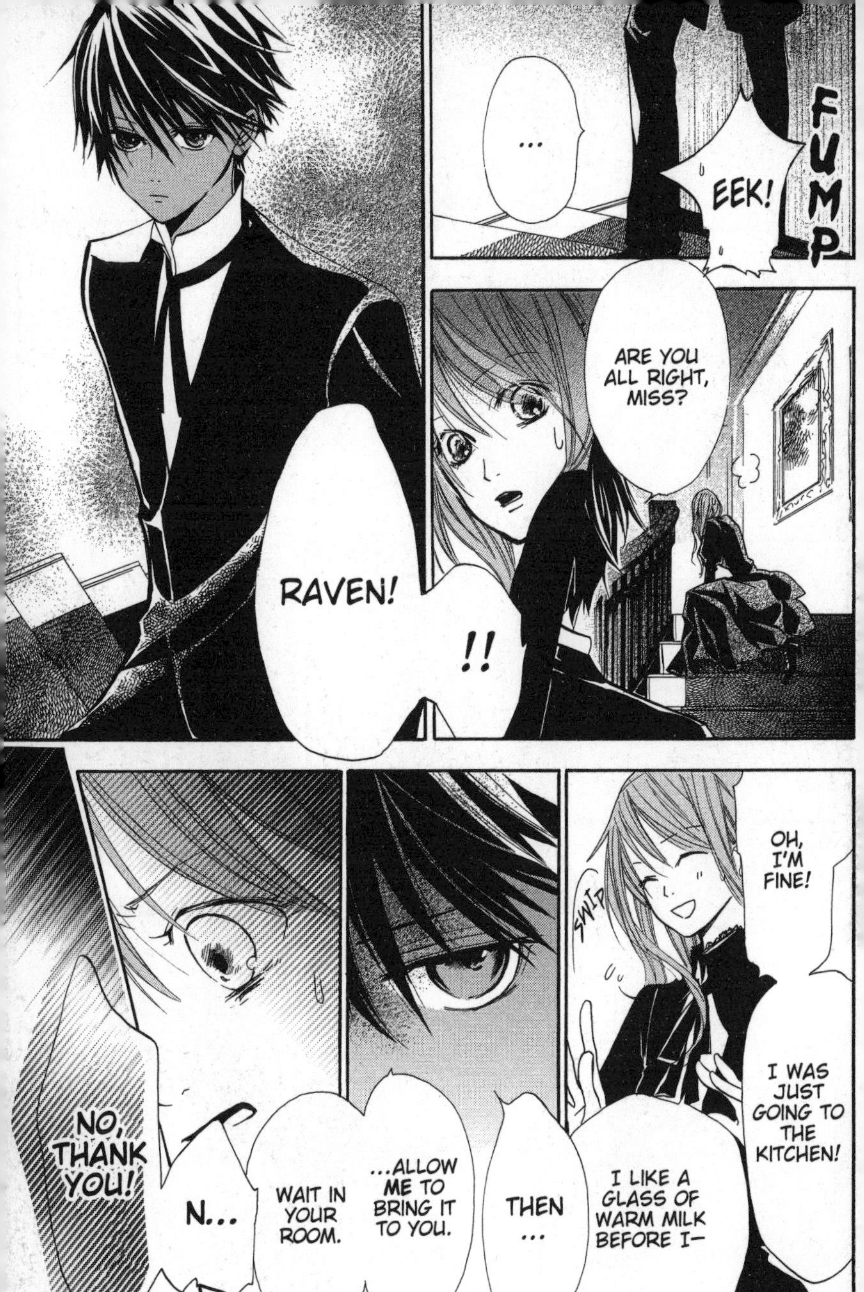

FUMP
EEK!
...
ARE YOU ALL RIGHT, MISS?
!!
RAVEN!
OH, I'M FINE!
SWIP
I WAS JUST GOING TO THE KITCHEN!
I LIKE A GLASS OF WARM MILK BEFORE I—
THEN ...
...ALLOW ME TO BRING IT TO YOU.
WAIT IN YOUR ROOM.
N...
NO, THANK YOU!

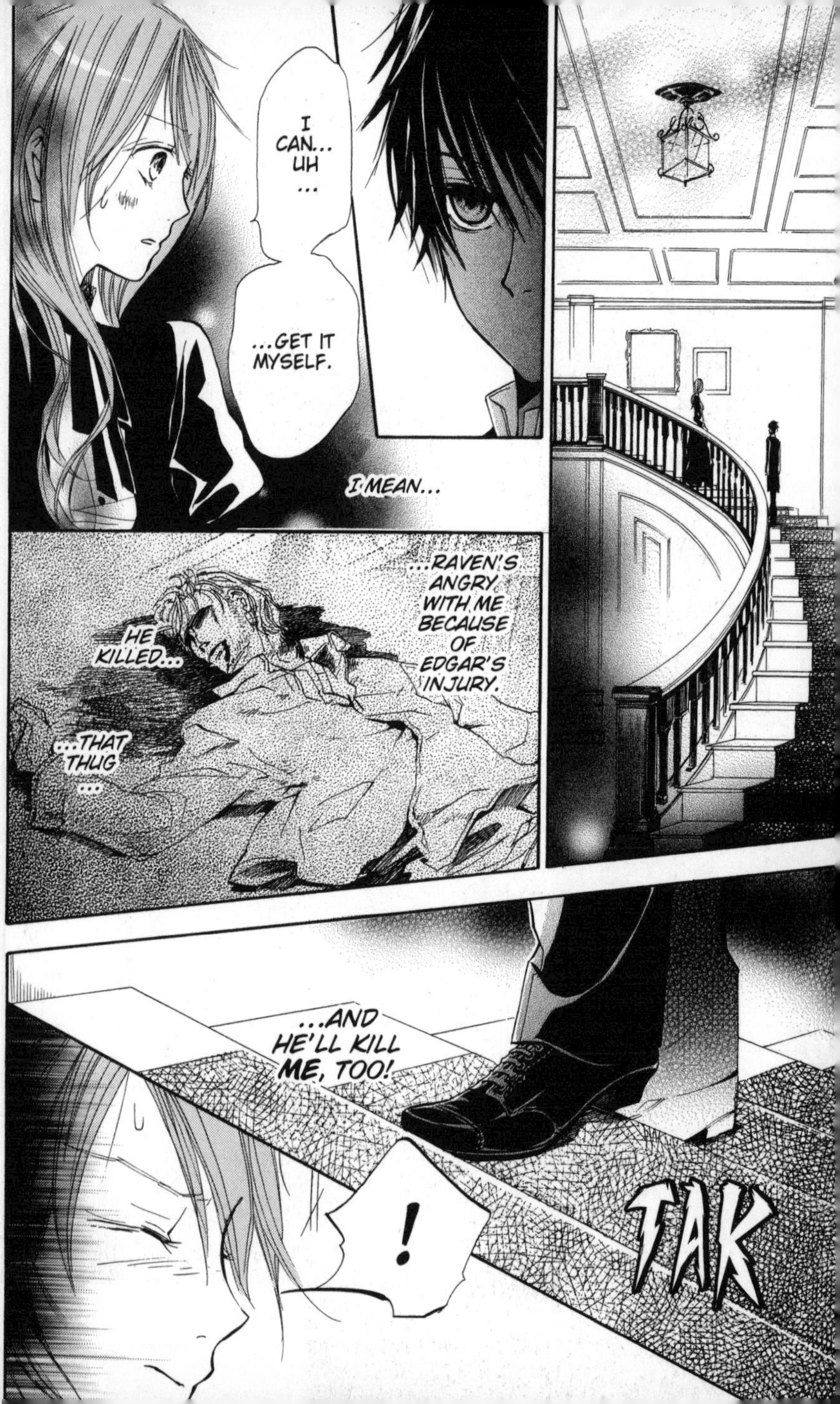
I CAN... UH...
...GET IT MYSELF.
I MEAN...
...RAVEN'S ANGRY WITH ME BECAUSE OF EDGAR'S INJURY.
HE KILLED...
...THAT THUG...
...AND HE'LL KILL ME, TOO!
!
TAK

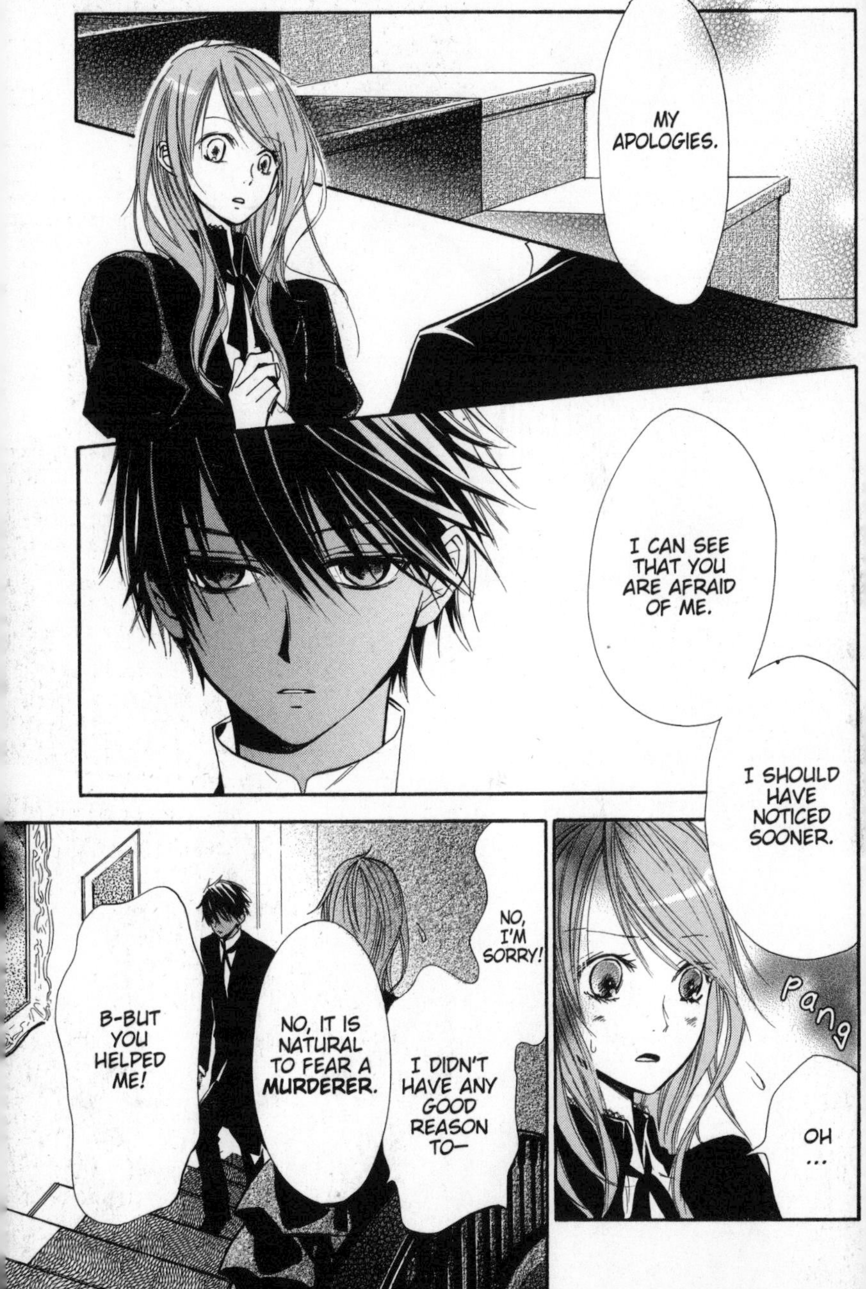
MY APOLOGIES.
I CAN SEE THAT YOU ARE AFRAID OF ME.
I SHOULD HAVE NOTICED SOONER.
Pang
OH ...
NO, I'M SORRY!
I DIDN'T HAVE ANY GOOD REASON TO—
NO, IT IS NATURAL TO FEAR A MURDERER.
B-BUT YOU HELPED ME!

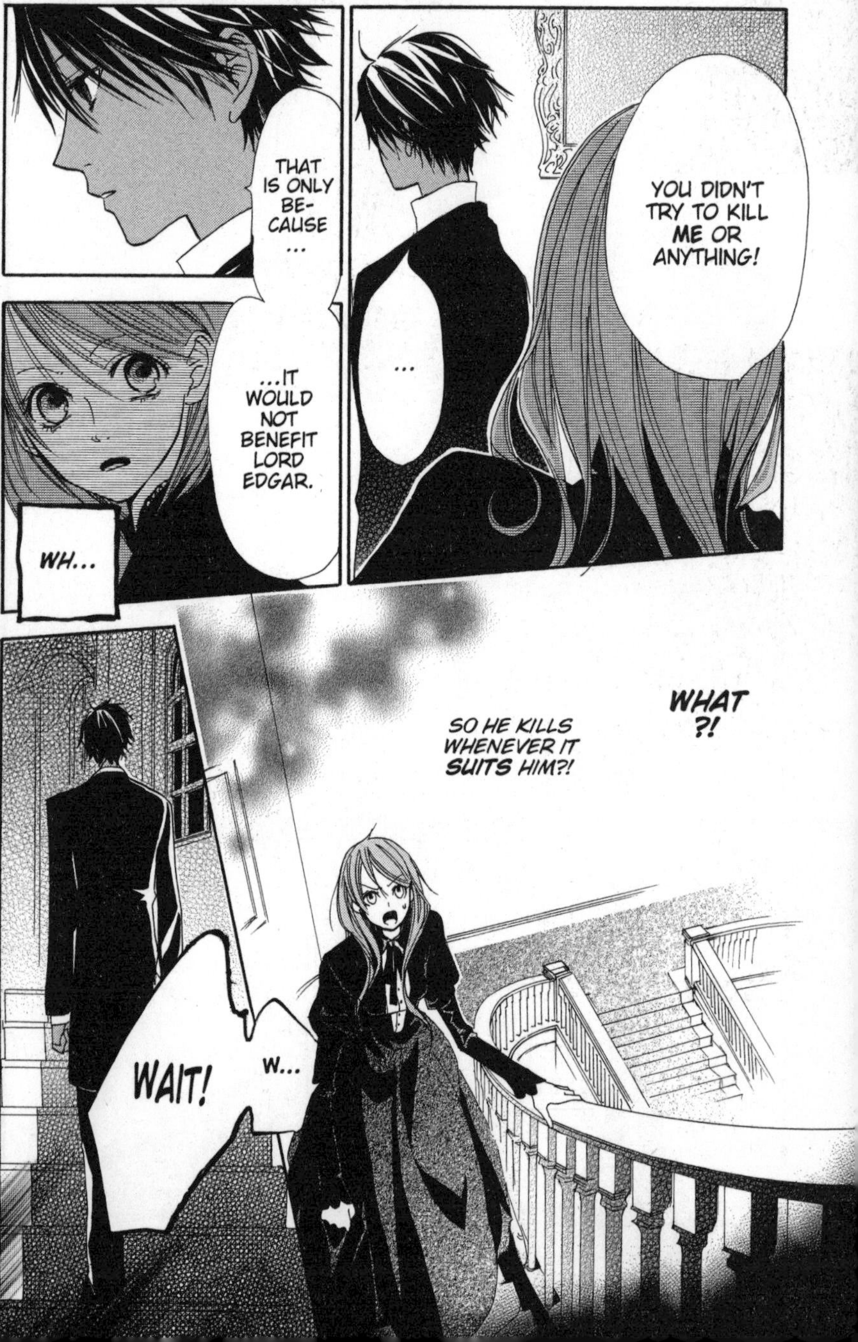
YOU DIDN'T TRY TO KILL ME OR ANYTHING!
...
THAT IS ONLY BE-CAUSE ...
...IT WOULD NOT BENEFIT LORD EDGAR.
WH...
WHAT ?!
SO HE KILLS WHENEVER IT SUITS HIM?!
W...
WAIT!

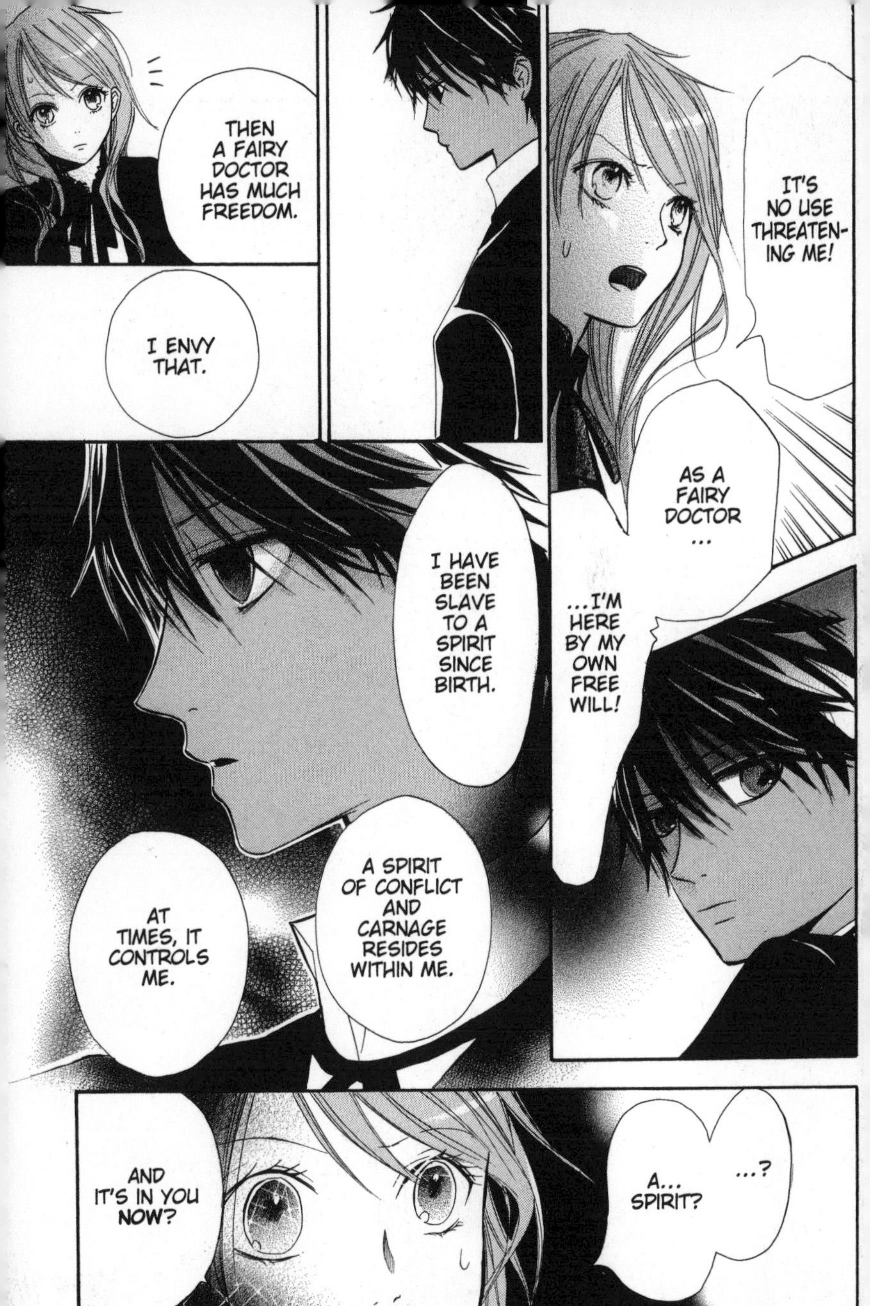
IT'S NO USE THREATEN-ING ME!
AS A FAIRY DOCTOR ...
...I'M HERE BY MY OWN FREE WILL!
THEN A FAIRY DOCTOR HAS MUCH FREEDOM.
I ENVY THAT.
I HAVE BEEN SLAVE TO A SPIRIT SINCE BIRTH.
A SPIRIT OF CONFLICT AND CARNAGE RESIDES WITHIN ME.
AT TIMES, IT CONTROLS ME.
...?
A... SPIRIT?
AND IT'S IN YOU NOW?

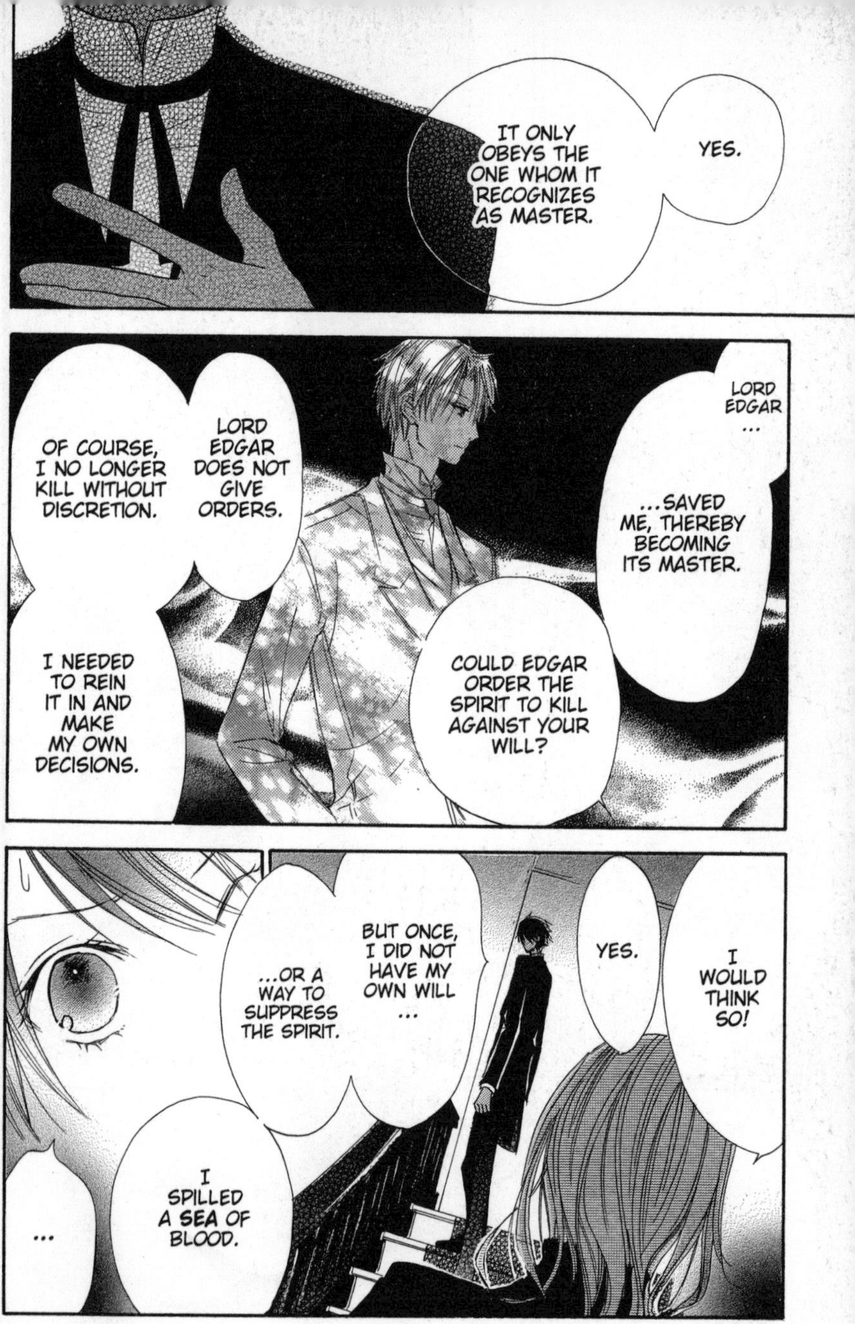
YES.
IT ONLY OBEYS THE ONE WHOM IT RECOGNIZES AS MASTER.
LORD EDGAR ...
...SAVED ME, THEREBY BECOMING ITS MASTER.
COULD EDGAR ORDER THE SPIRIT TO KILL AGAINST YOUR WILL?
LORD EDGAR DOES NOT GIVE ORDERS.
OF COURSE, I NO LONGER KILL WITHOUT DISCRETION.
I NEEDED TO REIN IT IN AND MAKE MY OWN DECISIONS.
I WOULD THINK SO!
YES.
BUT ONCE, I DID NOT HAVE MY OWN WILL ...
...OR A WAY TO SUPPRESS THE SPIRIT.
I SPILLED A SEA OF BLOOD.
...

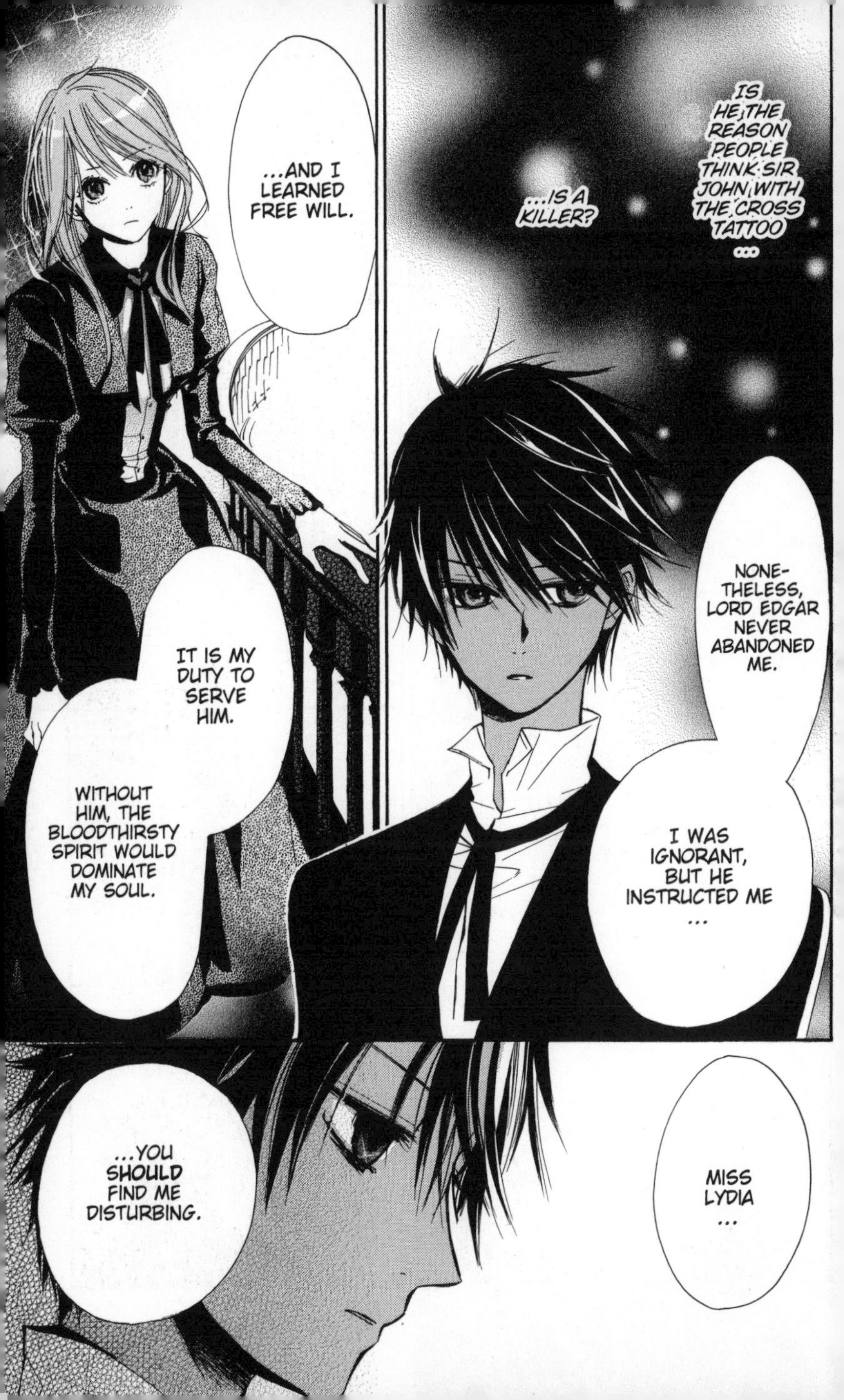
IS HE THE REASON PEOPLE THINK SIR JOHN WITH THE CROSS TATTOO...
...IS A KILLER?
NONE-THELESS, LORD EDGAR NEVER ABANDONED ME.
I WAS IGNORANT, BUT HE INSTRUCTED ME...
...AND I LEARNED FREE WILL.
IT IS MY DUTY TO SERVE HIM.
WITHOUT HIM, THE BLOODTHIRSTY SPIRIT WOULD DOMINATE MY SOUL.
MISS LYDIA...
...YOU SHOULD FIND ME DISTURBING.

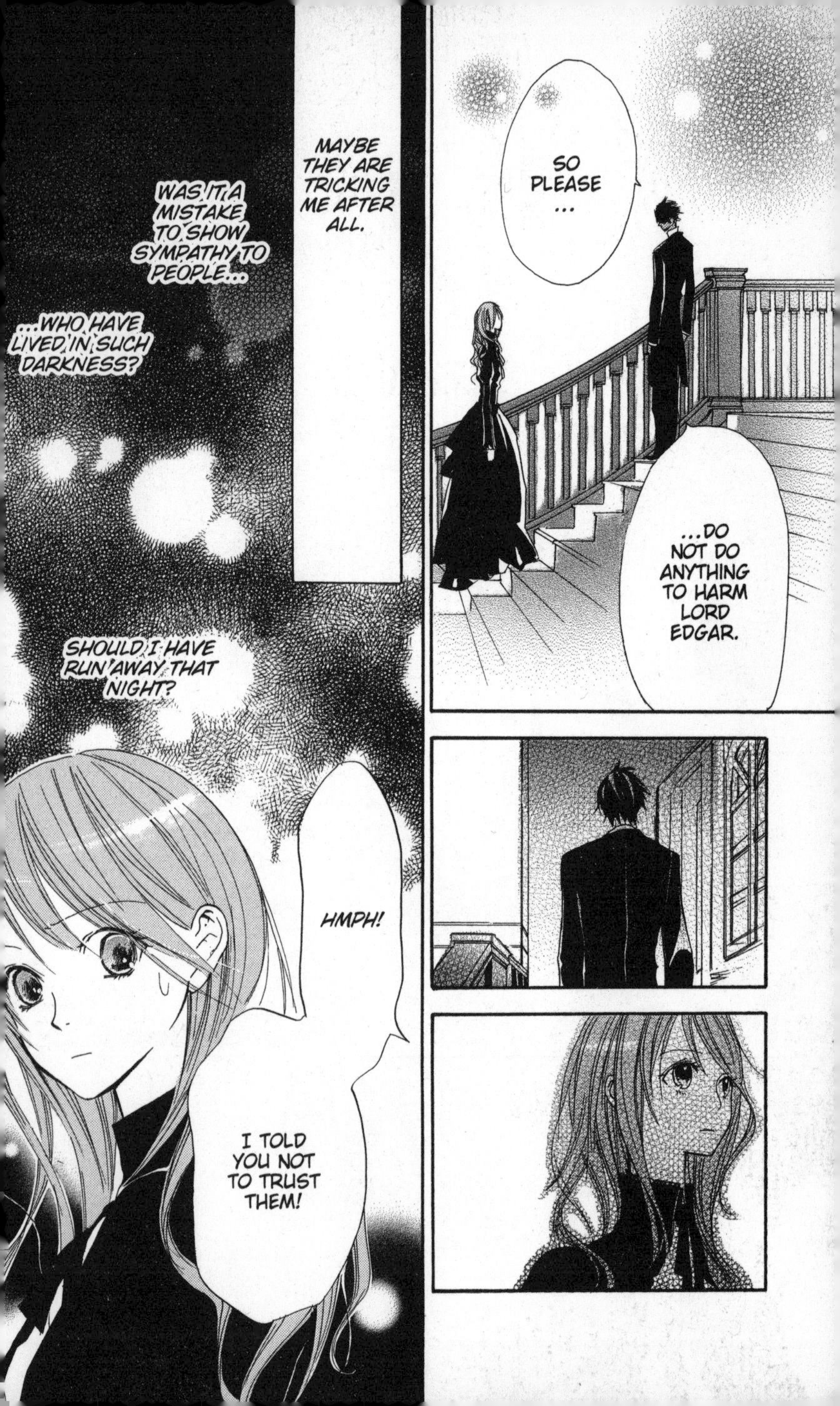
SO PLEASE ...
...DO NOT DO ANYTHING TO HARM LORD EDGAR.
MAYBE THEY ARE TRICKING ME AFTER ALL.
WAS IT A MISTAKE TO SHOW SYMPATHY TO PEOPLE...
...WHO HAVE LIVED IN SUCH DARKNESS?
SHOULD I HAVE RUN AWAY THAT NIGHT?
HMPH!
I TOLD YOU NOT TO TRUST THEM!

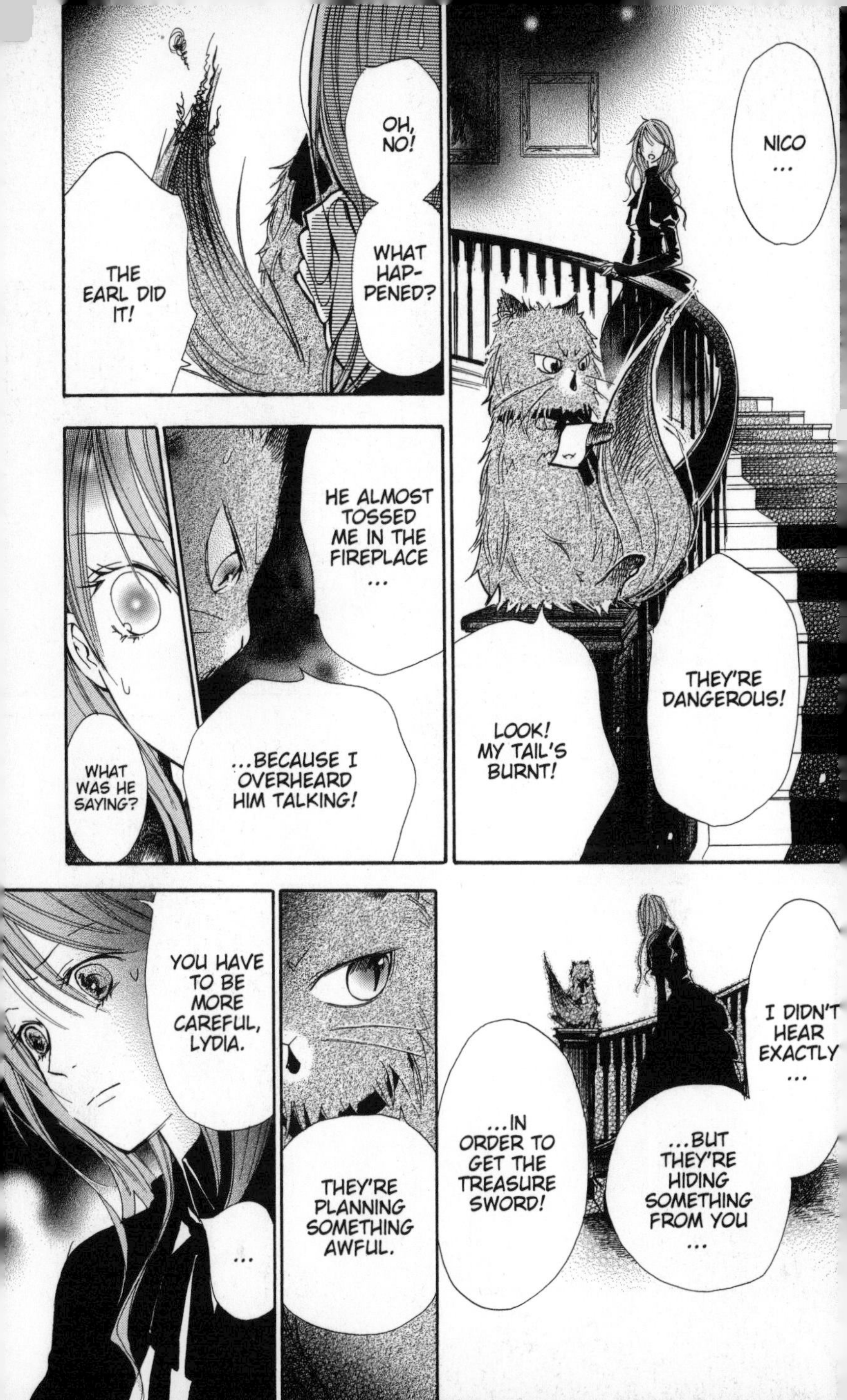

NICO ...
THEY'RE DANGEROUS!
LOOK! MY TAIL'S BURNT!
OH, NO!
WHAT HAP-PENED?
THE EARL DID IT!
HE ALMOST TOSSED ME IN THE FIREPLACE ...
...BECAUSE I OVERHEARD HIM TALKING!
WHAT WAS HE SAYING?
I DIDN'T HEAR EXACTLY ...
...BUT THEY'RE HIDING SOMETHING FROM YOU ...
...IN ORDER TO GET THE TREASURE SWORD!
THEY'RE PLANNING SOMETHING AWFUL.
YOU HAVE TO BE MORE CAREFUL, LYDIA.
...

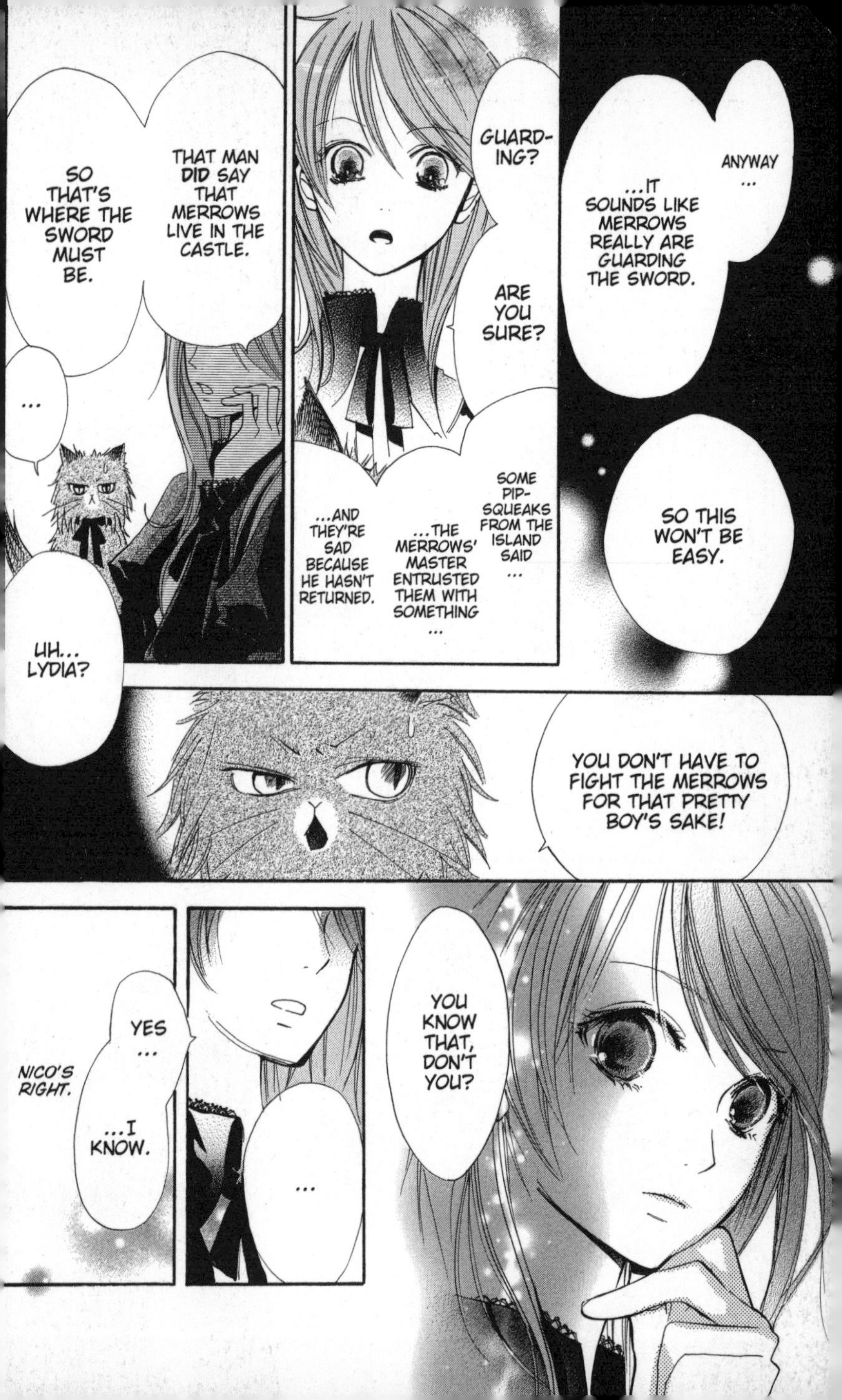
ANYWAY...
...IT SOUNDS LIKE MERROWS REALLY ARE GUARDING THE SWORD.
SO THIS WON'T BE EASY.
GUARDING?
ARE YOU SURE?
SOME PIP-SQUEAKS FROM THE ISLAND SAID...
...THE MERROWS' MASTER ENTRUSTED THEM WITH SOMETHING...
...AND THEY'RE SAD BECAUSE HE HASN'T RETURNED.
THAT MAN DID SAY THAT MERROWS LIVE IN THE CASTLE.
SO THAT'S WHERE THE SWORD MUST BE.
...
UH... LYDIA?
YOU DON'T HAVE TO FIGHT THE MERROWS FOR THAT PRETTY BOY'S SAKE!
YOU KNOW THAT, DON'T YOU?
...
YES...
...I KNOW.
NICO'S RIGHT.

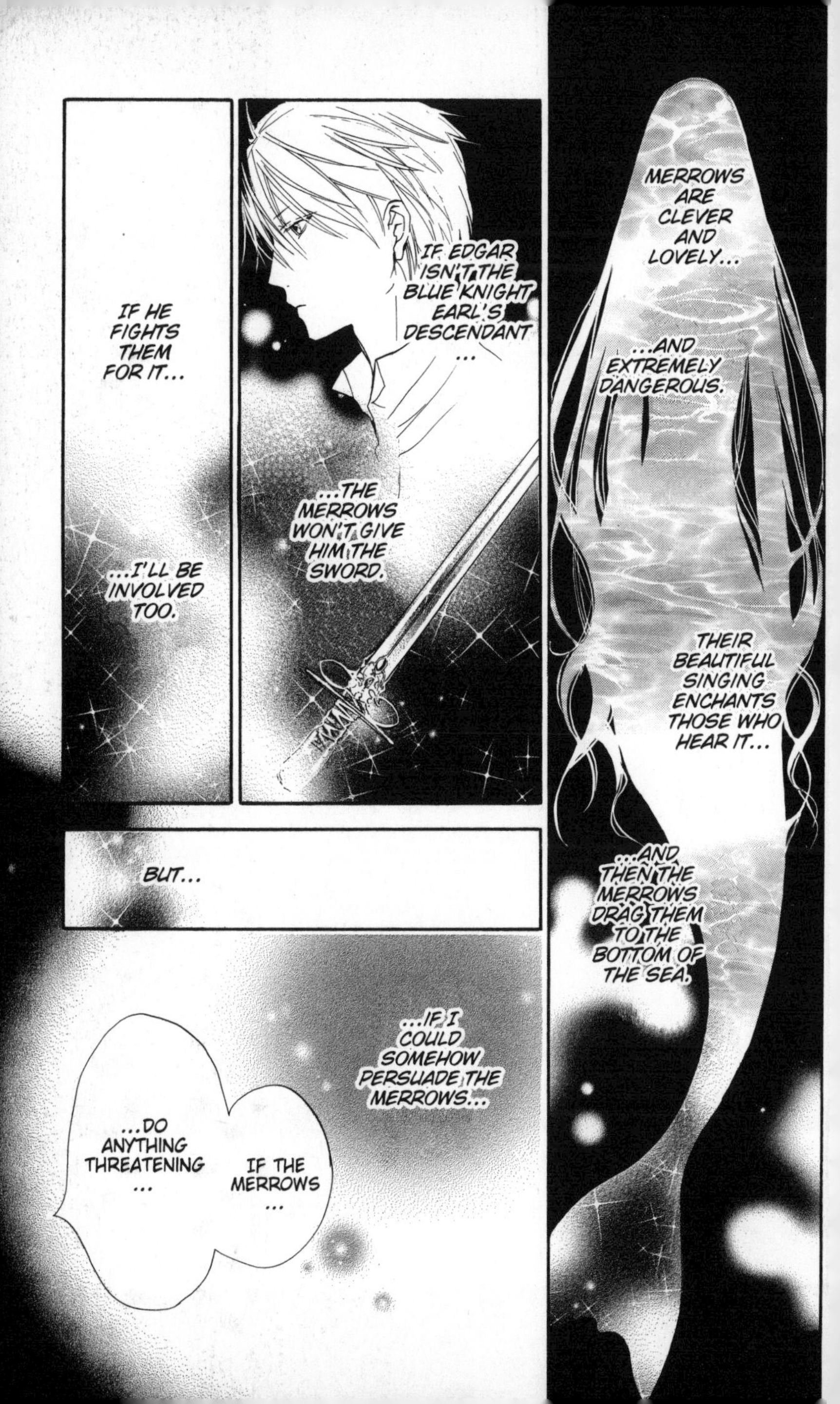
MERROWS ARE CLEVER AND LOVELY...
...AND EXTREMELY DANGEROUS.
THEIR BEAUTIFUL SINGING ENCHANTS THOSE WHO HEAR IT...
...AND THEN THE MERROWS DRAG THEM TO THE BOTTOM OF THE SEA.
IF EDGAR ISN'T THE BLUE KNIGHT EARL'S DESCENDANT ...
...THE MERROWS WON'T GIVE HIM THE SWORD.
IF HE FIGHTS THEM FOR IT...
...I'LL BE INVOLVED TOO.
BUT...
...IF I COULD SOMEHOW PERSUADE THE MERROWS...
IF THE MERROWS ...
...DO ANYTHING THREATENING ...

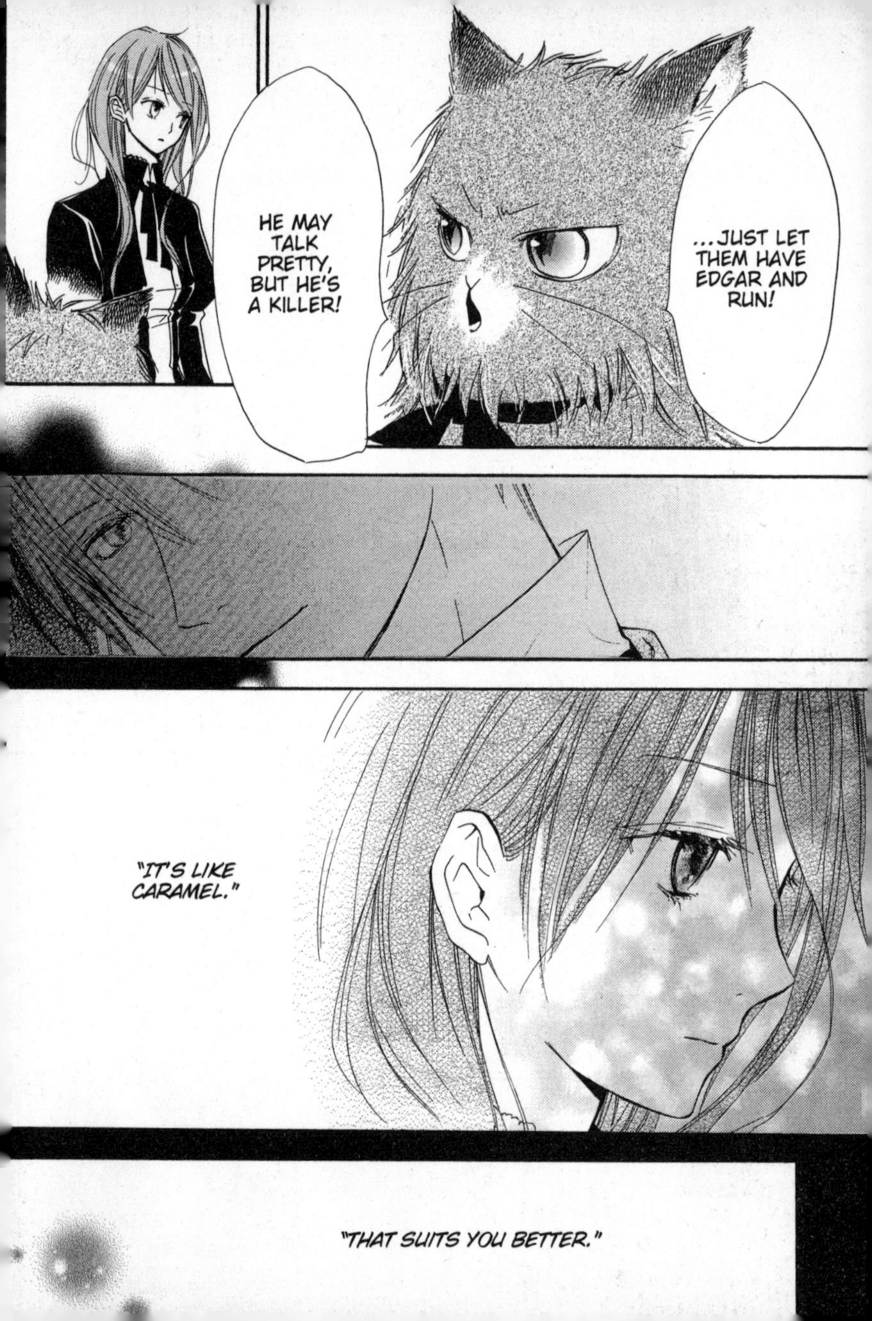
...JUST LET THEM HAVE EDGAR AND RUN!
HE MAY TALK PRETTY, BUT HE'S A KILLER!
"IT'S LIKE CARAMEL."
"THAT SUITS YOU BETTER."

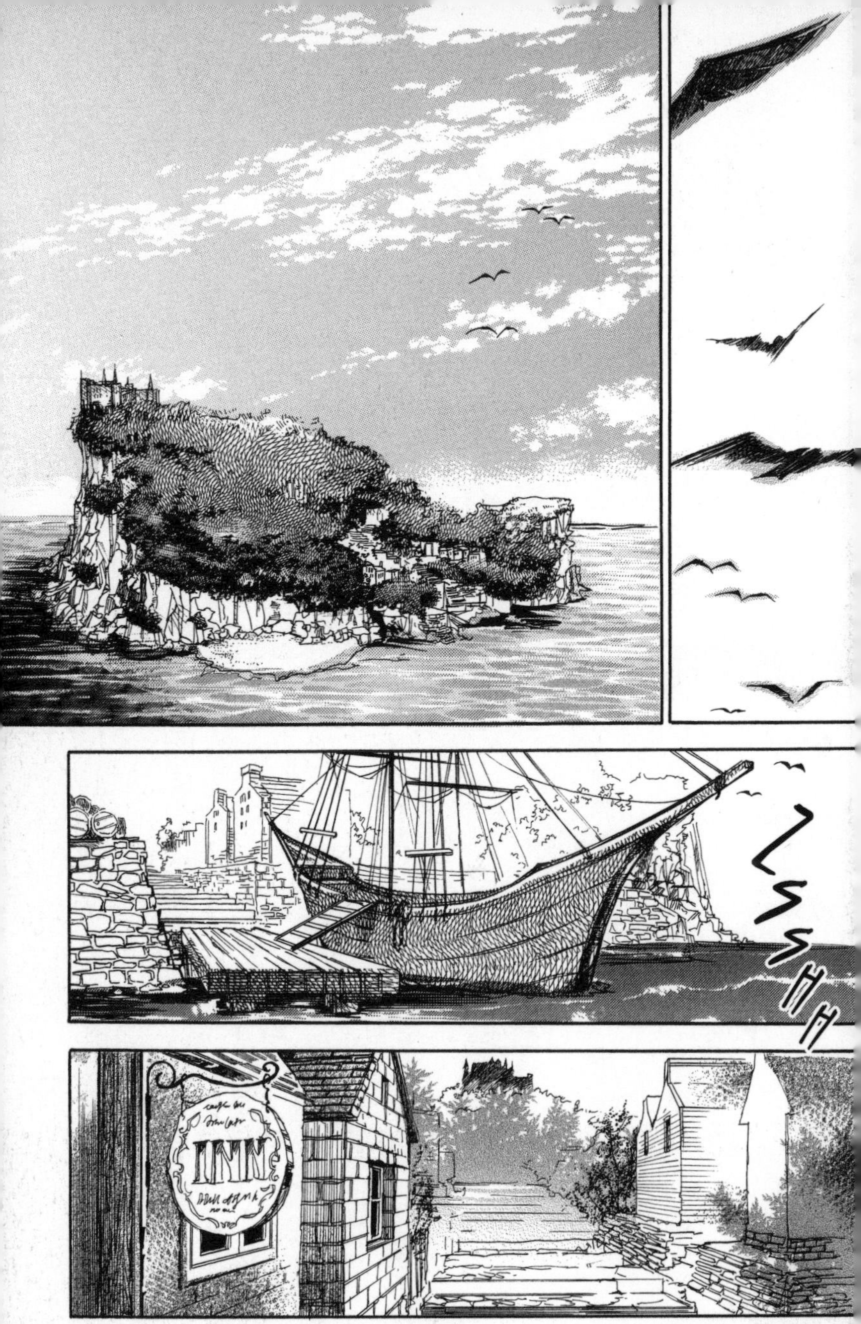
VSSHH
INN

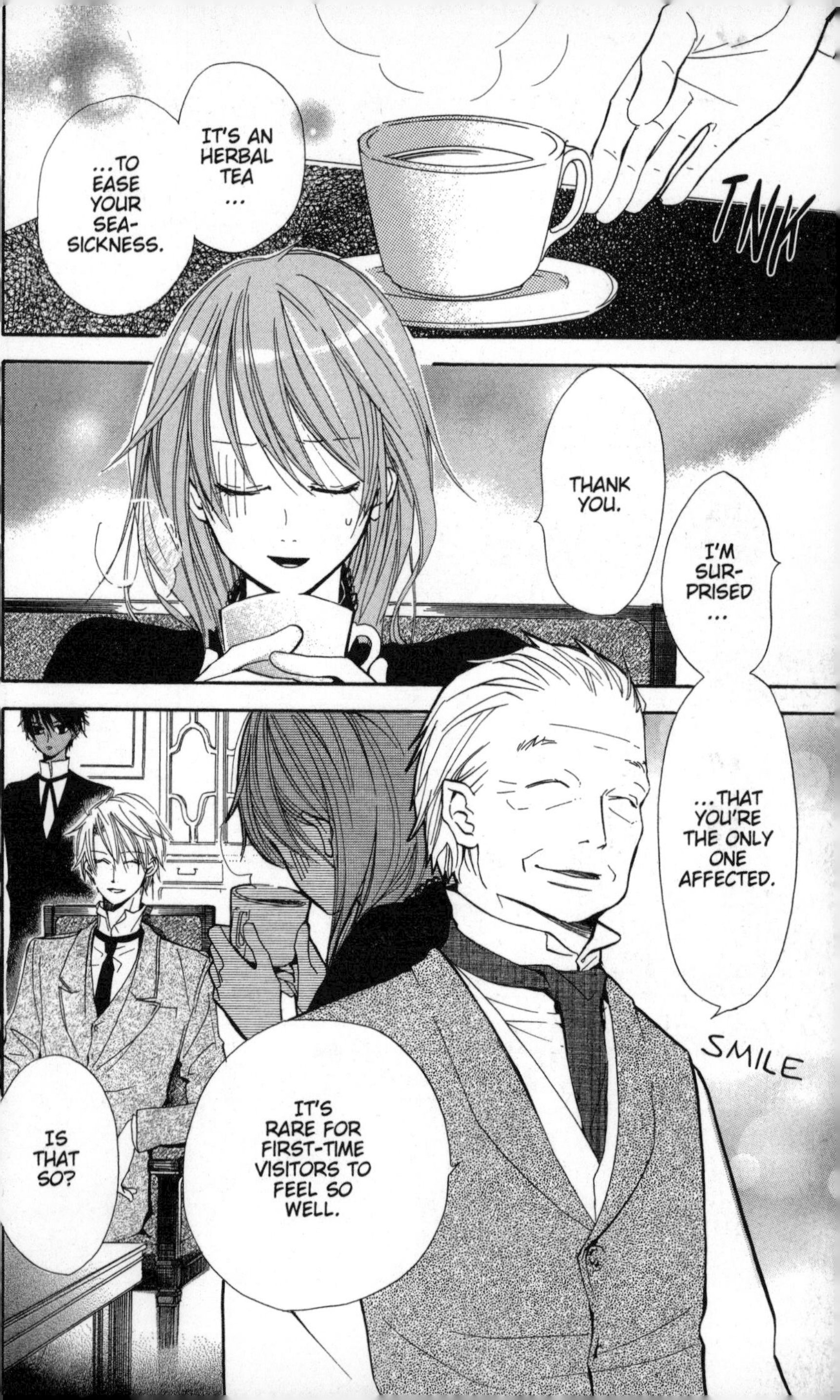
TNK
IT'S AN HERBAL TEA...
...TO EASE YOUR SEA-SICKNESS.
THANK YOU.
I'M SUR-PRISED...
...THAT YOU'RE THE ONLY ONE AFFECTED.
SMILE
IT'S RARE FOR FIRST-TIME VISITORS TO FEEL SO WELL.
IS THAT SO?

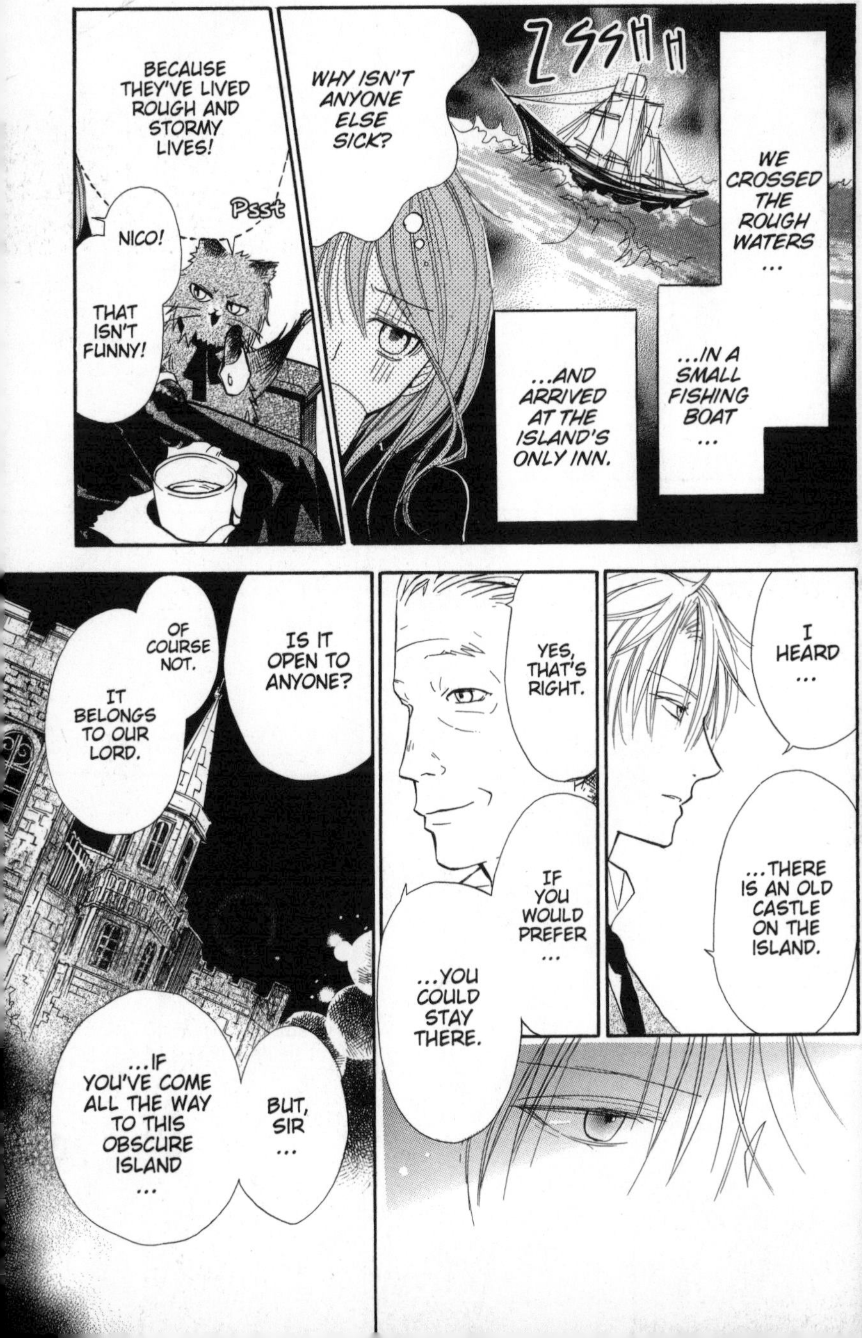
ZSSHH
WE CROSSED THE ROUGH WATERS ...
...IN A SMALL FISHING BOAT ...
...AND ARRIVED AT THE ISLAND'S ONLY INN.
WHY ISN'T ANYONE ELSE SICK?
BECAUSE THEY'VE LIVED ROUGH AND STORMY LIVES!
Psst
NICO!
THAT ISN'T FUNNY!
I HEARD ...
...THERE IS AN OLD CASTLE ON THE ISLAND.
YES, THAT'S RIGHT.
IF YOU WOULD PREFER ...
...YOU COULD STAY THERE.
IS IT OPEN TO ANYONE?
OF COURSE NOT.
IT BELONGS TO OUR LORD.
BUT, SIR ...
...IF YOU'VE COME ALL THE WAY TO THIS OBSCURE ISLAND ...

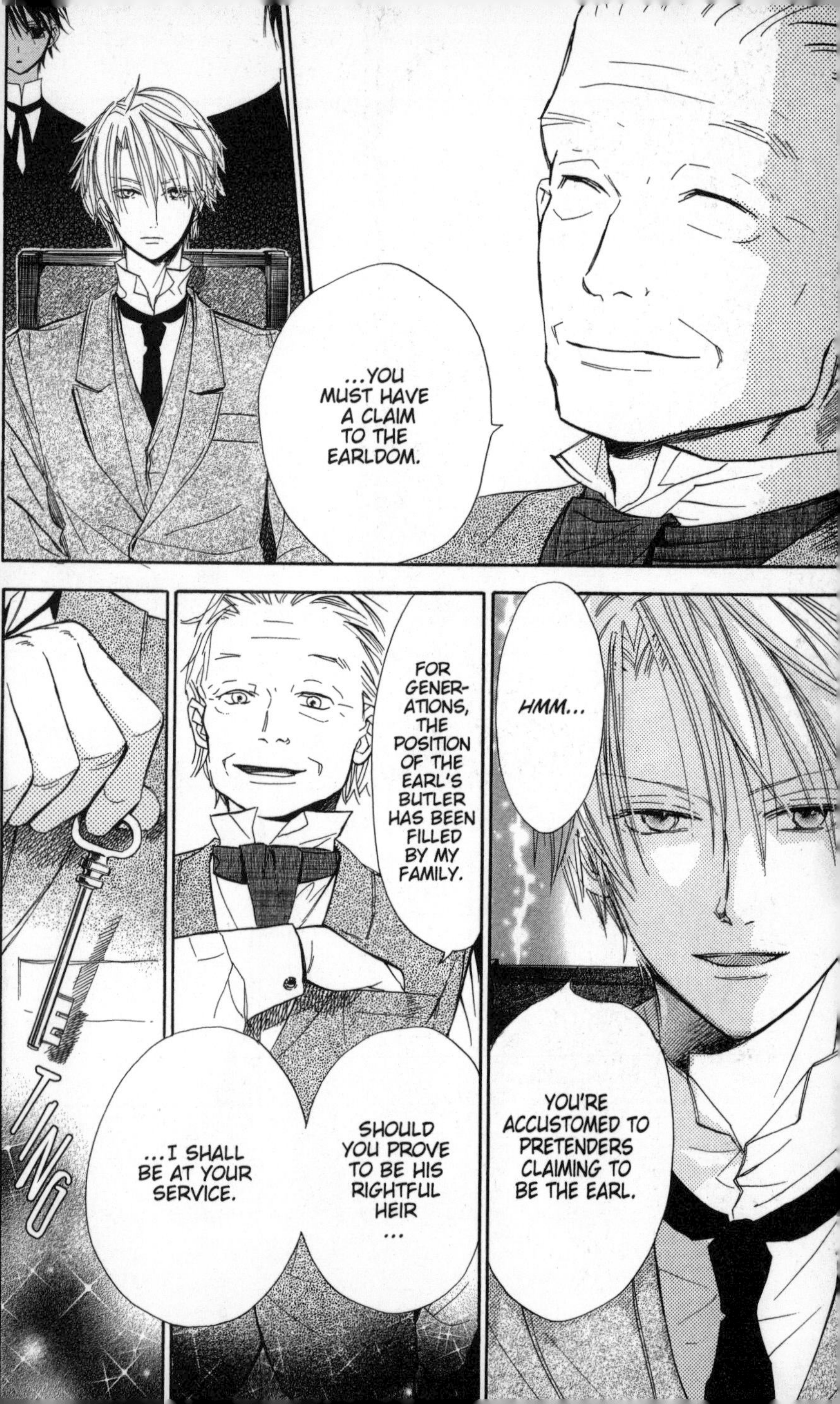
...YOU MUST HAVE A CLAIM TO THE EARLDOM.
HMM...
YOU'RE ACCUSTOMED TO PRETENDERS CLAIMING TO BE THE EARL.
FOR GENERATIONS, THE POSITION OF THE EARL'S BUTLER HAS BEEN FILLED BY MY FAMILY.
SHOULD YOU PROVE TO BE HIS RIGHTFUL HEIR ...
...I SHALL BE AT YOUR SERVICE.
TING

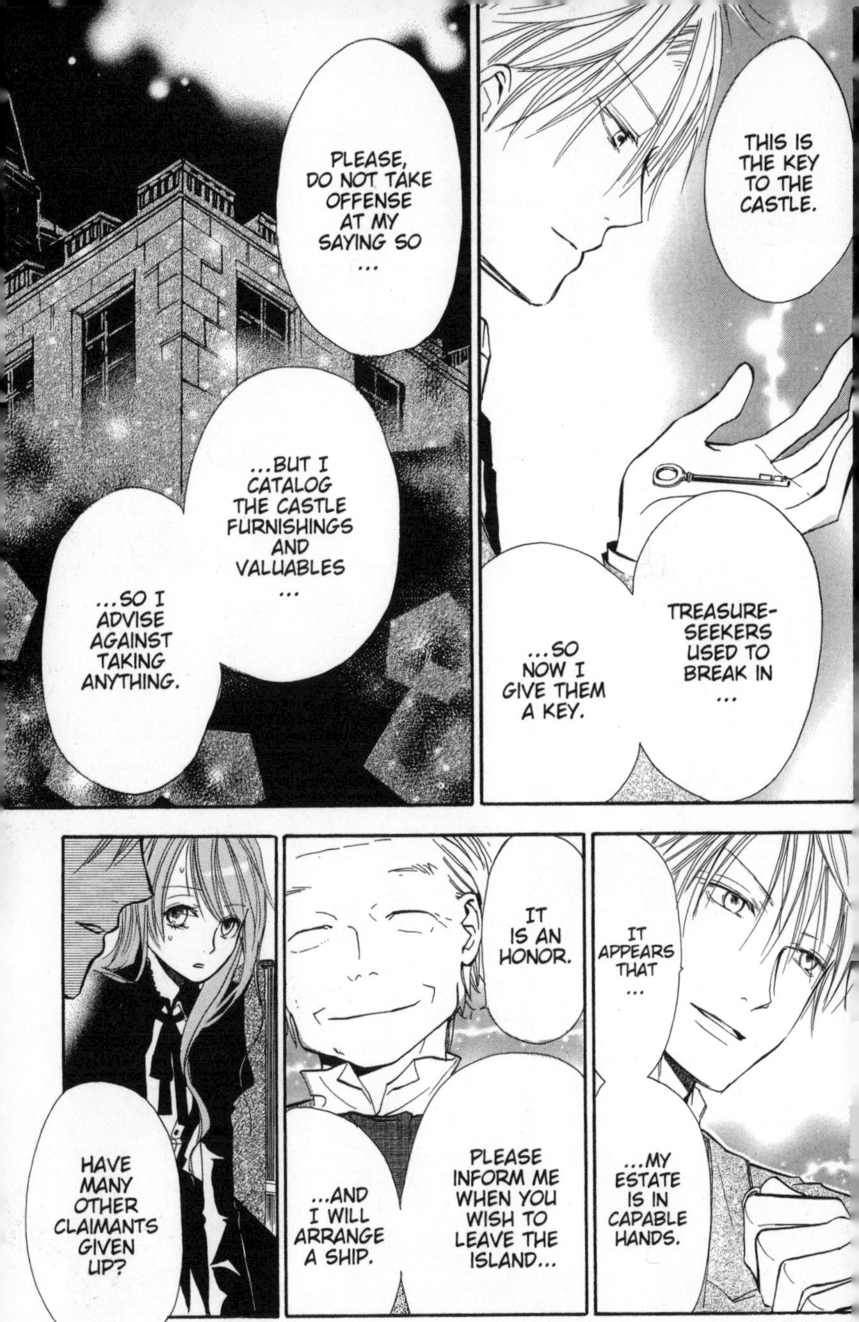
THIS IS THE KEY TO THE CASTLE.
TREASURE-SEEKERS USED TO BREAK IN ...
...SO NOW I GIVE THEM A KEY.
PLEASE, DO NOT TAKE OFFENSE AT MY SAYING SO ...
...BUT I CATALOG THE CASTLE FURNISHINGS AND VALUABLES ...
...SO I ADVISE AGAINST TAKING ANYTHING.
IT APPEARS THAT ...
...MY ESTATE IS IN CAPABLE HANDS.
IT IS AN HONOR.
PLEASE INFORM ME WHEN YOU WISH TO LEAVE THE ISLAND...
...AND I WILL ARRANGE A SHIP.
HAVE MANY OTHER CLAIMANTS GIVEN UP?

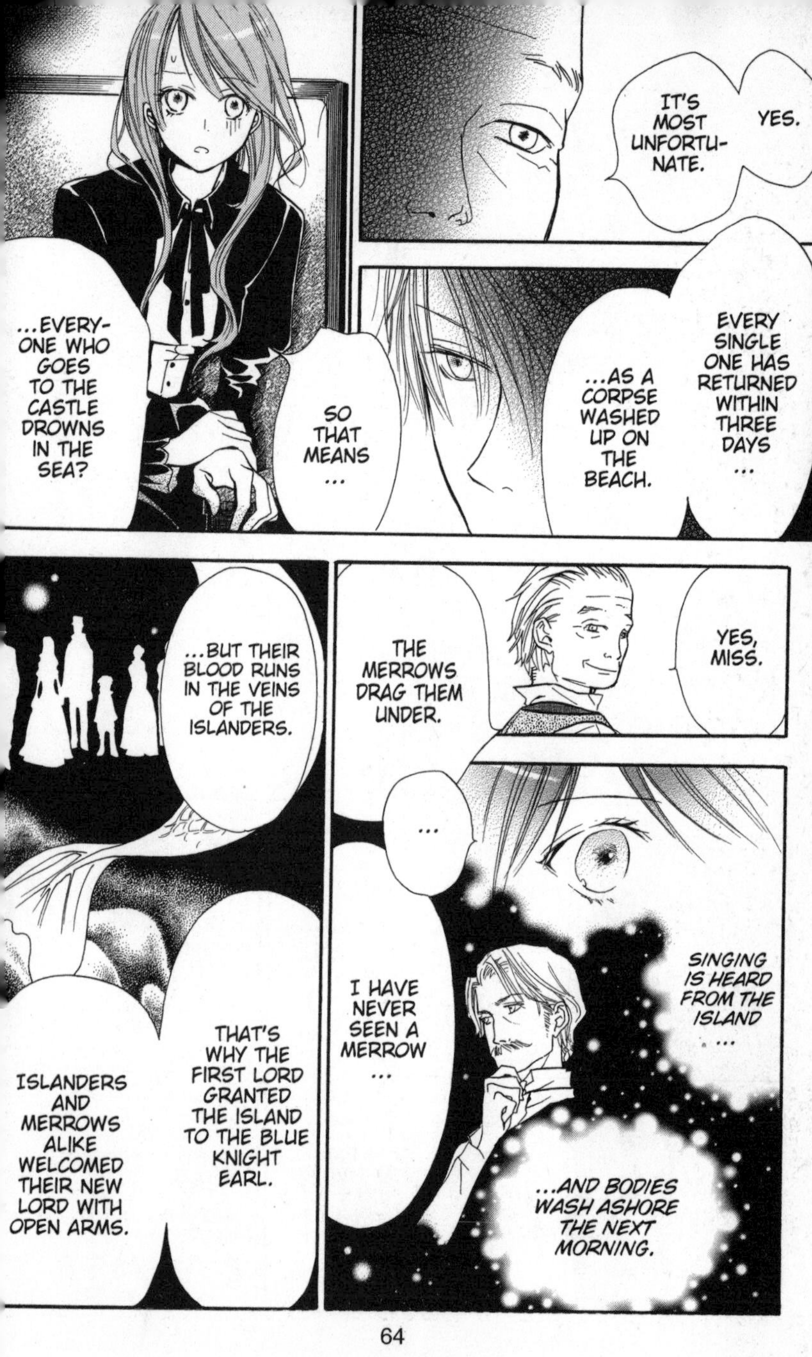
YES.
IT'S MOST UNFORTUNATE.
EVERY SINGLE ONE HAS RETURNED WITHIN THREE DAYS...
...AS A CORPSE WASHED UP ON THE BEACH.
SO THAT MEANS...
...EVERYONE WHO GOES TO THE CASTLE DROWNS IN THE SEA?
YES, MISS.
THE MERROWS DRAG THEM UNDER.
...
SINGING IS HEARD FROM THE ISLAND...
...AND BODIES WASH ASHORE THE NEXT MORNING.
I HAVE NEVER SEEN A MERROW...
...BUT THEIR BLOOD RUNS IN THE VEINS OF THE ISLANDERS.
THAT'S WHY THE FIRST LORD GRANTED THE ISLAND TO THE BLUE KNIGHT EARL.
ISLANDERS AND MERROWS ALIKE WELCOMED THEIR NEW LORD WITH OPEN ARMS.

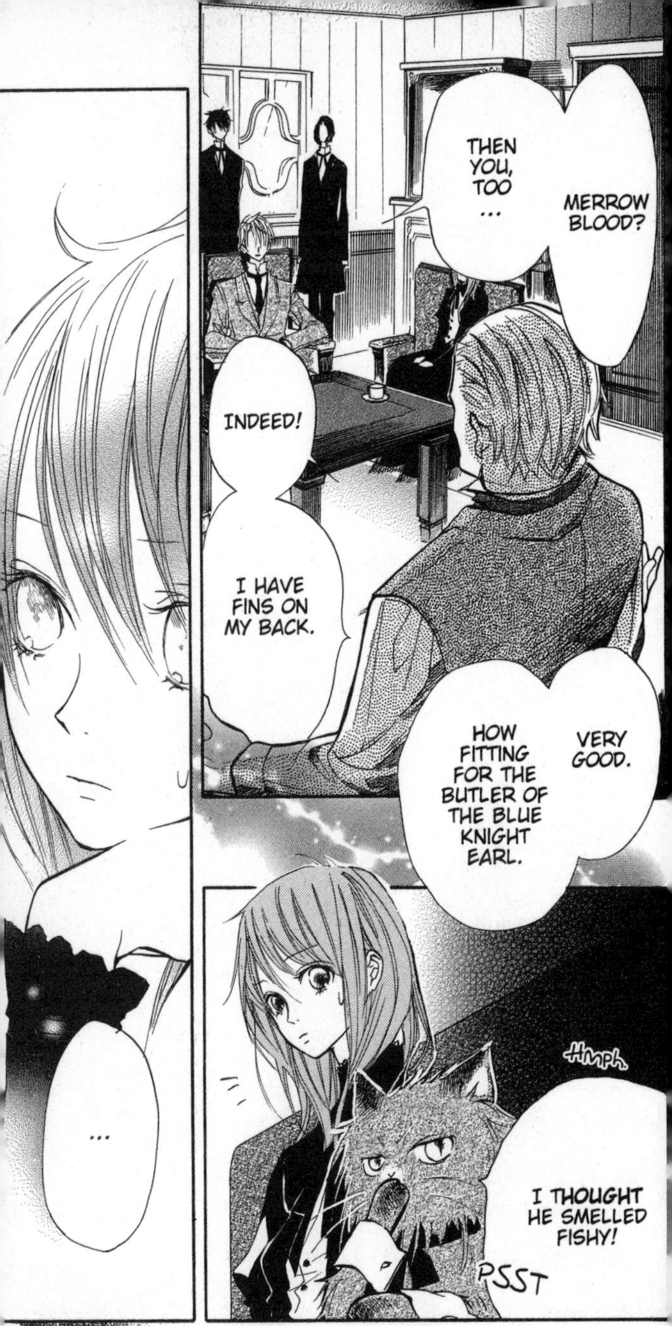
THEN YOU, TOO ...
MERROW BLOOD?
INDEED!
I HAVE FINS ON MY BACK.
VERY GOOD.
HOW FITTING FOR THE BUTLER OF THE BLUE KNIGHT EARL.
Hmph.
I THOUGHT HE SMELLED FISHY!
PSST
...

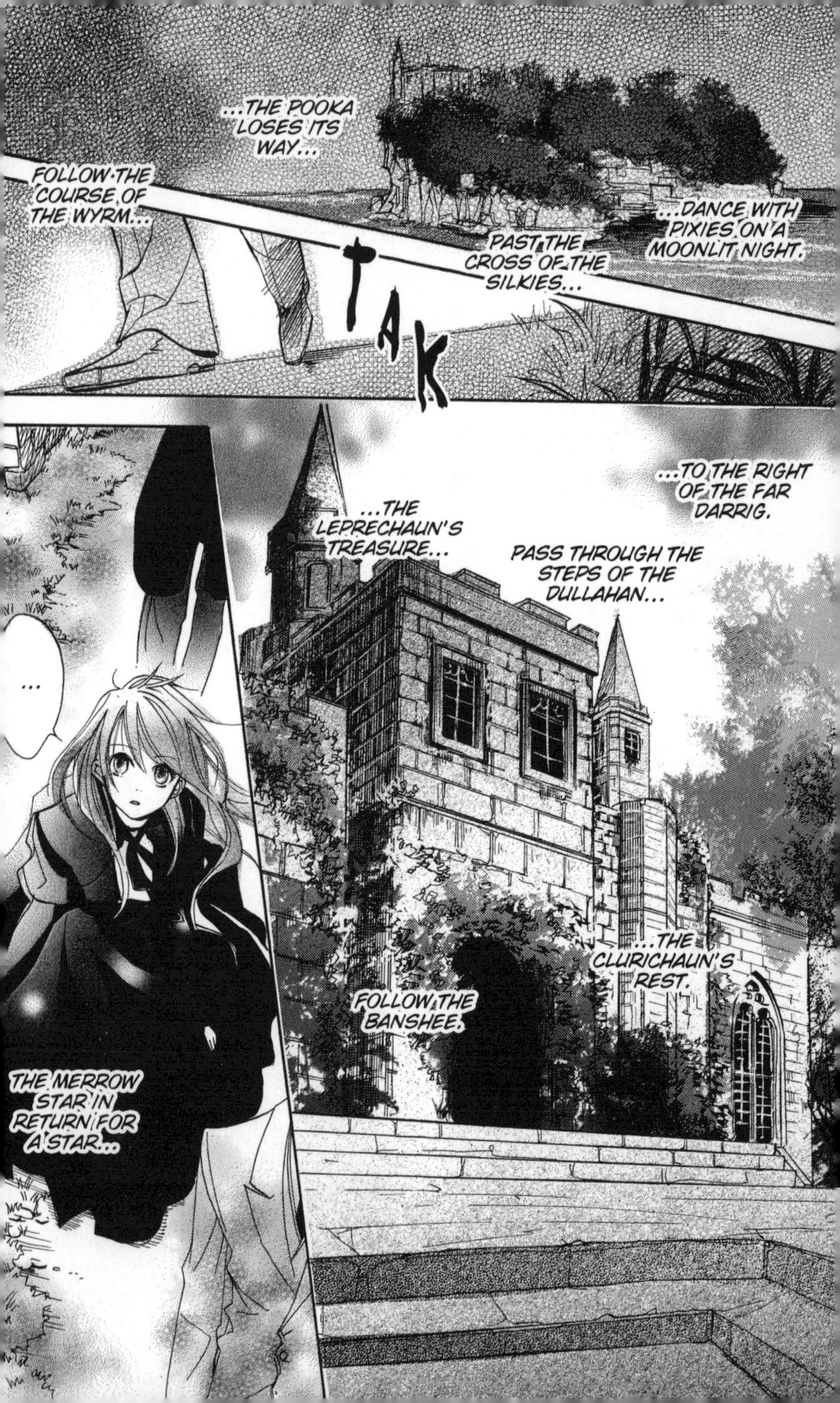
...DANCE WITH PIXIES ON A MOONLIT NIGHT.
PAST THE CROSS OF THE SILKIES...
...THE POOKA LOSES ITS WAY...
FOLLOW THE COURSE OF THE WYRM...
TAK
...TO THE RIGHT OF THE FAR DARRIG.
PASS THROUGH THE STEPS OF THE DULLAHAN...
...THE LEPRECHAUN'S TREASURE...
...THE CLURICHAUN'S REST.
FOLLOW THE BANSHEE.
...
THE MERROW STAR IN RETURN FOR A STAR...

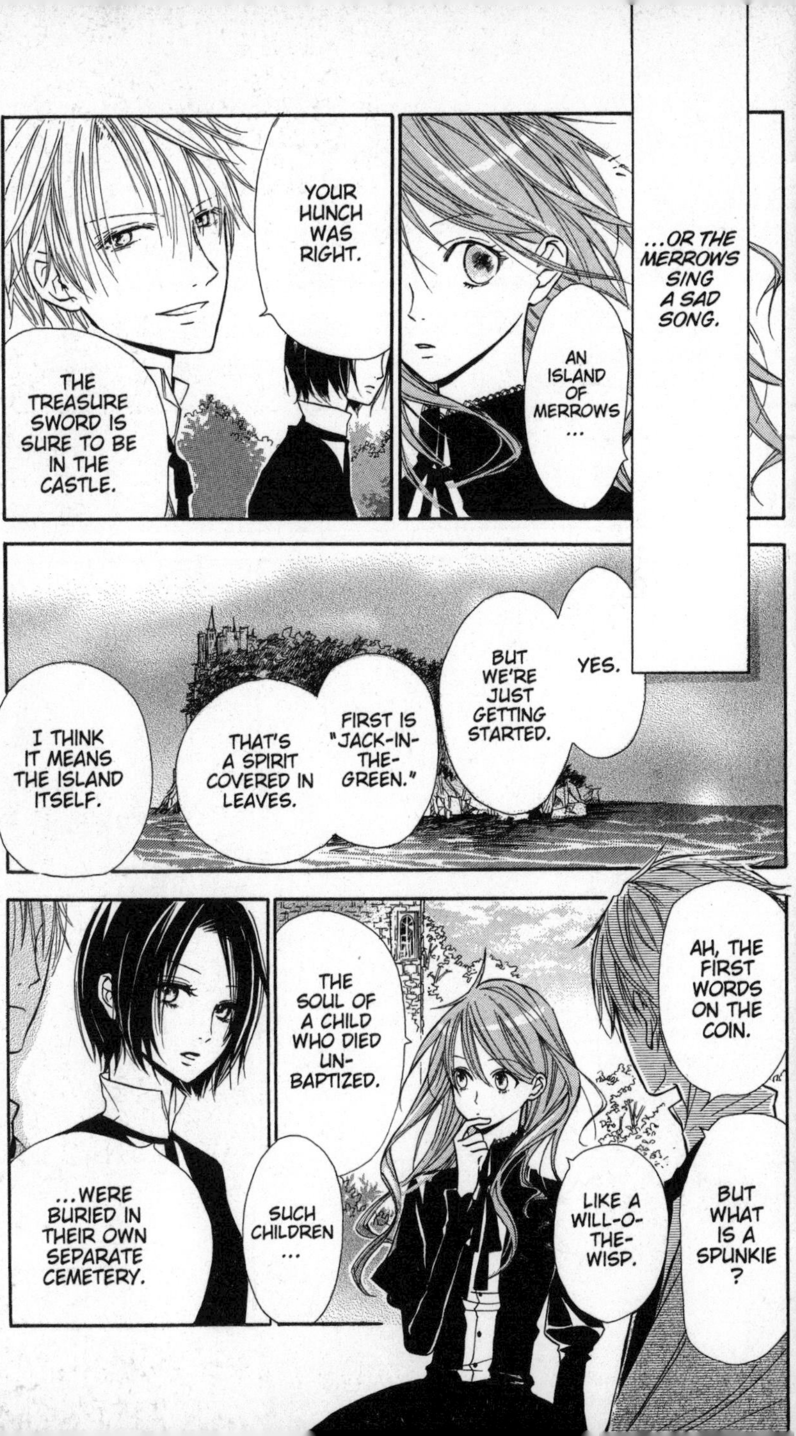
...OR THE MERROWS SING A SAD SONG.
AN ISLAND OF MERROWS...
YOUR HUNCH WAS RIGHT.
THE TREASURE SWORD IS SURE TO BE IN THE CASTLE.
YES.
BUT WE'RE JUST GETTING STARTED.
FIRST IS "JACK-IN-THE-GREEN."
THAT'S A SPIRIT COVERED IN LEAVES.
I THINK IT MEANS THE ISLAND ITSELF.
AH, THE FIRST WORDS ON THE COIN.
BUT WHAT IS A SPUNKIE?
LIKE A WILL-O-THE-WISP.
THE SOUL OF A CHILD WHO DIED UN-BAPTIZED.
SUCH CHILDREN...
...WERE BURIED IN THEIR OWN SEPARATE CEMETERY.

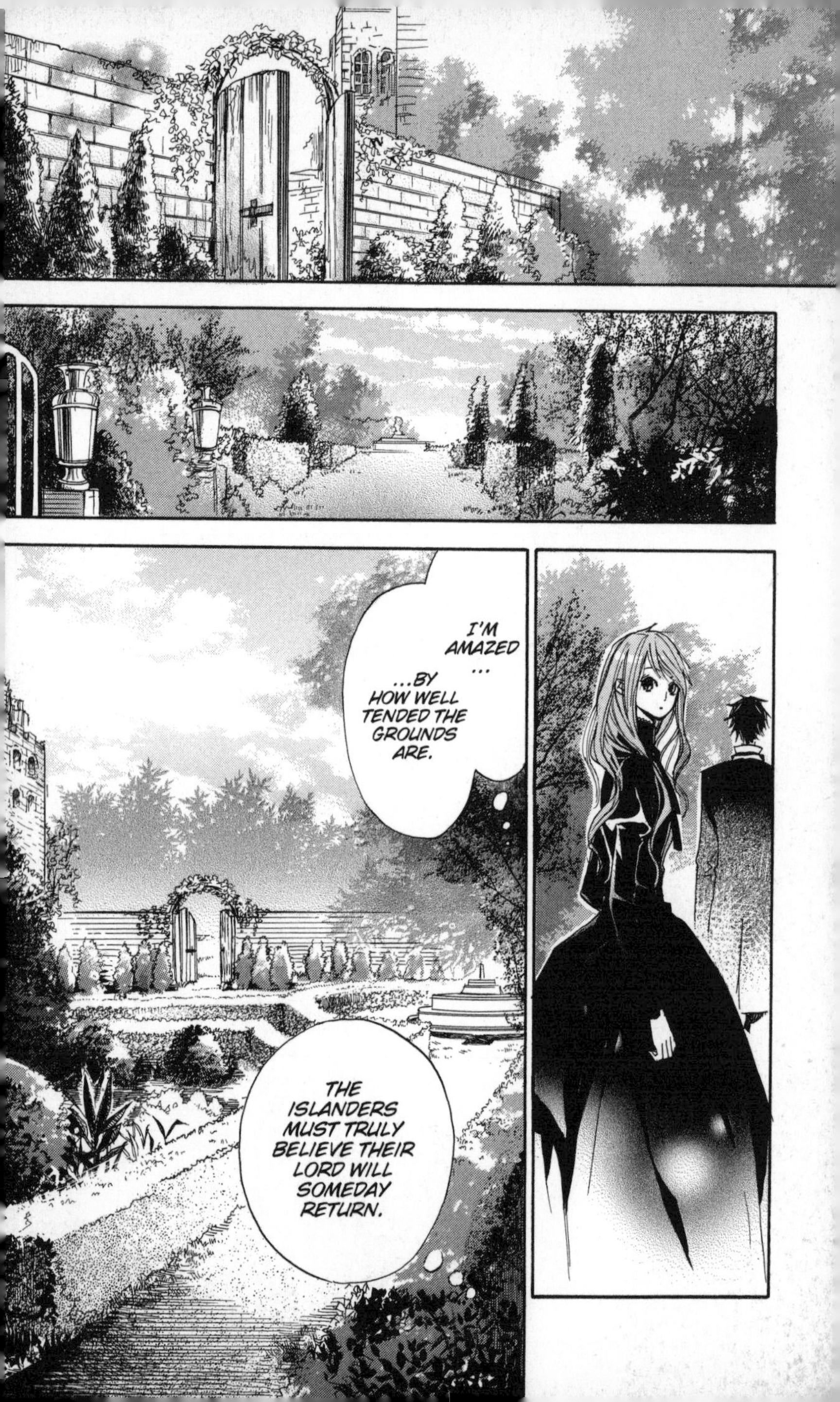
I'M AMAZED...
...BY HOW WELL TENDED THE GROUNDS ARE.
THE ISLANDERS MUST TRULY BELIEVE THEIR LORD WILL SOMEDAY RETURN.

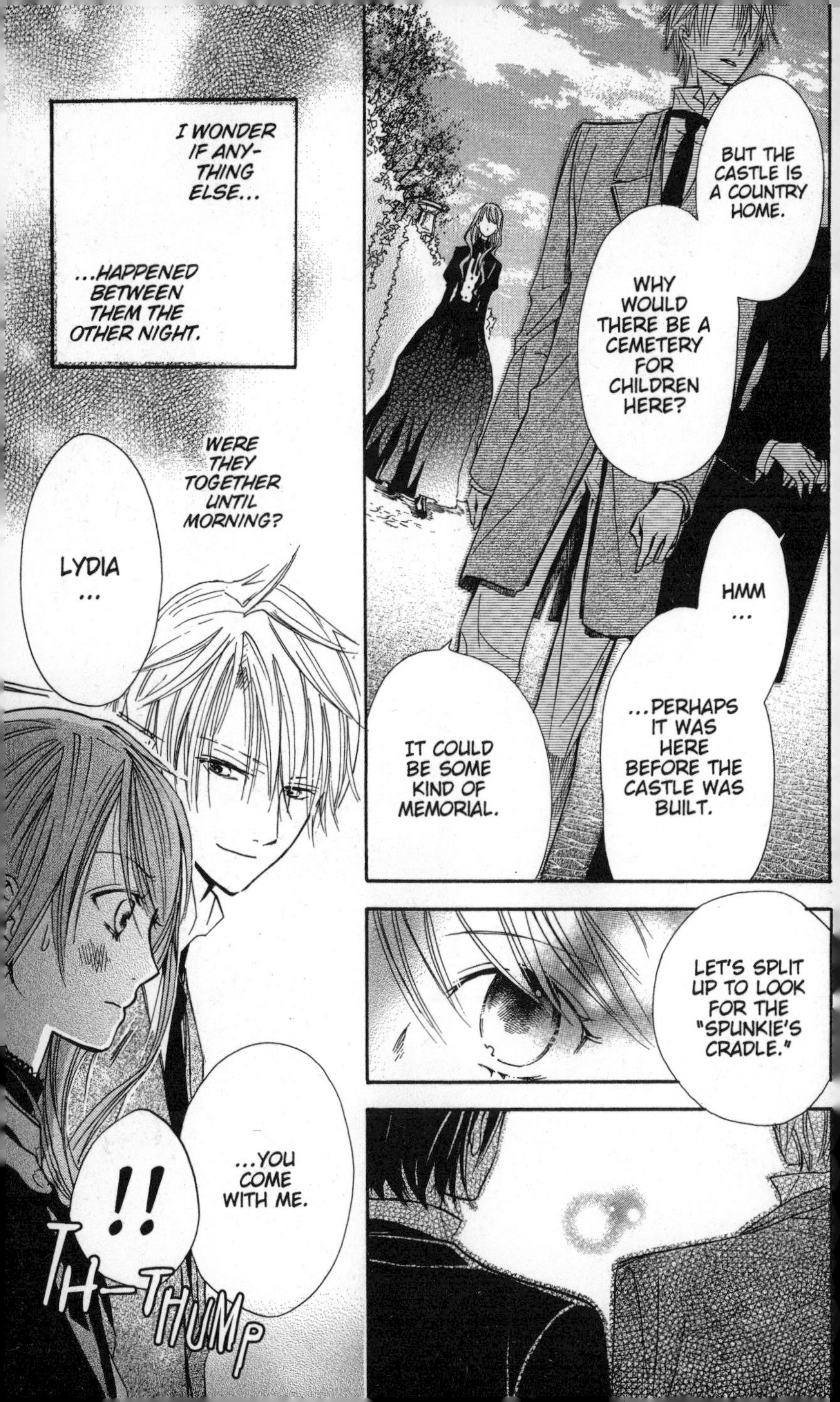
BUT THE CASTLE IS A COUNTRY HOME.
WHY WOULD THERE BE A CEMETERY FOR CHILDREN HERE?
HMM...
...PERHAPS IT WAS HERE BEFORE THE CASTLE WAS BUILT.
IT COULD BE SOME KIND OF MEMORIAL.
LET'S SPLIT UP TO LOOK FOR THE "SPUNKIE'S CRADLE."
I WONDER IF ANY-THING ELSE...
...HAPPENED BETWEEN THEM THE OTHER NIGHT.
WERE THEY TOGETHER UNTIL MORNING?
LYDIA...
...YOU COME WITH ME.
!!
TH-THUMP

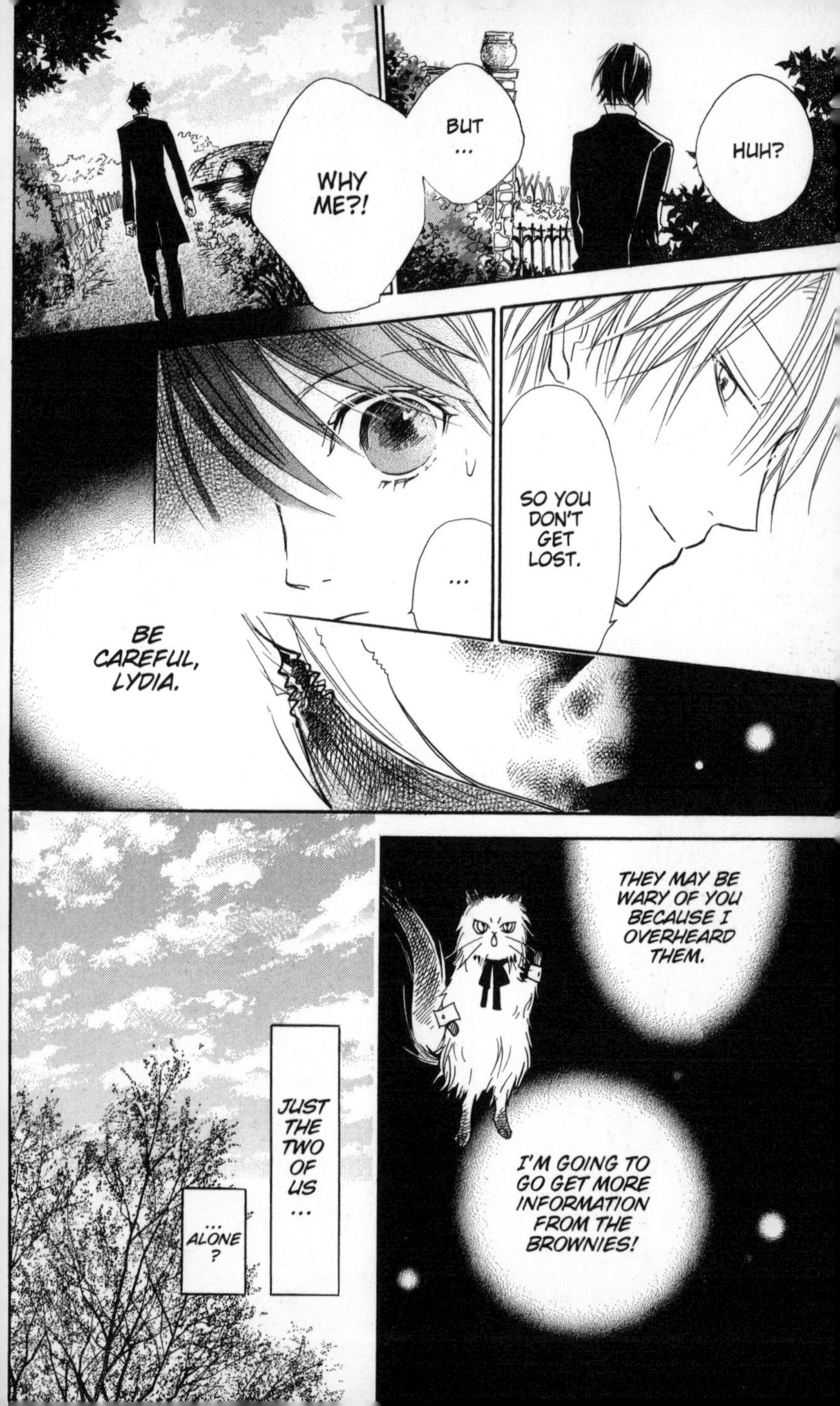
HUH?
BUT...
WHY ME?!
SO YOU DON'T GET LOST.
...
BE CAREFUL, LYDIA.
THEY MAY BE WARY OF YOU BECAUSE I OVERHEARD THEM.
I'M GOING TO GO GET MORE INFORMATION FROM THE BROWNIES!
JUST THE TWO OF US...
...ALONE?

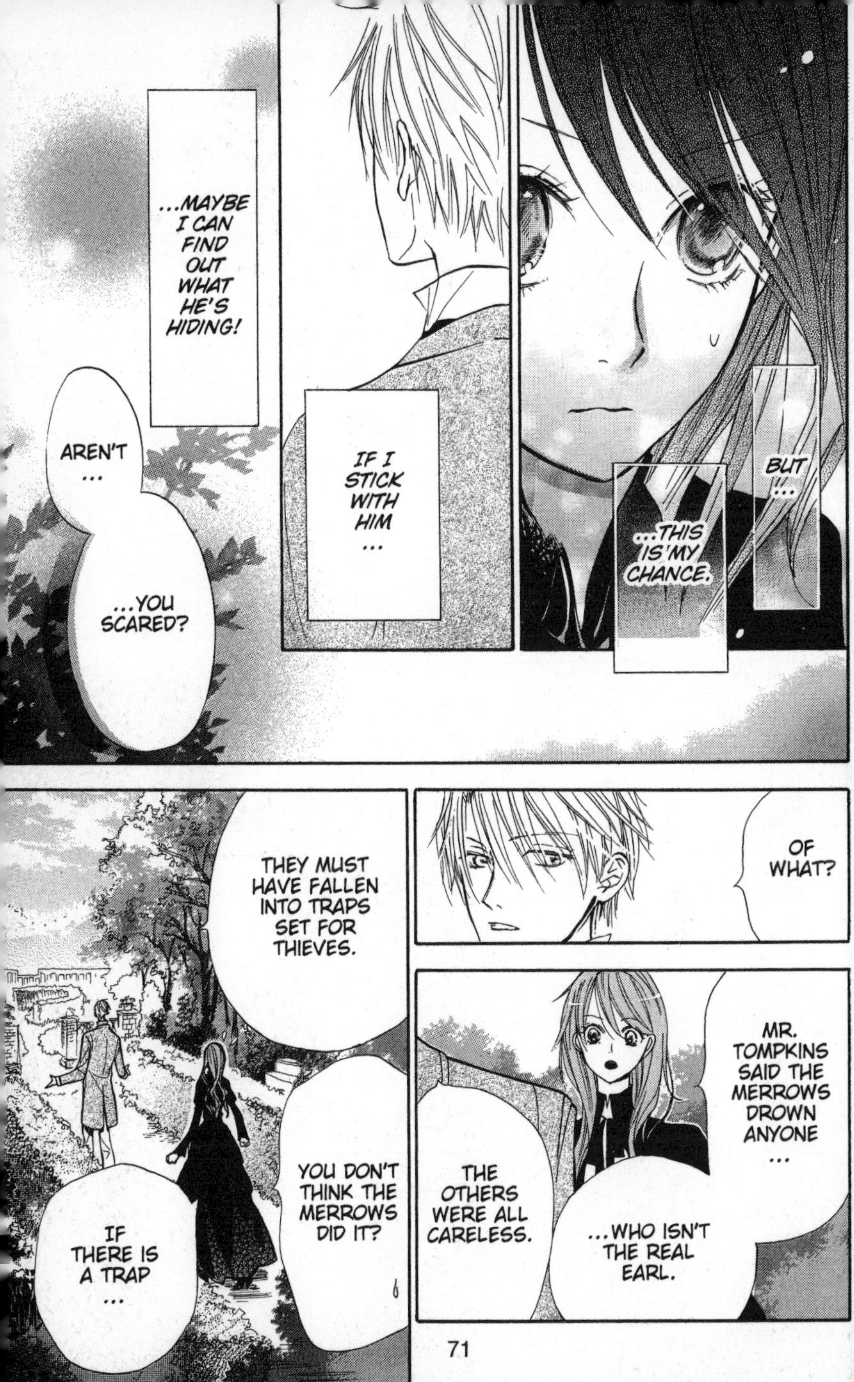
BUT...
...THIS IS MY CHANCE.
IF I STICK WITH HIM...
...MAYBE I CAN FIND OUT WHAT HE'S HIDING!
AREN'T...
...YOU SCARED?
OF WHAT?
MR. TOMPKINS SAID THE MERROWS DROWN ANYONE...
...WHO ISN'T THE REAL EARL.
THE OTHERS WERE ALL CARELESS.
THEY MUST HAVE FALLEN INTO TRAPS SET FOR THIEVES.
YOU DON'T THINK THE MERROWS DID IT?
IF THERE IS A TRAP...

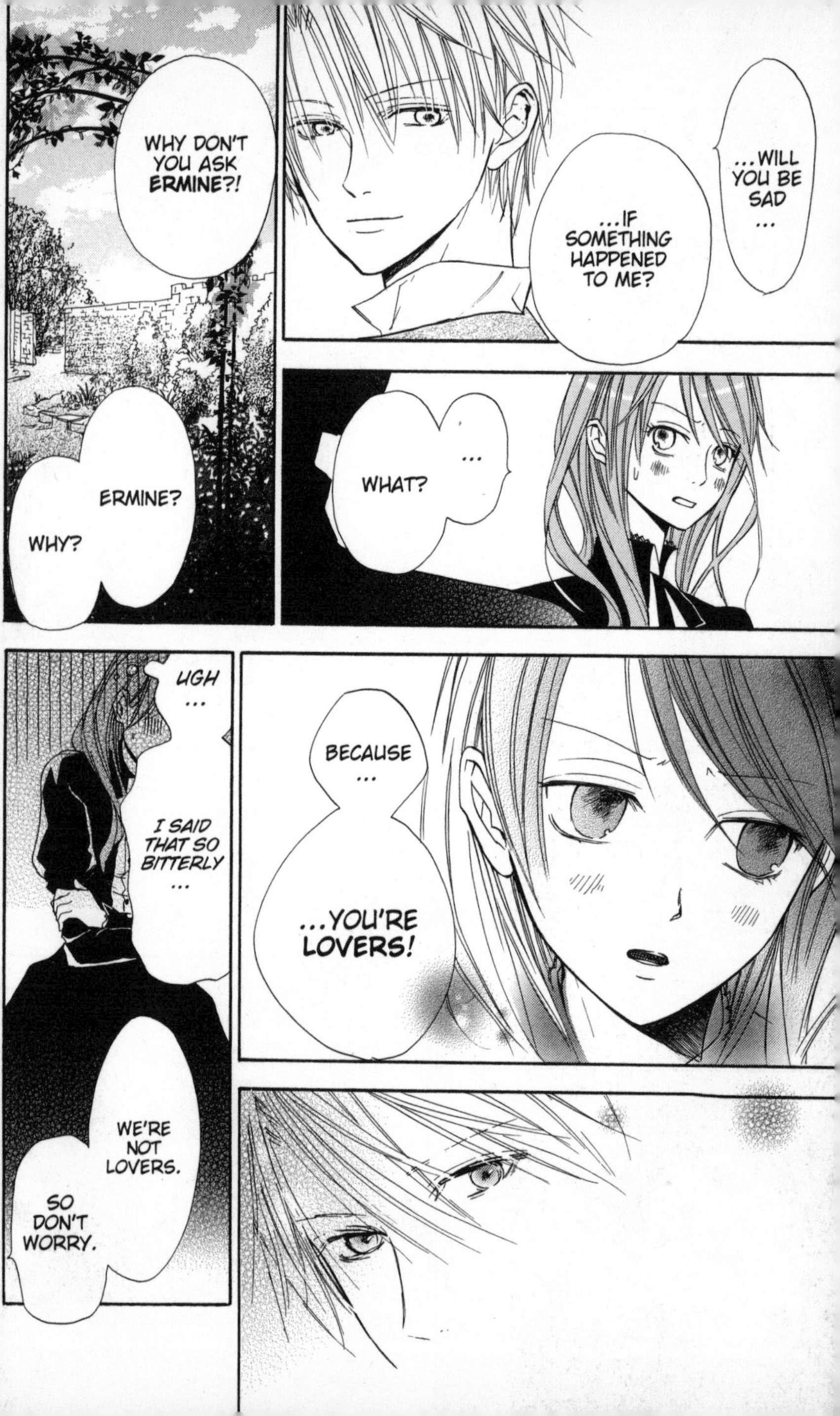
...WILL YOU BE SAD...
...IF SOMETHING HAPPENED TO ME?
...
WHAT?
WHY DON'T YOU ASK ERMINE?!
ERMINE?
WHY?
BECAUSE...
...YOU'RE LOVERS!
UGH...
I SAID THAT SO BITTERLY...
WE'RE NOT LOVERS.
SO DON'T WORRY.

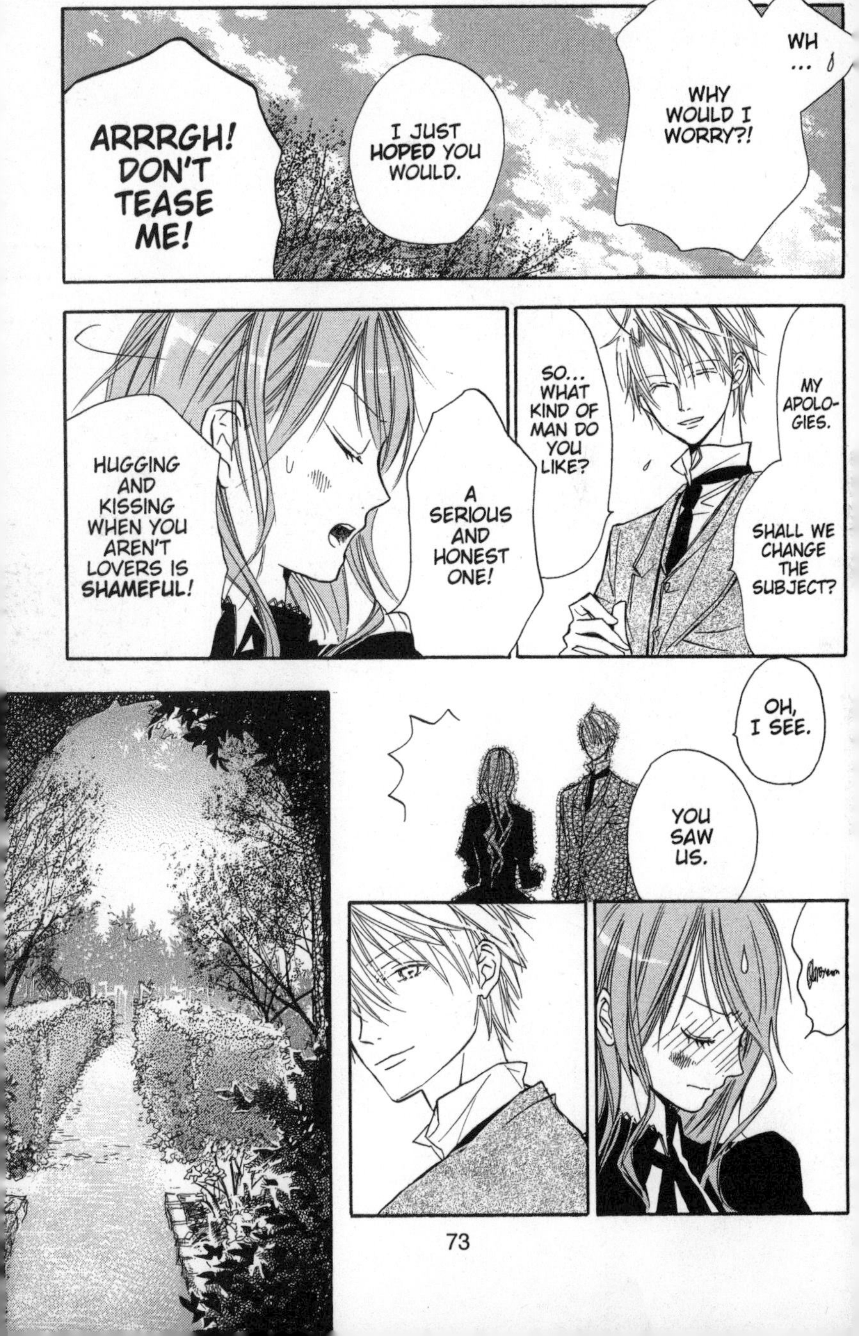
WH... WHY WOULD I WORRY?!
I JUST HOPED YOU WOULD.
ARRRGH! DON'T TEASE ME!
MY APOLOGIES.
SHALL WE CHANGE THE SUBJECT?
SO... WHAT KIND OF MAN DO YOU LIKE?
A SERIOUS AND HONEST ONE!
HUGGING AND KISSING WHEN YOU AREN'T LOVERS IS SHAMEFUL!
OH, I SEE.
YOU SAW US.

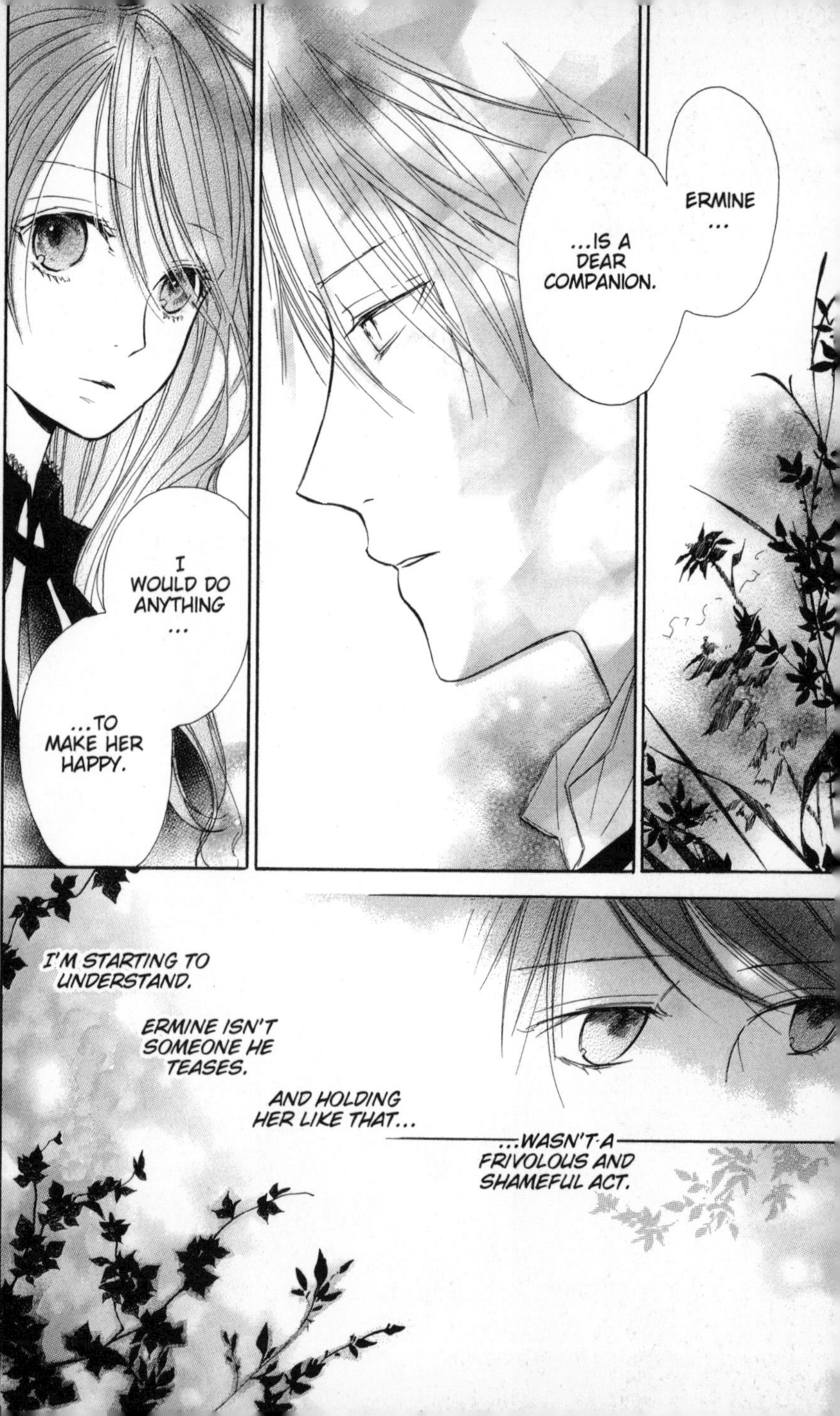
ERMINE ...
...IS A DEAR COMPANION.
I WOULD DO ANYTHING ...
...TO MAKE HER HAPPY.
I'M STARTING TO UNDERSTAND.
ERMINE ISN'T SOMEONE HE TEASES.
AND HOLDING HER LIKE THAT...
...WASN'T A FRIVOLOUS AND SHAMEFUL ACT.

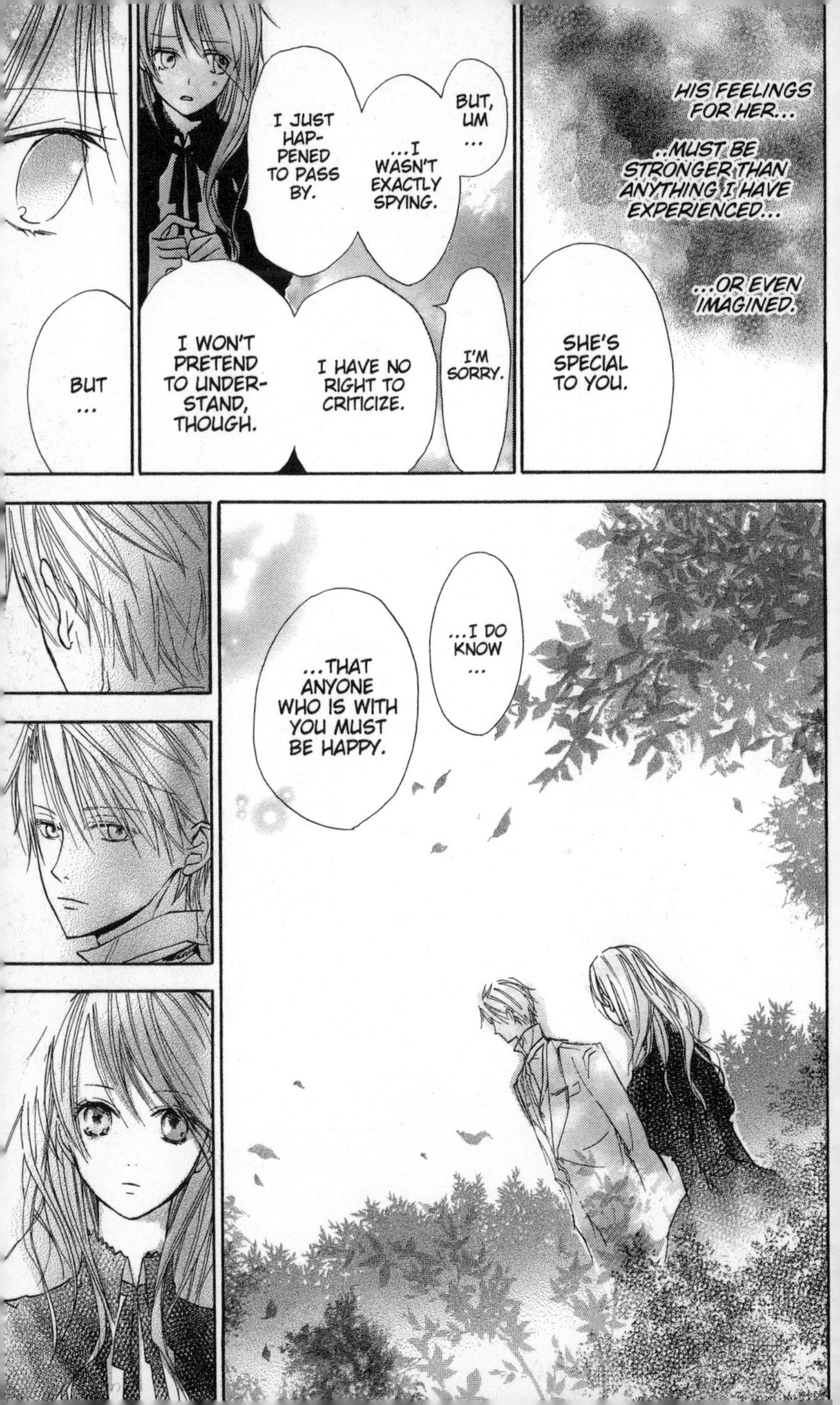
HIS FEELINGS FOR HER...
..MUST BE STRONGER THAN ANYTHING I HAVE EXPERIENCED...
...OR EVEN IMAGINED.
SHE'S SPECIAL TO YOU.
BUT, UM ...
...I WASN'T EXACTLY SPYING.
I JUST HAP-PENED TO PASS BY.
I'M SORRY.
I HAVE NO RIGHT TO CRITICIZE.
I WON'T PRETEND TO UNDER-STAND, THOUGH.
BUT ...
...I DO KNOW ...
...THAT ANYONE WHO IS WITH YOU MUST BE HAPPY.

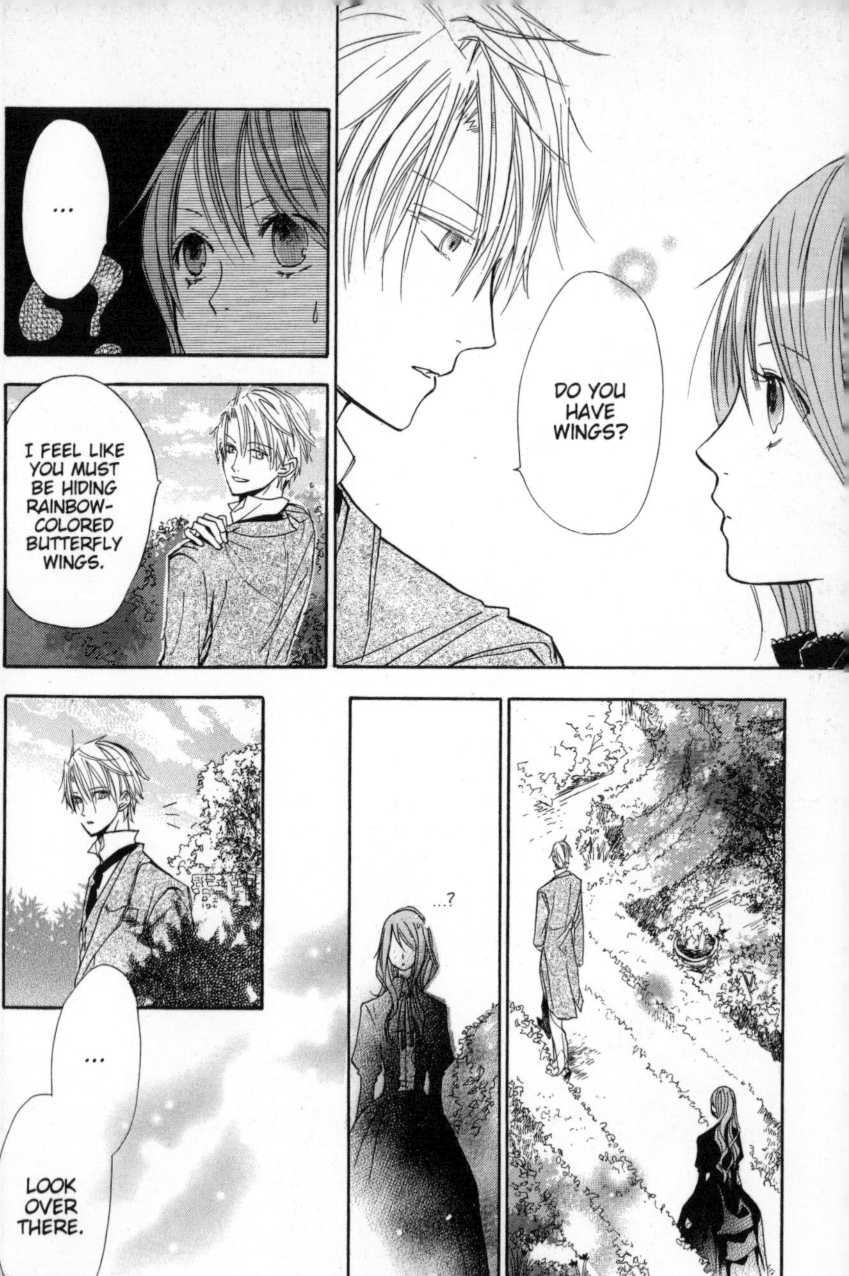
DO YOU HAVE WINGS?
...
I FEEL LIKE YOU MUST BE HIDING RAINBOW-COLORED BUTTERFLY WINGS.
...?
...
LOOK OVER THERE.

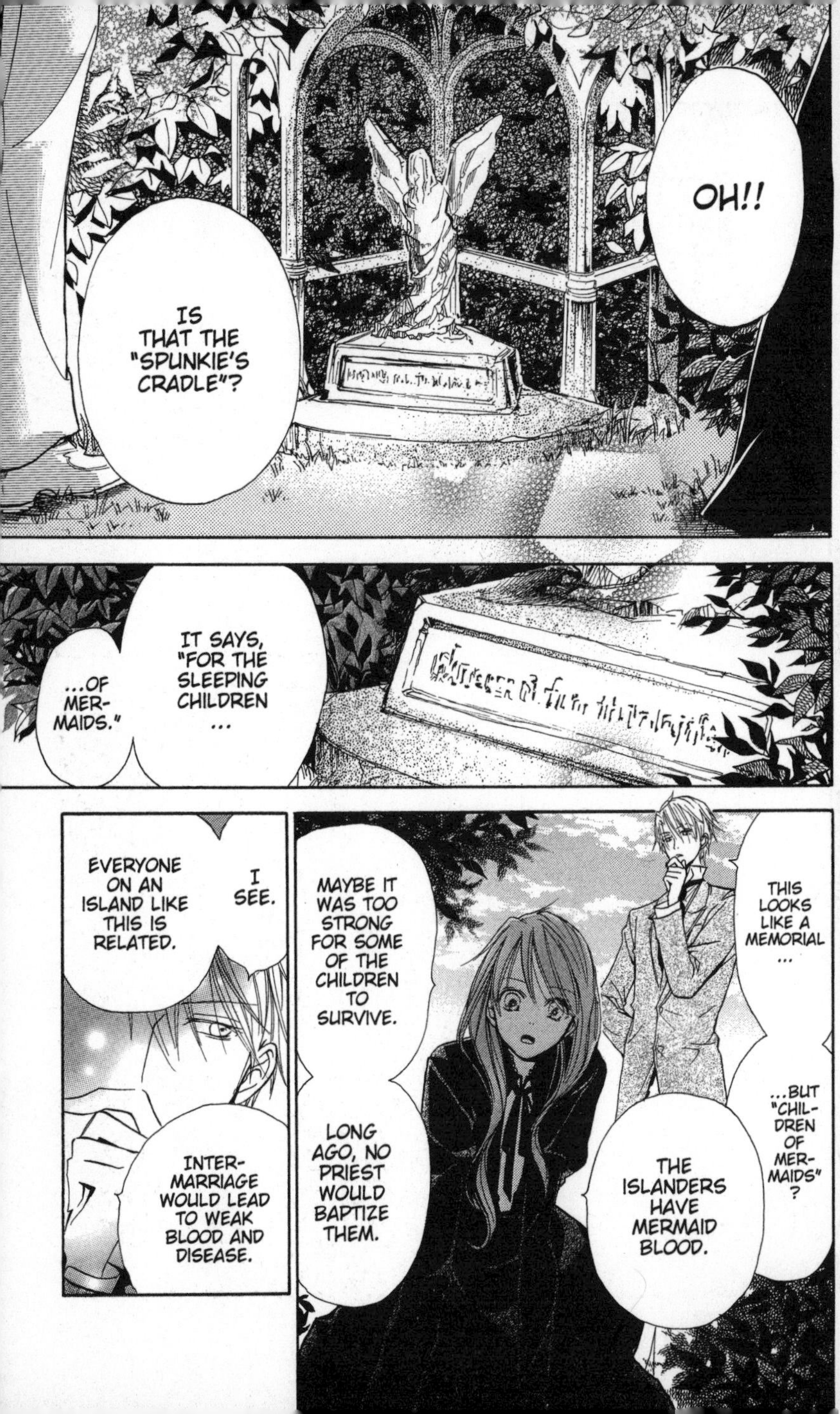
OH!!
IS THAT THE "SPUNKIE'S CRADLE"?
IT SAYS, "FOR THE SLEEPING CHILDREN ...
...OF MER-MAIDS."
THIS LOOKS LIKE A MEMORIAL ...
...BUT "CHIL-DREN OF MER-MAIDS"?
THE ISLANDERS HAVE MERMAID BLOOD.
MAYBE IT WAS TOO STRONG FOR SOME OF THE CHILDREN TO SURVIVE.
LONG AGO, NO PRIEST WOULD BAPTIZE THEM.
I SEE.
EVERYONE ON AN ISLAND LIKE THIS IS RELATED.
INTER-MARRIAGE WOULD LEAD TO WEAK BLOOD AND DISEASE.

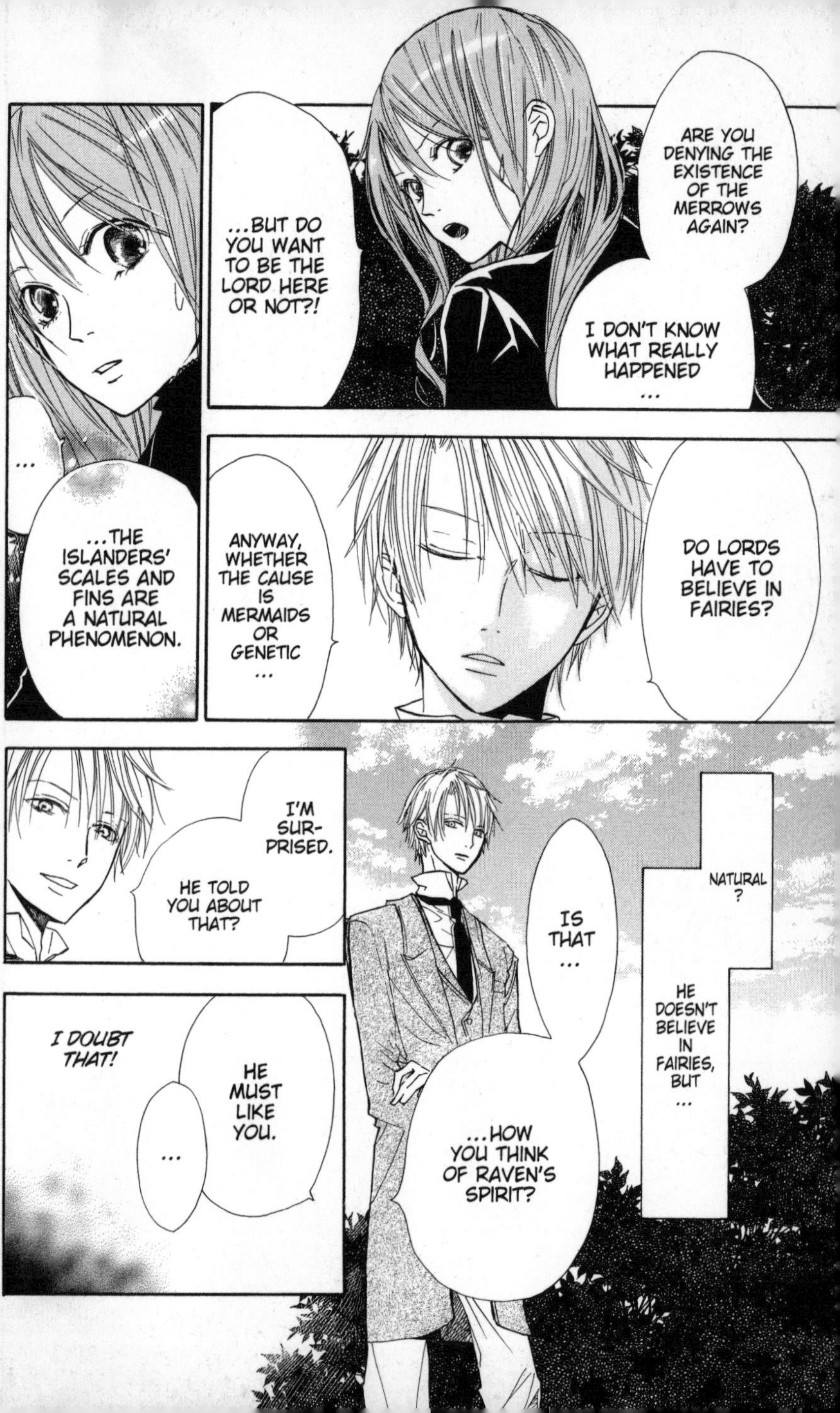
ARE YOU DENYING THE EXISTENCE OF THE MERROWS AGAIN?
I DON'T KNOW WHAT REALLY HAPPENED ...
...BUT DO YOU WANT TO BE THE LORD HERE OR NOT?!
DO LORDS HAVE TO BELIEVE IN FAIRIES?
ANYWAY, WHETHER THE CAUSE IS MERMAIDS OR GENETIC ...
...
...THE ISLANDERS' SCALES AND FINS ARE A NATURAL PHENOMENON.
NATURAL?
HE DOESN'T BELIEVE IN FAIRIES, BUT ...
IS THAT ...
...HOW YOU THINK OF RAVEN'S SPIRIT?
I'M SUR-PRISED.
HE TOLD YOU ABOUT THAT?
HE MUST LIKE YOU.
...
I DOUBT THAT!

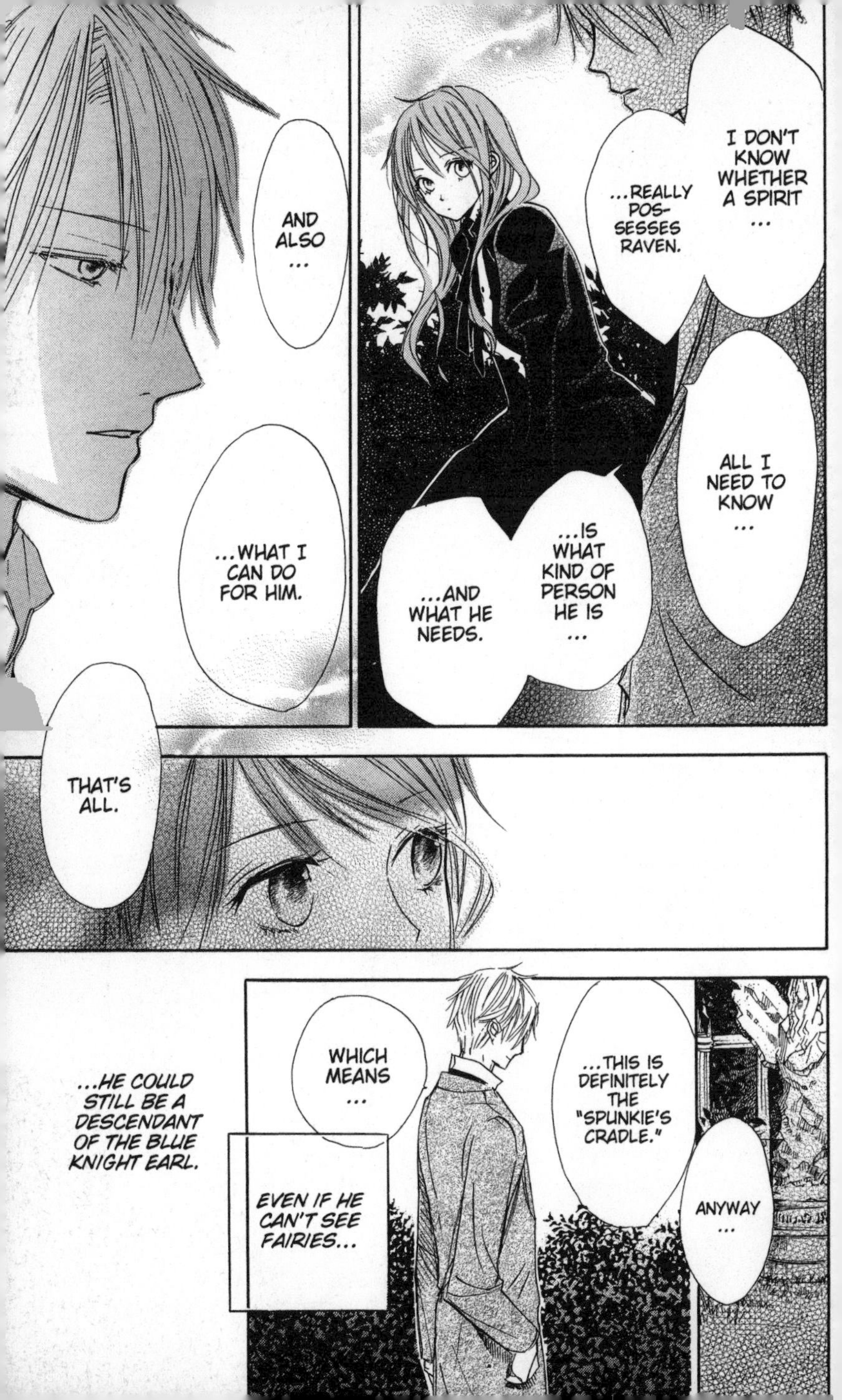
I DON'T KNOW WHETHER A SPIRIT ...
...REALLY POS-SESSES RAVEN.
ALL I NEED TO KNOW ...
...IS WHAT KIND OF PERSON HE IS ...
...AND WHAT HE NEEDS.
AND ALSO ...
...WHAT I CAN DO FOR HIM.
THAT'S ALL.
ANYWAY ...
...THIS IS DEFINITELY THE "SPUNKIE'S CRADLE."
WHICH MEANS ...
EVEN IF HE CAN'T SEE FAIRIES...
...HE COULD STILL BE A DESCENDANT OF THE BLUE KNIGHT EARL.

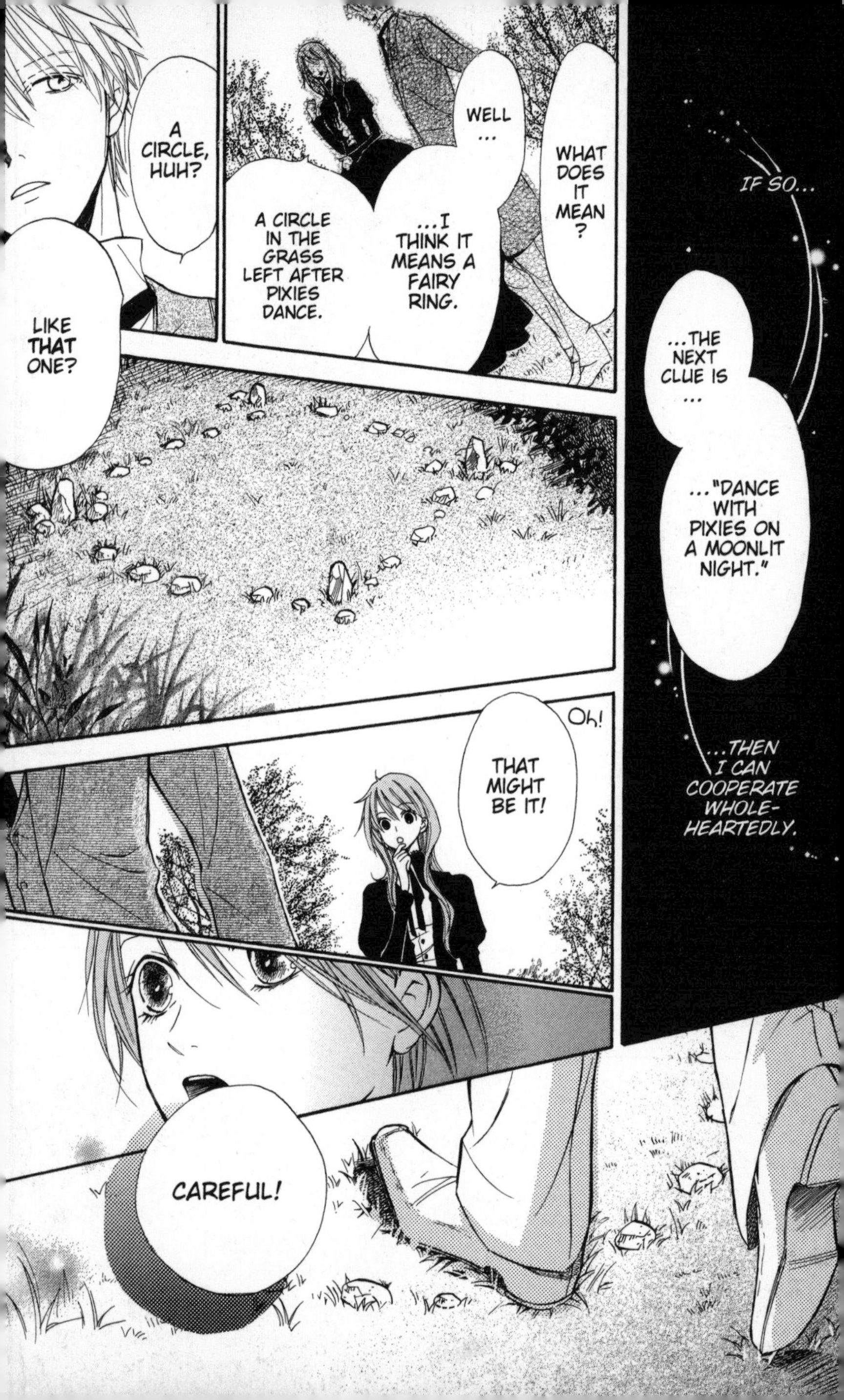
IF SO...
...THE NEXT CLUE IS...
..."DANCE WITH PIXIES ON A MOONLIT NIGHT."
...THEN I CAN COOPERATE WHOLE-HEARTEDLY.
WHAT DOES IT MEAN?
WELL...
...I THINK IT MEANS A FAIRY RING.
A CIRCLE IN THE GRASS LEFT AFTER PIXIES DANCE.
A CIRCLE, HUH?
LIKE THAT ONE?
Oh!
THAT MIGHT BE IT!
CAREFUL!

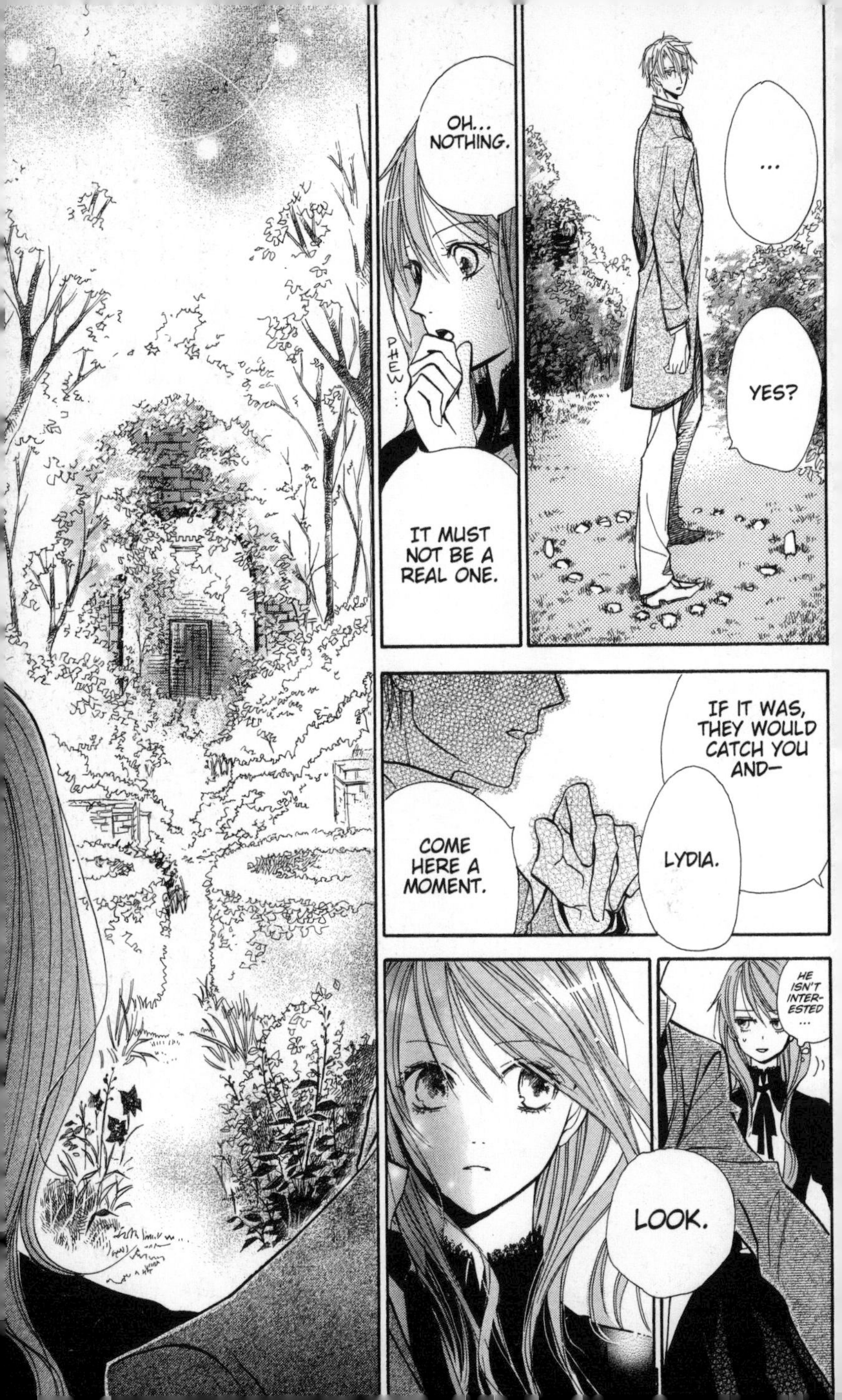
...
YES?
OH... NOTHING.
PHEW...
IT MUST NOT BE A REAL ONE.
IF IT WAS, THEY WOULD CATCH YOU AND—
LYDIA.
COME HERE A MOMENT.
HE ISN'T INTERESTED...
LOOK.

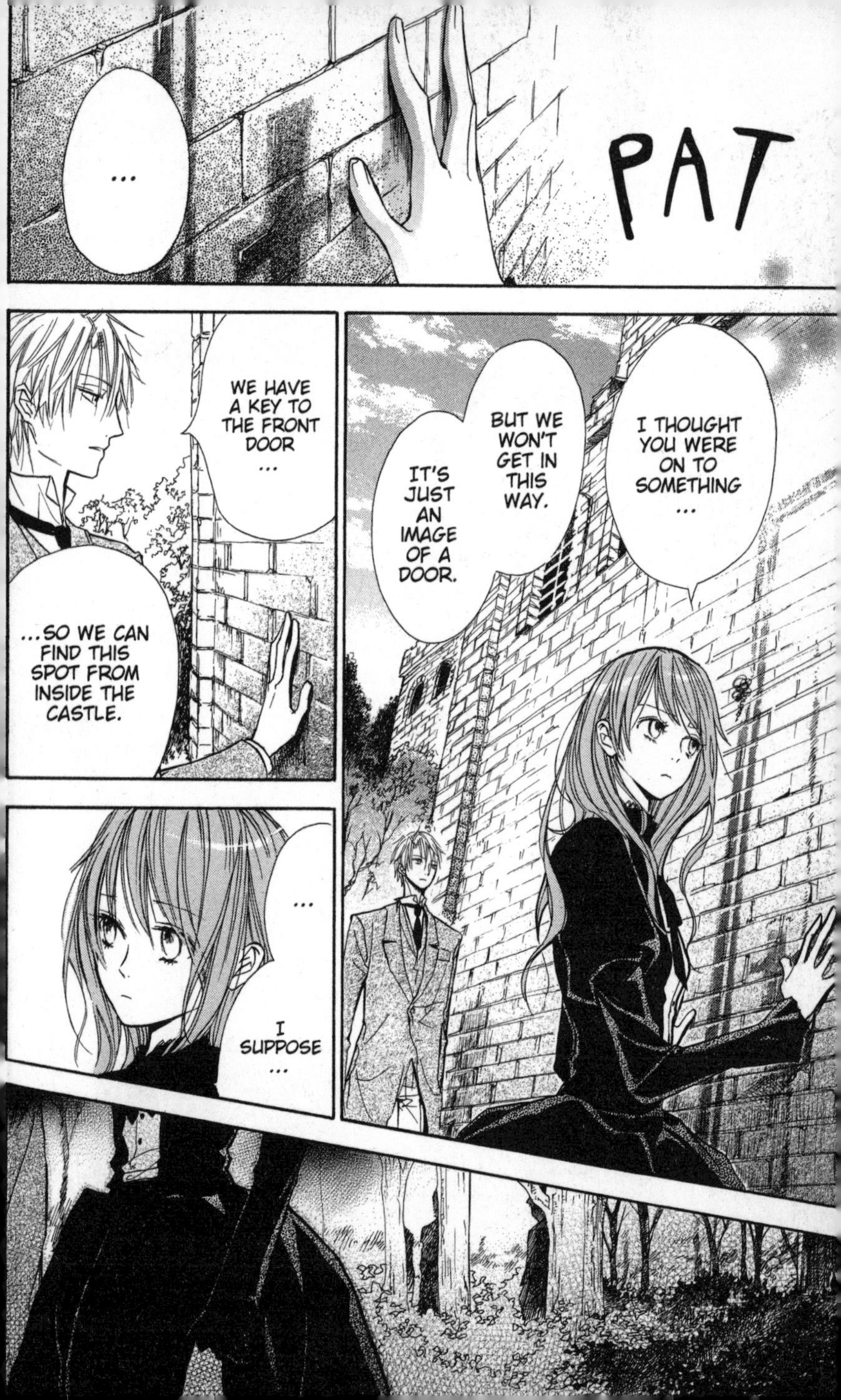
PAT
...
I THOUGHT YOU WERE ON TO SOMETHING ...
BUT WE WON'T GET IN THIS WAY.
IT'S JUST AN IMAGE OF A DOOR.
WE HAVE A KEY TO THE FRONT DOOR ...
...SO WE CAN FIND THIS SPOT FROM INSIDE THE CASTLE.
...
I SUPPOSE ...

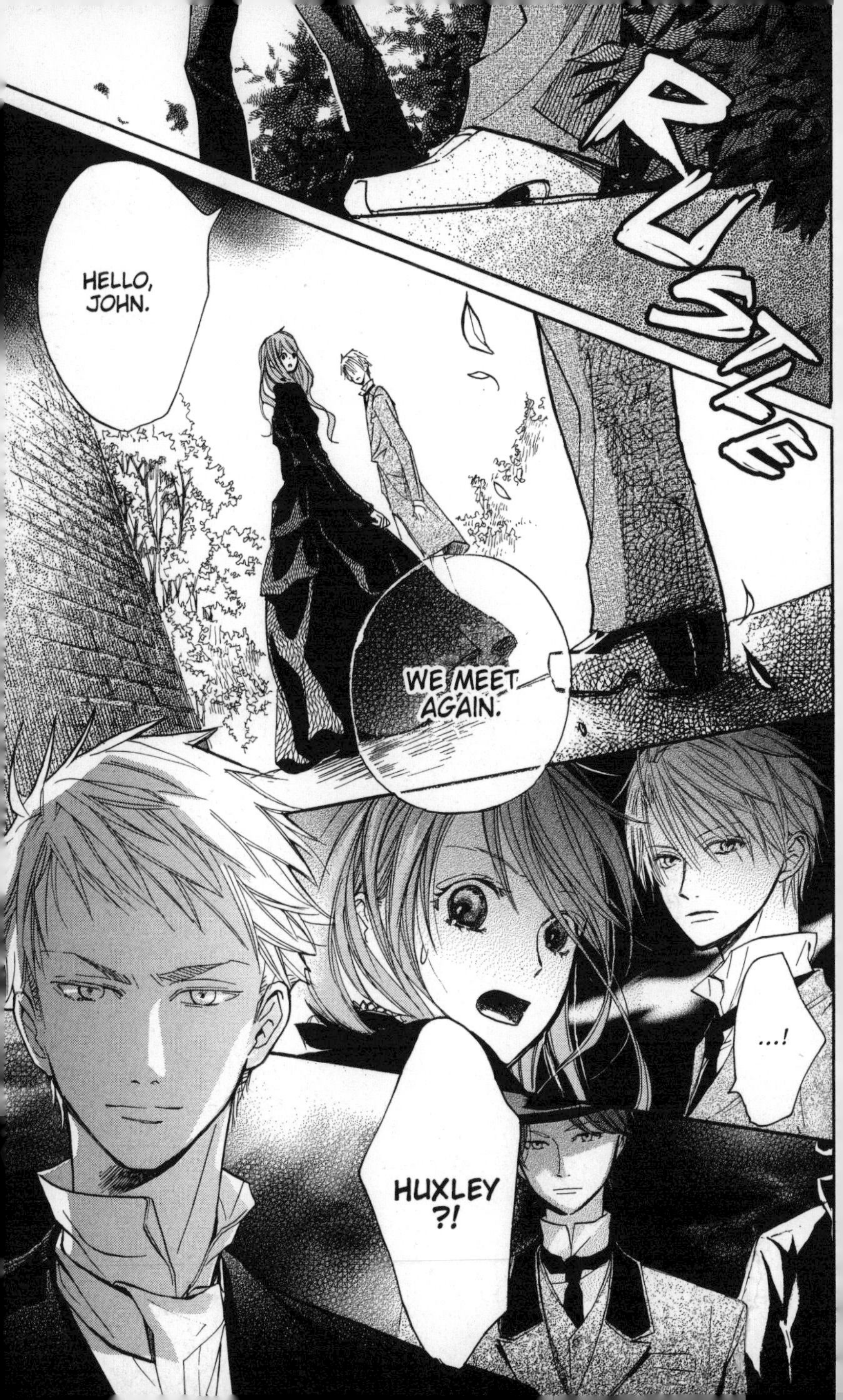
RUSTLE
HELLO, JOHN.
WE MEET AGAIN.
...!
HUXLEY ?!

The Earl & the Fairy

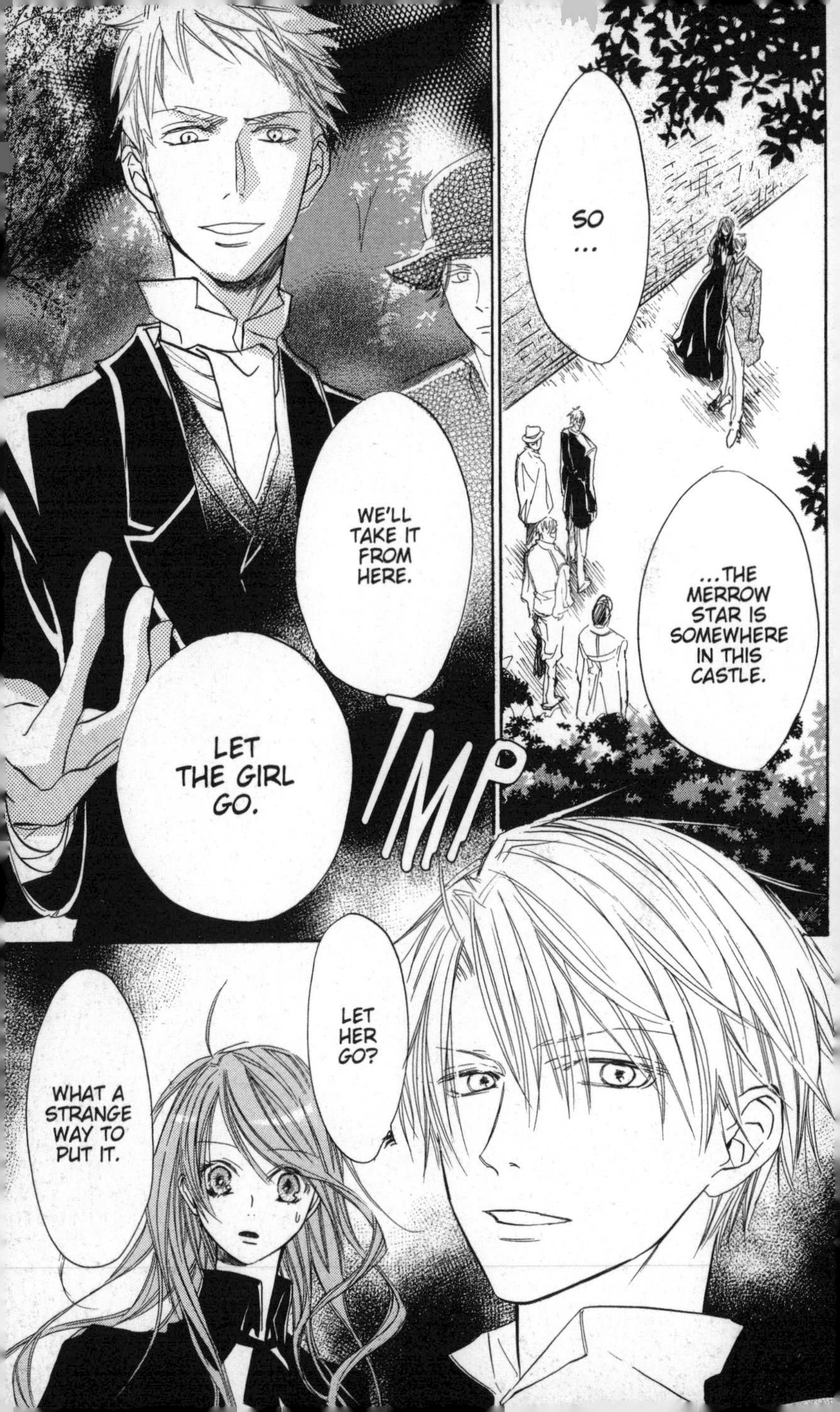
SO ...
...THE MERROW STAR IS SOMEWHERE IN THIS CASTLE.
WE'LL TAKE IT FROM HERE.
LET THE GIRL GO.
TMP
LET HER GO?
WHAT A STRANGE WAY TO PUT IT.

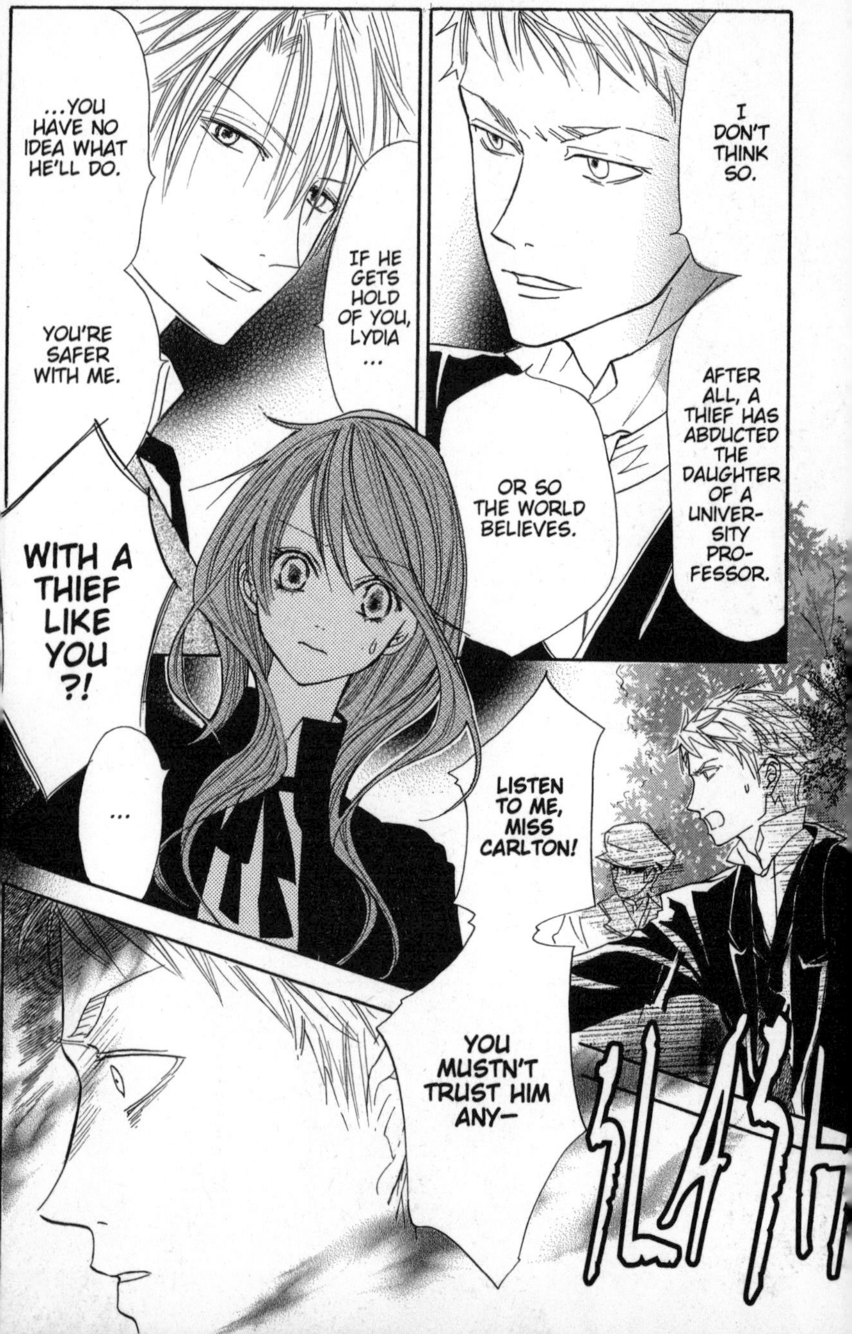

I DON'T THINK SO.
AFTER ALL, A THIEF HAS ABDUCTED THE DAUGHTER OF A UNIVER-SITY PRO-FESSOR.
OR SO THE WORLD BELIEVES.
...YOU HAVE NO IDEA WHAT HE'LL DO.
IF HE GETS HOLD OF YOU, LYDIA...
YOU'RE SAFER WITH ME.
WITH A THIEF LIKE YOU?!
...
LISTEN TO ME, MISS CARLTON!
YOU MUSTN'T TRUST HIM ANY—
SLASH

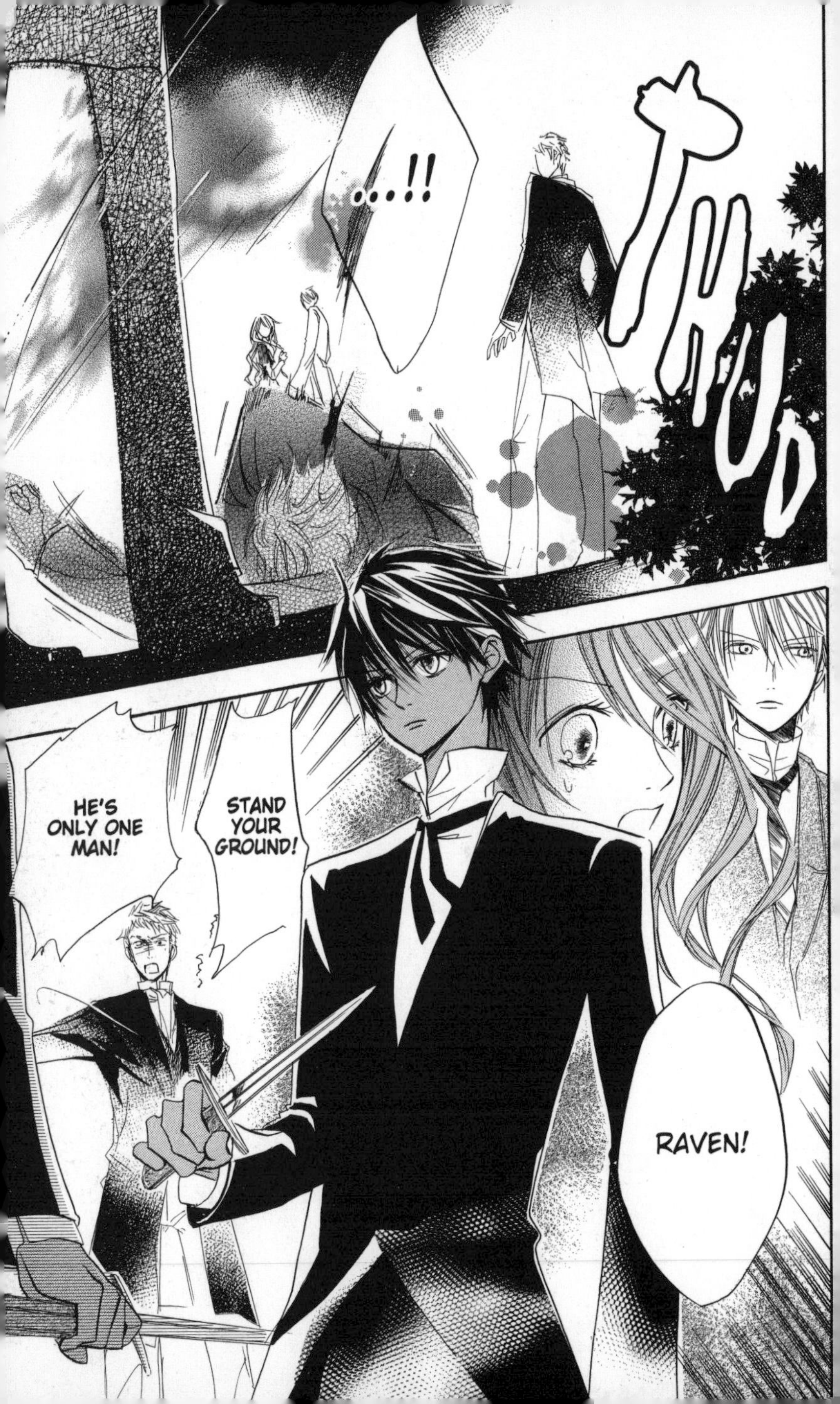
THUD
...!!
RAVEN!
STAND YOUR GROUND!
HE'S ONLY ONE MAN!

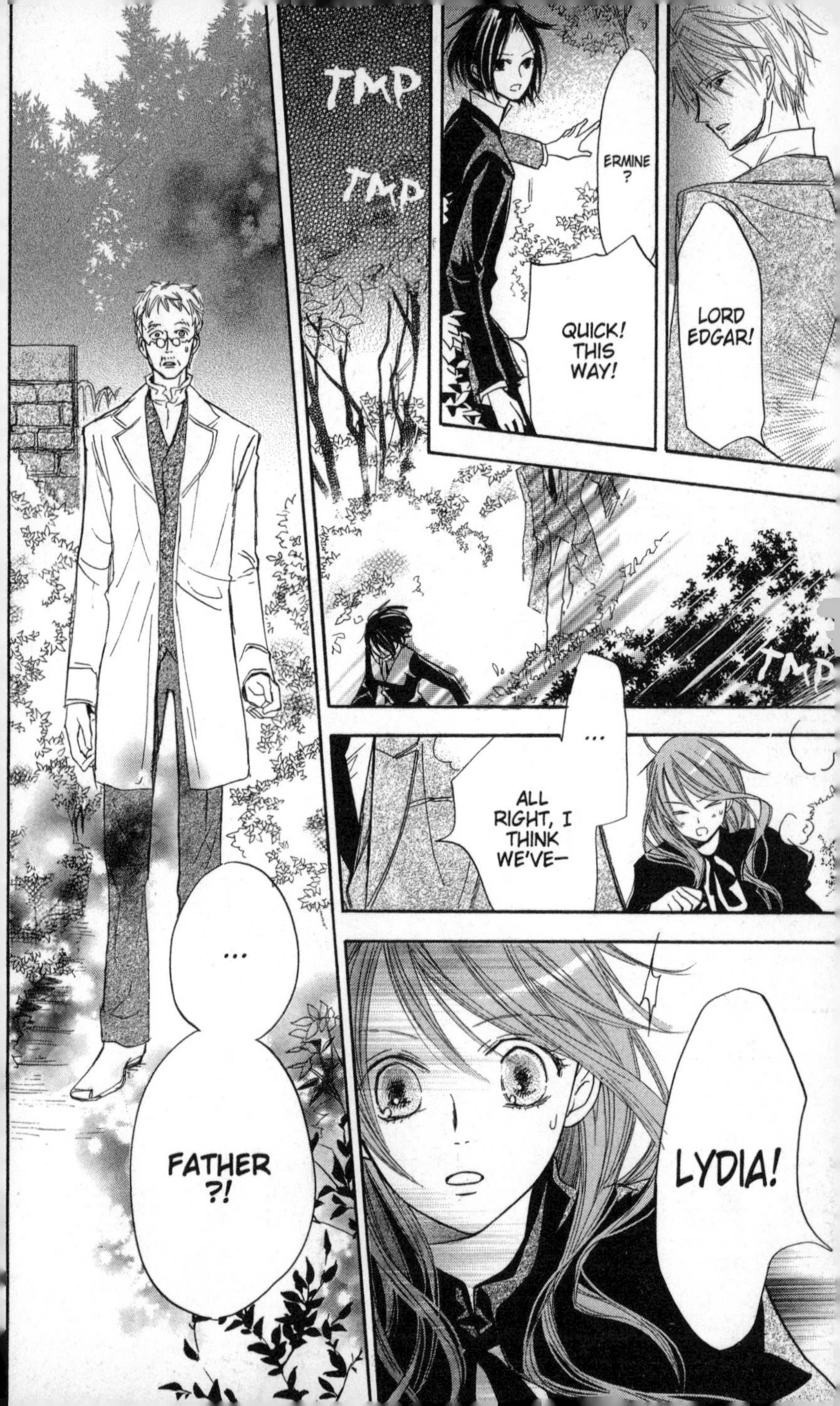

LORD EDGAR!
ERMINE?
QUICK! THIS WAY!
TMP
TMP
TMP
...
ALL RIGHT, I THINK WE'VE—
LYDIA!
...
FATHER?!

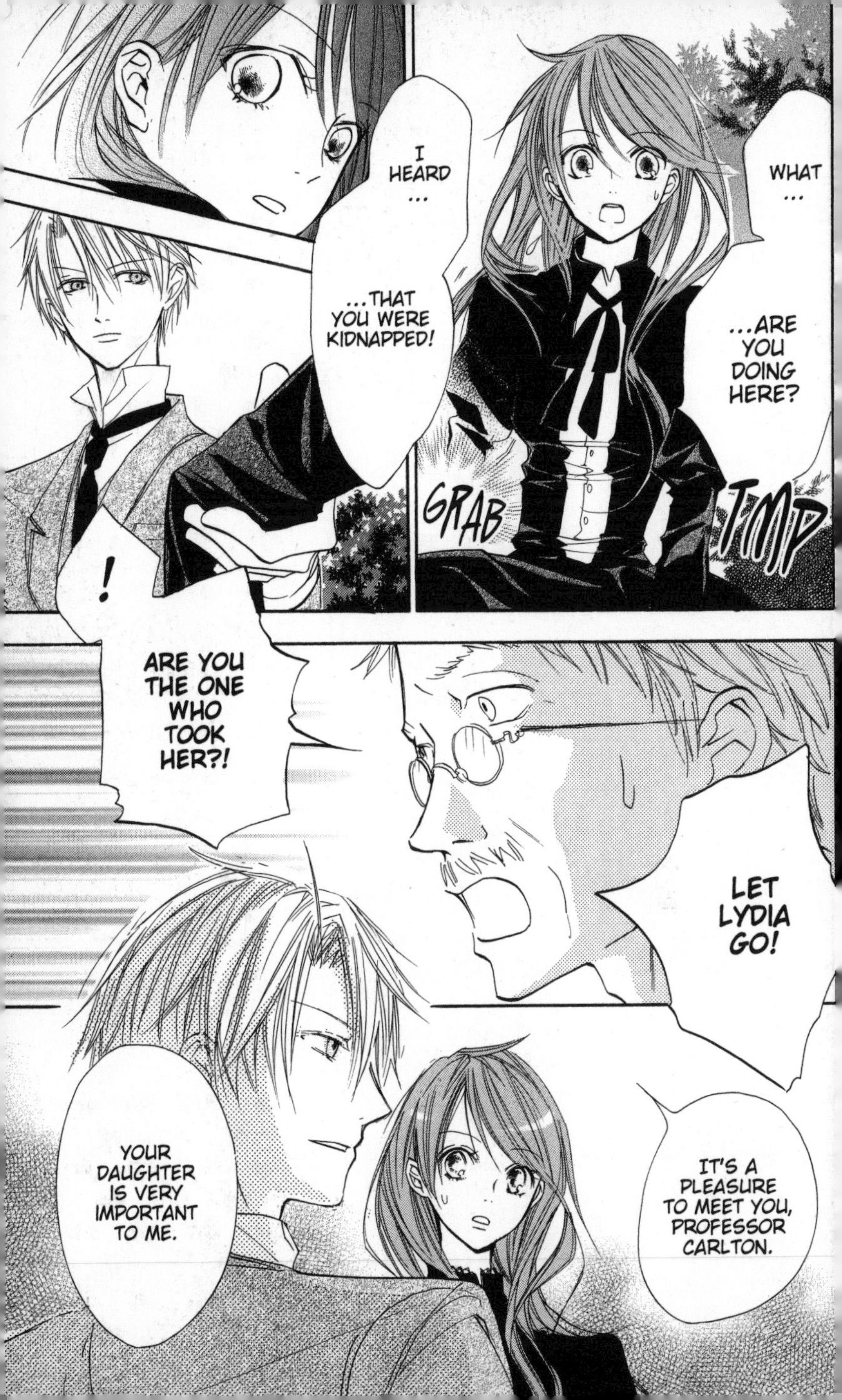

WHAT...
...ARE YOU DOING HERE?
TMP
GRAB
I HEARD...
...THAT YOU WERE KIDNAPPED!
!
ARE YOU THE ONE WHO TOOK HER?!
LET LYDIA GO!
IT'S A PLEASURE TO MEET YOU, PROFESSOR CARLTON.
YOUR DAUGHTER IS VERY IMPORTANT TO ME.

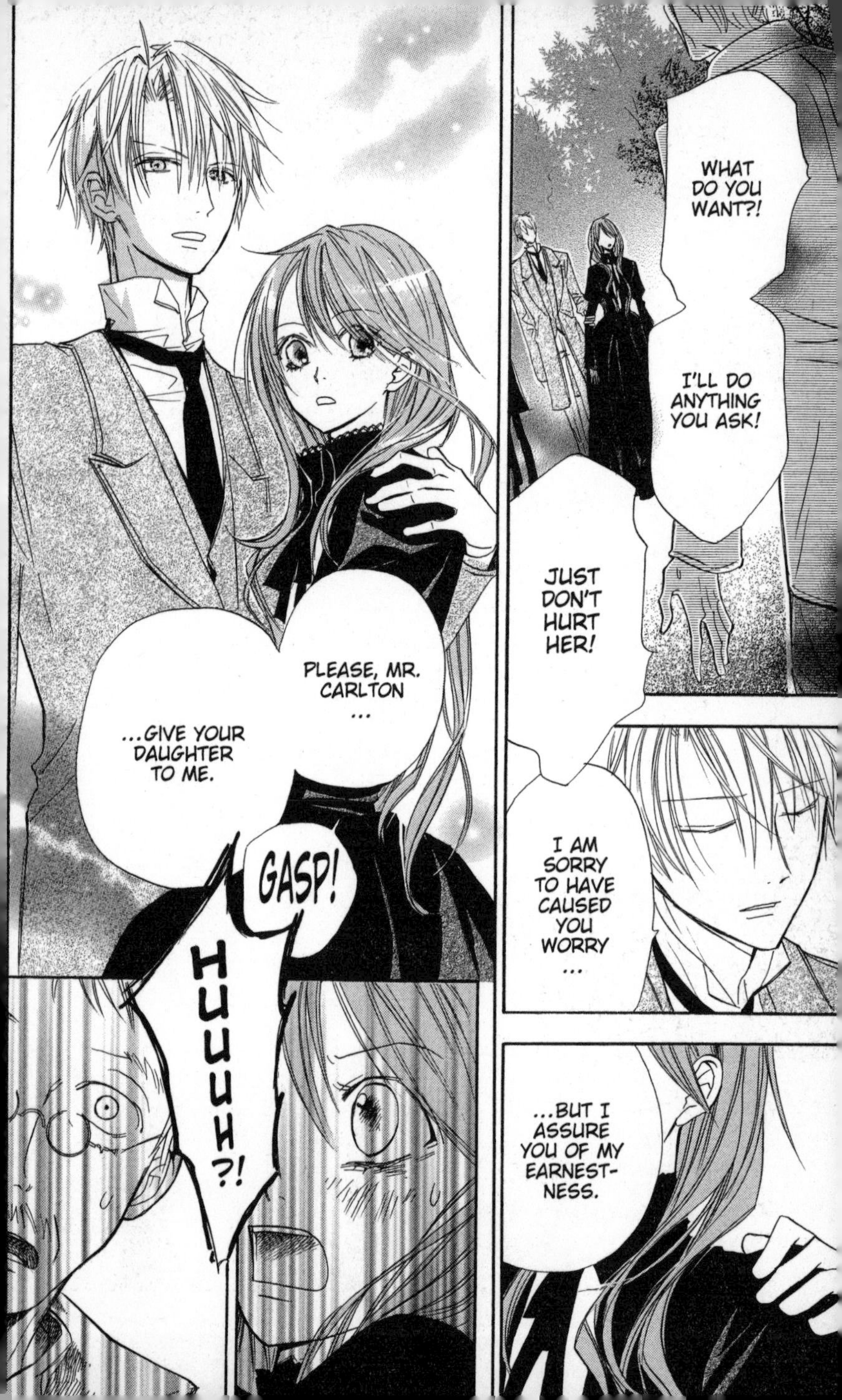
WHAT DO YOU WANT?!
I'LL DO ANYTHING YOU ASK!
JUST DON'T HURT HER!
I AM SORRY TO HAVE CAUSED YOU WORRY ...
...BUT I ASSURE YOU OF MY EARNEST-NESS.
PLEASE, MR. CARLTON ...
...GIVE YOUR DAUGHTER TO ME.
GASP!
HUUUH?!

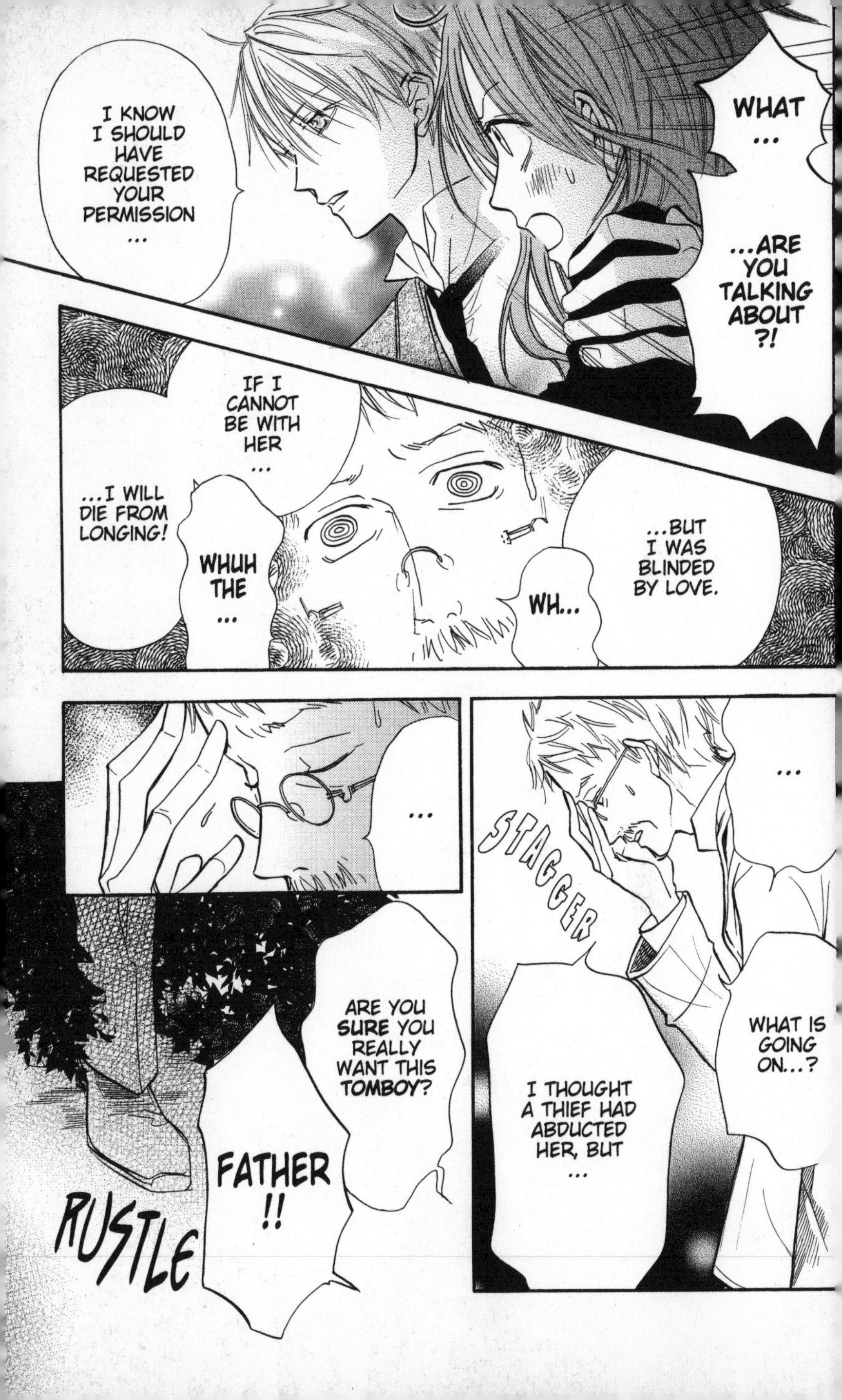
WHAT ...
...ARE YOU TALKING ABOUT?!
I KNOW I SHOULD HAVE REQUESTED YOUR PERMISSION ...
...BUT I WAS BLINDED BY LOVE.
WH...
IF I CANNOT BE WITH HER ...
WHUH THE ...
...I WILL DIE FROM LONGING!
...
STAGGER
...
WHAT IS GOING ON...?
I THOUGHT A THIEF HAD ABDUCTED HER, BUT ...
ARE YOU SURE YOU REALLY WANT THIS TOMBOY?
FATHER !!
RUSTLE

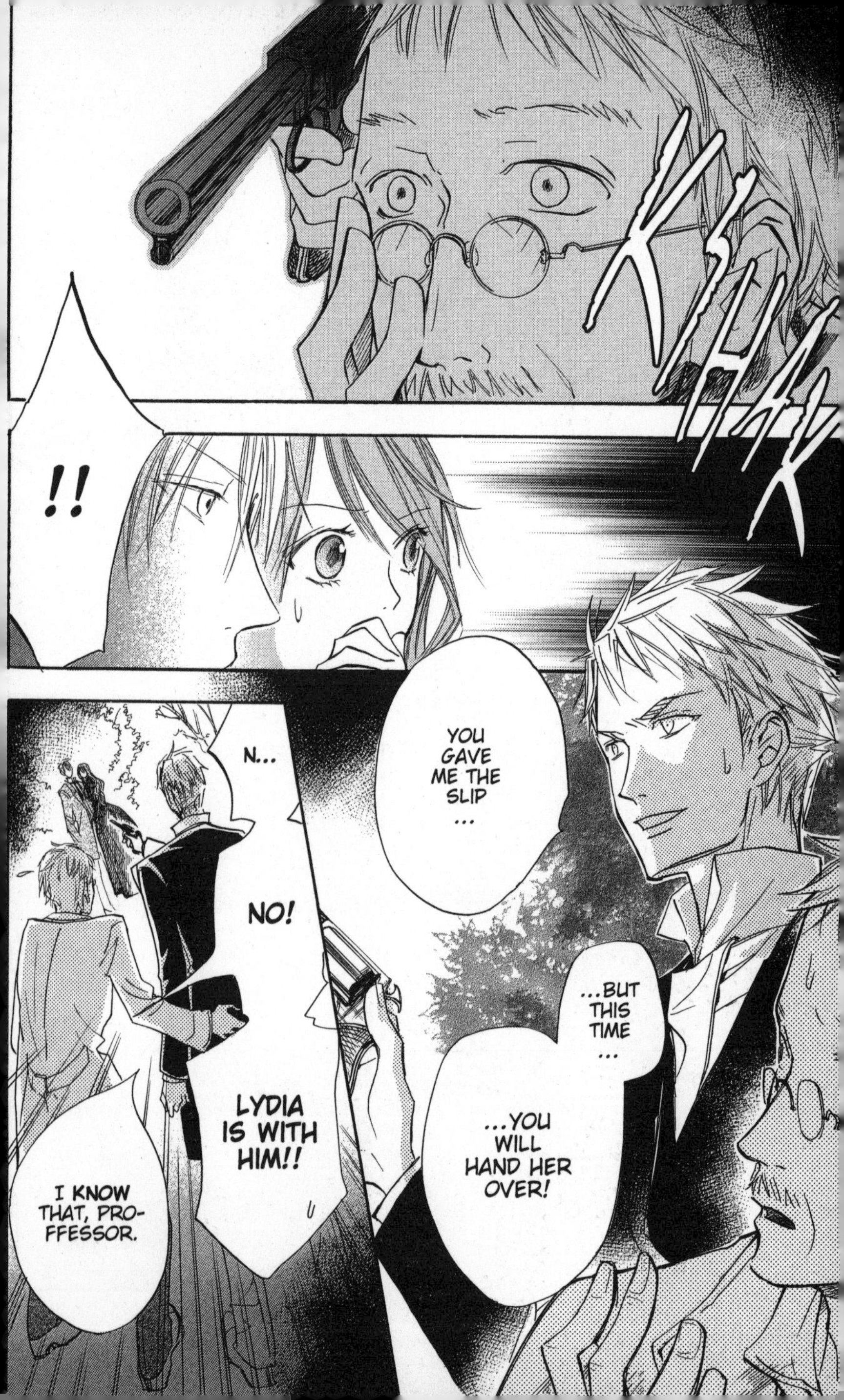
KSHAK
!!
YOU GAVE ME THE SLIP...
...BUT THIS TIME...
...YOU WILL HAND HER OVER!
N...
NO!
LYDIA IS WITH HIM!!
I KNOW THAT, PRO-FFESSOR.

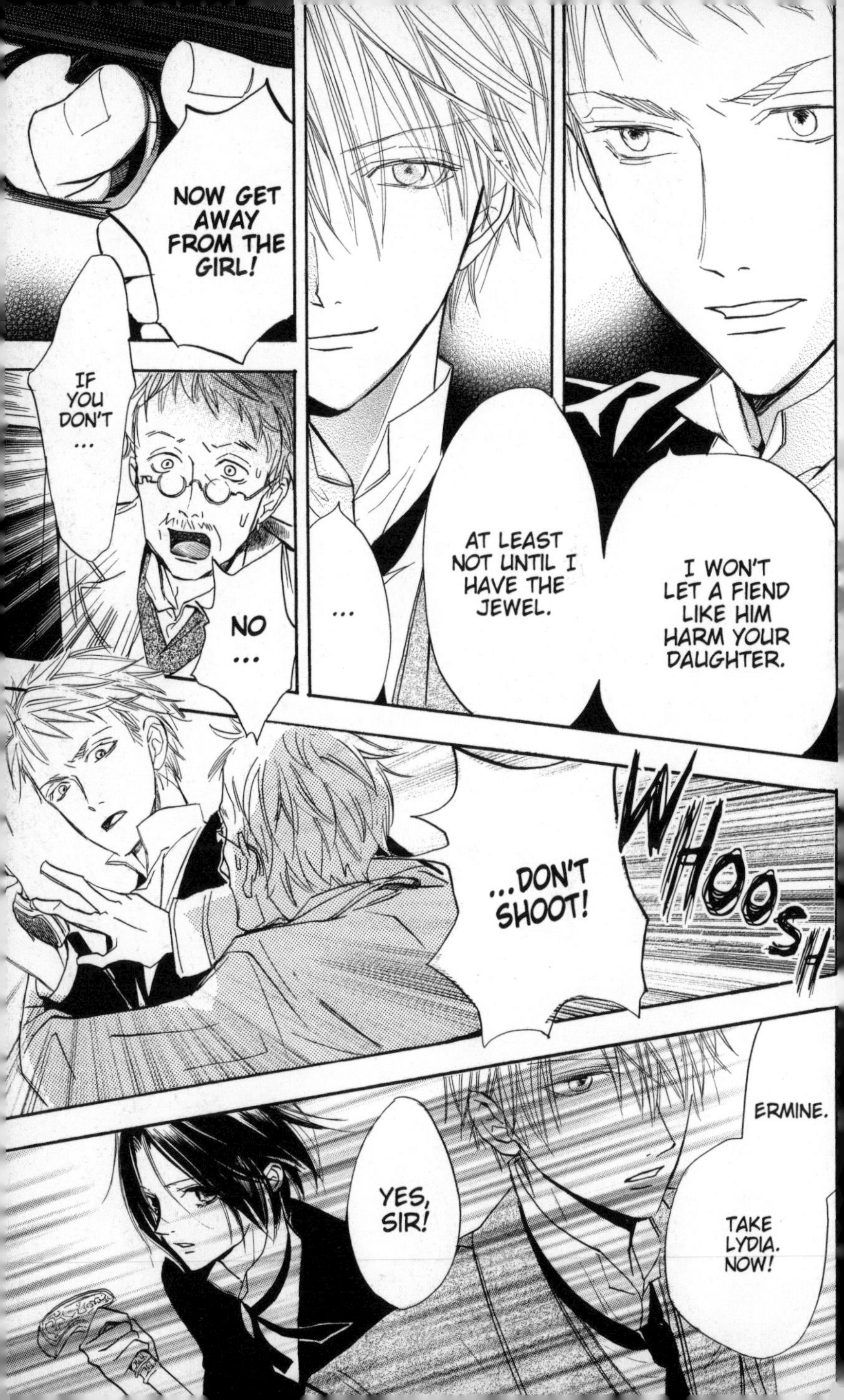

I WON'T LET A FIEND LIKE HIM HARM YOUR DAUGHTER.
AT LEAST NOT UNTIL I HAVE THE JEWEL.
...
NOW GET AWAY FROM THE GIRL!
IF YOU DON'T...
NO...
WHOOSH
...DON'T SHOOT!
ERMINE.
TAKE LYDIA. NOW!
YES, SIR!

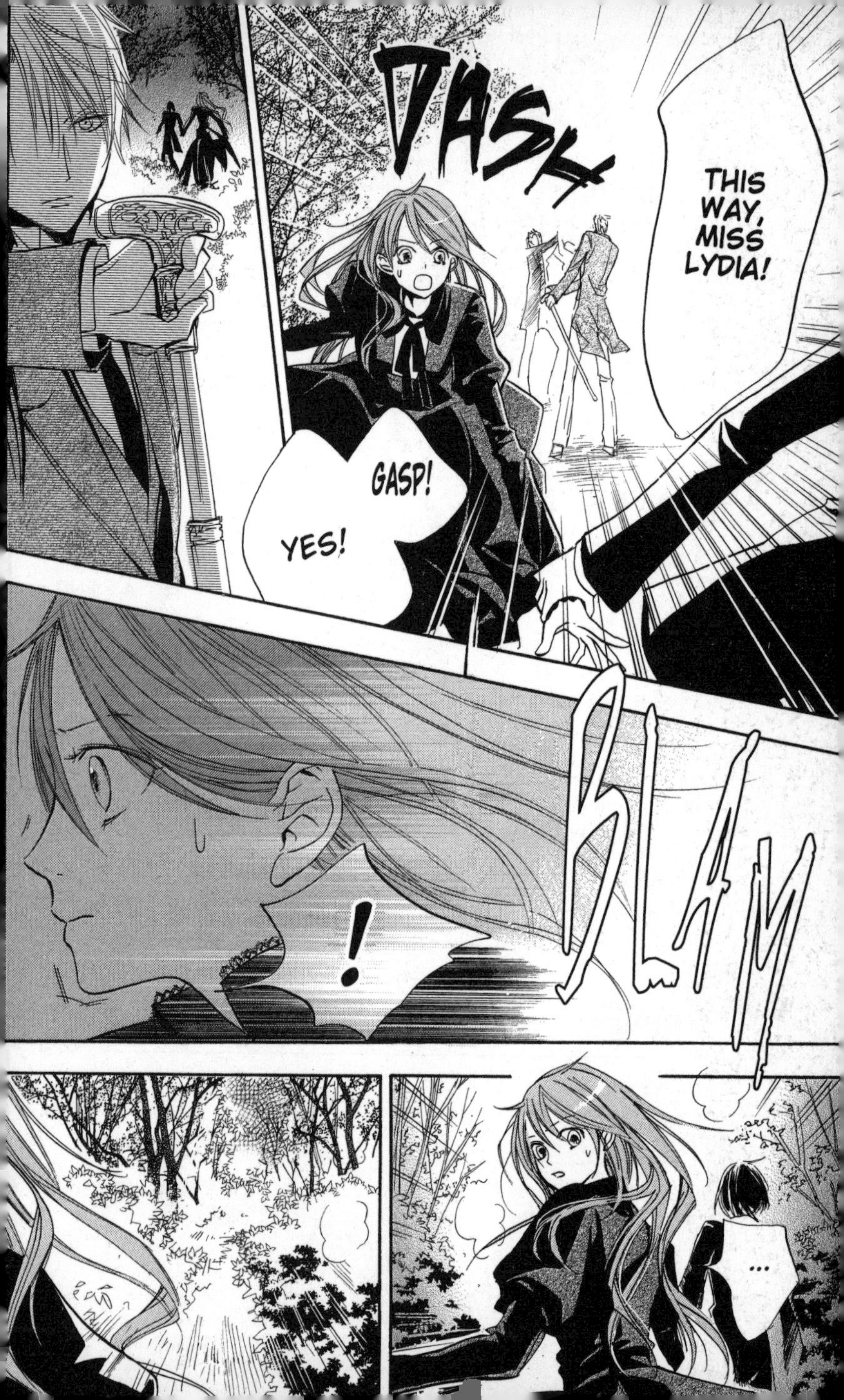
THIS WAY, MISS LYDIA!
DASH
GASP!
YES!
BLAM
!
...

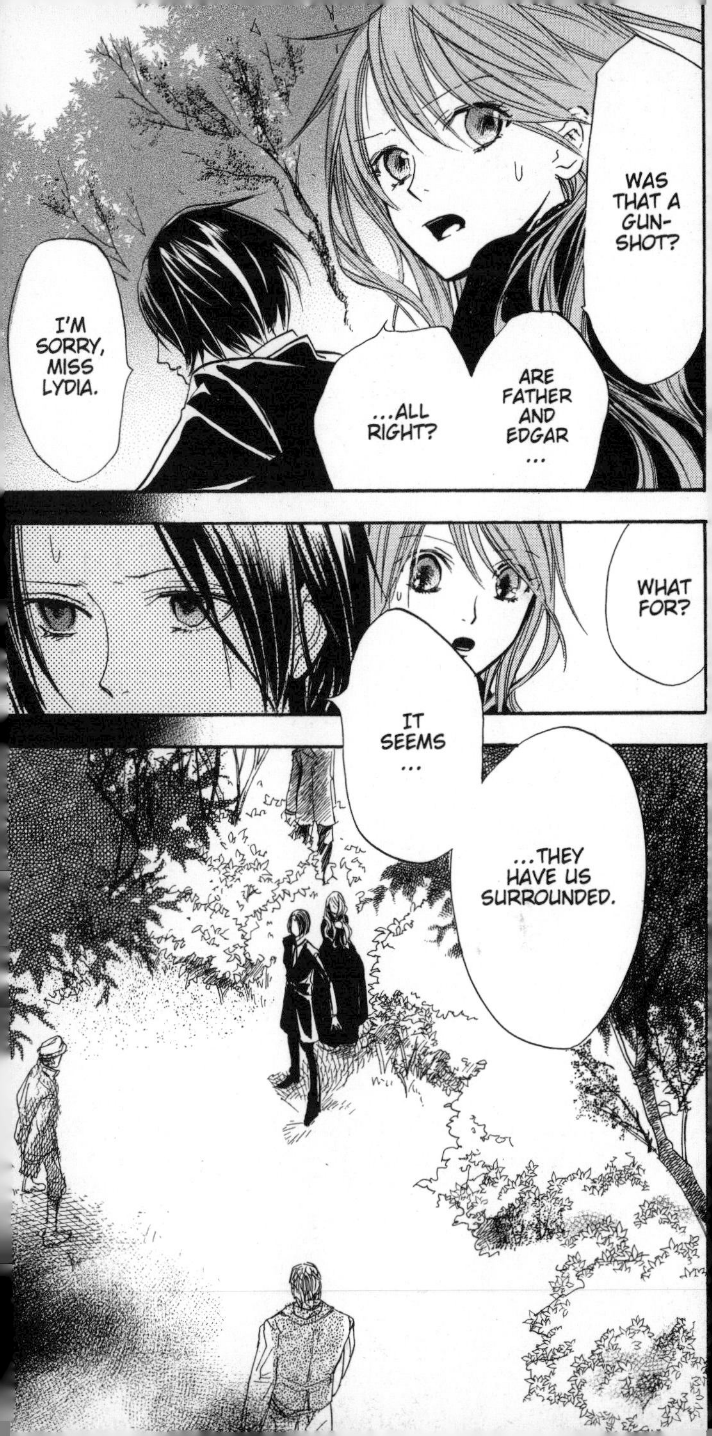
WAS THAT A GUN-SHOT?
ARE FATHER AND EDGAR ...
...ALL RIGHT?
I'M SORRY, MISS LYDIA.
WHAT FOR?
IT SEEMS ...
...THEY HAVE US SURROUNDED.

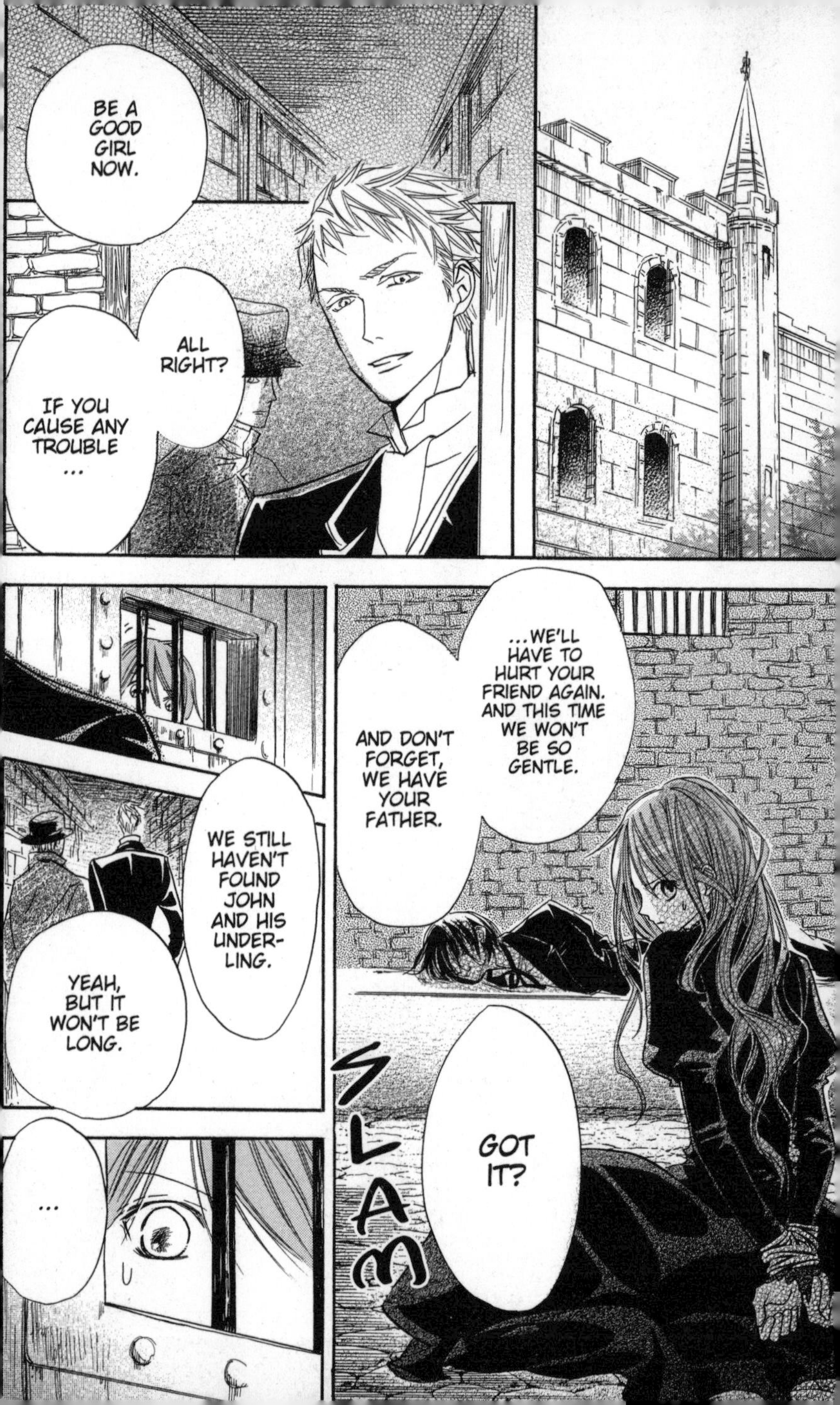
BE A GOOD GIRL NOW.
ALL RIGHT?
IF YOU CAUSE ANY TROUBLE ...
...WE'LL HAVE TO HURT YOUR FRIEND AGAIN. AND THIS TIME WE WON'T BE SO GENTLE.
AND DON'T FORGET, WE HAVE YOUR FATHER.
GOT IT?
SLAM
WE STILL HAVEN'T FOUND JOHN AND HIS UNDER-LING.
YEAH, BUT IT WON'T BE LONG.
...

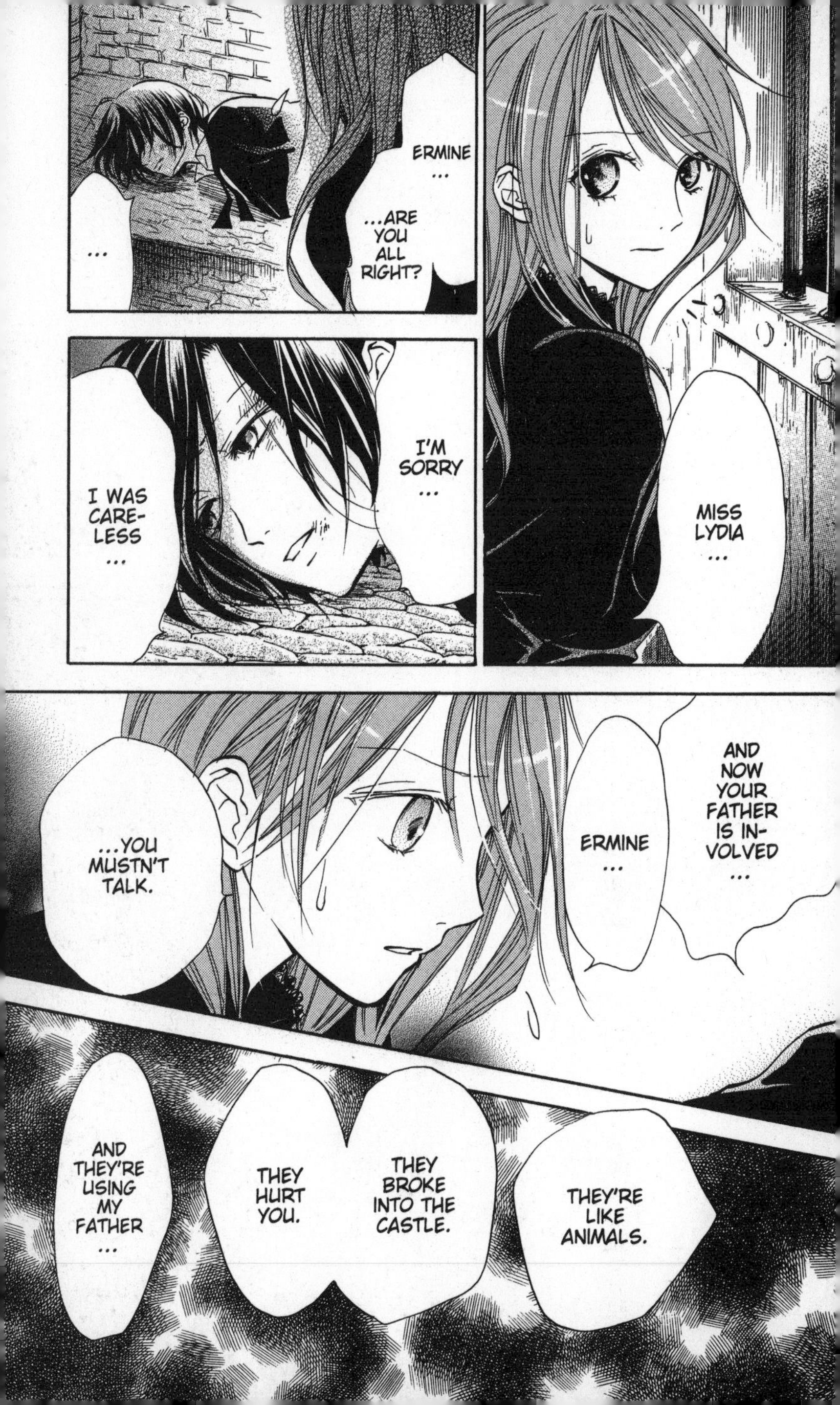
MISS LYDIA ...
ERMINE ...
...ARE YOU ALL RIGHT?
...
I'M SORRY ...
I WAS CARE-LESS ...
AND NOW YOUR FATHER IS IN-VOLVED ...
ERMINE ...
...YOU MUSTN'T TALK.
THEY'RE LIKE ANIMALS.
THEY BROKE INTO THE CASTLE.
THEY HURT YOU.
AND THEY'RE USING MY FATHER ...

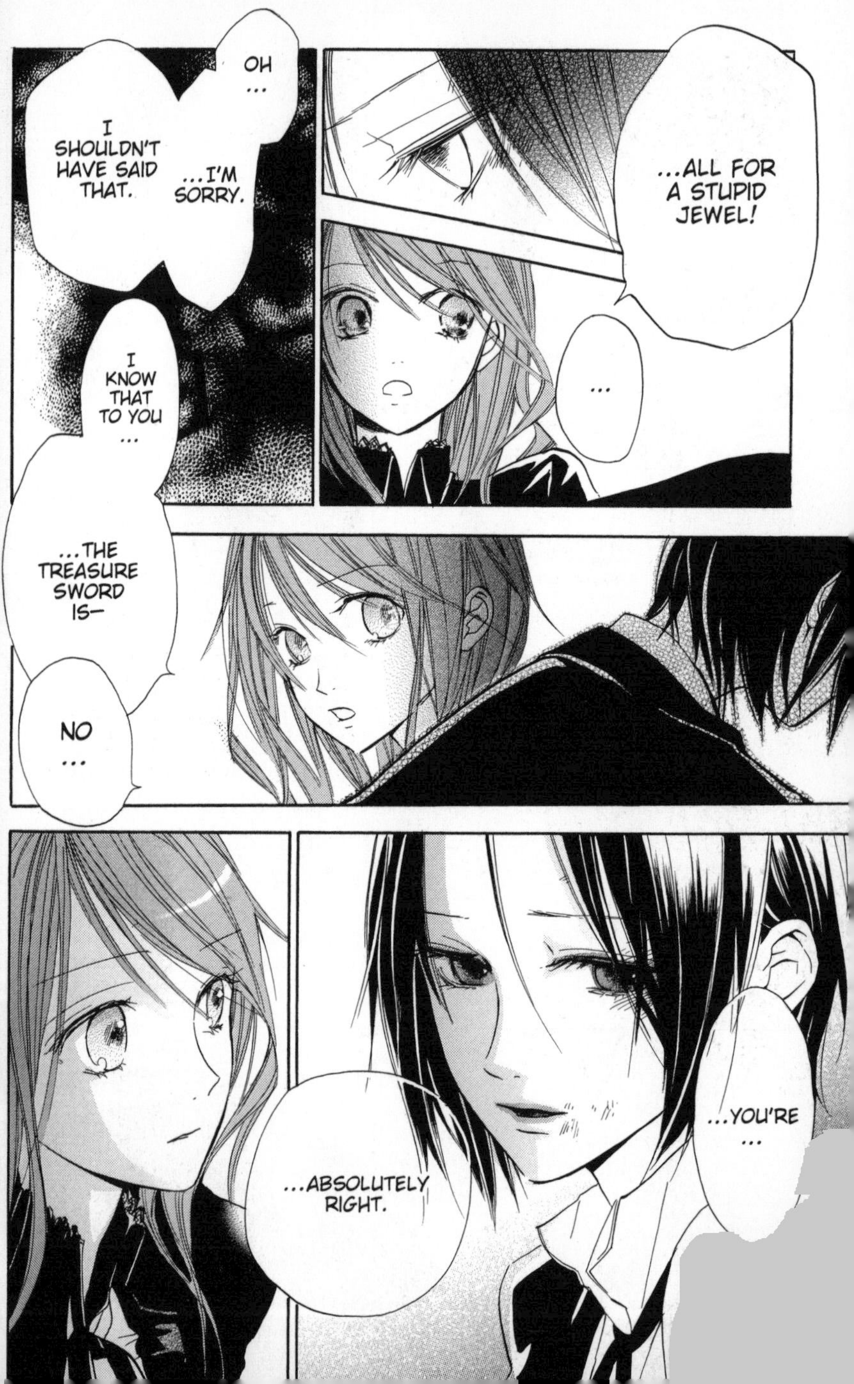
...ALL FOR A STUPID JEWEL!
...
OH ...
...I'M SORRY.
I SHOULDN'T HAVE SAID THAT.
I KNOW THAT TO YOU ...
...THE TREASURE SWORD IS—
NO ...
...YOU'RE ...
...ABSOLUTELY RIGHT.

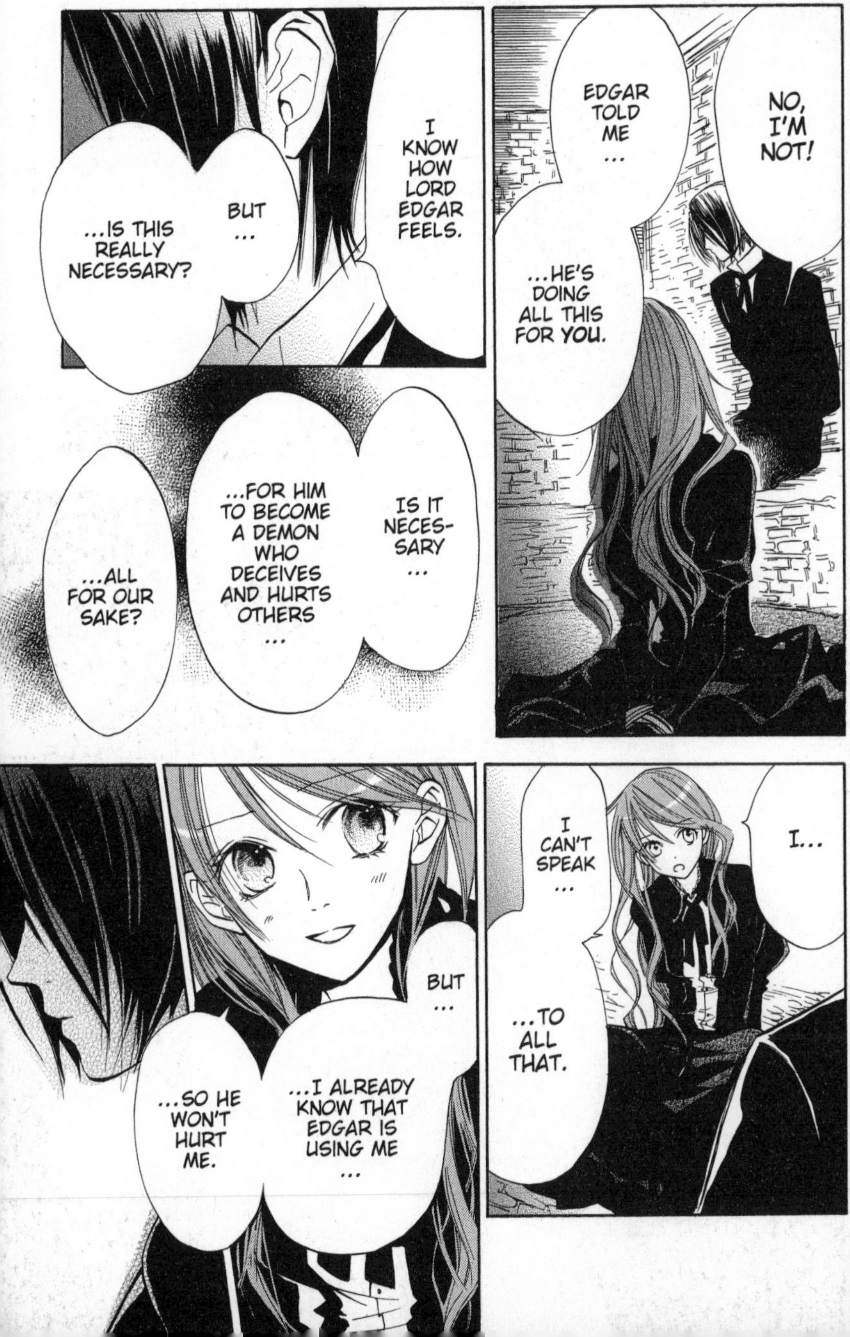
NO, I'M NOT!
EDGAR TOLD ME ...
...HE'S DOING ALL THIS FOR YOU.
I KNOW HOW LORD EDGAR FEELS.
BUT ...
...IS THIS REALLY NECESSARY?
IS IT NECES-SARY ...
...FOR HIM TO BECOME A DEMON WHO DECEIVES AND HURTS OTHERS ...
...ALL FOR OUR SAKE?
I...
I CAN'T SPEAK ...
...TO ALL THAT.
BUT ...
...I ALREADY KNOW THAT EDGAR IS USING ME ...
...SO HE WON'T HURT ME.

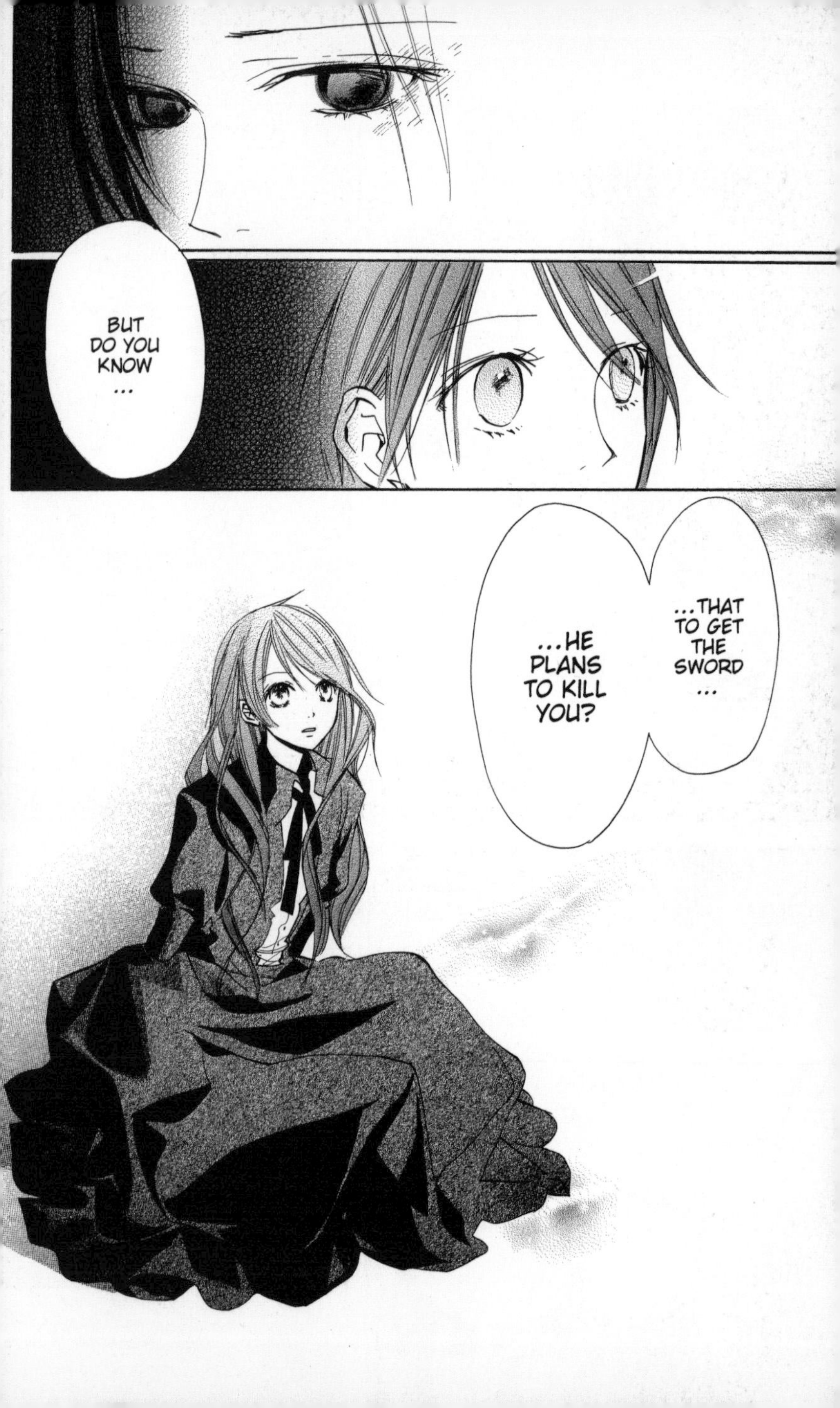
BUT DO YOU KNOW ...
...THAT TO GET THE SWORD ...
...HE PLANS TO KILL YOU?

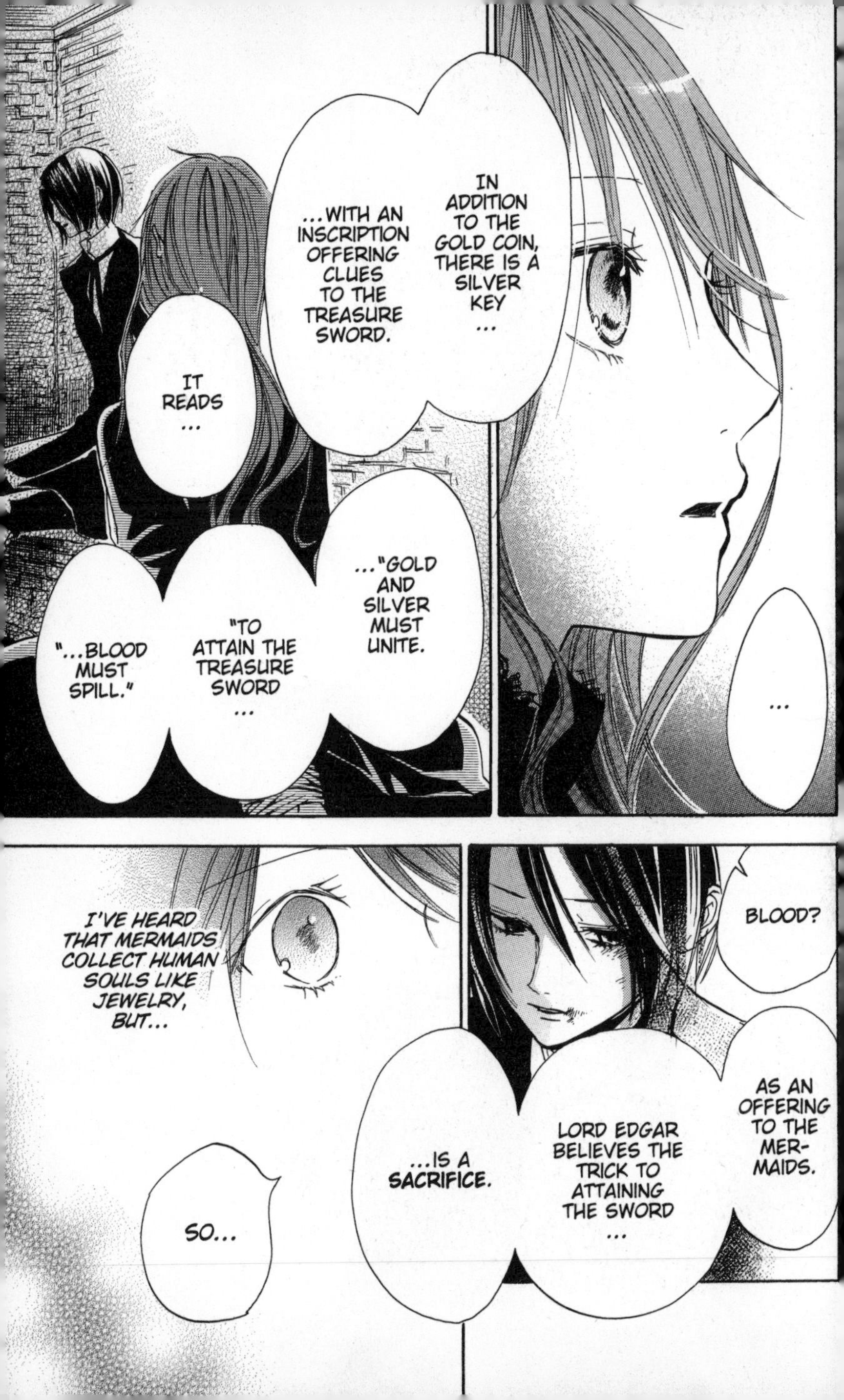
...
IN ADDITION TO THE GOLD COIN, THERE IS A SILVER KEY...
...WITH AN INSCRIPTION OFFERING CLUES TO THE TREASURE SWORD.
IT READS...
..."GOLD AND SILVER MUST UNITE.
"TO ATTAIN THE TREASURE SWORD...
"...BLOOD MUST SPILL."
BLOOD?
AS AN OFFERING TO THE MER-MAIDS.
LORD EDGAR BELIEVES THE TRICK TO ATTAINING THE SWORD...
...IS A SACRIFICE.
I'VE HEARD THAT MERMAIDS COLLECT HUMAN SOULS LIKE JEWELRY, BUT...
SO...

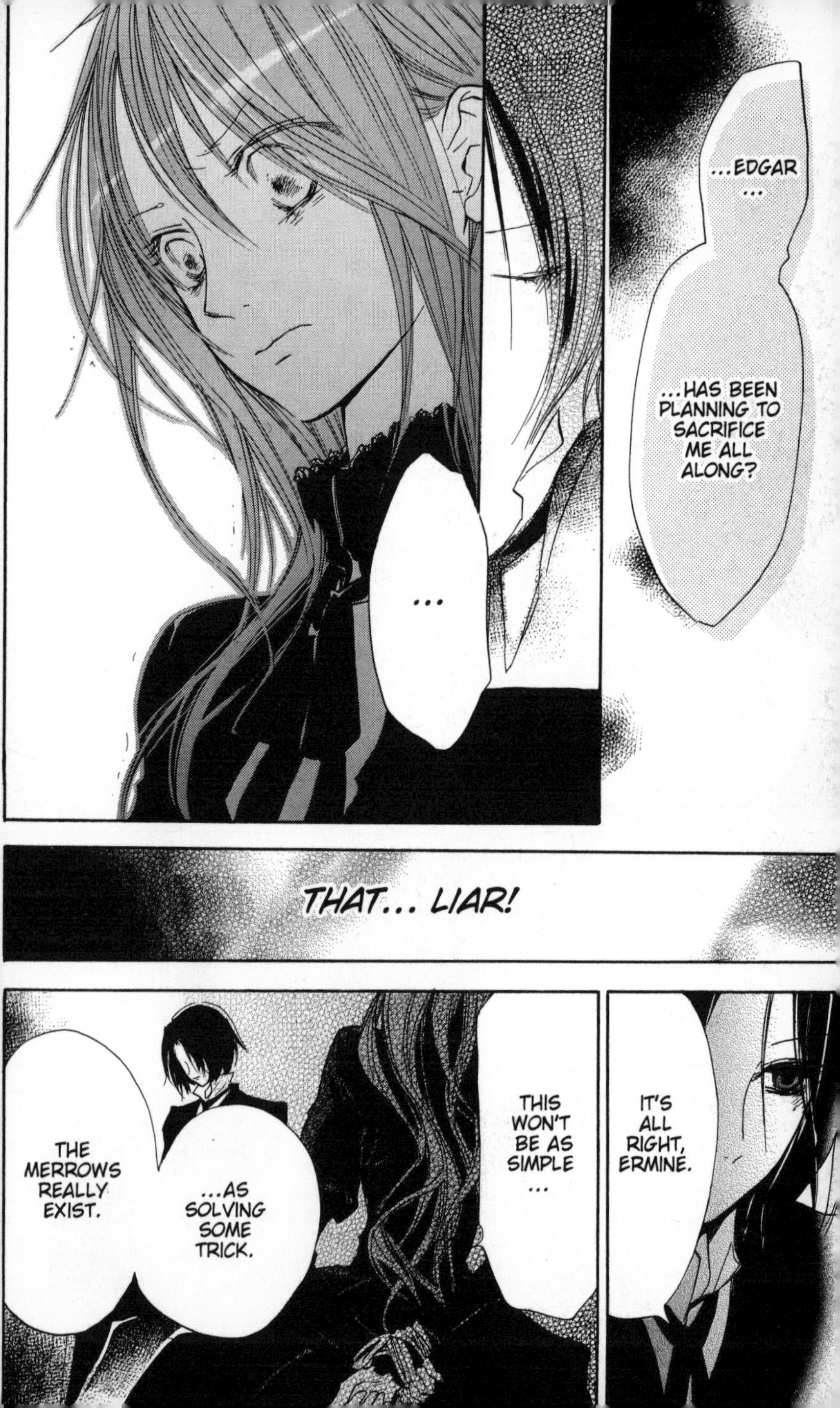
...EDGAR ...
...HAS BEEN PLANNING TO SACRIFICE ME ALL ALONG?
...
THAT... LIAR!
IT'S ALL RIGHT, ERMINE.
THIS WON'T BE AS SIMPLE ...
...AS SOLVING SOME TRICK.
THE MERROWS REALLY EXIST.

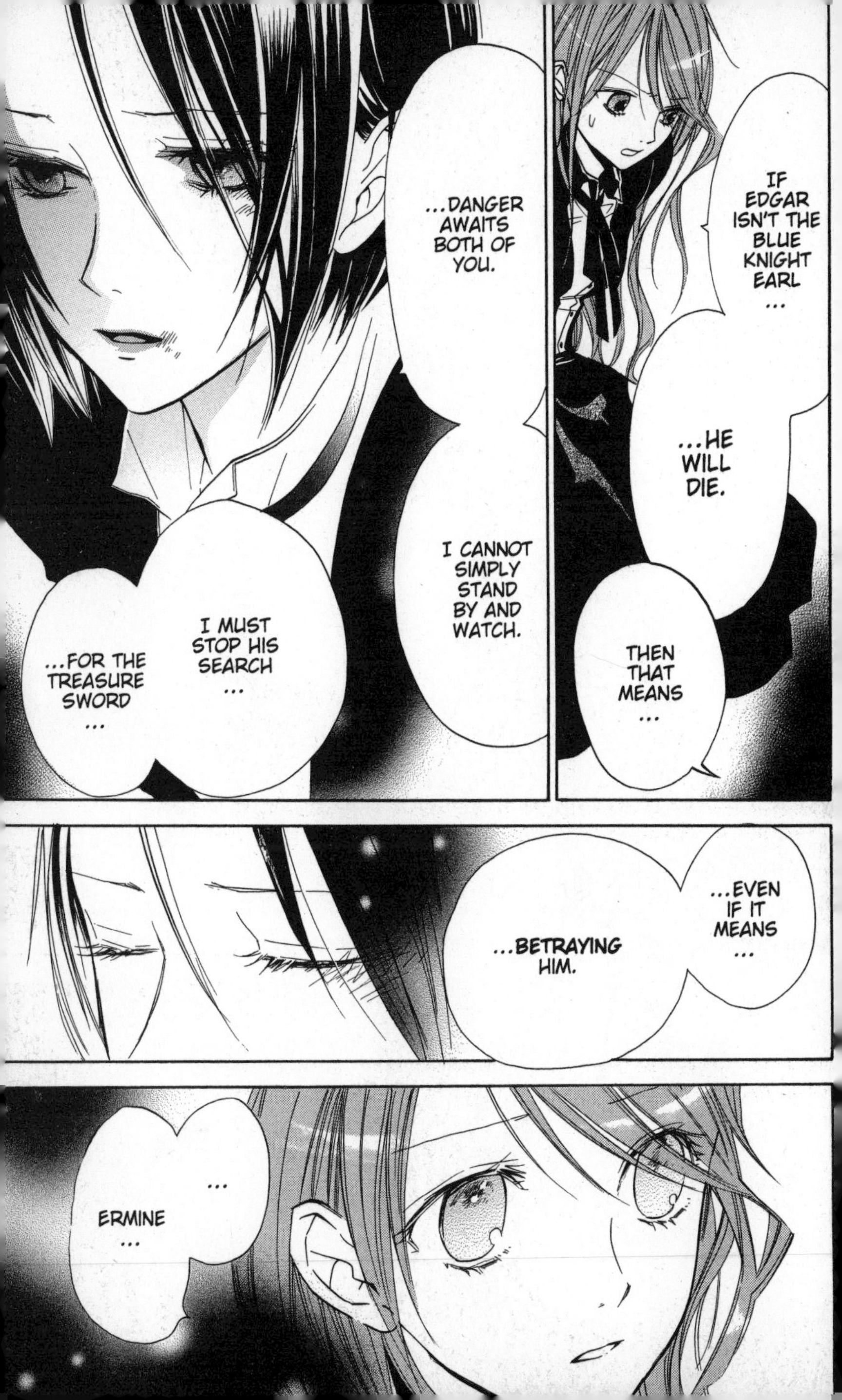
IF EDGAR ISN'T THE BLUE KNIGHT EARL ...
...HE WILL DIE.
THEN THAT MEANS ...
...DANGER AWAITS BOTH OF YOU.
I CANNOT SIMPLY STAND BY AND WATCH.
I MUST STOP HIS SEARCH ...
...FOR THE TREASURE SWORD ...
...EVEN IF IT MEANS ...
...BETRAYING HIM.
... ERMINE ...

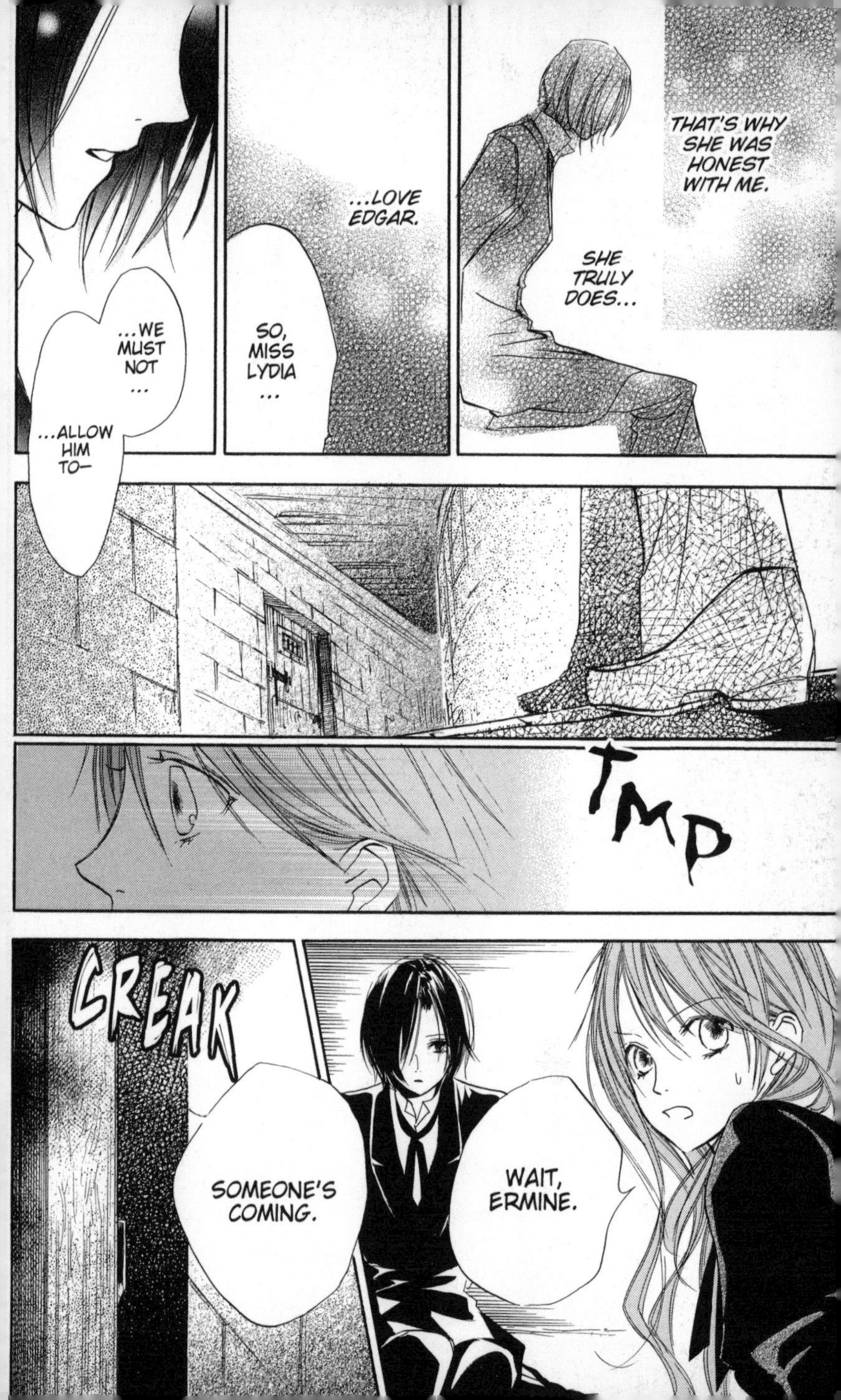

THAT'S WHY SHE WAS HONEST WITH ME.
SHE TRULY DOES...
...LOVE EDGAR.
SO, MISS LYDIA...
...WE MUST NOT...
...ALLOW HIM TO—
TMP
CREAK
WAIT, ERMINE.
SOMEONE'S COMING.

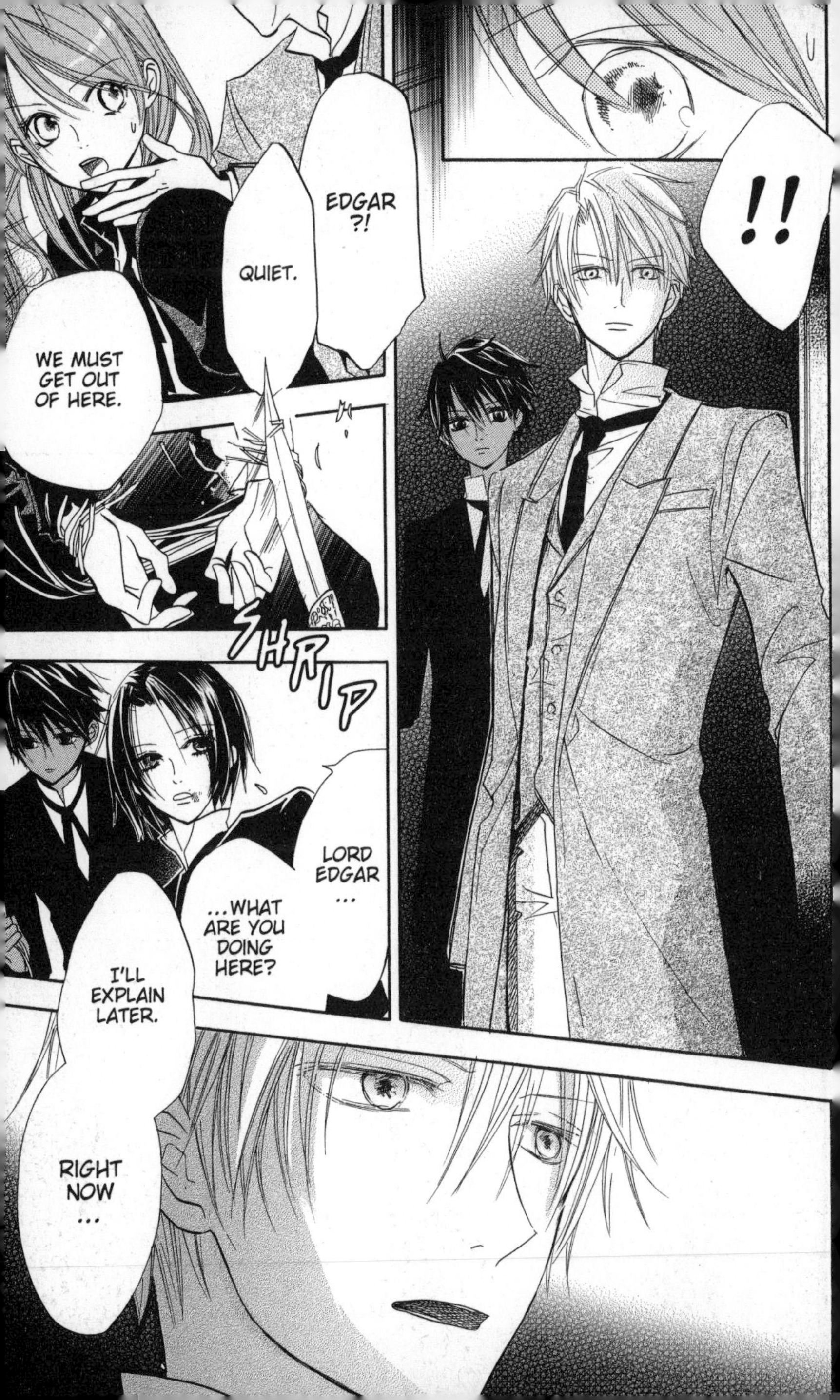
!!
EDGAR ?!
QUIET.
WE MUST GET OUT OF HERE.
SHRIP
LORD EDGAR ...
...WHAT ARE YOU DOING HERE?
I'LL EXPLAIN LATER.
RIGHT NOW ...

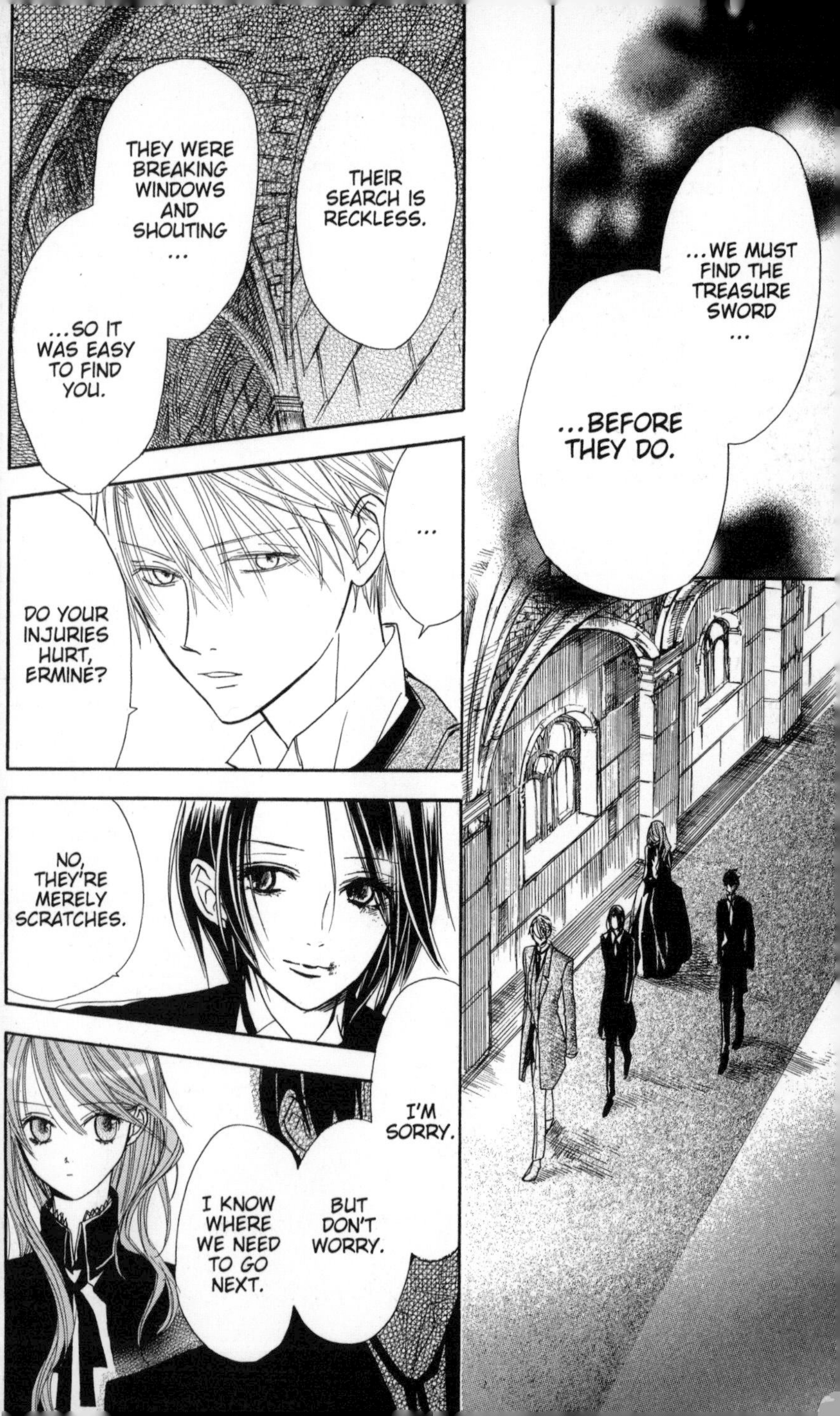
...WE MUST FIND THE TREASURE SWORD ...
...BEFORE THEY DO.
THEIR SEARCH IS RECKLESS.
THEY WERE BREAKING WINDOWS AND SHOUTING ...
...SO IT WAS EASY TO FIND YOU.
...
DO YOUR INJURIES HURT, ERMINE?
NO, THEY'RE MERELY SCRATCHES.
I'M SORRY.
BUT DON'T WORRY.
I KNOW WHERE WE NEED TO GO NEXT.

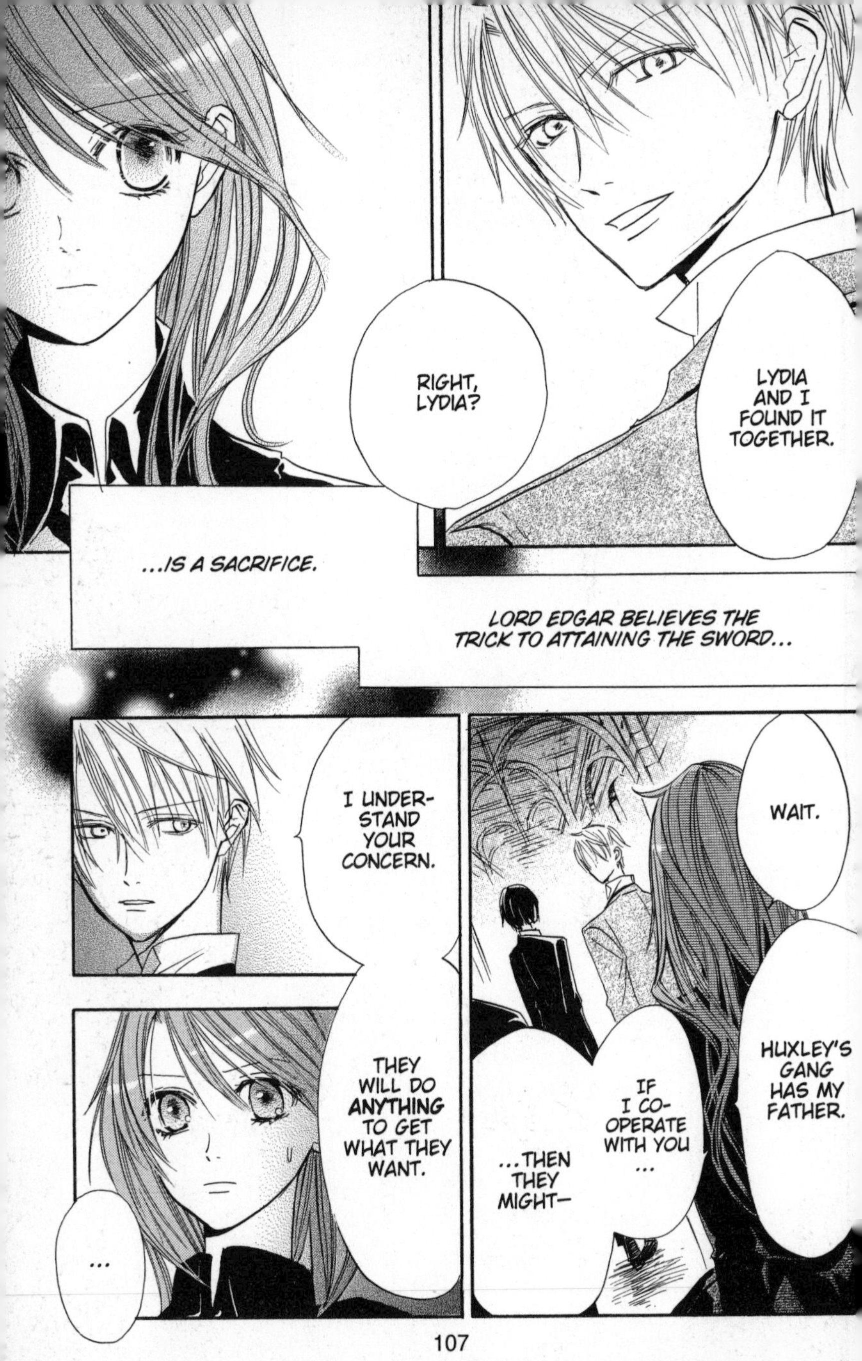
LYDIA AND I FOUND IT TOGETHER.
RIGHT, LYDIA?
LORD EDGAR BELIEVES THE TRICK TO ATTAINING THE SWORD...
...IS A SACRIFICE.
WAIT.
HUXLEY'S GANG HAS MY FATHER.
IF I CO-OPERATE WITH YOU...
...THEN THEY MIGHT–
I UNDER-STAND YOUR CONCERN.
THEY WILL DO **ANYTHING** TO GET WHAT THEY WANT.
...

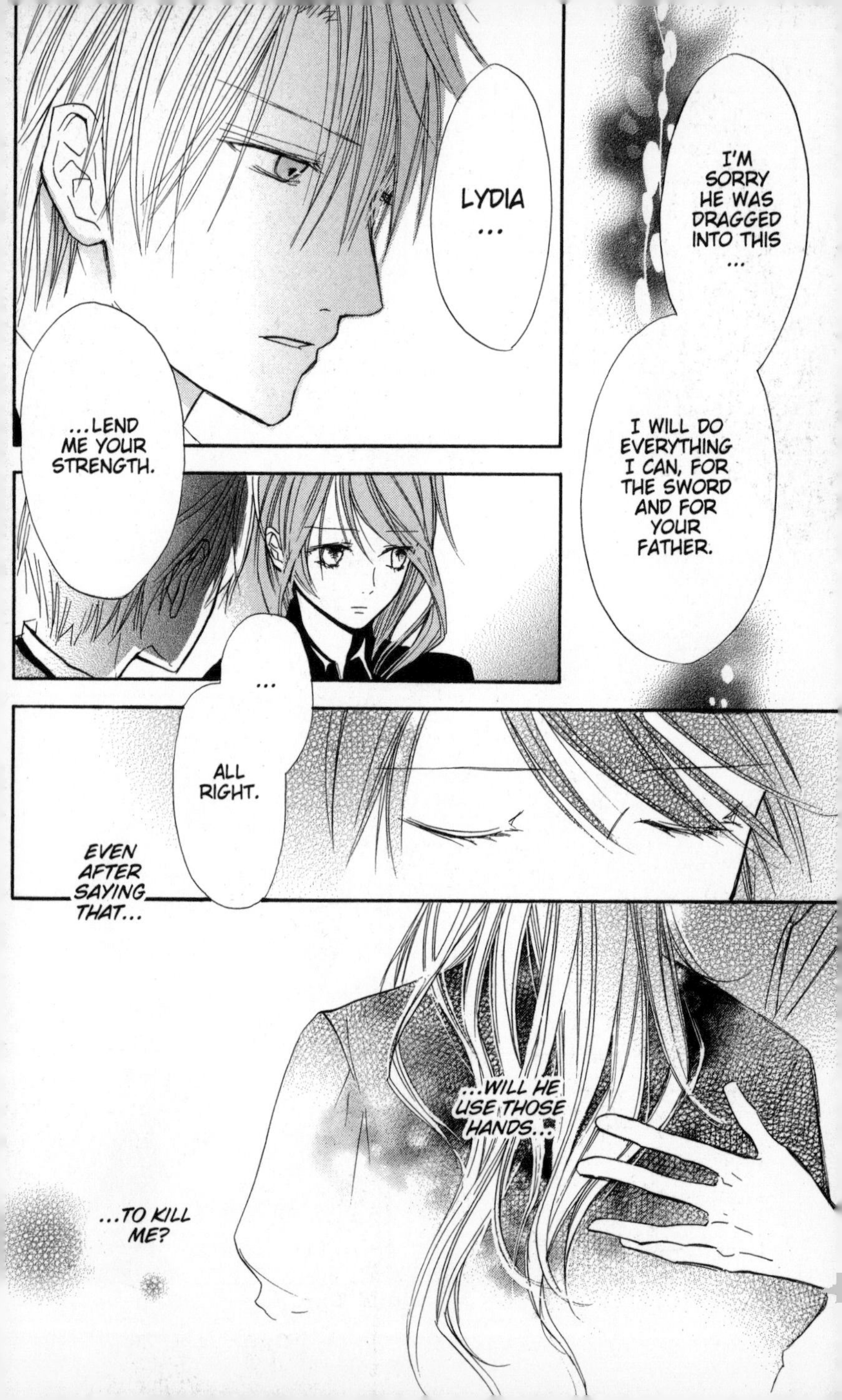
I'M SORRY HE WAS DRAGGED INTO THIS ...
I WILL DO EVERYTHING I CAN, FOR THE SWORD AND FOR YOUR FATHER.
LYDIA ...
...LEND ME YOUR STRENGTH.
...
ALL RIGHT.
EVEN AFTER SAYING THAT...
...WILL HE USE THOSE HANDS...
...TO KILL ME?

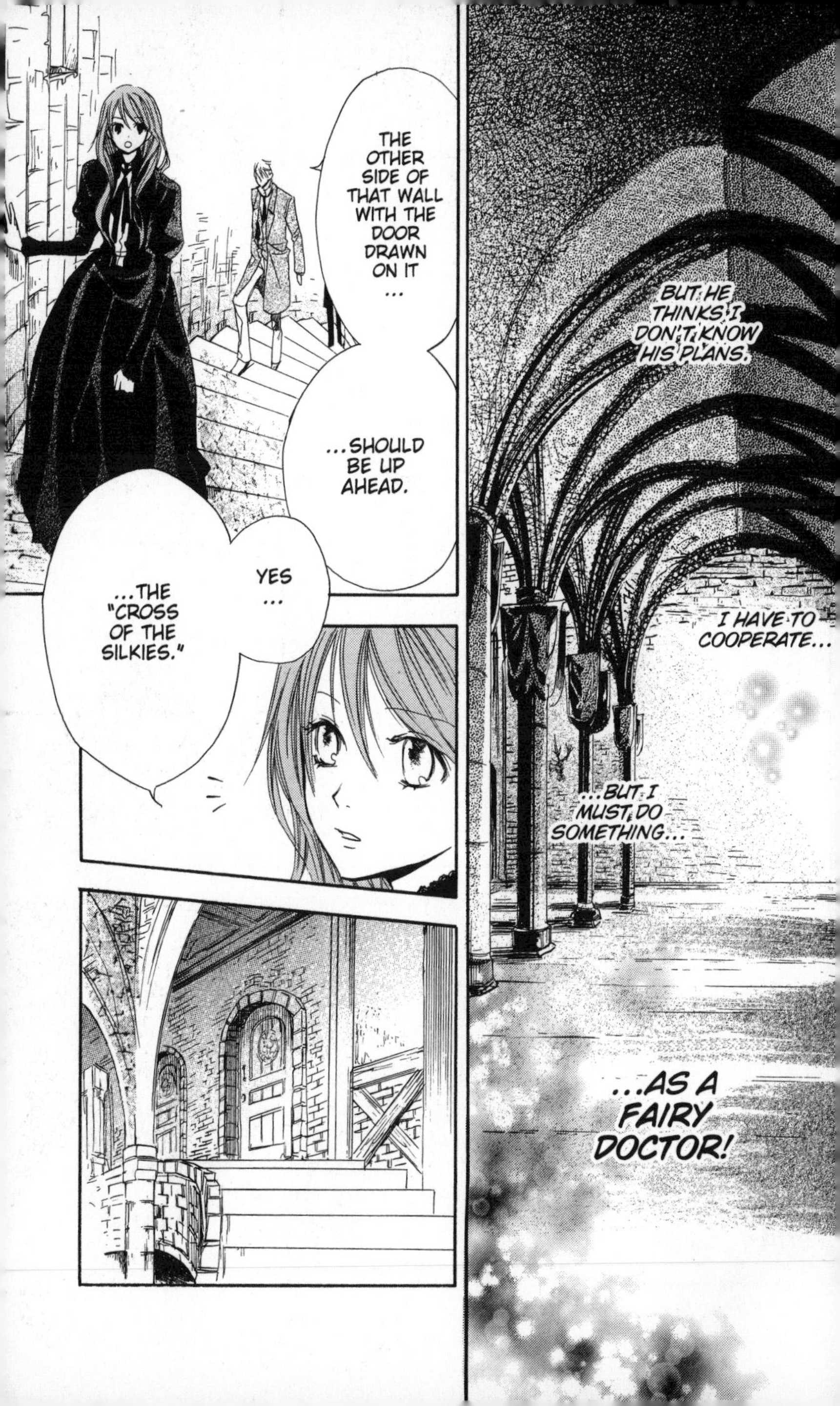
BUT HE THINKS I DON'T KNOW HIS PLANS.
I HAVE TO COOPERATE...
...BUT I MUST DO SOMETHING...
...AS A FAIRY DOCTOR!
THE OTHER SIDE OF THAT WALL WITH THE DOOR DRAWN ON IT ...
...SHOULD BE UP AHEAD.
YES ...
...THE "CROSS OF THE SILKIES."

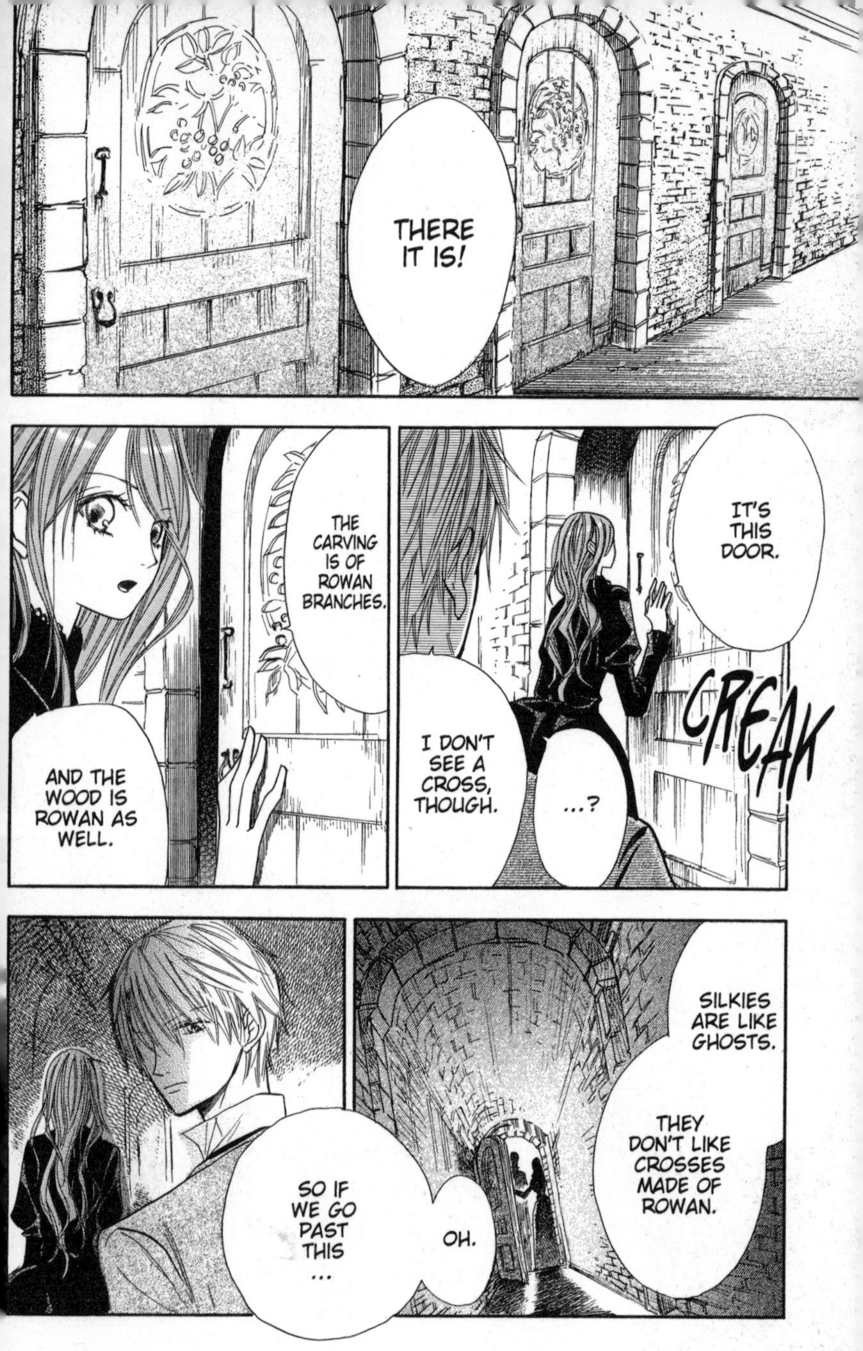
THERE IT IS!
IT'S THIS DOOR.
CREAK
...?
I DON'T SEE A CROSS, THOUGH.
THE CARVING IS OF ROWAN BRANCHES.
AND THE WOOD IS ROWAN AS WELL.
SILKIES ARE LIKE GHOSTS.
THEY DON'T LIKE CROSSES MADE OF ROWAN.
OH.
SO IF WE GO PAST THIS ...

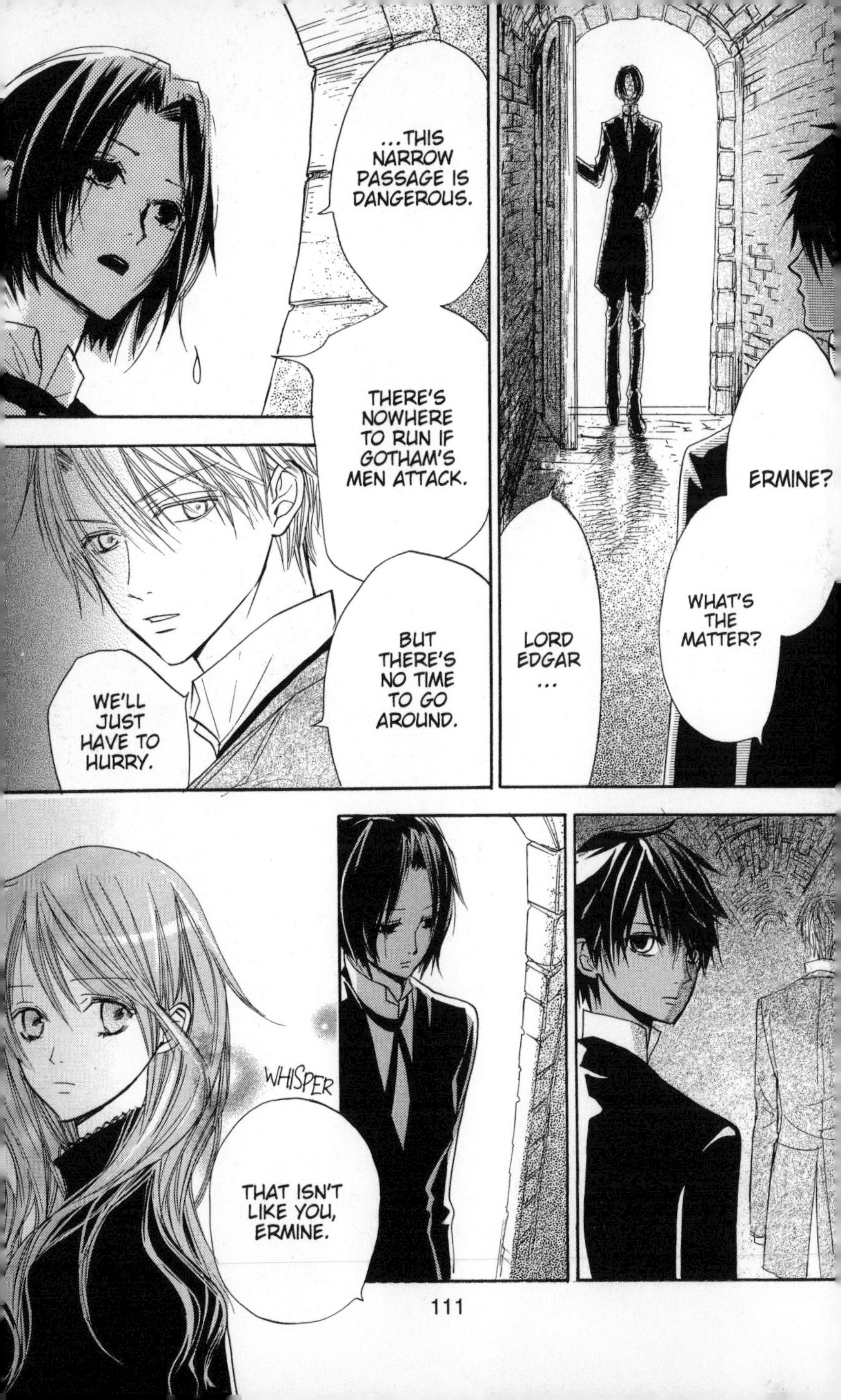
ERMINE?
WHAT'S THE MATTER?
LORD EDGAR ...
...THIS NARROW PASSAGE IS DANGEROUS.
THERE'S NOWHERE TO RUN IF GOTHAM'S MEN ATTACK.
BUT THERE'S NO TIME TO GO AROUND.
WE'LL JUST HAVE TO HURRY.
WHISPER
THAT ISN'T LIKE YOU, ERMINE.

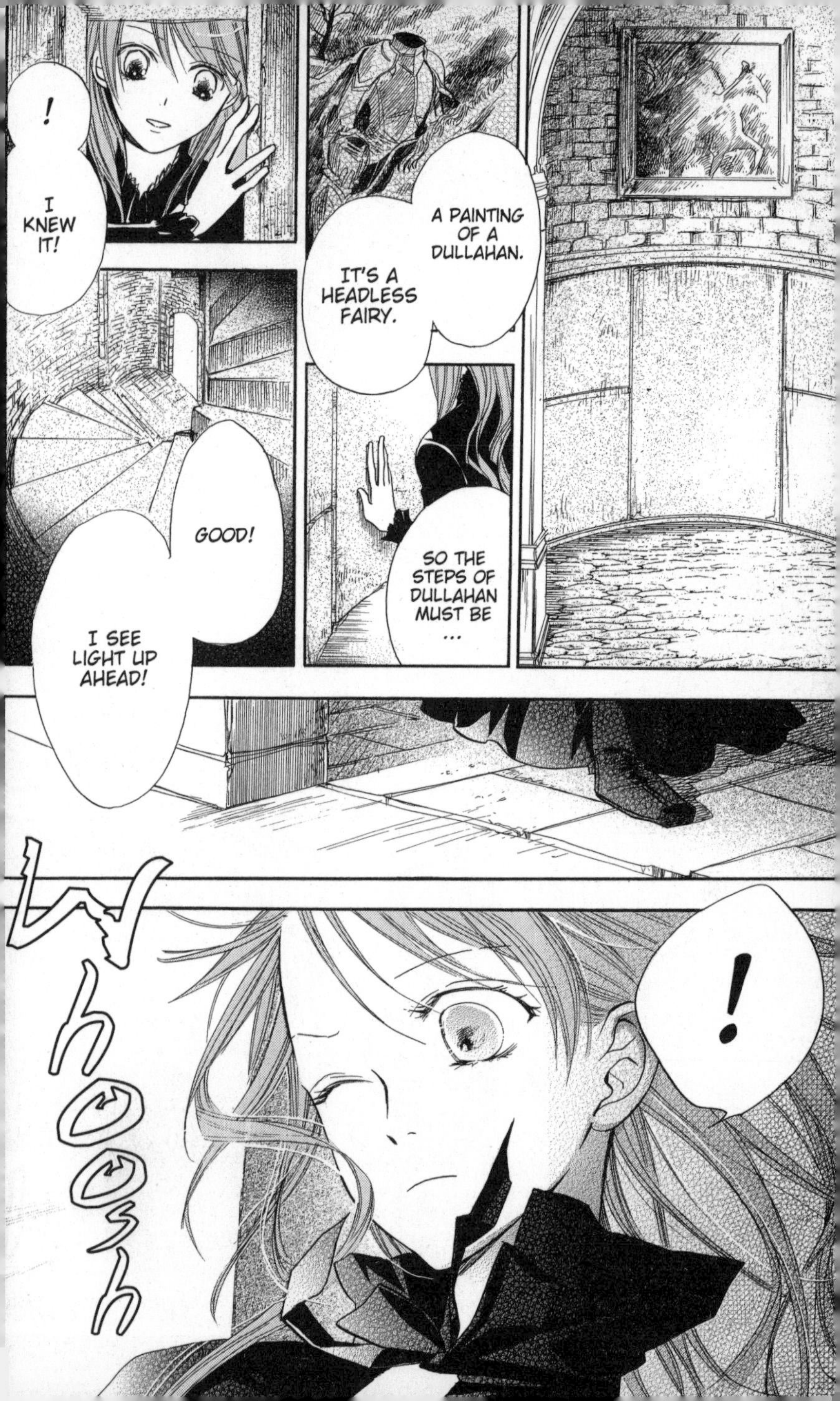
A PAINTING OF A DULLAHAN.
IT'S A HEADLESS FAIRY.
!
I KNEW IT!
SO THE STEPS OF DULLAHAN MUST BE ...
GOOD!
I SEE LIGHT UP AHEAD!
!
Whoosh

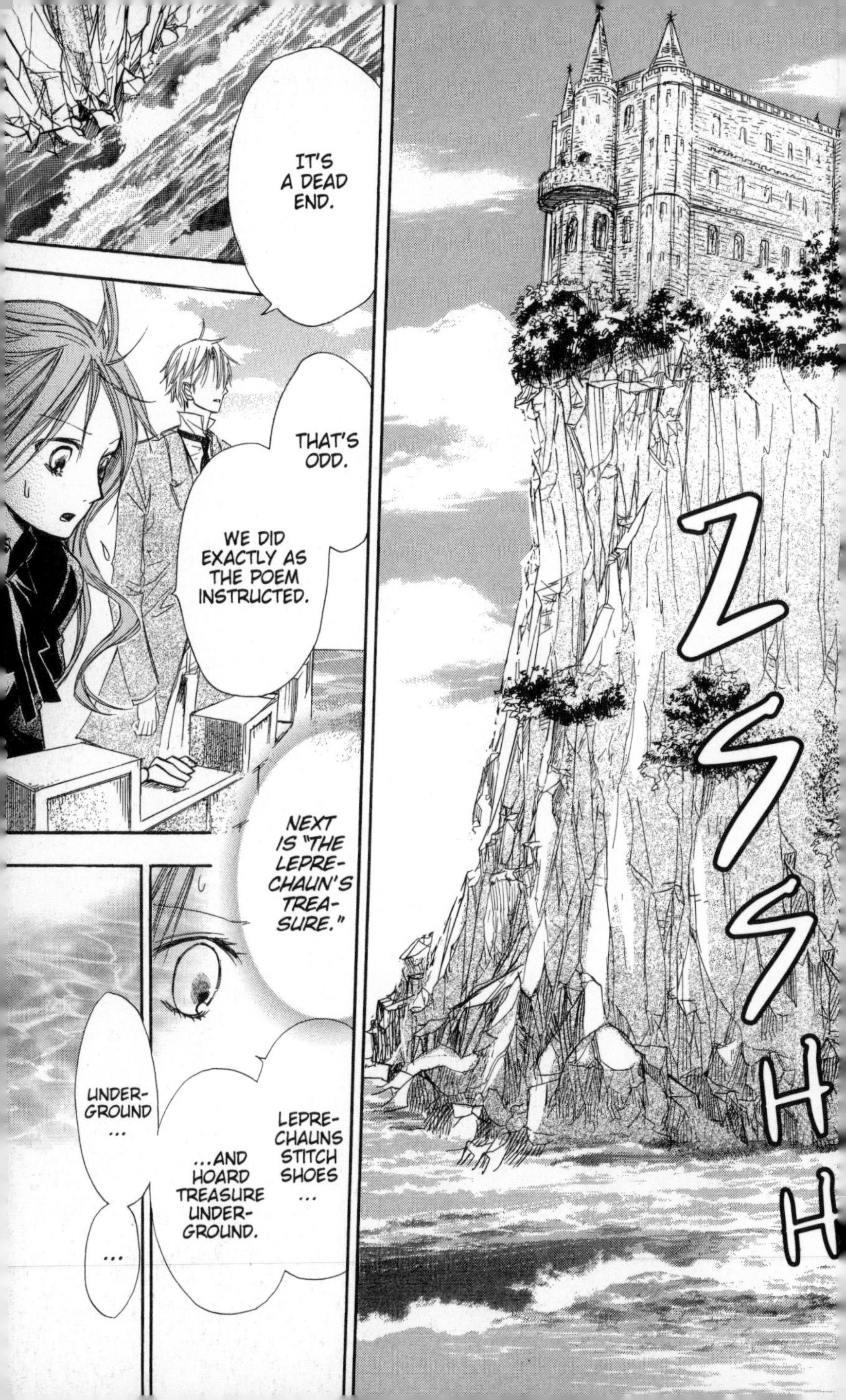
ZSSHH
IT'S A DEAD END.
THAT'S ODD.
WE DID EXACTLY AS THE POEM INSTRUCTED.
NEXT IS "THE LEPRECHAUN'S TREASURE."
LEPRECHAUNS STITCH SHOES...
...AND HOARD TREASURE UNDERGROUND.
UNDERGROUND...
...

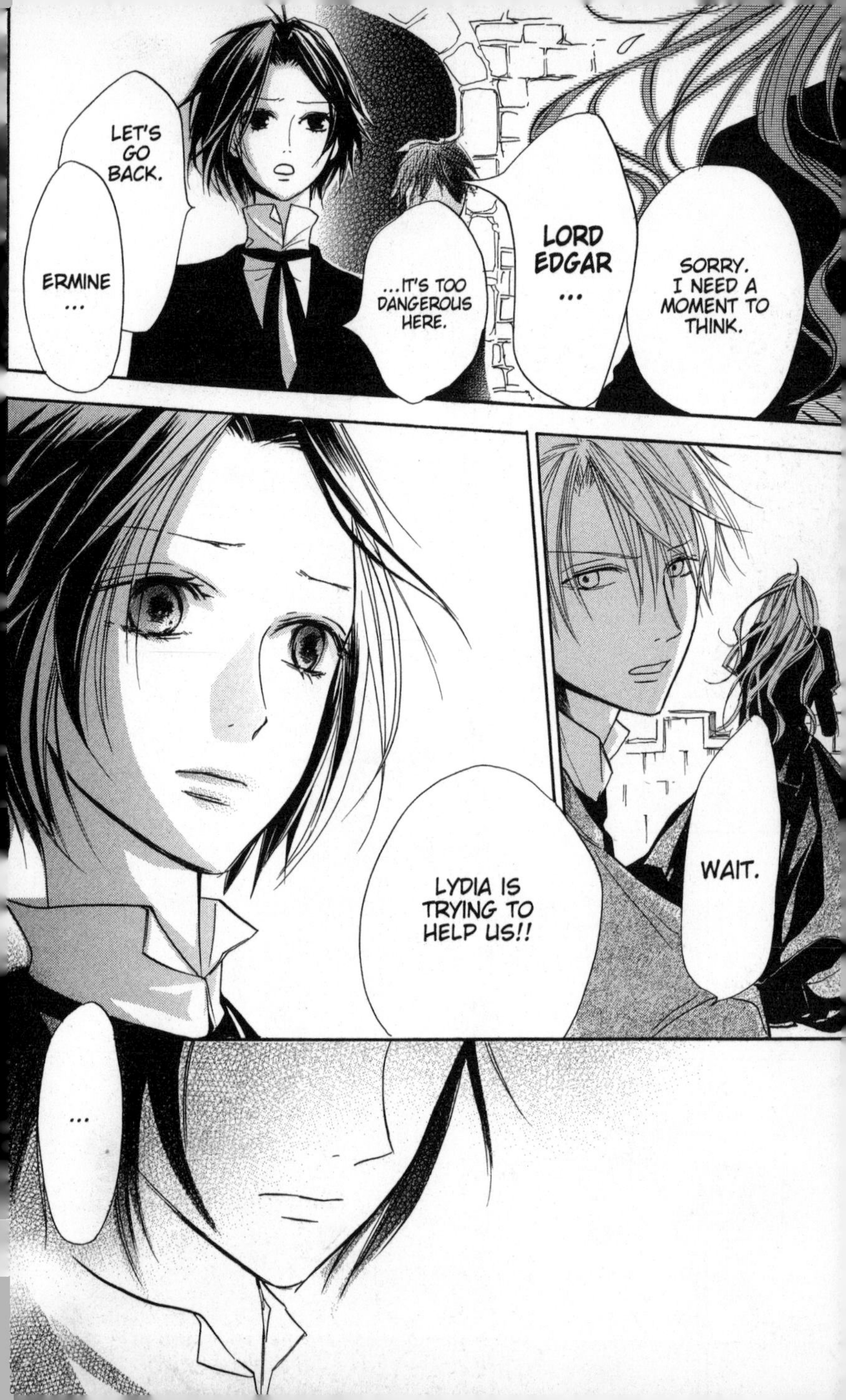
SORRY. I NEED A MOMENT TO THINK.
LORD EDGAR ...
LET'S GO BACK.
...IT'S TOO DANGEROUS HERE.
ERMINE ...
WAIT.
LYDIA IS TRYING TO HELP US!!
...

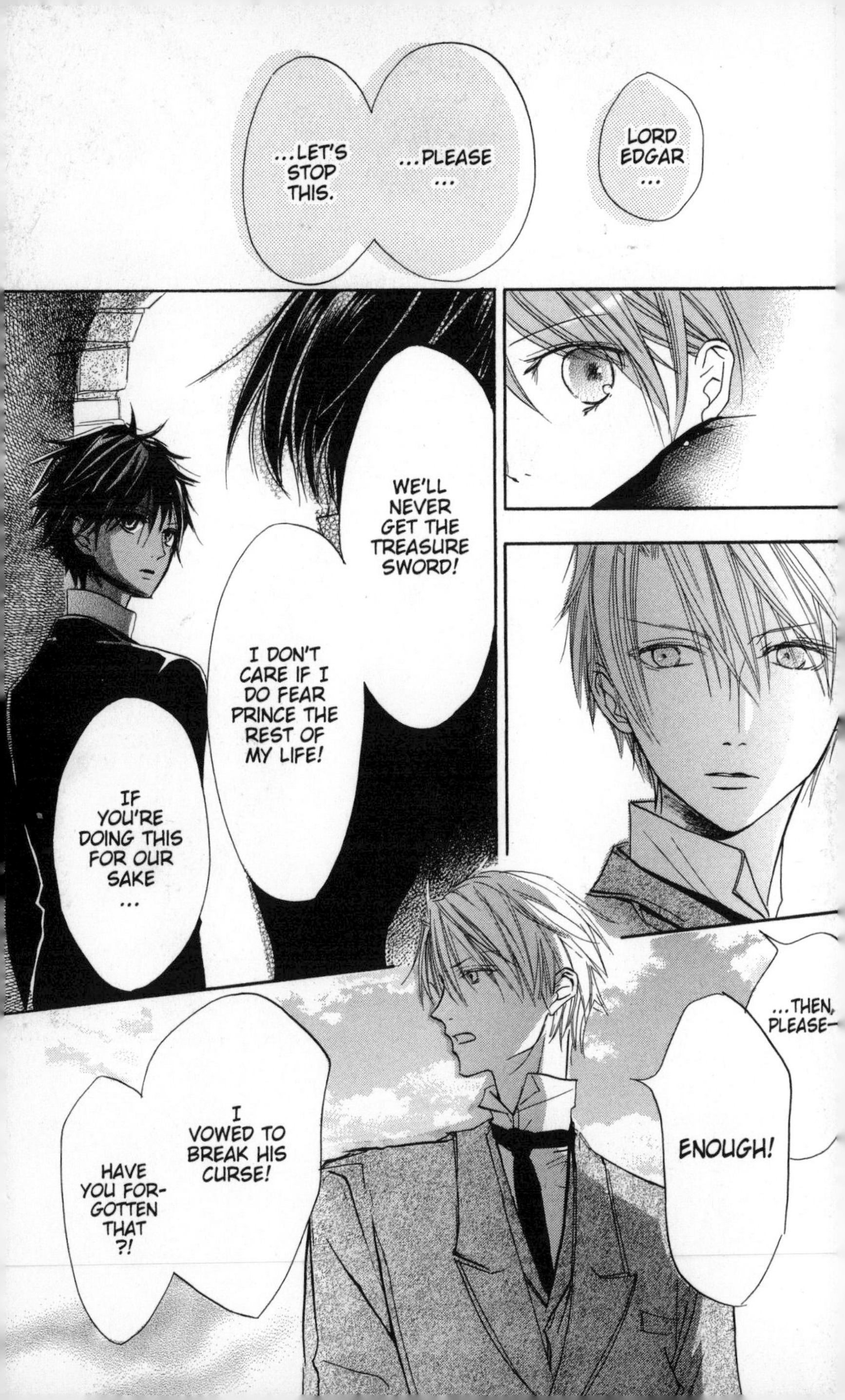

LORD EDGAR...
...PLEASE...
...LET'S STOP THIS.
WE'LL NEVER GET THE TREASURE SWORD!
I DON'T CARE IF I DO FEAR PRINCE THE REST OF MY LIFE!
IF YOU'RE DOING THIS FOR OUR SAKE...
...THEN, PLEASE—
ENOUGH!
I VOWED TO BREAK HIS CURSE!
HAVE YOU FOR-GOTTEN THAT?!

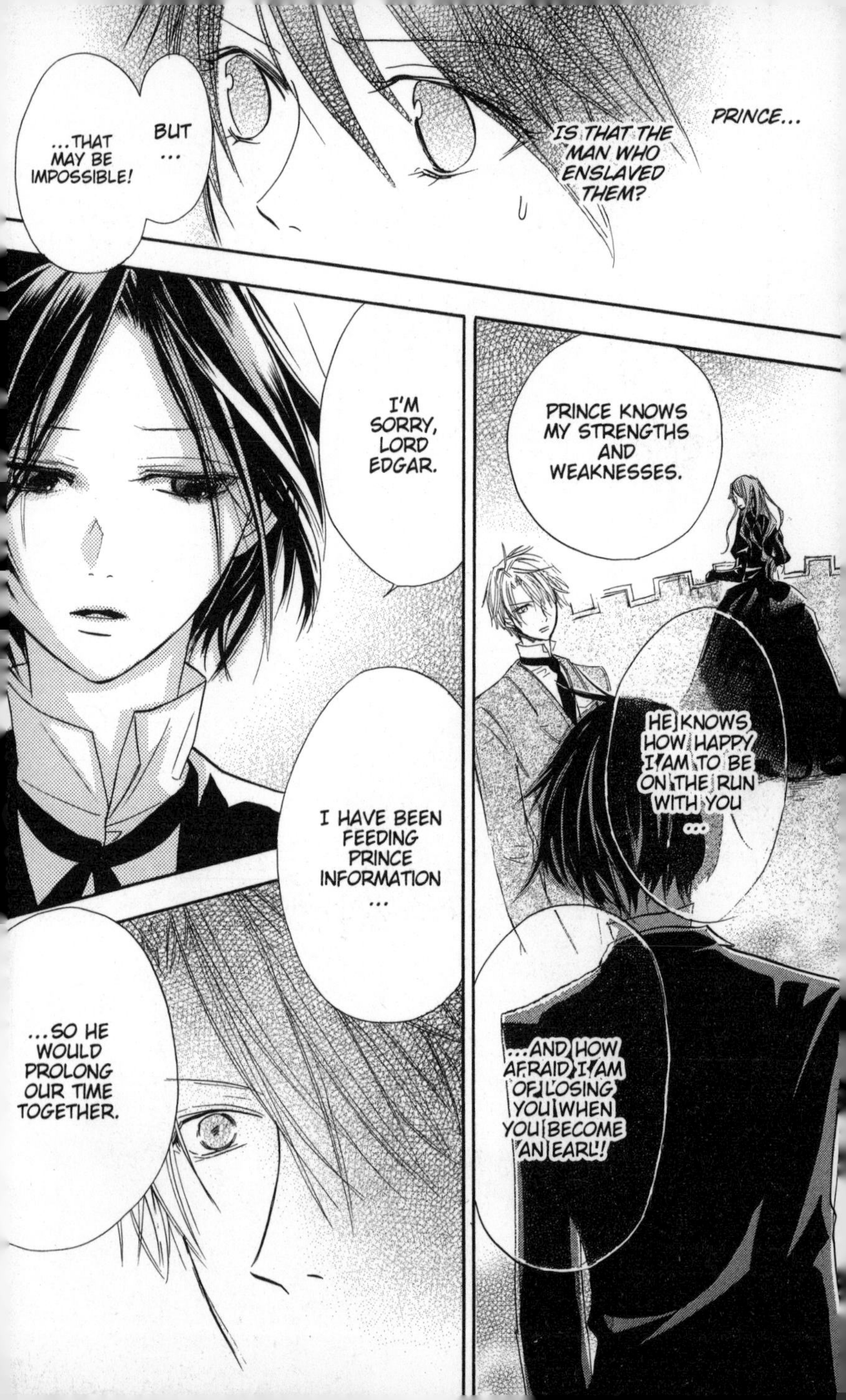
PRINCE...
IS THAT THE MAN WHO ENSLAVED THEM?
BUT...
...THAT MAY BE IMPOSSIBLE!
PRINCE KNOWS MY STRENGTHS AND WEAKNESSES.
HE KNOWS HOW HAPPY I AM TO BE ON THE RUN WITH YOU...
...AND HOW AFRAID I AM OF LOSING YOU WHEN YOU BECOME AN EARL!
I'M SORRY, LORD EDGAR.
I HAVE BEEN FEEDING PRINCE INFORMATION...
...SO HE WOULD PROLONG OUR TIME TOGETHER.

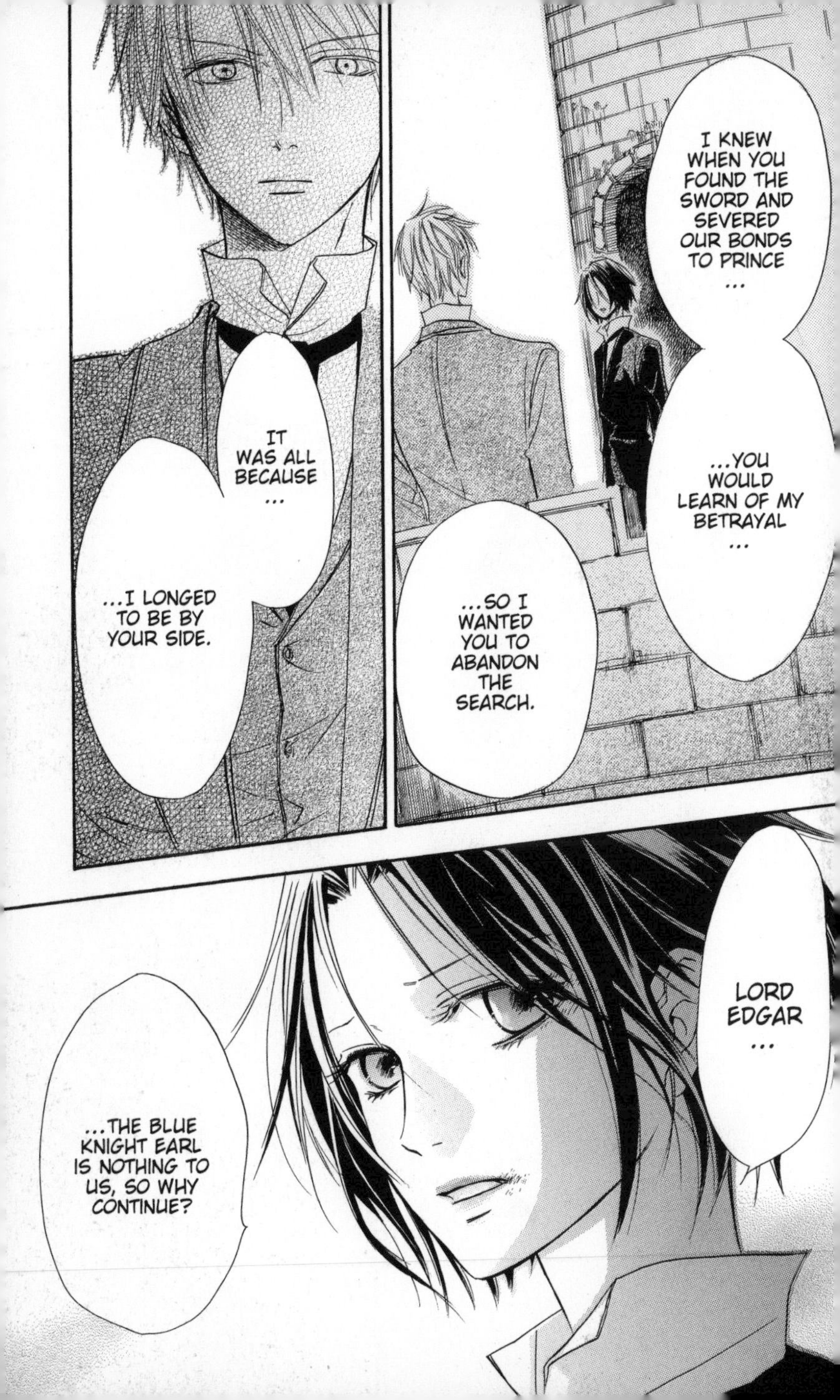
I KNEW WHEN YOU FOUND THE SWORD AND SEVERED OUR BONDS TO PRINCE ...
...YOU WOULD LEARN OF MY BETRAYAL ...
...SO I WANTED YOU TO ABANDON THE SEARCH.
IT WAS ALL BECAUSE ...
...I LONGED TO BE BY YOUR SIDE.
LORD EDGAR ...
...THE BLUE KNIGHT EARL IS NOTHING TO US, SO WHY CONTINUE?

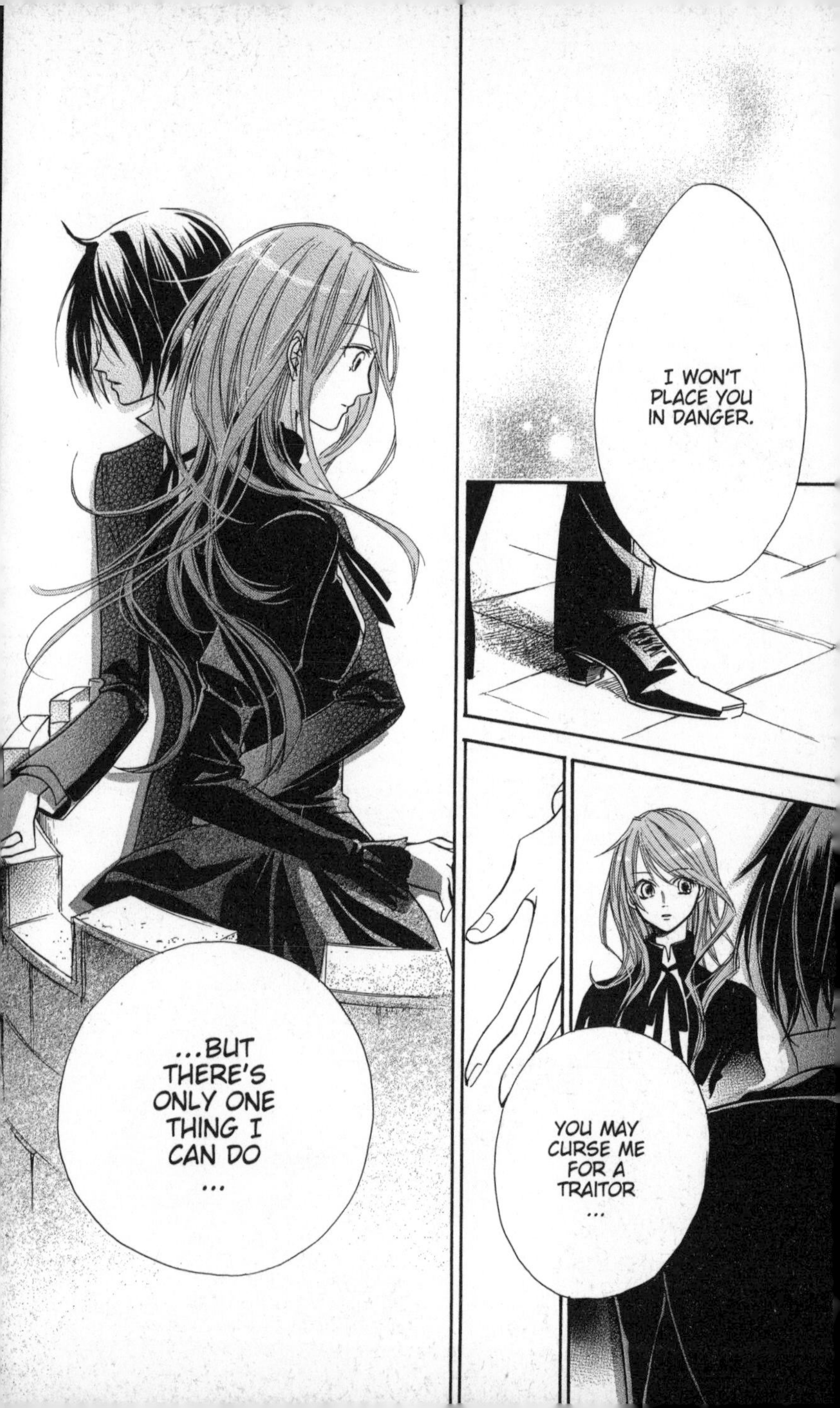
I WON'T PLACE YOU IN DANGER.
YOU MAY CURSE ME FOR A TRAITOR ...
...BUT THERE'S ONLY ONE THING I CAN DO ...

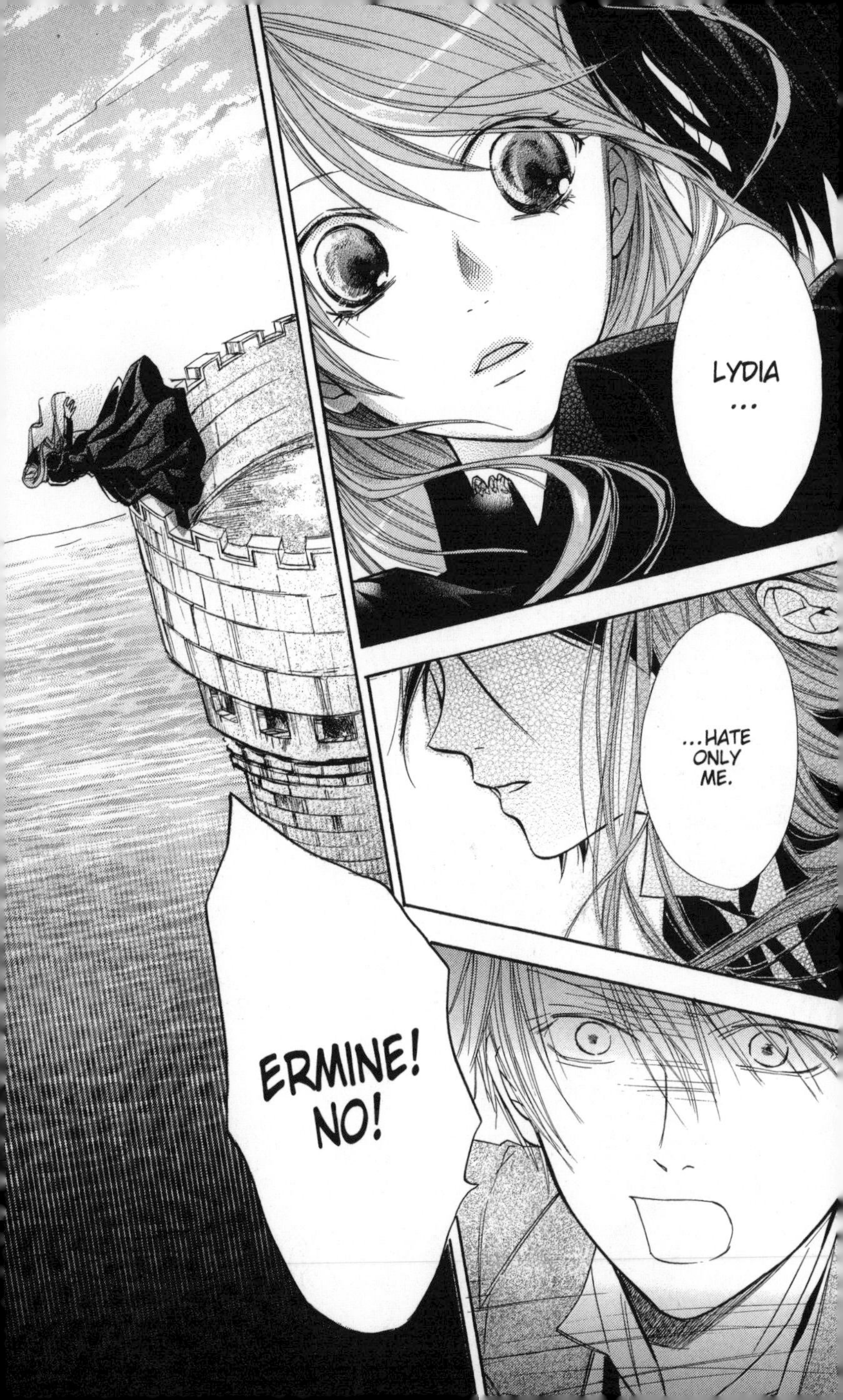
LYDIA ...
...HATE ONLY ME.
ERMINE! NO!

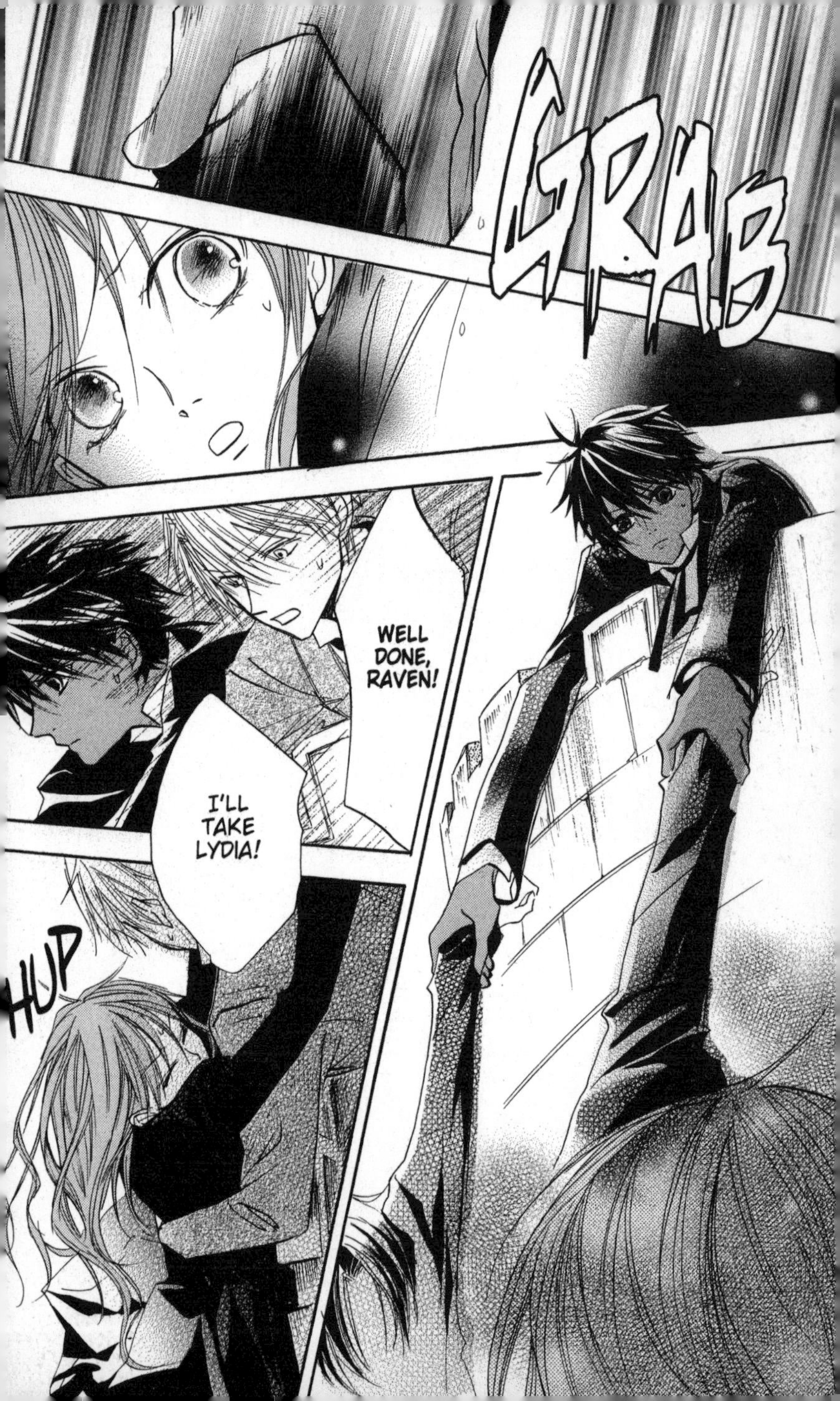
GRAB
WELL DONE, RAVEN!
I'LL TAKE LYDIA!
HUP

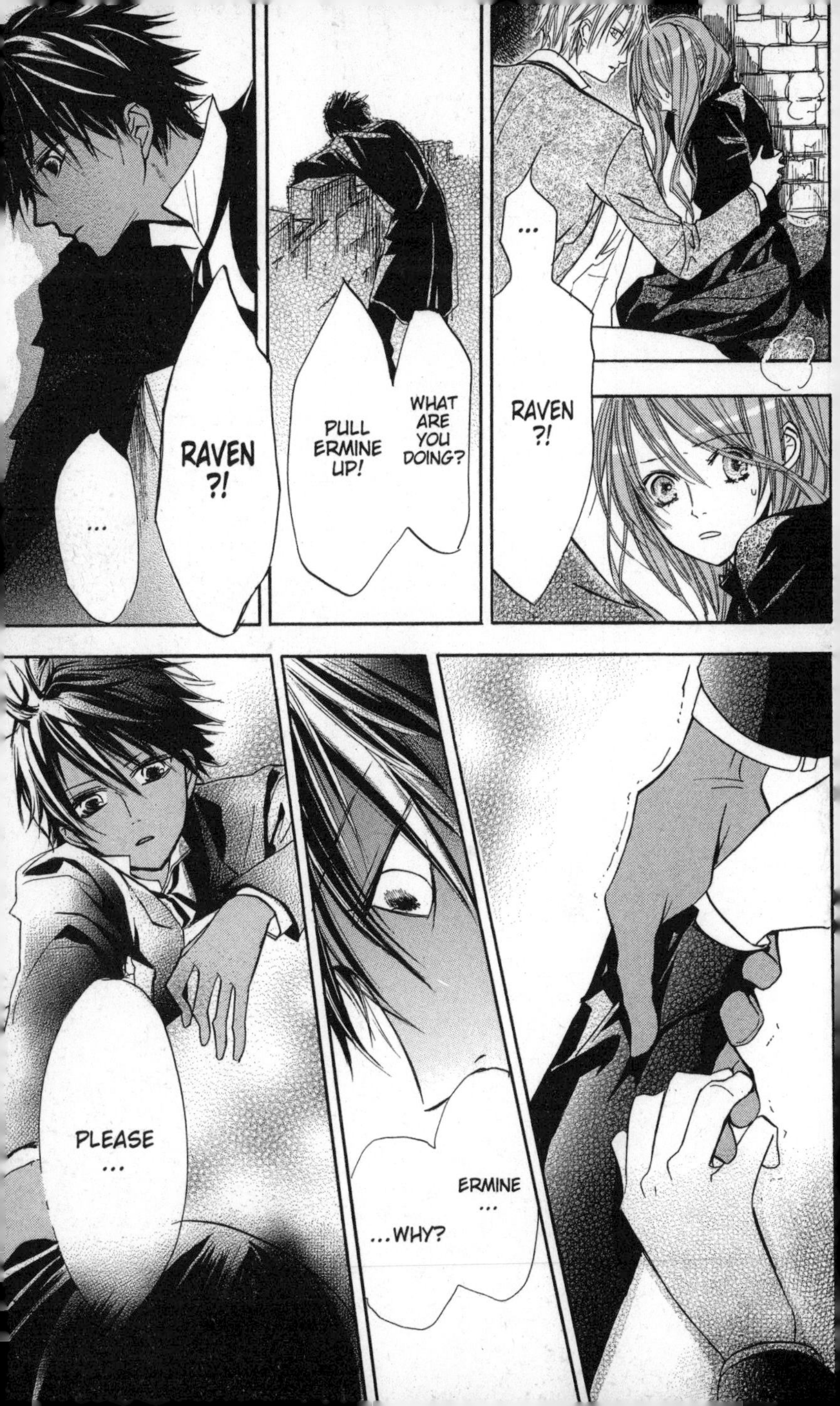
...
RAVEN ?!
WHAT ARE YOU DOING?
PULL ERMINE UP!
RAVEN ?!
...
ERMINE ...
...WHY?
PLEASE ...

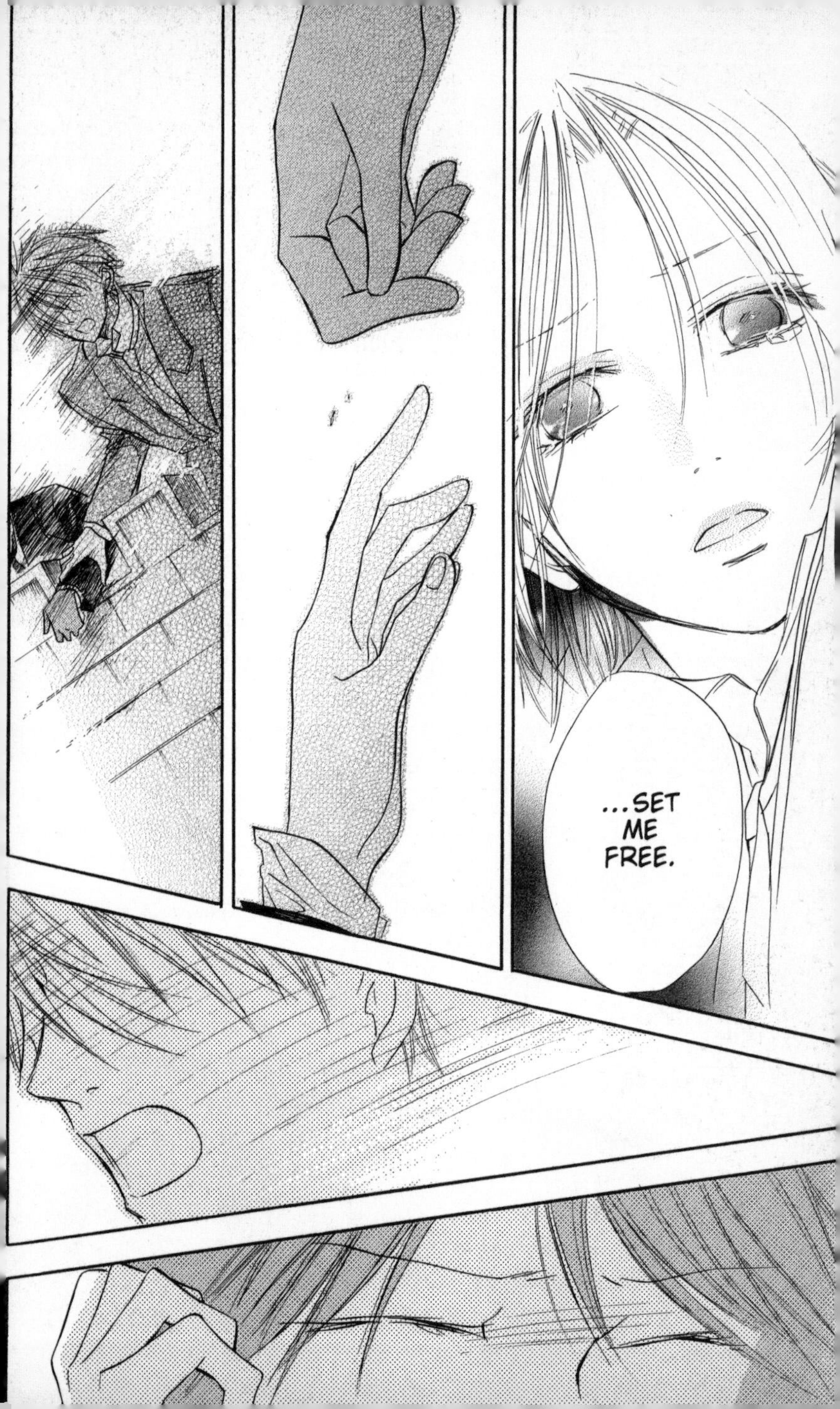
...SET ME FREE.

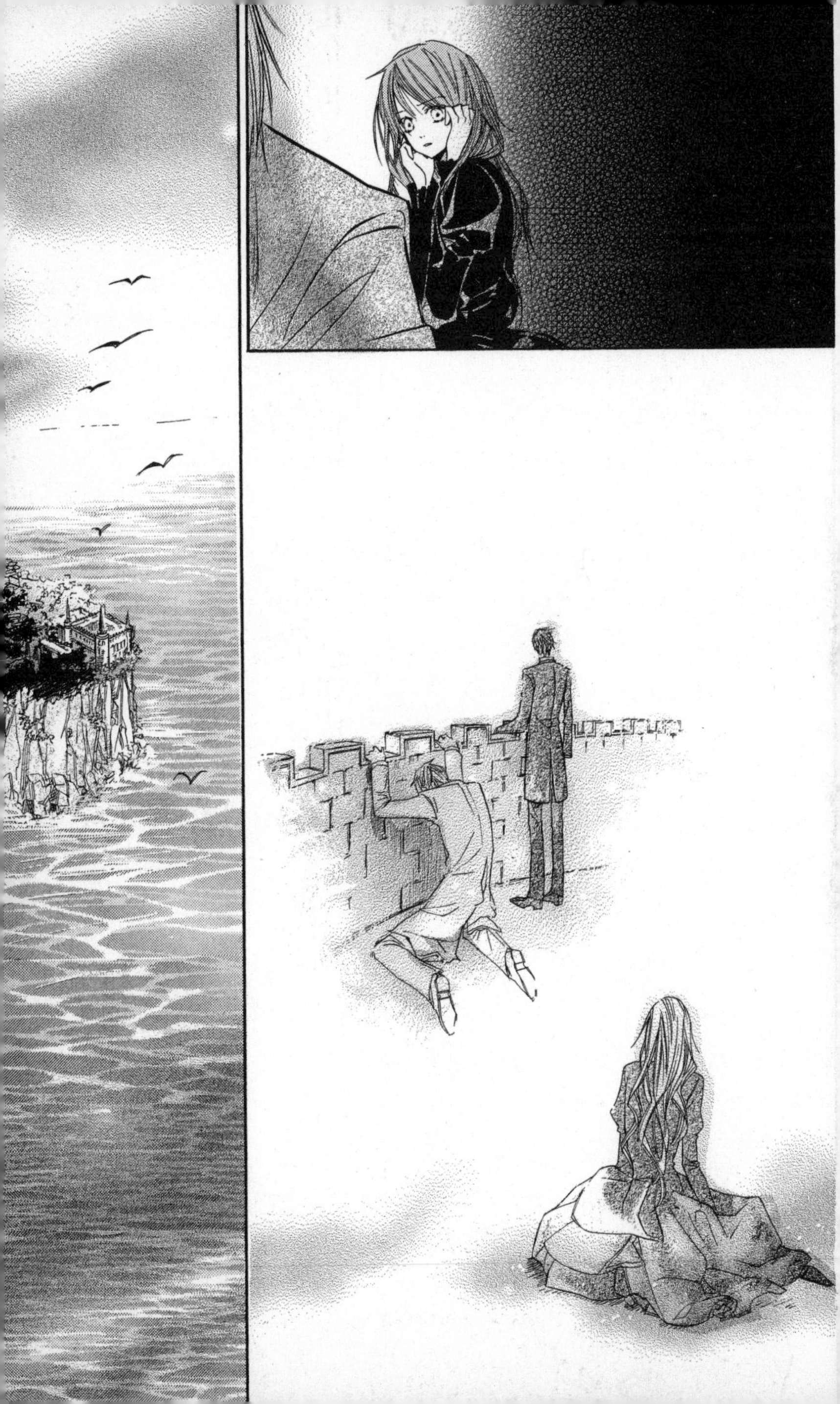

The Earl & the Fairy

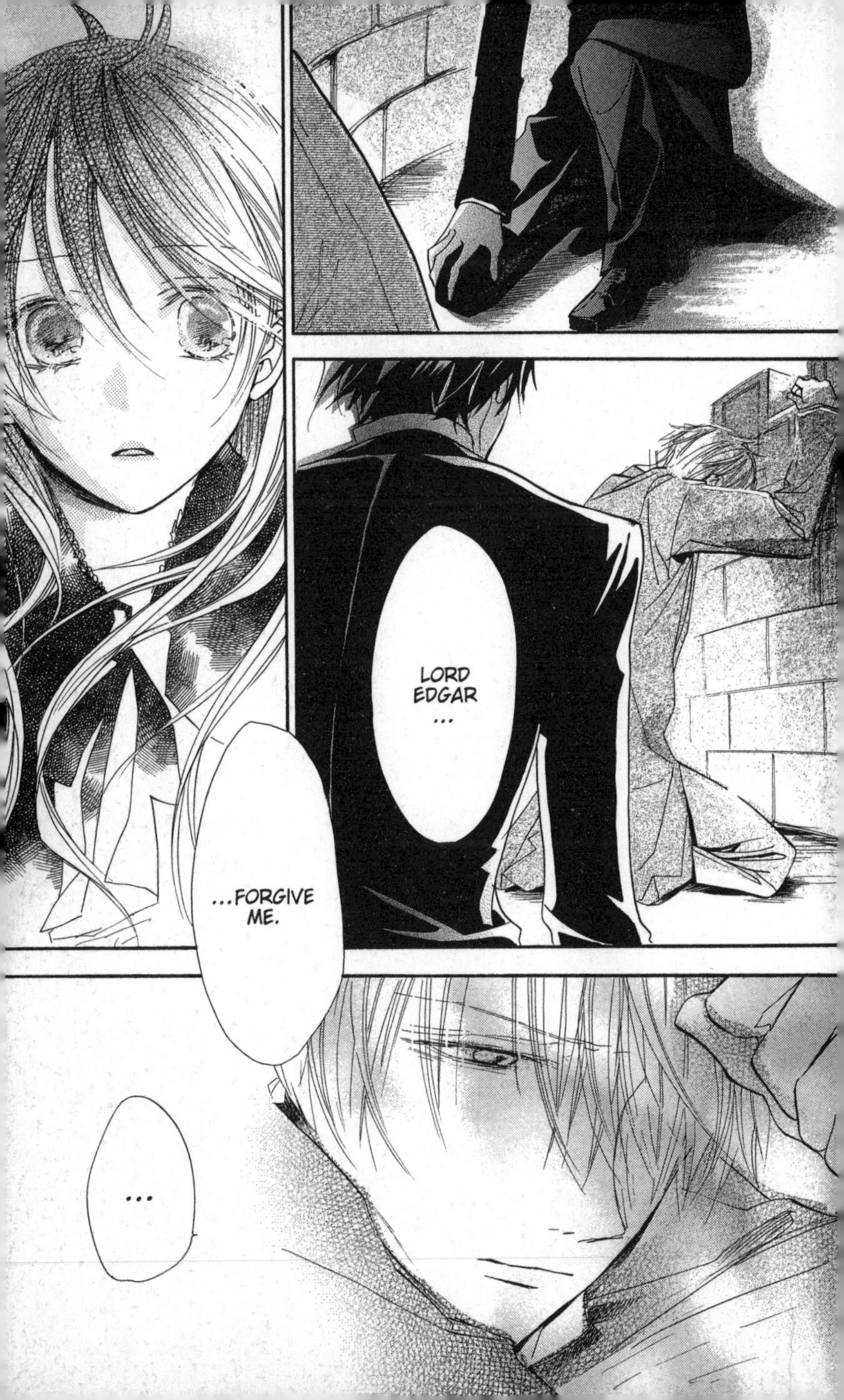
LORD EDGAR ...
...FORGIVE ME.
...

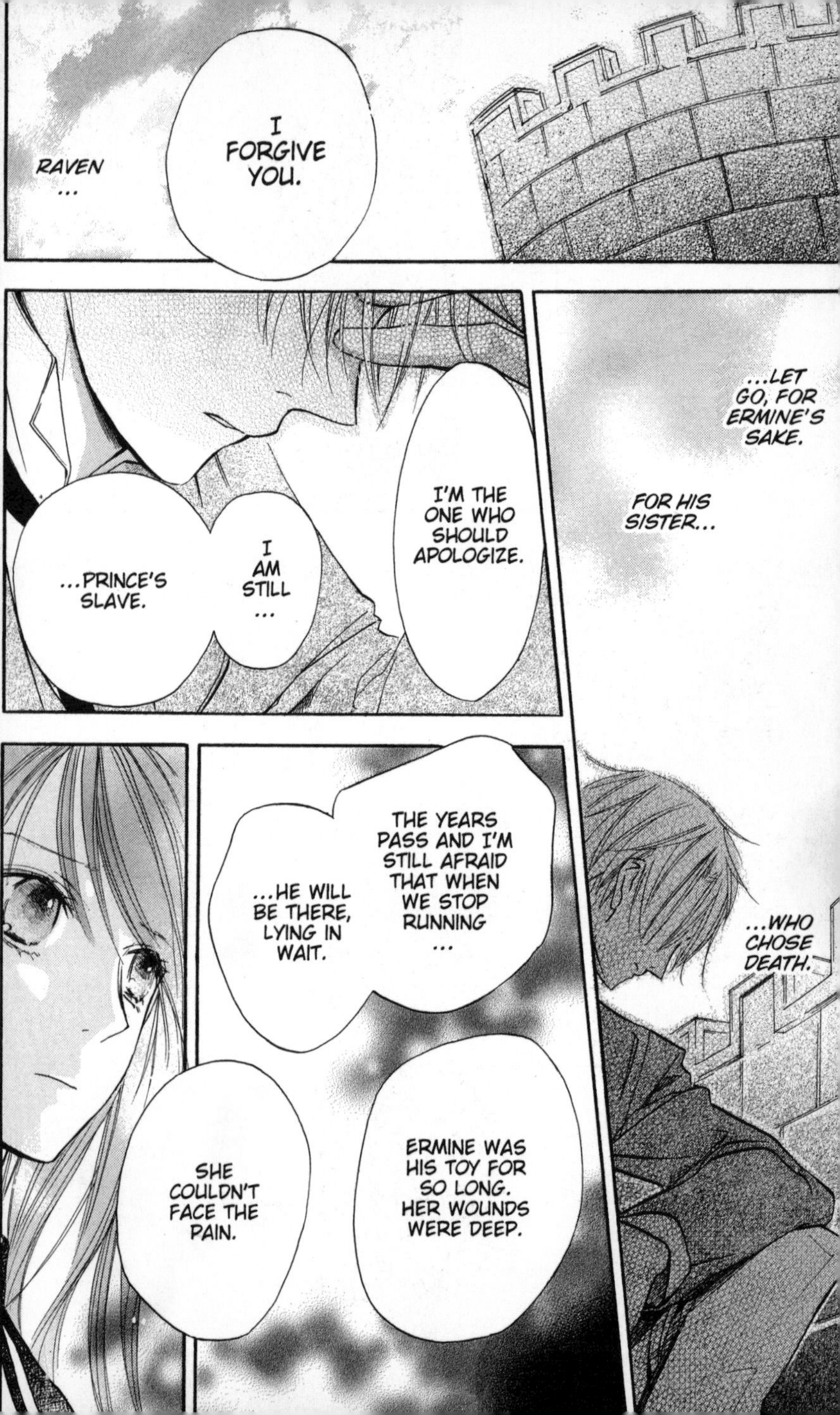
I FORGIVE YOU.
RAVEN ...
...LET GO, FOR ERMINE'S SAKE.
FOR HIS SISTER...
...WHO CHOSE DEATH.
I'M THE ONE WHO SHOULD APOLOGIZE.
I AM STILL ...
...PRINCE'S SLAVE.
THE YEARS PASS AND I'M STILL AFRAID THAT WHEN WE STOP RUNNING ...
...HE WILL BE THERE, LYING IN WAIT.
ERMINE WAS HIS TOY FOR SO LONG. HER WOUNDS WERE DEEP.
SHE COULDN'T FACE THE PAIN.

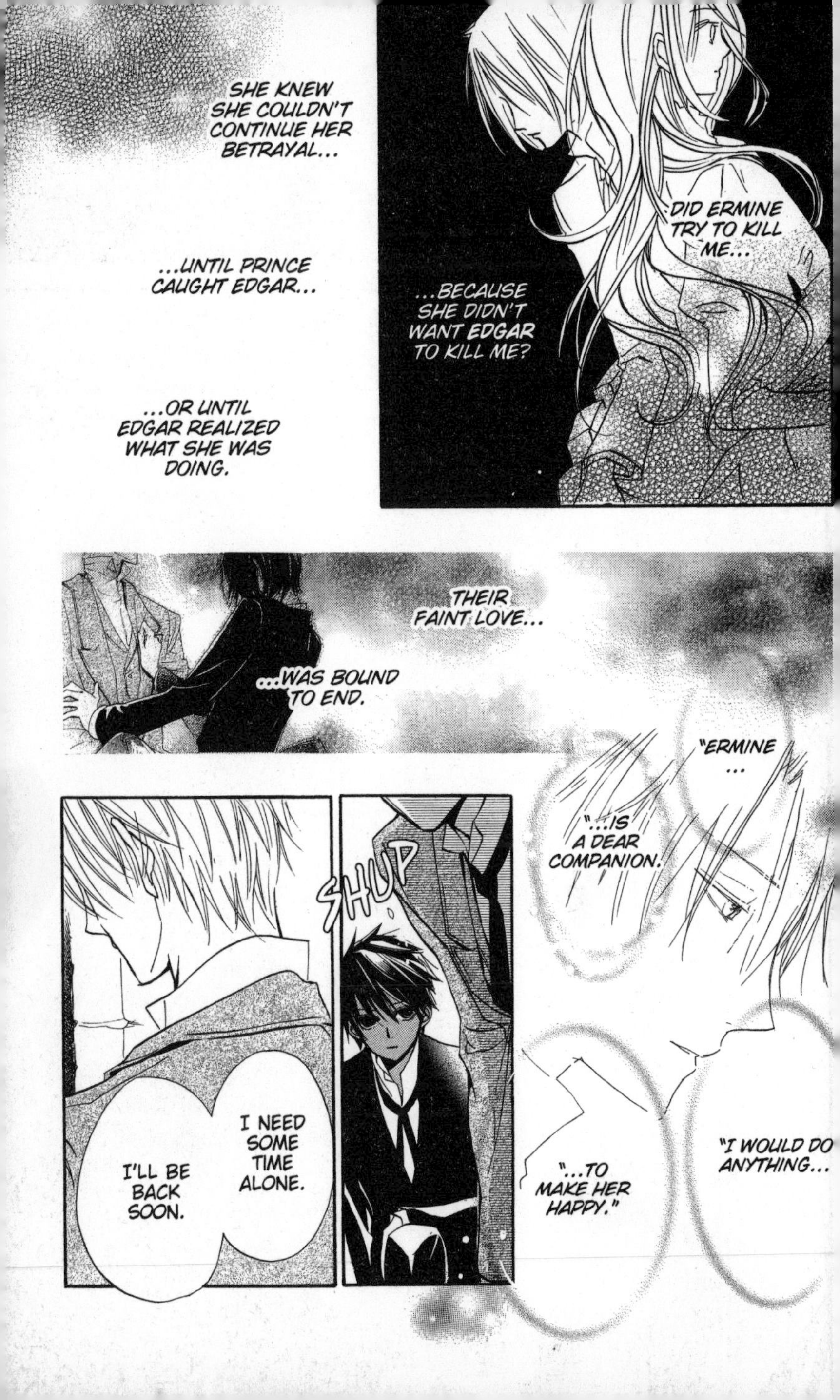
DID ERMINE TRY TO KILL ME...
...BECAUSE SHE DIDN'T WANT EDGAR TO KILL ME?
SHE KNEW SHE COULDN'T CONTINUE HER BETRAYAL...
...UNTIL PRINCE CAUGHT EDGAR...
...OR UNTIL EDGAR REALIZED WHAT SHE WAS DOING.
THEIR FAINT LOVE...
...WAS BOUND TO END.
"ERMINE...
"...IS A DEAR COMPANION.
"I WOULD DO ANYTHING...
"...TO MAKE HER HAPPY."
SHUP
I NEED SOME TIME ALONE.
I'LL BE BACK SOON.

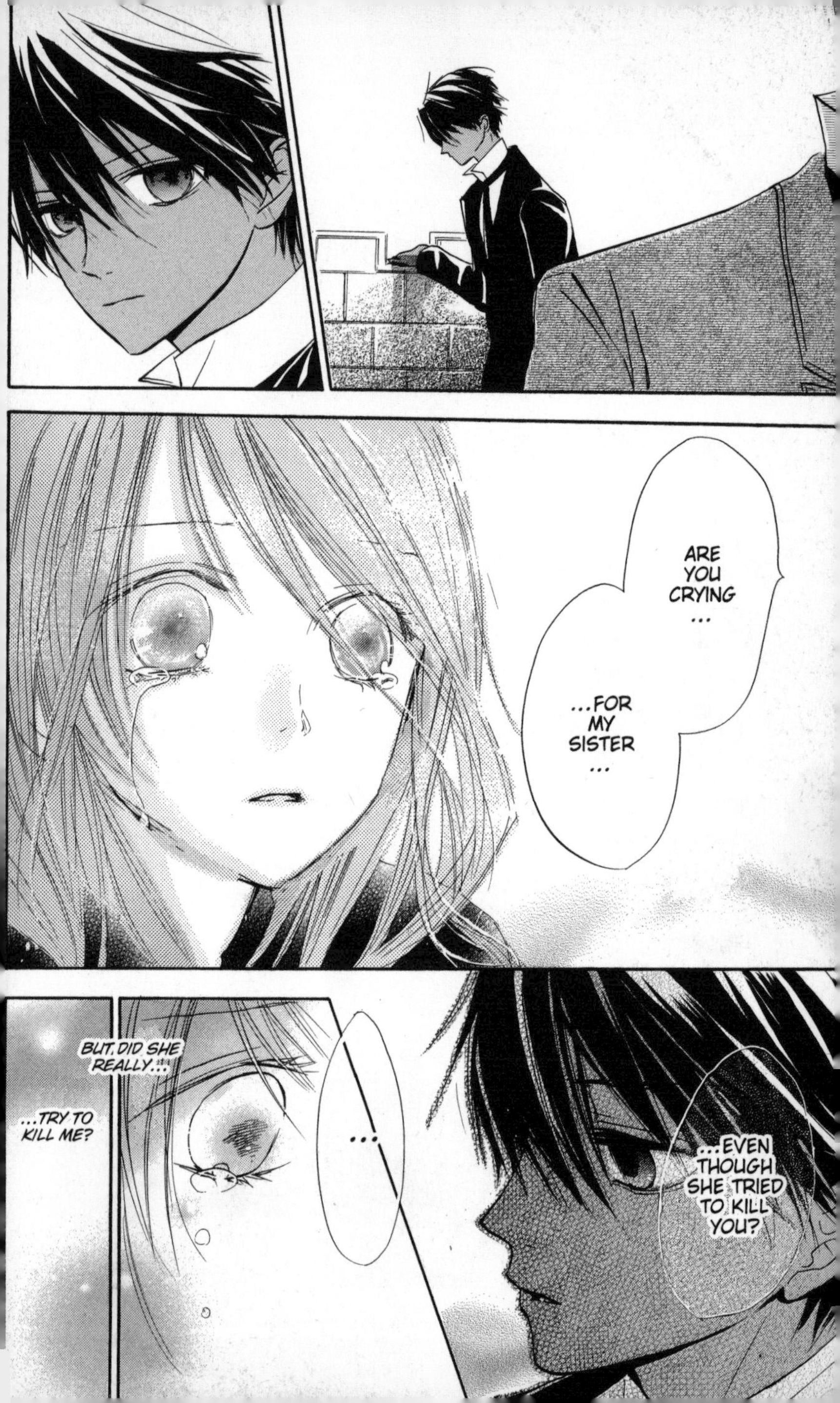
ARE YOU CRYING ...
...FOR MY SISTER ...
...EVEN THOUGH SHE TRIED TO KILL YOU?
...
BUT, DID SHE REALLY...
...TRY TO KILL ME?

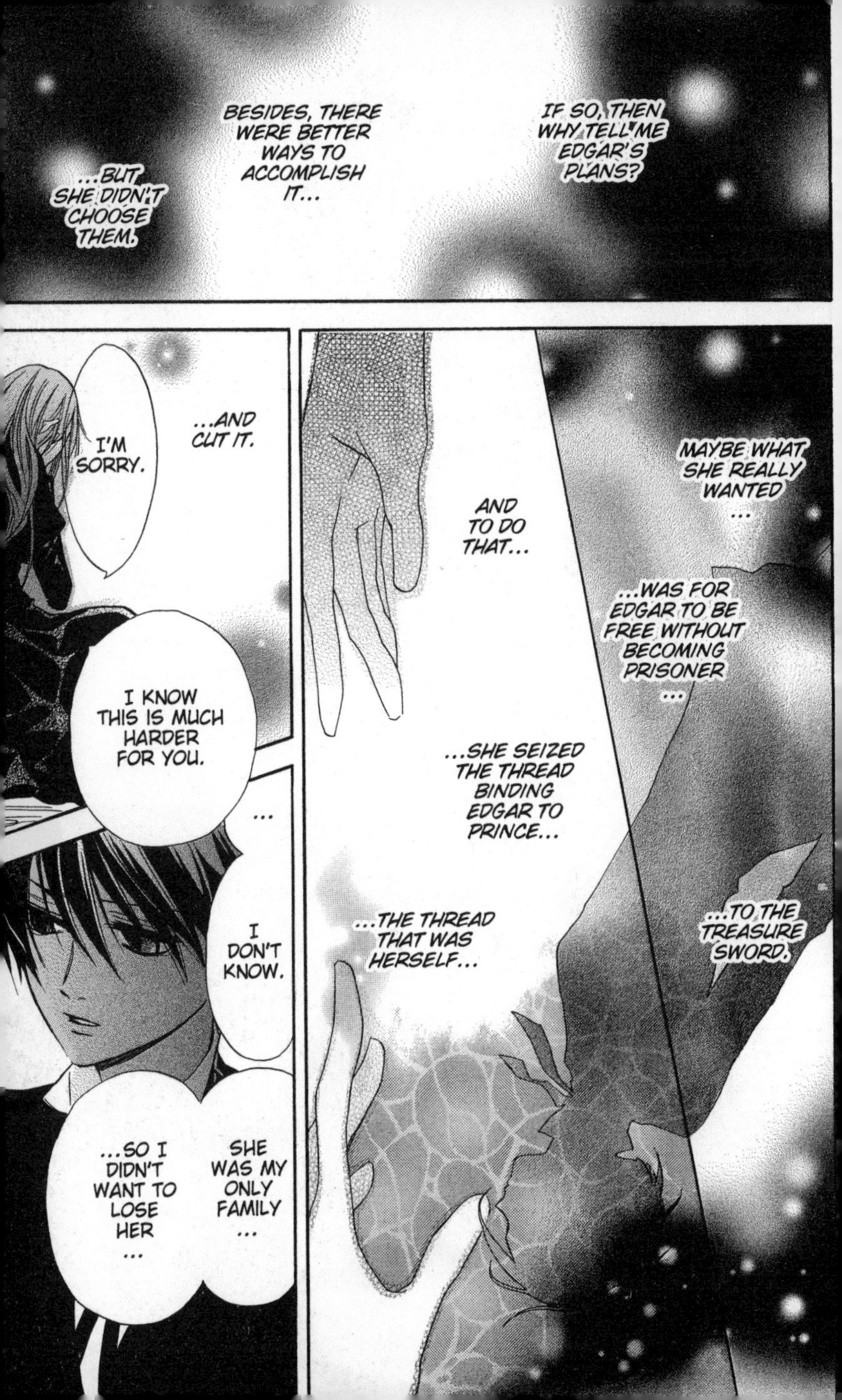
IF SO, THEN WHY TELL ME EDGAR'S PLANS?
BESIDES, THERE WERE BETTER WAYS TO ACCOMPLISH IT...
...BUT SHE DIDN'T CHOOSE THEM.
MAYBE WHAT SHE REALLY WANTED ...
...WAS FOR EDGAR TO BE FREE WITHOUT BECOMING PRISONER ...
...TO THE TREASURE SWORD.
AND TO DO THAT...
...SHE SEIZED THE THREAD BINDING EDGAR TO PRINCE...
...THE THREAD THAT WAS HERSELF...
...AND CUT IT.
I'M SORRY.
I KNOW THIS IS MUCH HARDER FOR YOU.
...
I DON'T KNOW.
SHE WAS MY ONLY FAMILY ...
...SO I DIDN'T WANT TO LOSE HER ...

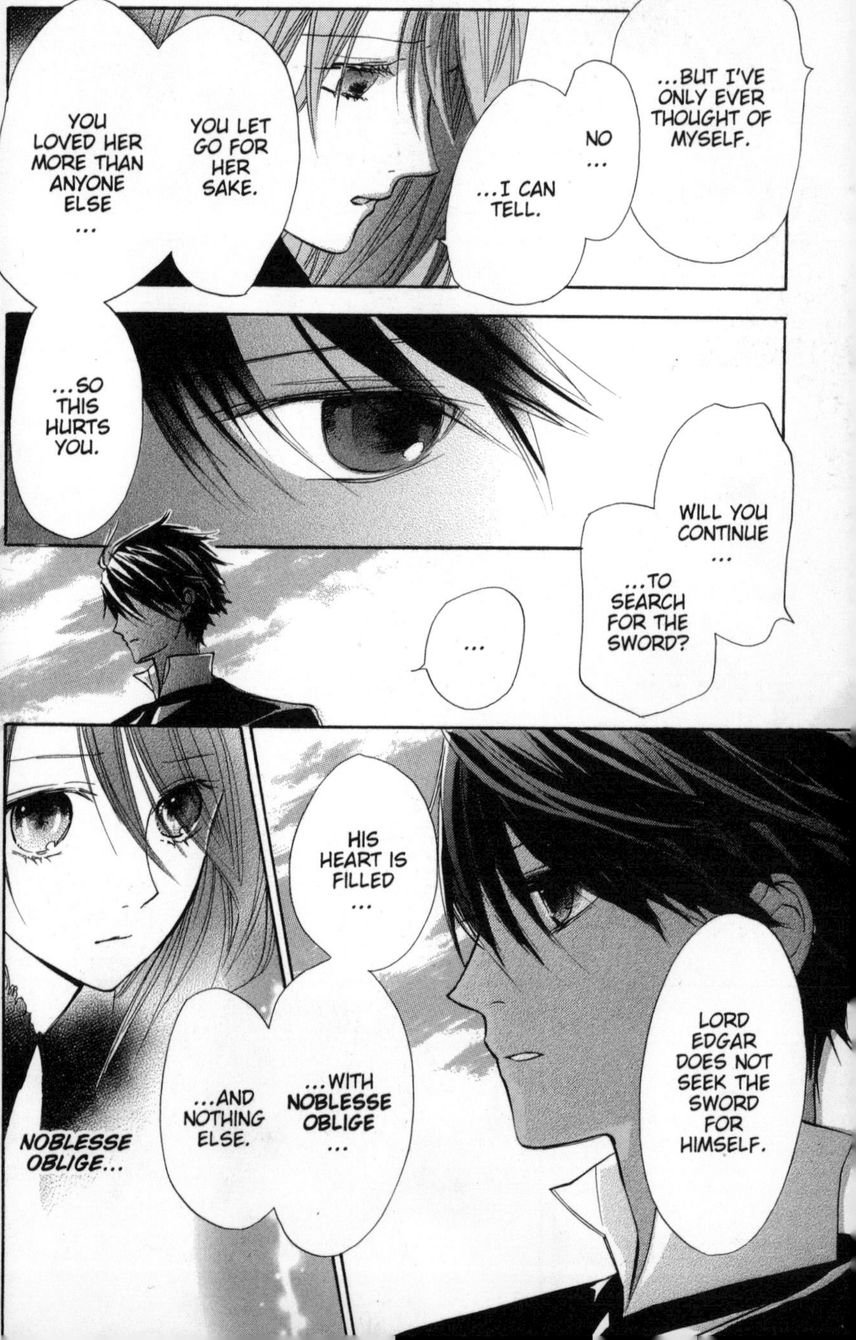
...BUT I'VE ONLY EVER THOUGHT OF MYSELF.
NO...
...I CAN TELL.
YOU LET GO FOR HER SAKE.
YOU LOVED HER MORE THAN ANYONE ELSE...
...SO THIS HURTS YOU.
WILL YOU CONTINUE...
...TO SEARCH FOR THE SWORD?
...
LORD EDGAR DOES NOT SEEK THE SWORD FOR HIMSELF.
HIS HEART IS FILLED...
...WITH NOBLESSE OBLIGE...
...AND NOTHING ELSE.
NOBLESSE OBLIGE...

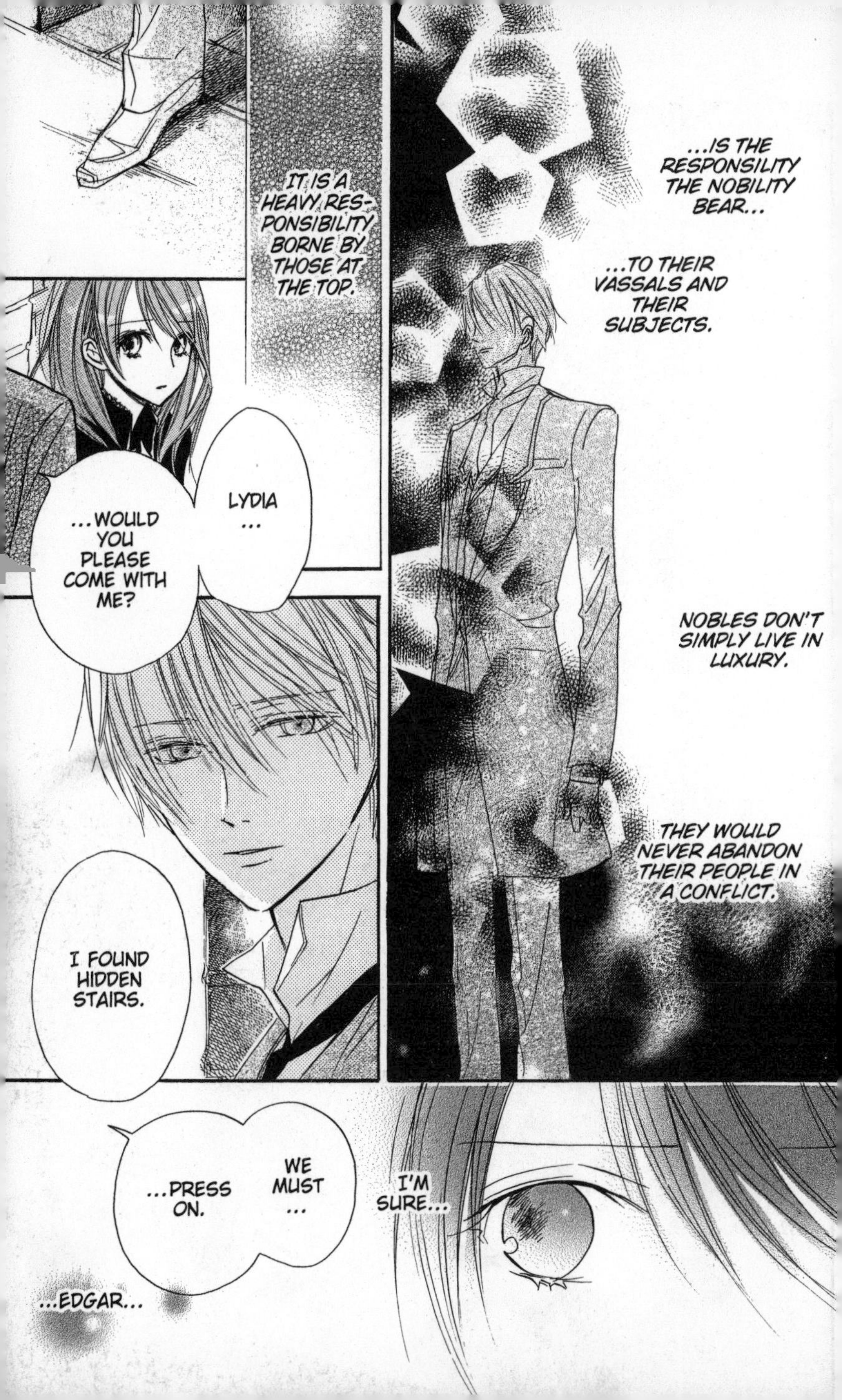

...IS THE RESPONSILITY THE NOBILITY BEAR...
...TO THEIR VASSALS AND THEIR SUBJECTS.
NOBLES DON'T SIMPLY LIVE IN LUXURY.
THEY WOULD NEVER ABANDON THEIR PEOPLE IN A CONFLICT.
IT IS A HEAVY RES-PONSIBILITY BORNE BY THOSE AT THE TOP.
LYDIA ...
...WOULD YOU PLEASE COME WITH ME?
I FOUND HIDDEN STAIRS.
I'M SURE...
WE MUST ...
...PRESS ON.
...EDGAR...

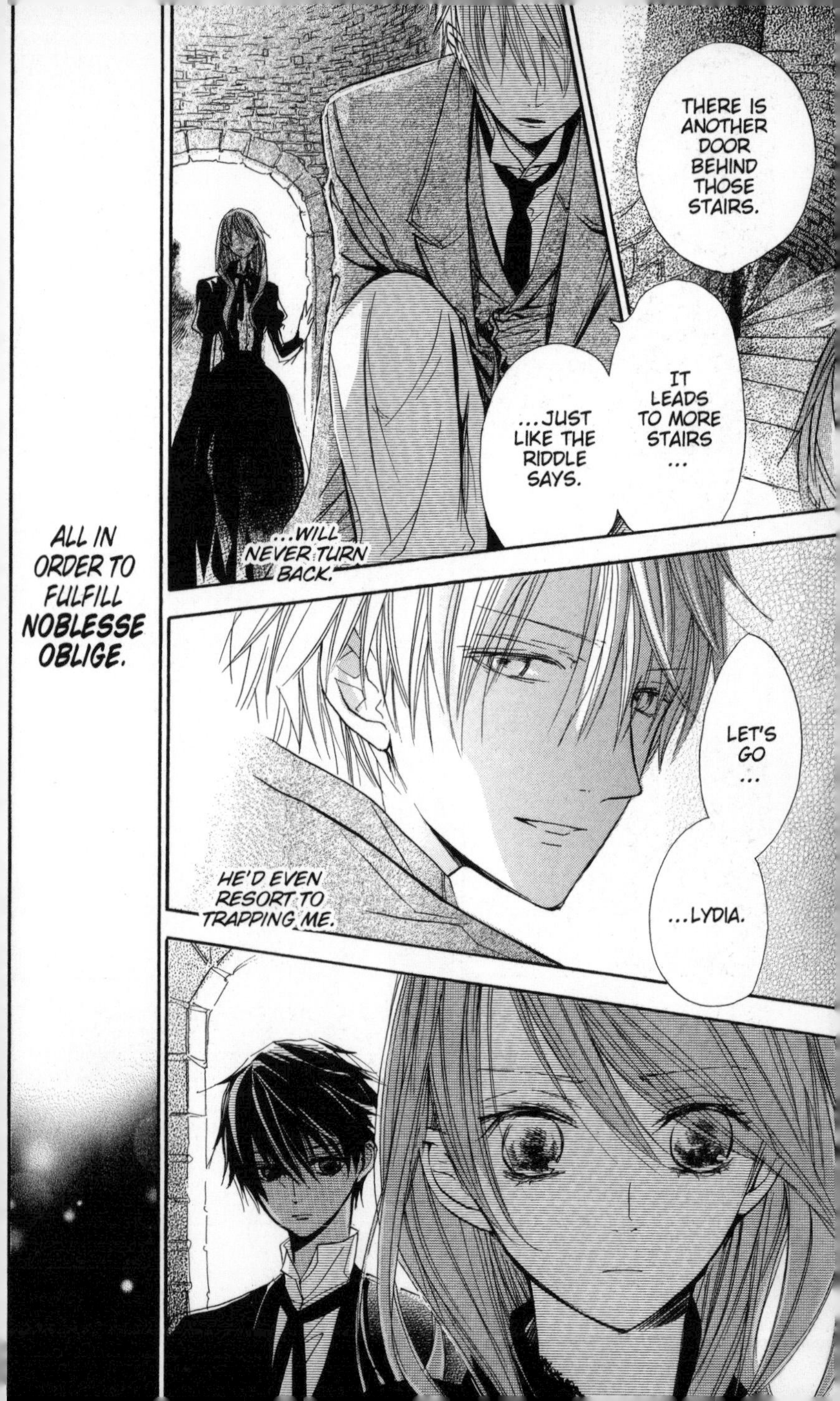
THERE IS ANOTHER DOOR BEHIND THOSE STAIRS.
IT LEADS TO MORE STAIRS...
...JUST LIKE THE RIDDLE SAYS.
...WILL NEVER TURN BACK.
ALL IN ORDER TO FULFILL NOBLESSE OBLIGE.
LET'S GO...
...LYDIA.
HE'D EVEN RESORT TO TRAPPING ME.

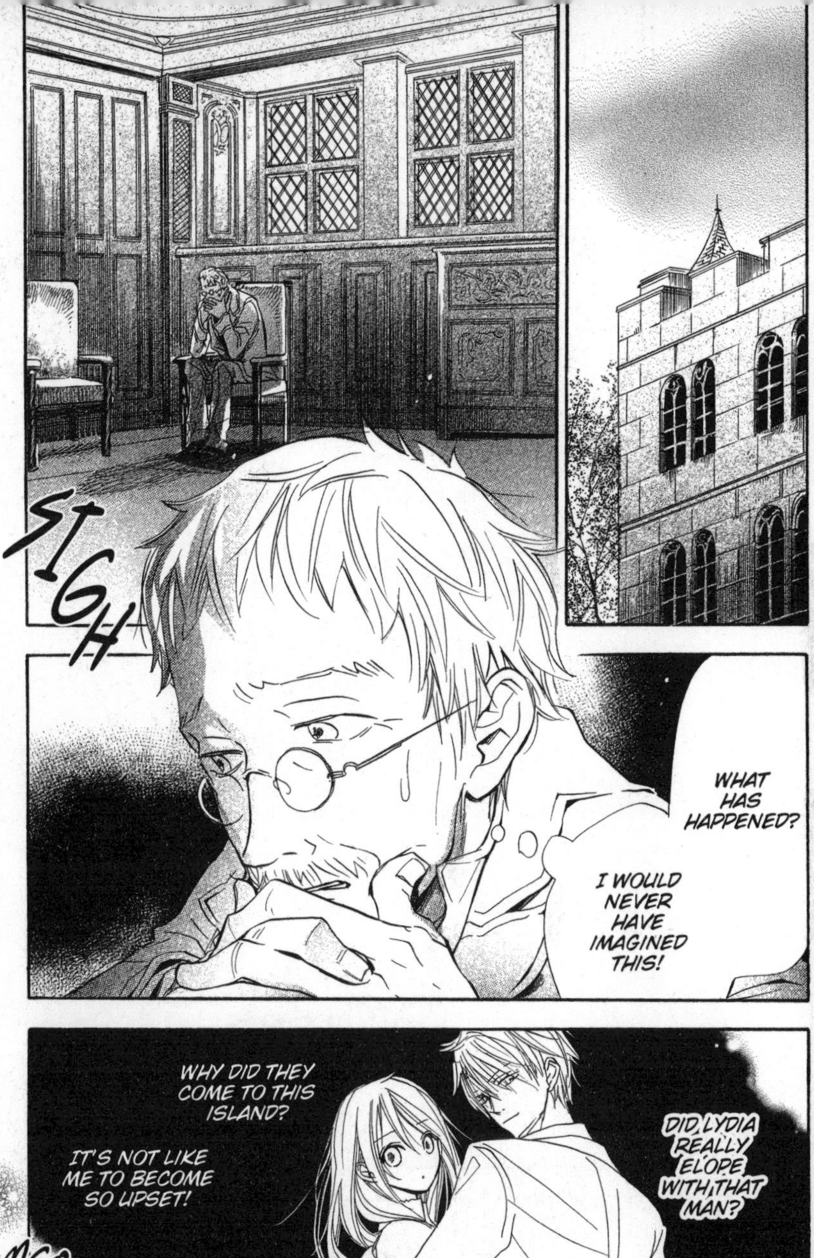
SIGH
WHAT HAS HAPPENED?
I WOULD NEVER HAVE IMAGINED THIS!
DID LYDIA REALLY ELOPE WITH THAT MAN?
WHY DID THEY COME TO THIS ISLAND?
IT'S NOT LIKE ME TO BECOME SO UPSET!
MEOW

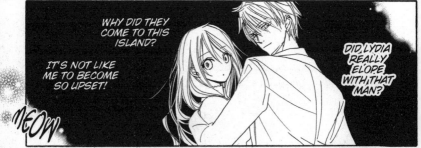

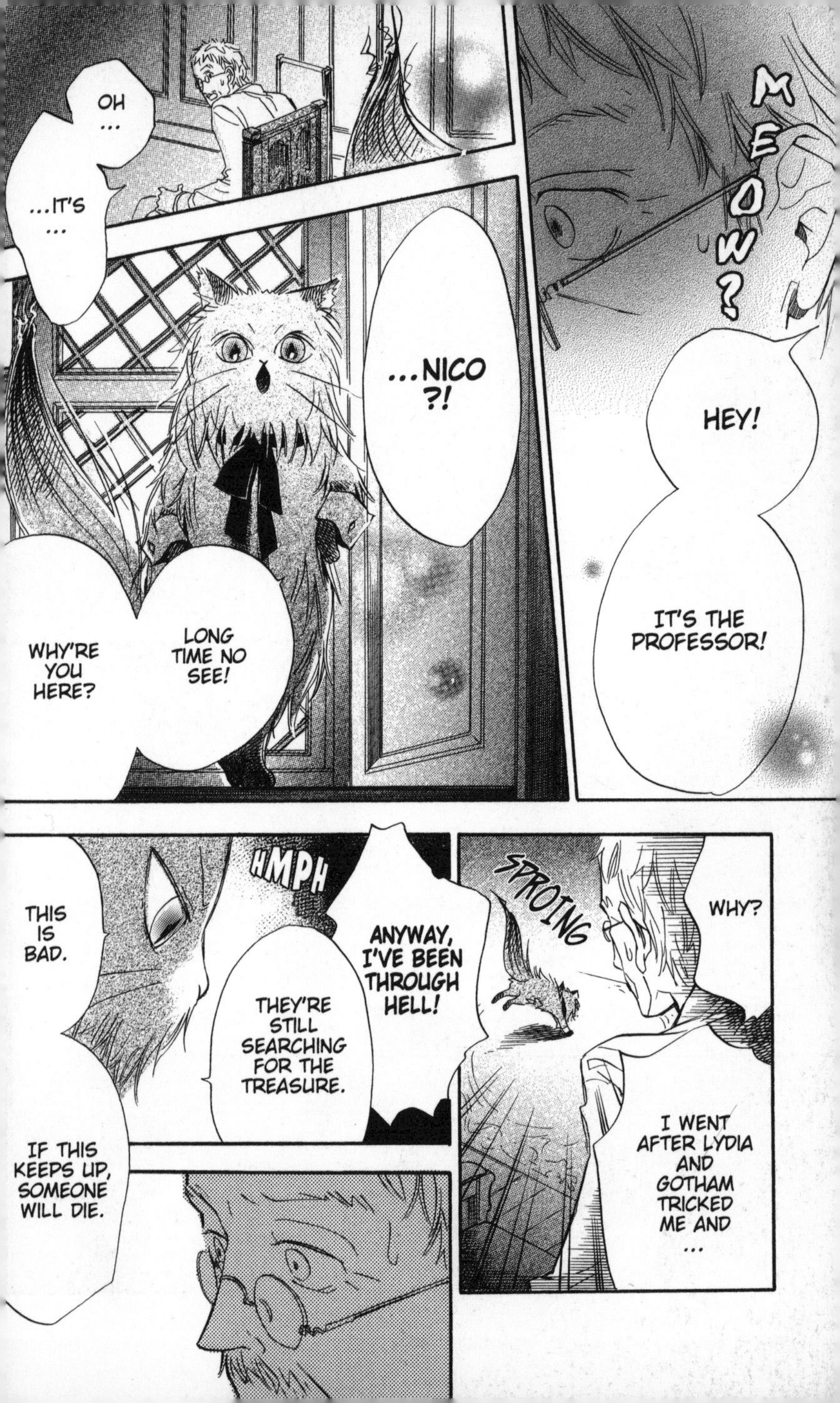
MEOW?
HEY!
IT'S THE PROFESSOR!
OH ...
...IT'S ...
...NICO ?!
LONG TIME NO SEE!
WHY'RE YOU HERE?
SPROING
WHY?
I WENT AFTER LYDIA AND GOTHAM TRICKED ME AND ...
HMPH
ANYWAY, I'VE BEEN THROUGH HELL!
THEY'RE STILL SEARCHING FOR THE TREASURE.
THIS IS BAD.
IF THIS KEEPS UP, SOMEONE WILL DIE.

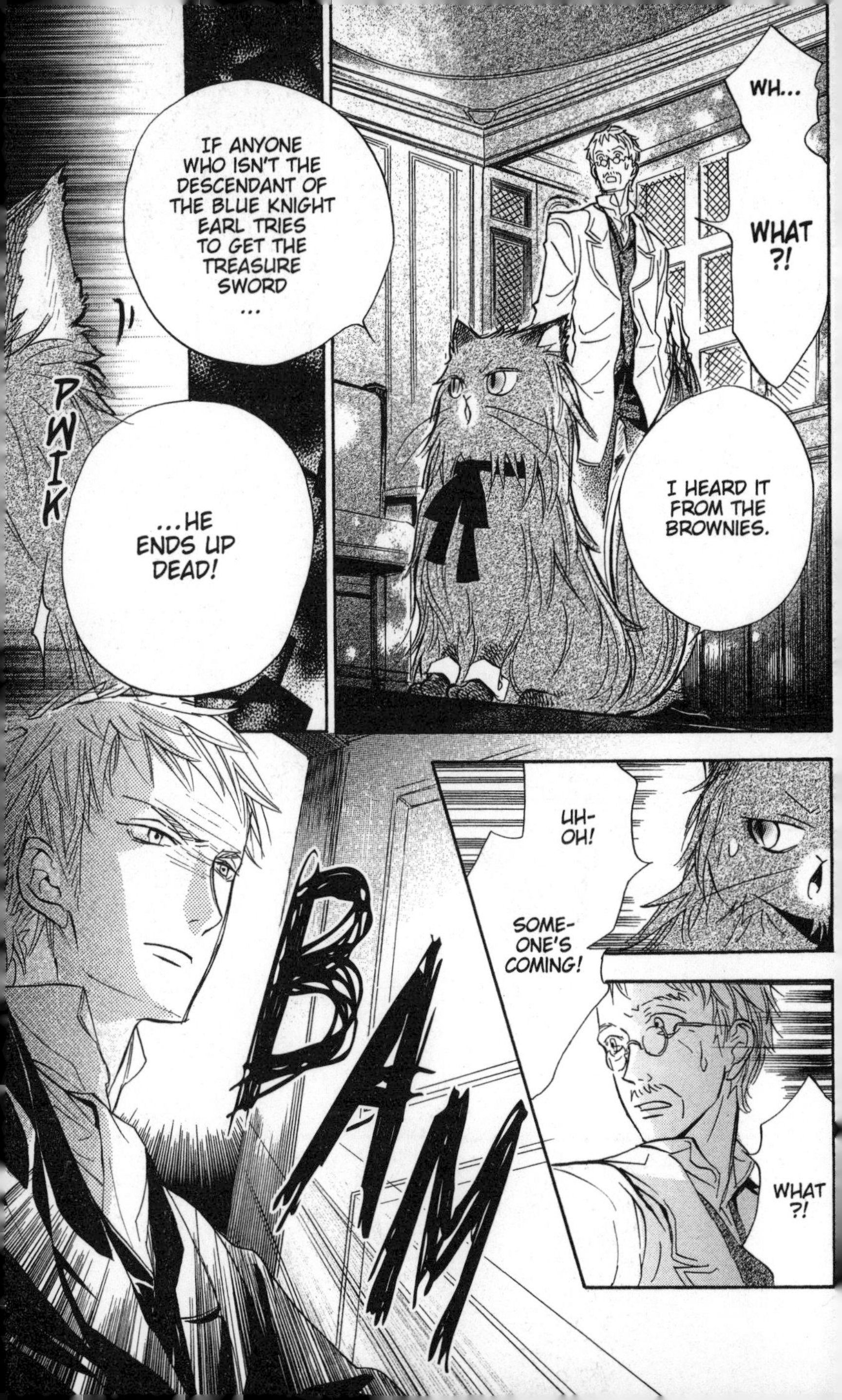
WH...
WHAT ?!
I HEARD IT FROM THE BROWNIES.
IF ANYONE WHO ISN'T THE DESCENDANT OF THE BLUE KNIGHT EARL TRIES TO GET THE TREASURE SWORD ...
PWIK
...HE ENDS UP DEAD!
UH-OH!
SOME-ONE'S COMING!
WHAT ?!
BAM

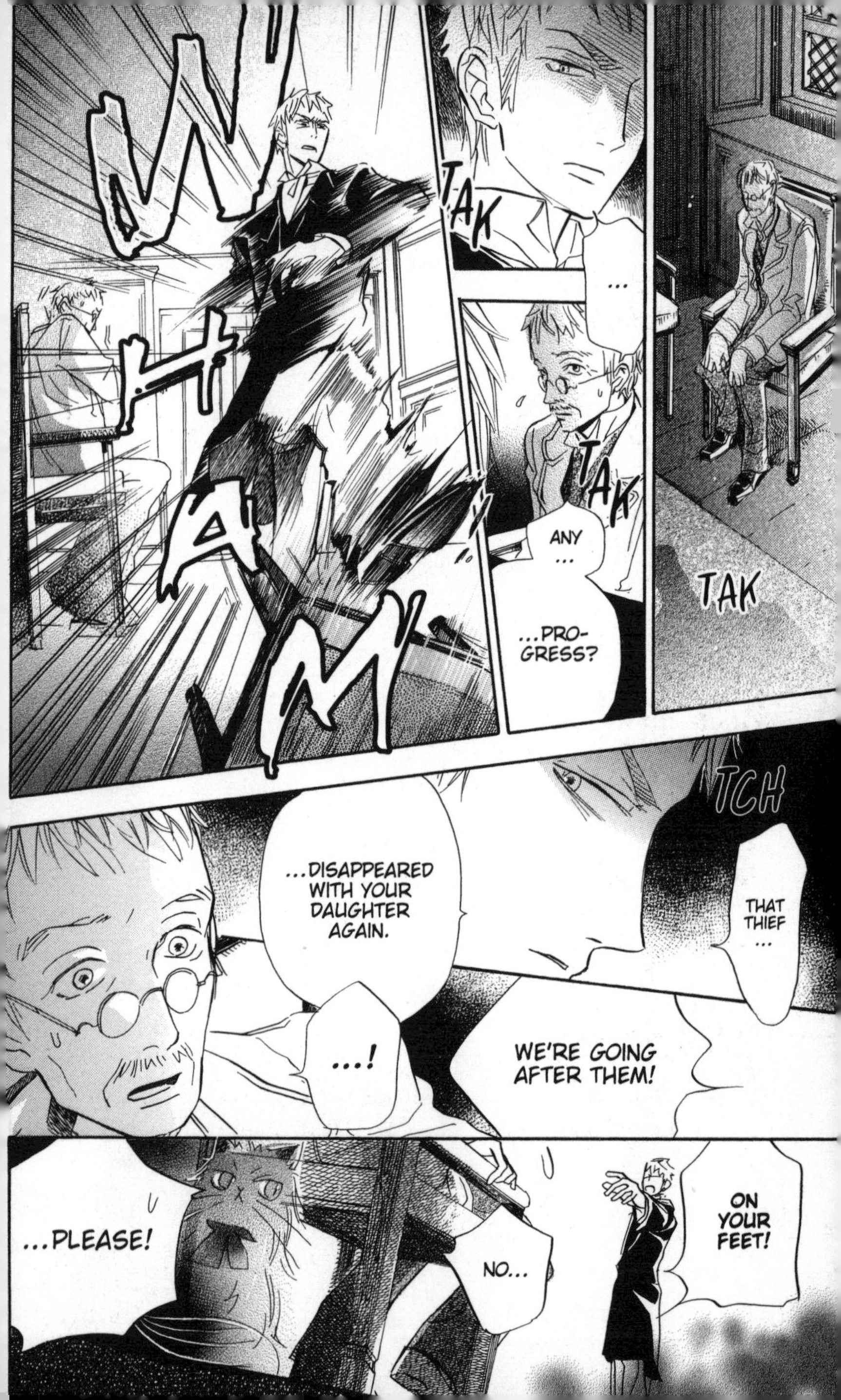
TAK
TAK
...
TAK
ANY ...
...PRO-GRESS?
WHAM
TCH
THAT THIEF ...
...DISAPPEARED WITH YOUR DAUGHTER AGAIN.
WE'RE GOING AFTER THEM!
...!
ON YOUR FEET!
NO...
...PLEASE!

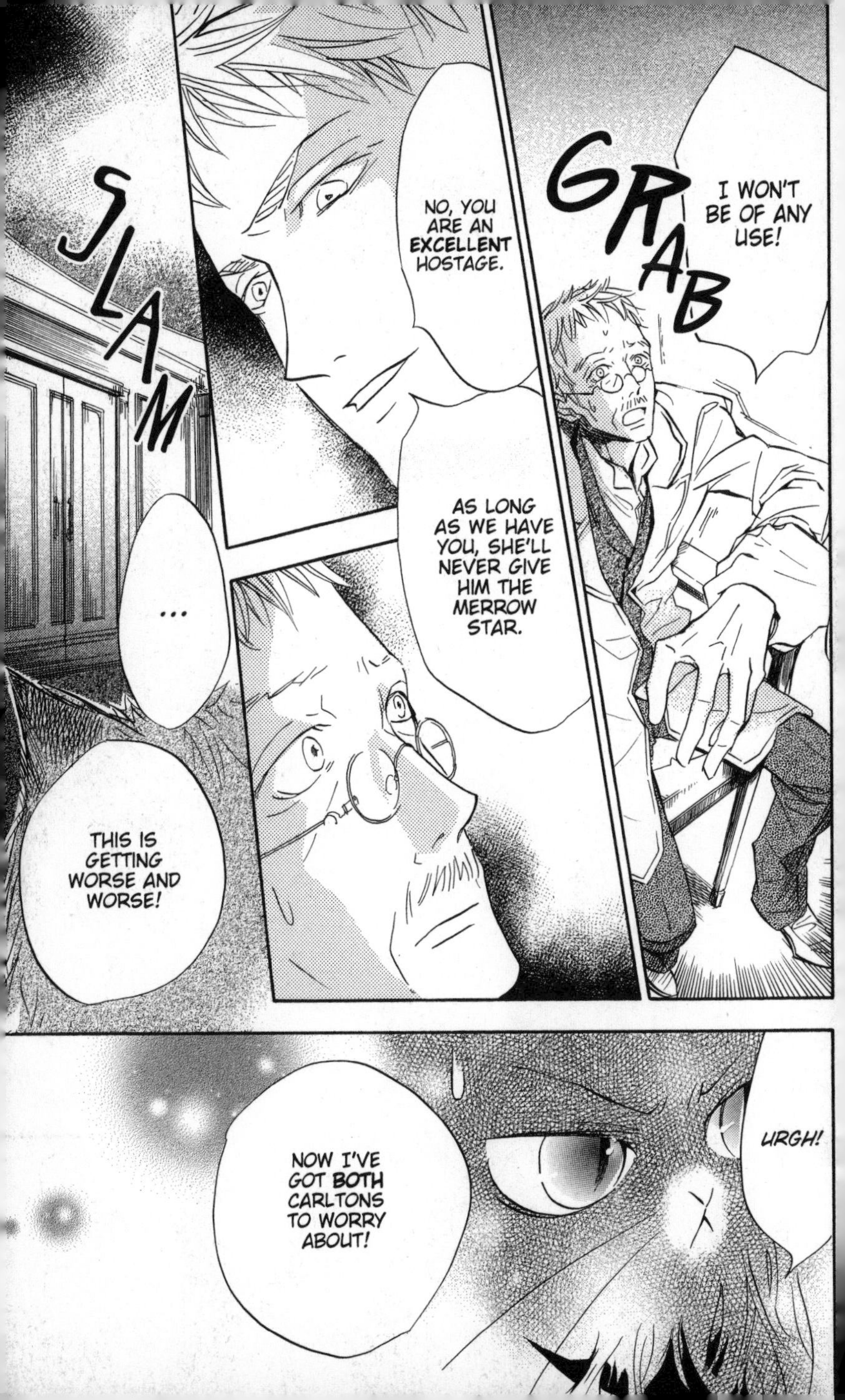
GRAB
I WON'T BE OF ANY USE!
NO, YOU ARE AN EXCELLENT HOSTAGE.
AS LONG AS WE HAVE YOU, SHE'LL NEVER GIVE HIM THE MERROW STAR.
SLAM
...
THIS IS GETTING WORSE AND WORSE!
URGH!
NOW I'VE GOT BOTH CARLTONS TO WORRY ABOUT!

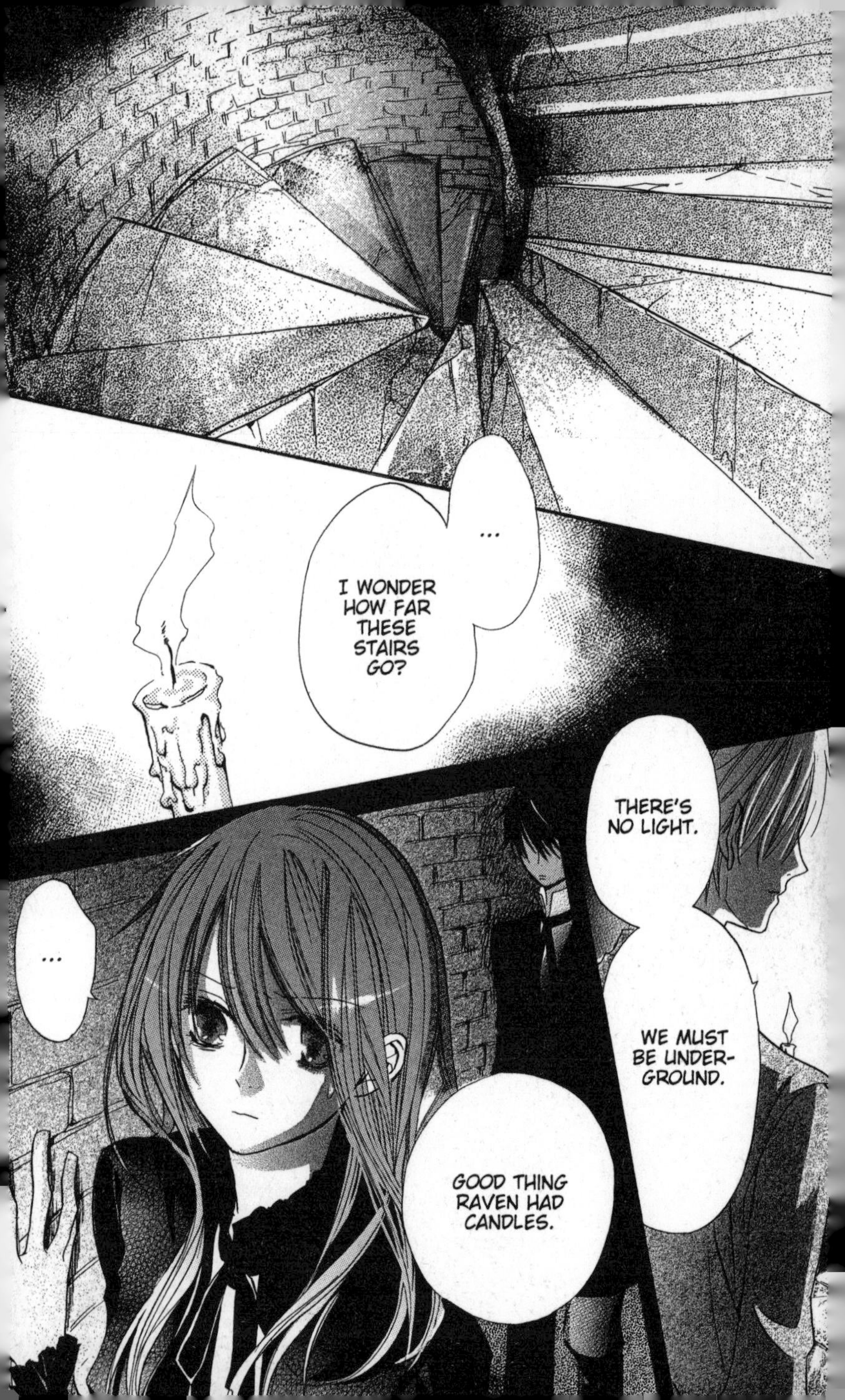
...
I WONDER HOW FAR THESE STAIRS GO?
THERE'S NO LIGHT.
WE MUST BE UNDER-GROUND.
GOOD THING RAVEN HAD CANDLES.
...

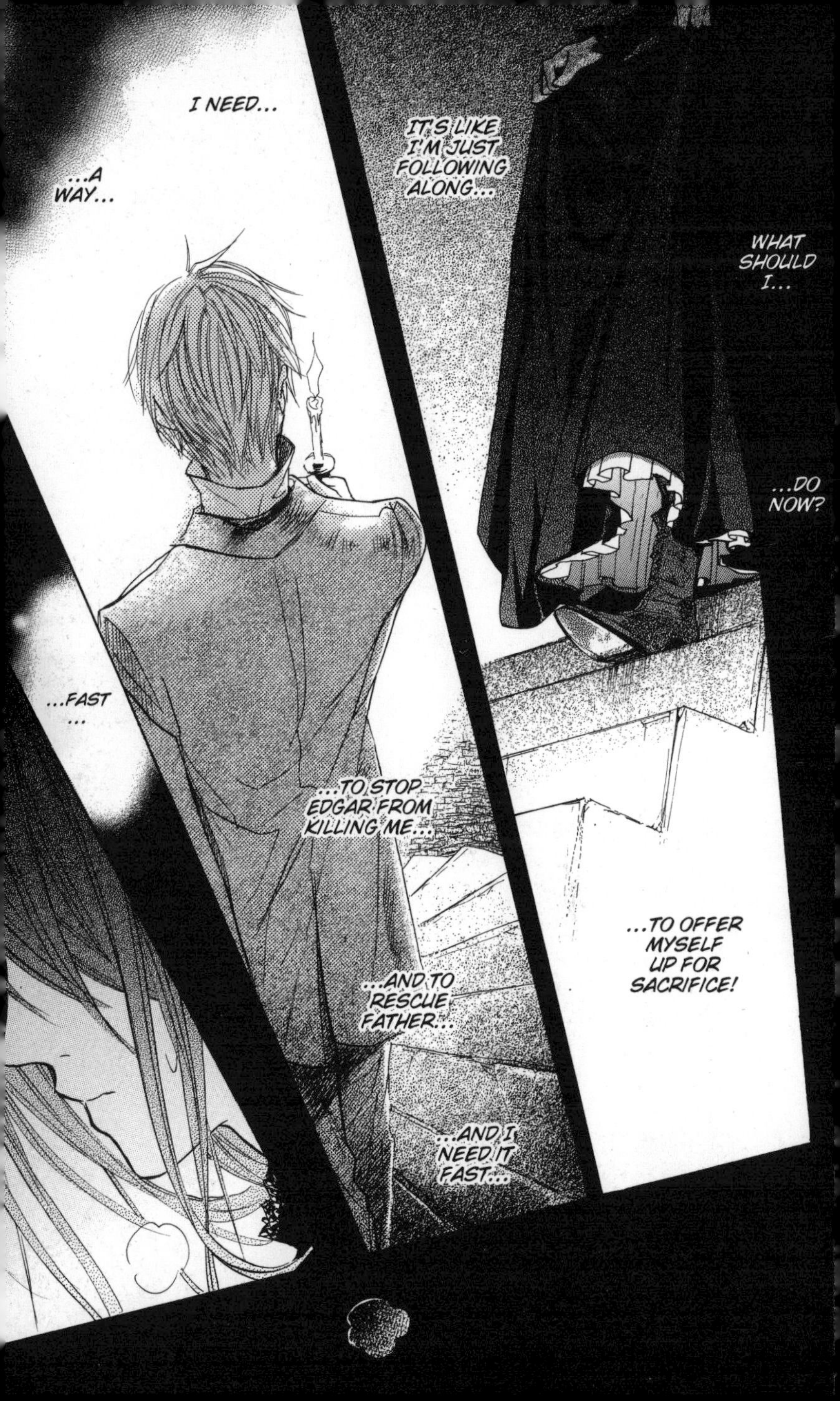
WHAT SHOULD I...
...DO NOW?
IT'S LIKE I'M JUST FOLLOWING ALONG...
I NEED...
...A WAY...
...TO OFFER MYSELF UP FOR SACRIFICE!
...TO STOP EDGAR FROM KILLING ME...
...AND TO RESCUE FATHER...
...AND I NEED IT FAST...
...FAST...

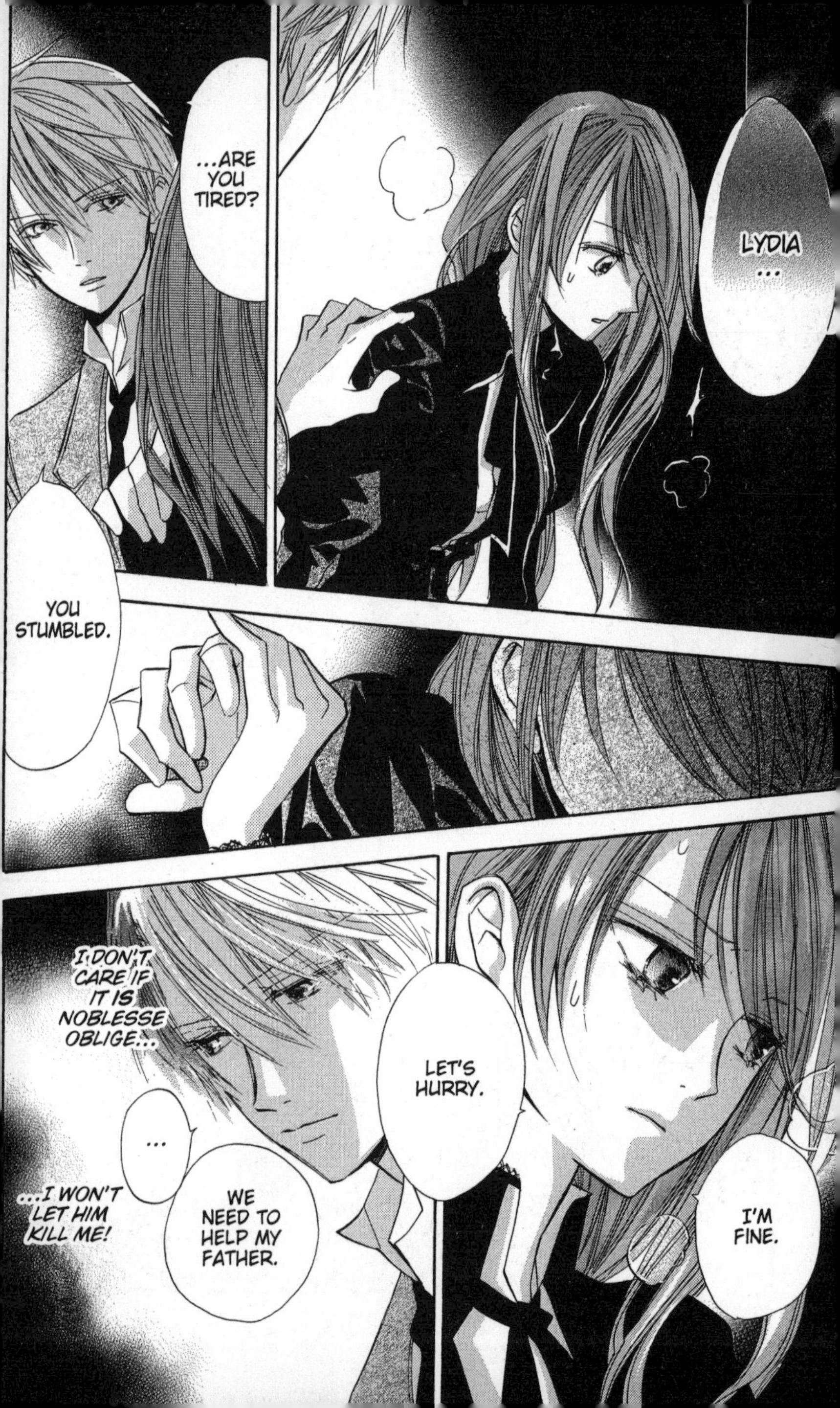
LYDIA …
…ARE YOU TIRED?
YOU STUMBLED.
I'M FINE.
LET'S HURRY.
…
WE NEED TO HELP MY FATHER.
I DON'T CARE IF IT IS NOBLESSE OBLIGE…
…I WON'T LET HIM KILL ME!

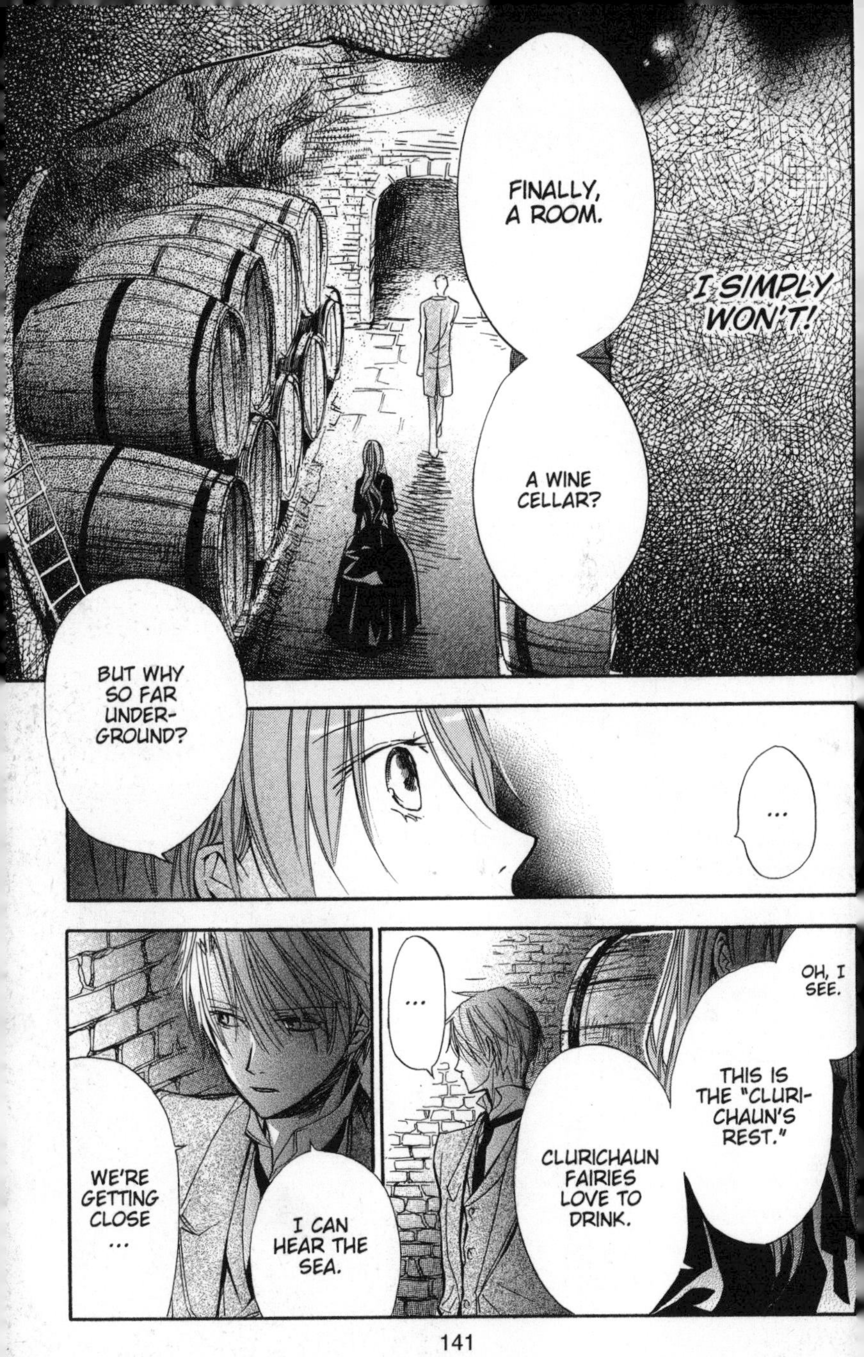
I SIMPLY WON'T!
FINALLY, A ROOM.
A WINE CELLAR?
BUT WHY SO FAR UNDER-GROUND?
...
OH, I SEE.
THIS IS THE "CLURICHAUN'S REST."
CLURICHAUN FAIRIES LOVE TO DRINK.
...
WE'RE GETTING CLOSE ...
I CAN HEAR THE SEA.

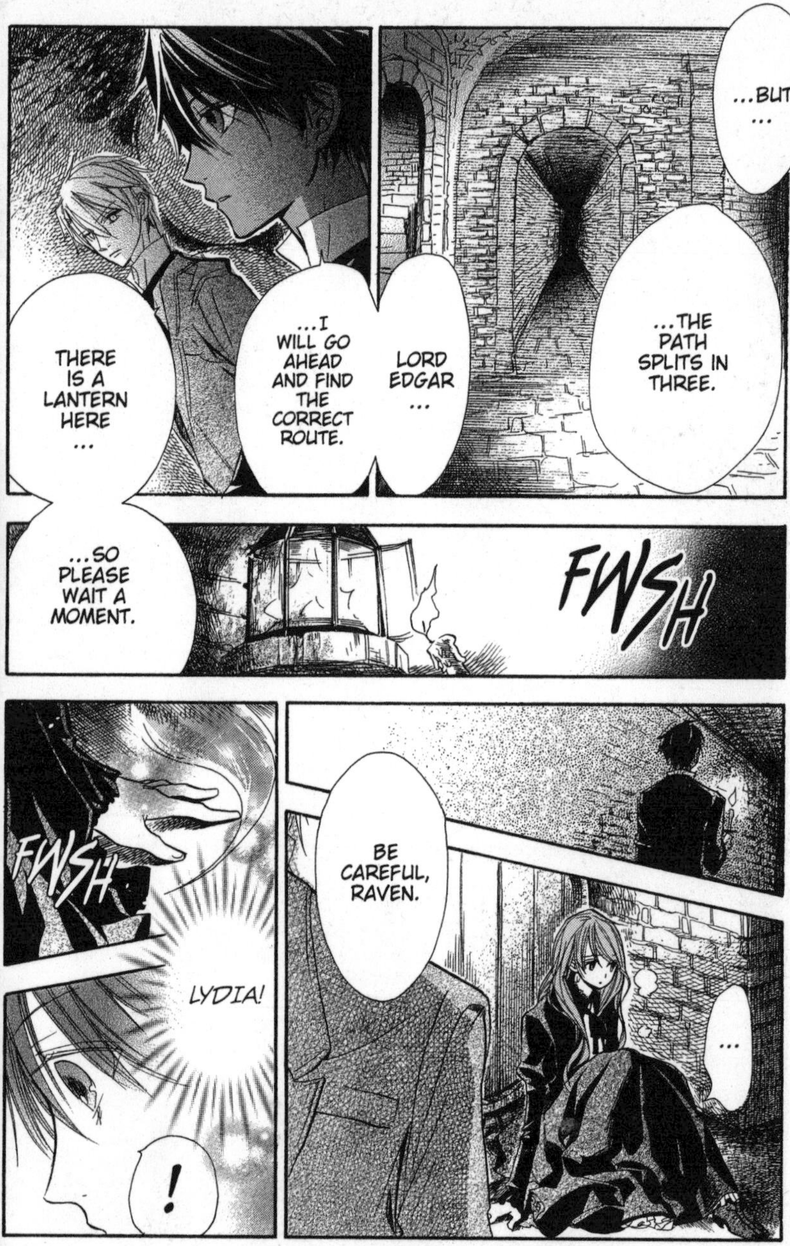

...BUT ...
...THE PATH SPLITS IN THREE.
LORD EDGAR ...
...I WILL GO AHEAD AND FIND THE CORRECT ROUTE.
THERE IS A LANTERN HERE ...
FWSH
...SO PLEASE WAIT A MOMENT.
BE CAREFUL, RAVEN.
...
FWSH
LYDIA!
!

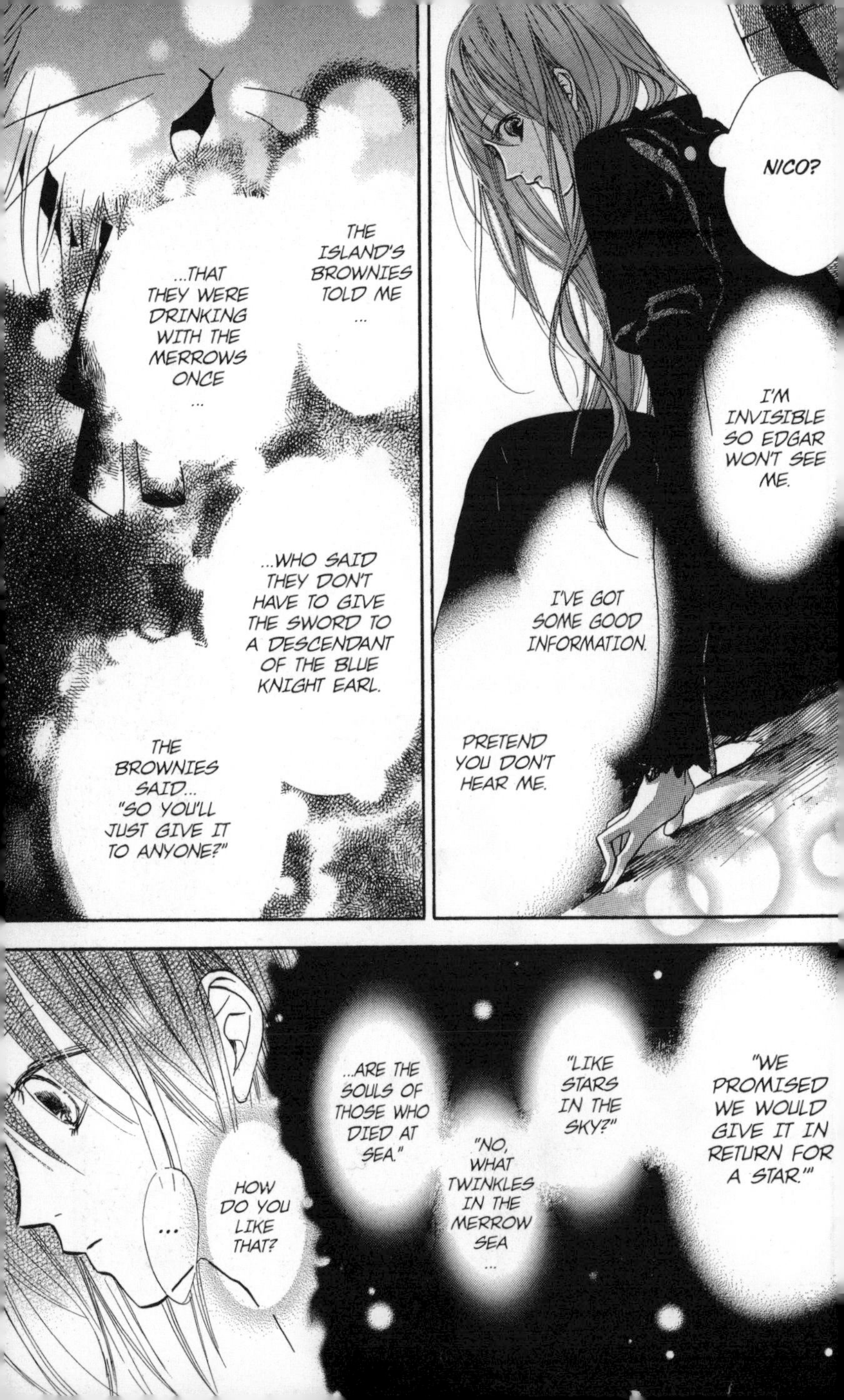
NICO?
I'M INVISIBLE SO EDGAR WON'T SEE ME.
I'VE GOT SOME GOOD INFORMATION.
PRETEND YOU DON'T HEAR ME.
THE ISLAND'S BROWNIES TOLD ME ...
...THAT THEY WERE DRINKING WITH THE MERROWS ONCE ...
...WHO SAID THEY DON'T HAVE TO GIVE THE SWORD TO A DESCENDANT OF THE BLUE KNIGHT EARL.
THE BROWNIES SAID... "SO YOU'LL JUST GIVE IT TO ANYONE?"
"WE PROMISED WE WOULD GIVE IT IN RETURN FOR A STAR.'"
"LIKE STARS IN THE SKY?"
"NO, WHAT TWINKLES IN THE MERROW SEA ...
...ARE THE SOULS OF THOSE WHO DIED AT SEA."
HOW DO YOU LIKE THAT?
...

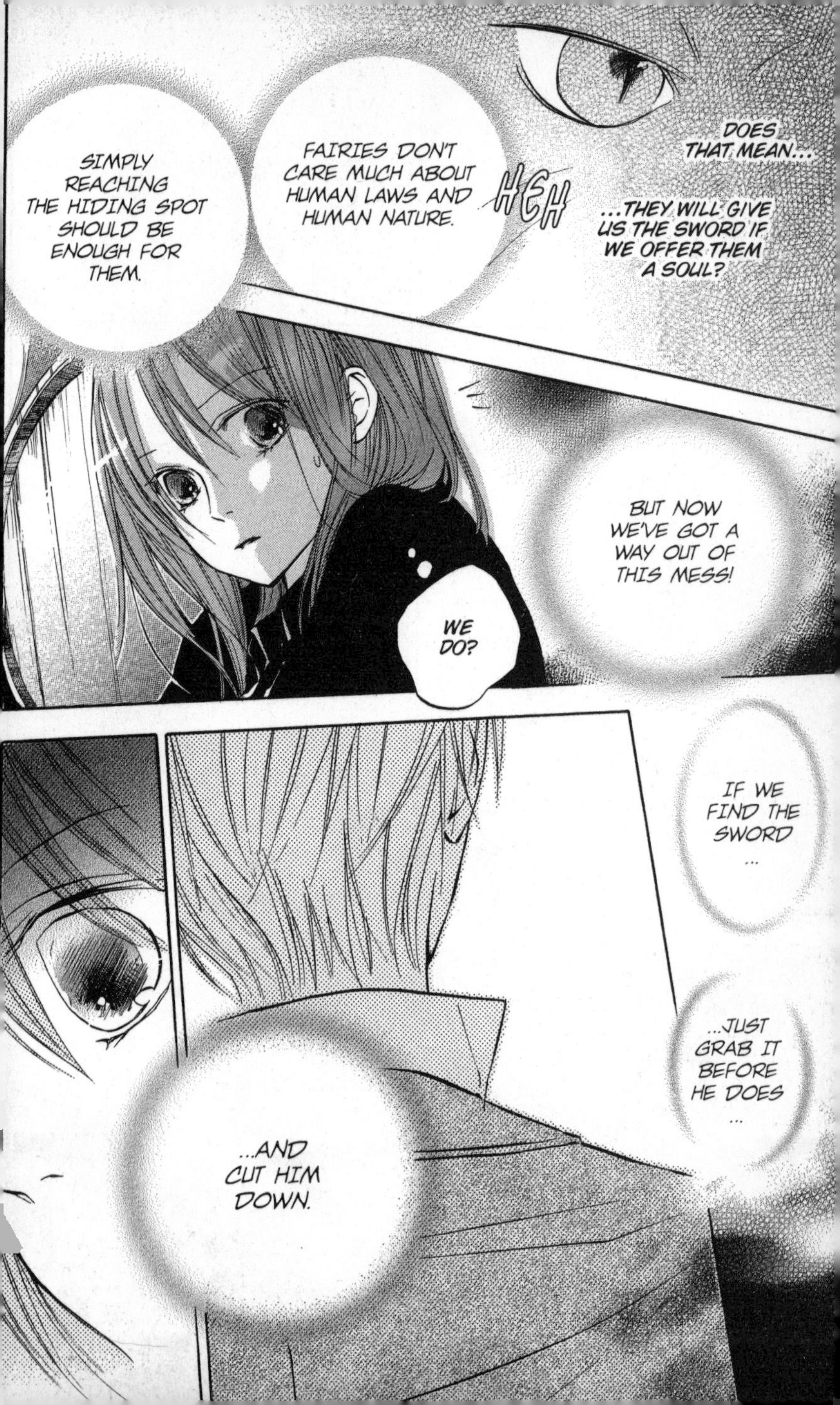
DOES THAT MEAN...
...THEY WILL GIVE US THE SWORD IF WE OFFER THEM A SOUL?
HEH
FAIRIES DON'T CARE MUCH ABOUT HUMAN LAWS AND HUMAN NATURE.
SIMPLY REACHING THE HIDING SPOT SHOULD BE ENOUGH FOR THEM.
BUT NOW WE'VE GOT A WAY OUT OF THIS MESS!
WE DO?
IF WE FIND THE SWORD...
...JUST GRAB IT BEFORE HE DOES...
...AND CUT HIM DOWN.

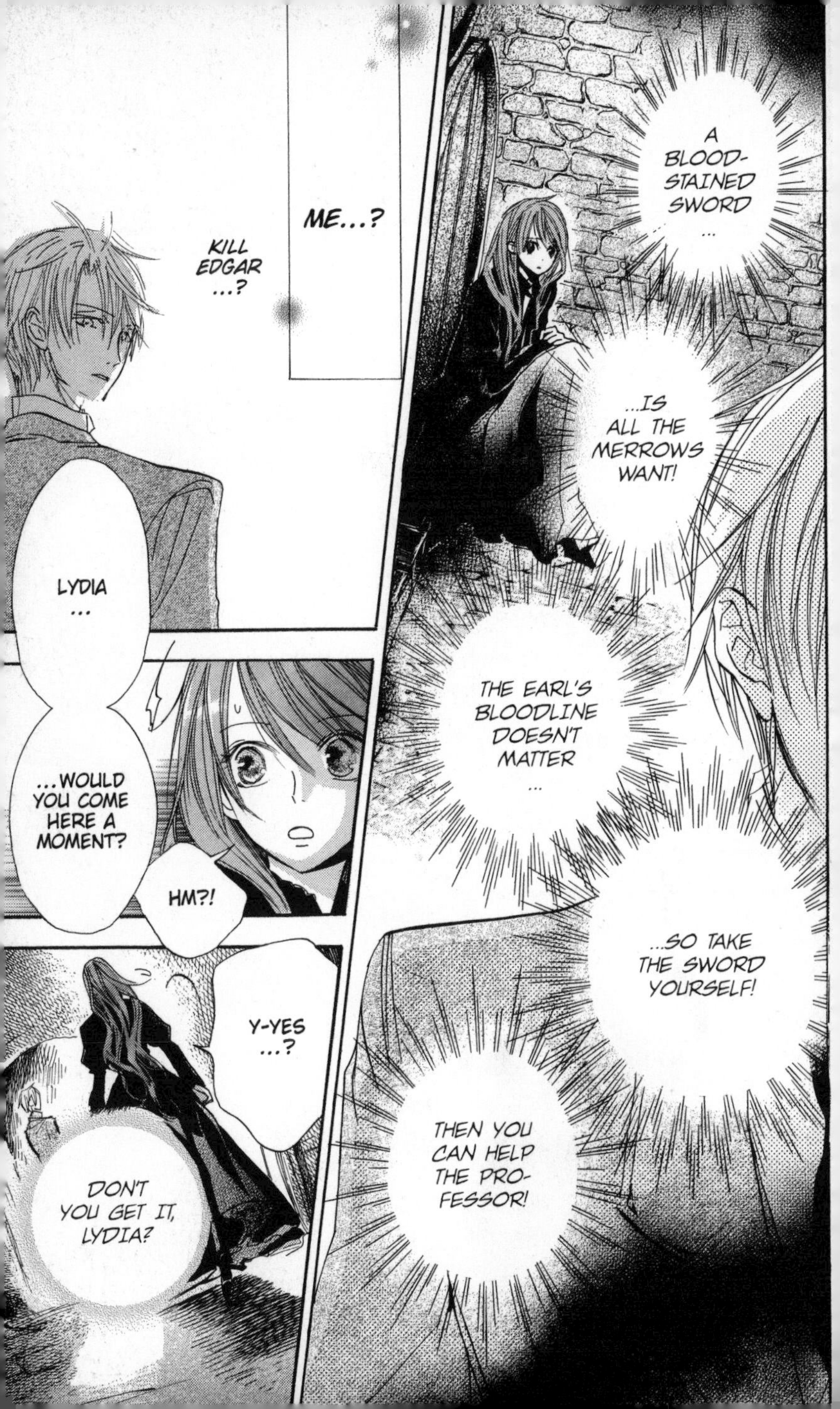
A BLOOD-STAINED SWORD...
...IS ALL THE MERROWS WANT!
THE EARL'S BLOODLINE DOESN'T MATTER...
...SO TAKE THE SWORD YOURSELF!
THEN YOU CAN HELP THE PRO-FESSOR!
ME...?
KILL EDGAR...?
LYDIA...
...WOULD YOU COME HERE A MOMENT?
HM?!
Y-YES...?
DON'T YOU GET IT, LYDIA?

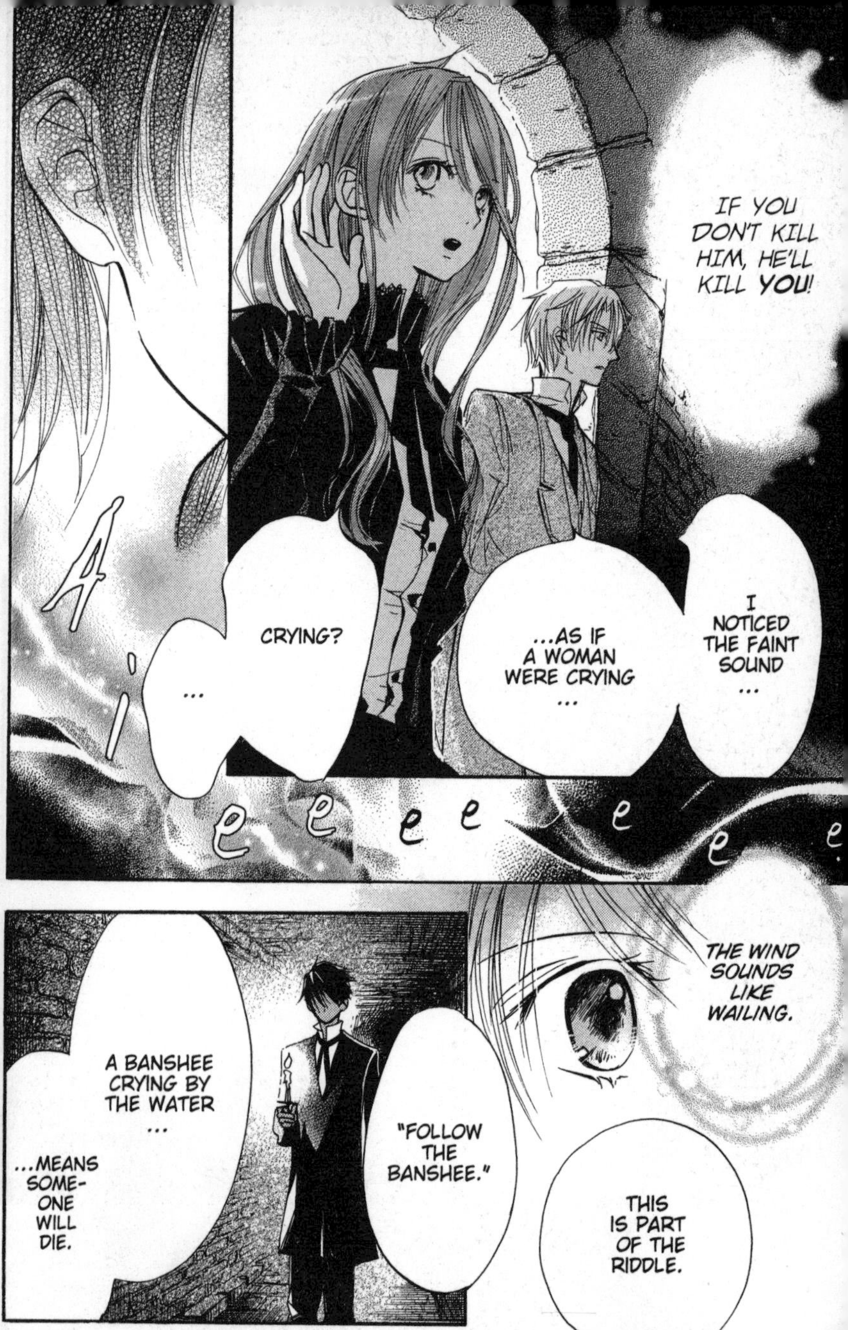
IF YOU DON'T KILL HIM, HE'LL KILL YOU!
I NOTICED THE FAINT SOUND ...
...AS IF A WOMAN WERE CRYING ...
CRYING?
...
Aieeeeeee
THE WIND SOUNDS LIKE WAILING.
THIS IS PART OF THE RIDDLE.
"FOLLOW THE BANSHEE."
A BANSHEE CRYING BY THE WATER ...
...MEANS SOME-ONE WILL DIE.

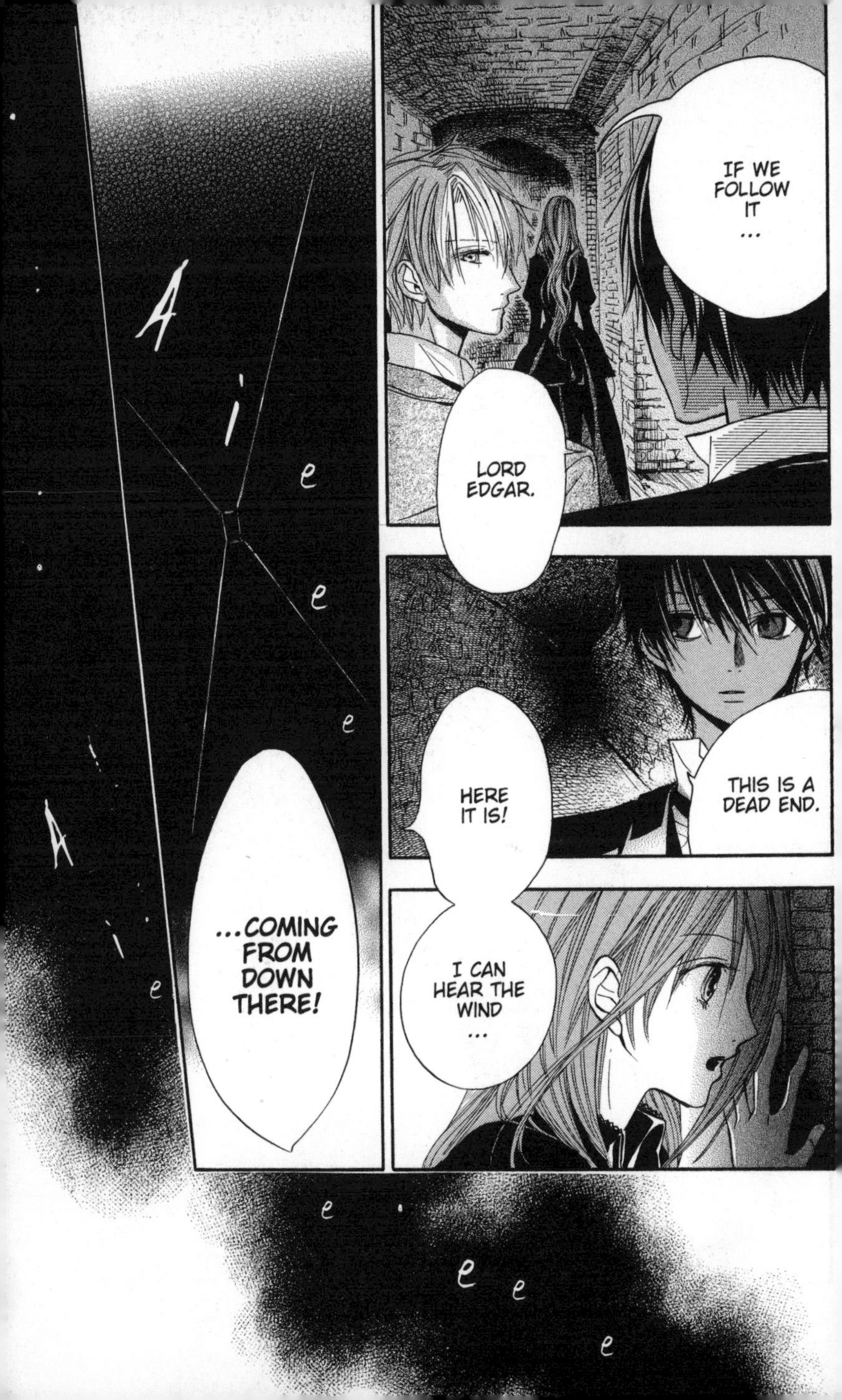

IF WE FOLLOW IT ...
LORD EDGAR.
THIS IS A DEAD END.
HERE IT IS!
I CAN HEAR THE WIND ...
...COMING FROM DOWN THERE!
Aieee
Aieeeee

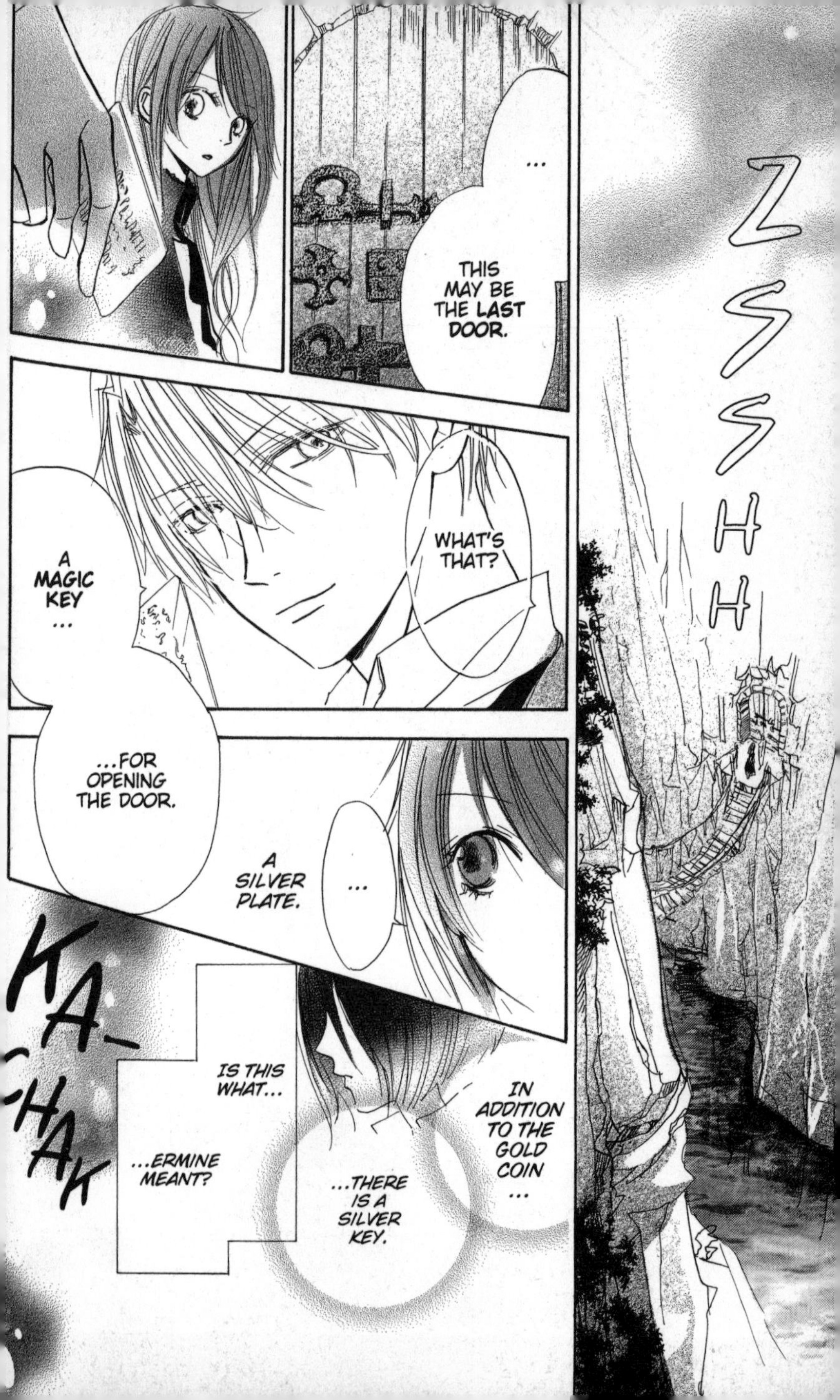
ZSSHHH
...
THIS MAY BE THE LAST DOOR.
WHAT'S THAT?
A MAGIC KEY ...
...FOR OPENING THE DOOR.
...
A SILVER PLATE.
IN ADDITION TO THE GOLD COIN ...
...THERE IS A SILVER KEY.
IS THIS WHAT...
...ERMINE MEANT?
KA-CHAK

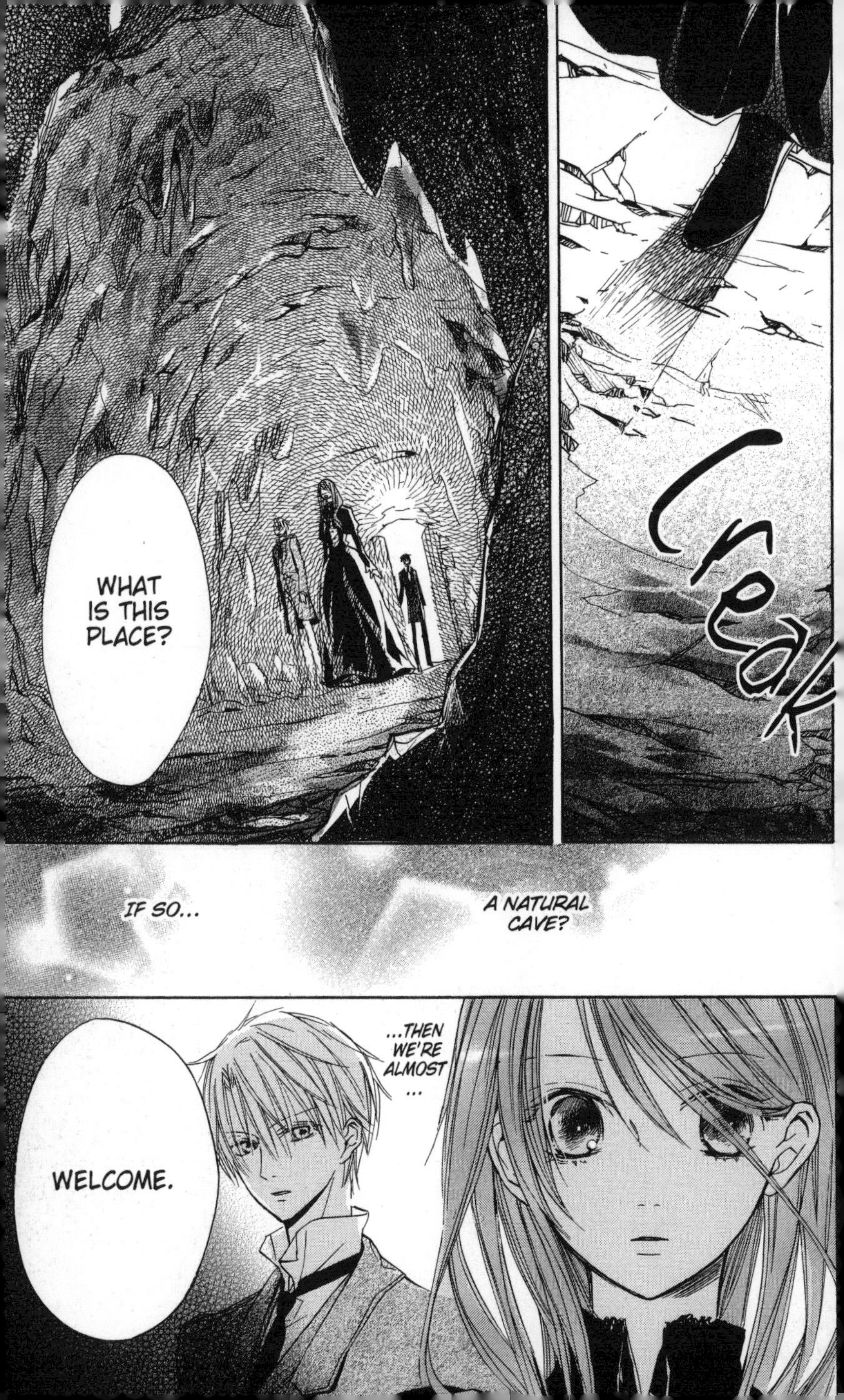
Creak
WHAT IS THIS PLACE?
A NATURAL CAVE?
IF SO...
...THEN WE'RE ALMOST ...
WELCOME.

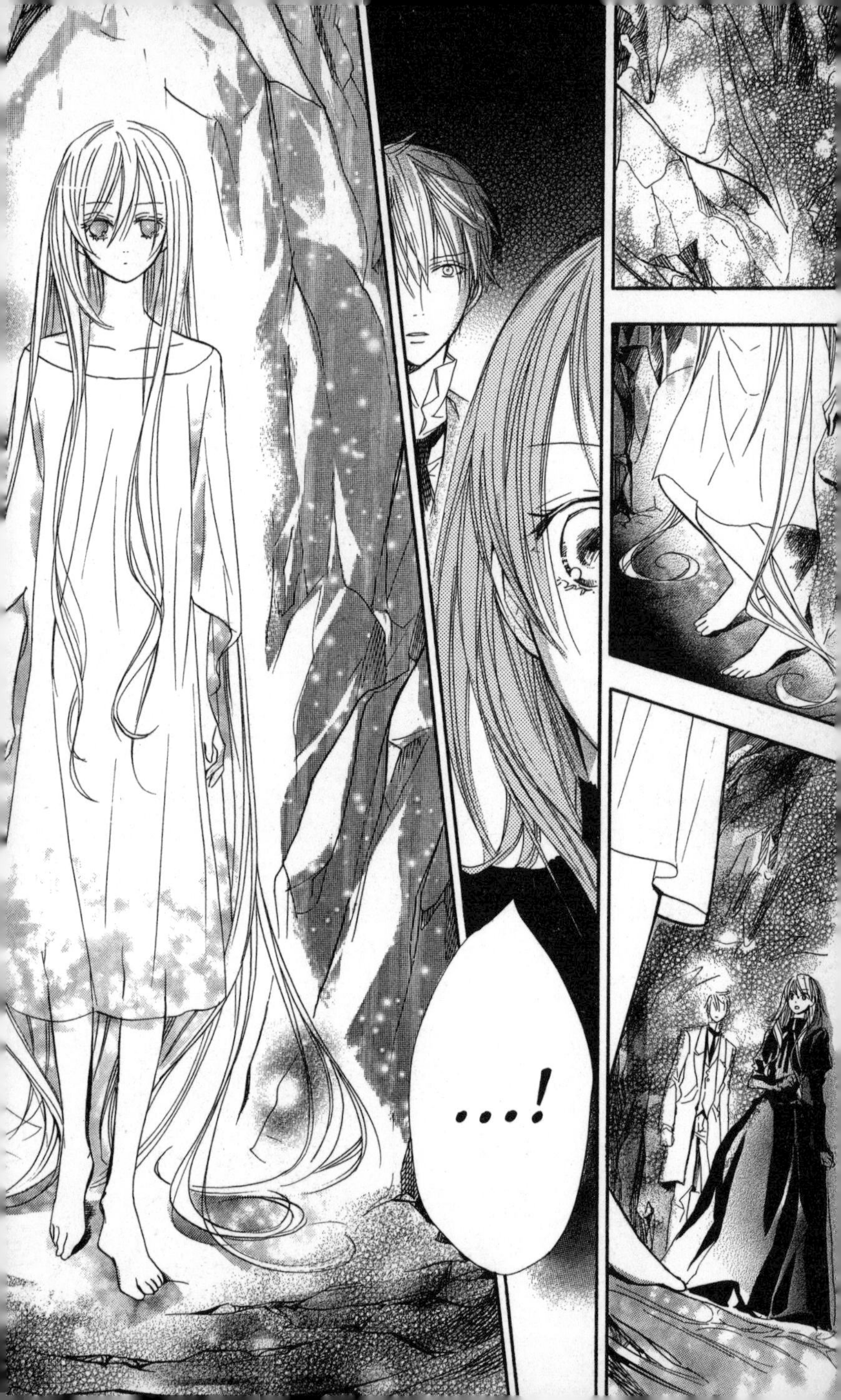
...!

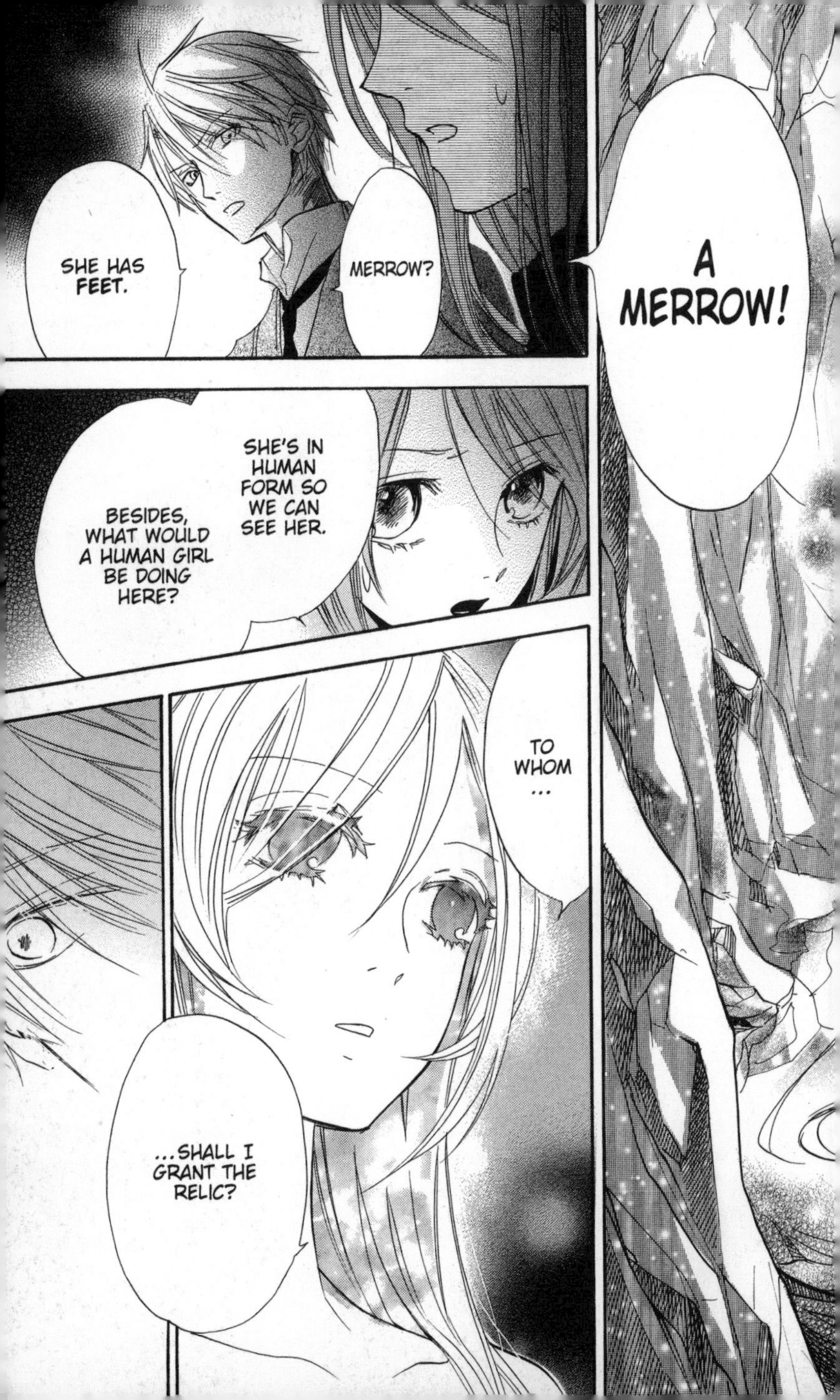
A MERROW!
MERROW?
SHE HAS FEET.
SHE'S IN HUMAN FORM SO WE CAN SEE HER.
BESIDES, WHAT WOULD A HUMAN GIRL BE DOING HERE?
TO WHOM ...
...SHALL I GRANT THE RELIC?

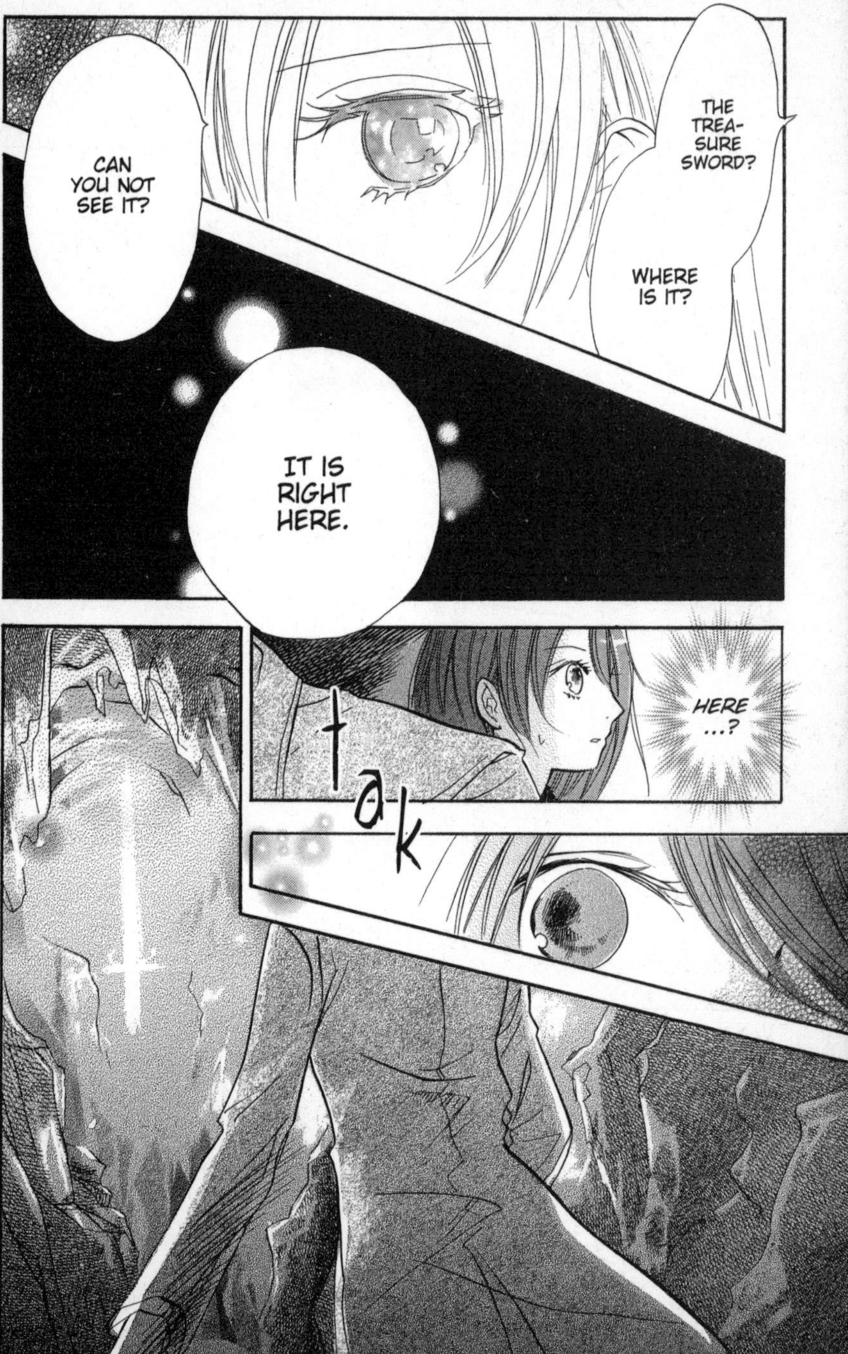
THE TREA-SURE SWORD?
WHERE IS IT?
CAN YOU NOT SEE IT?
IT IS RIGHT HERE.
HERE ...?
tak

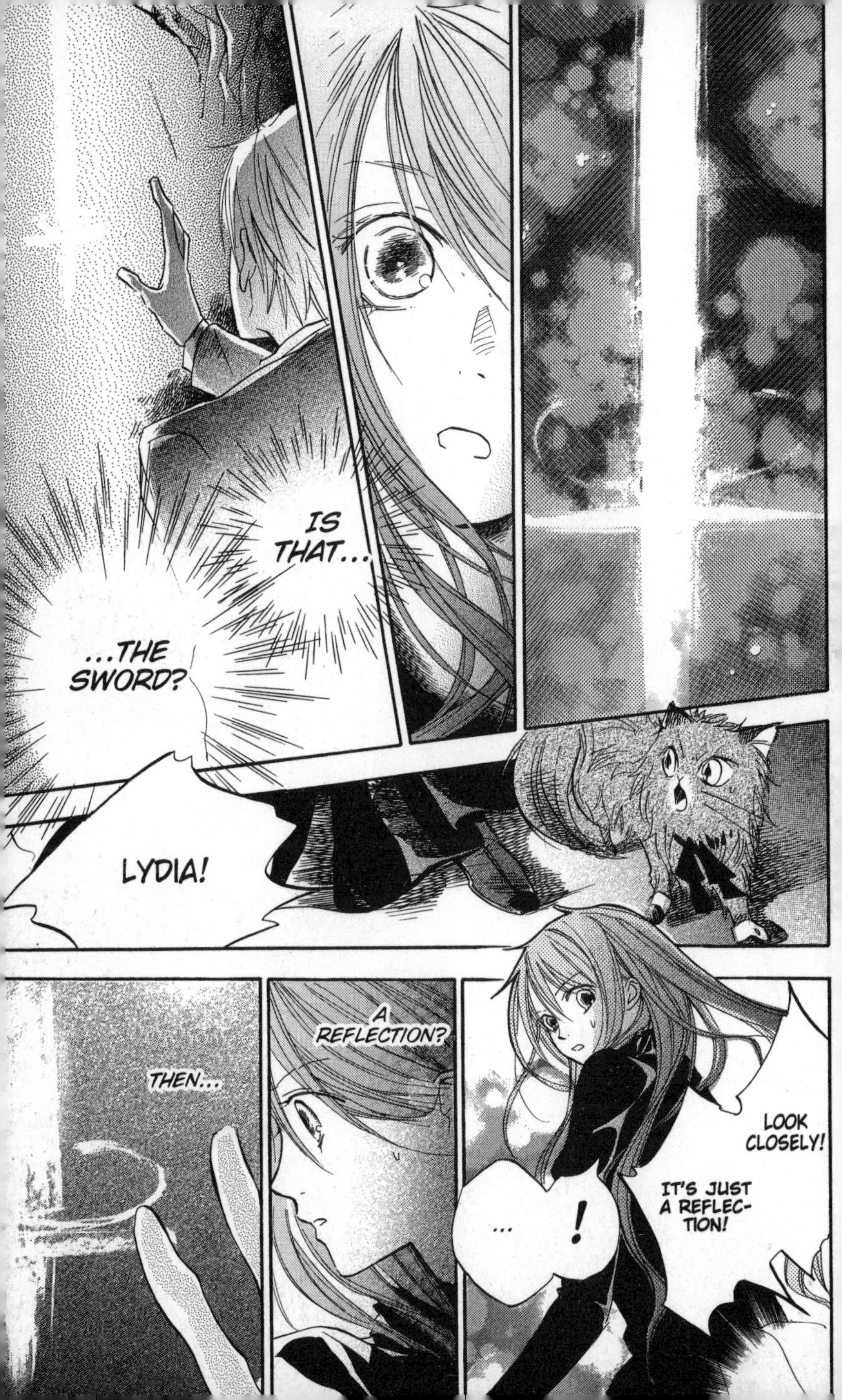
IS THAT...
...THE SWORD?
LYDIA!
LOOK CLOSELY!
IT'S JUST A REFLECTION!
!
...
A REFLECTION?
THEN...

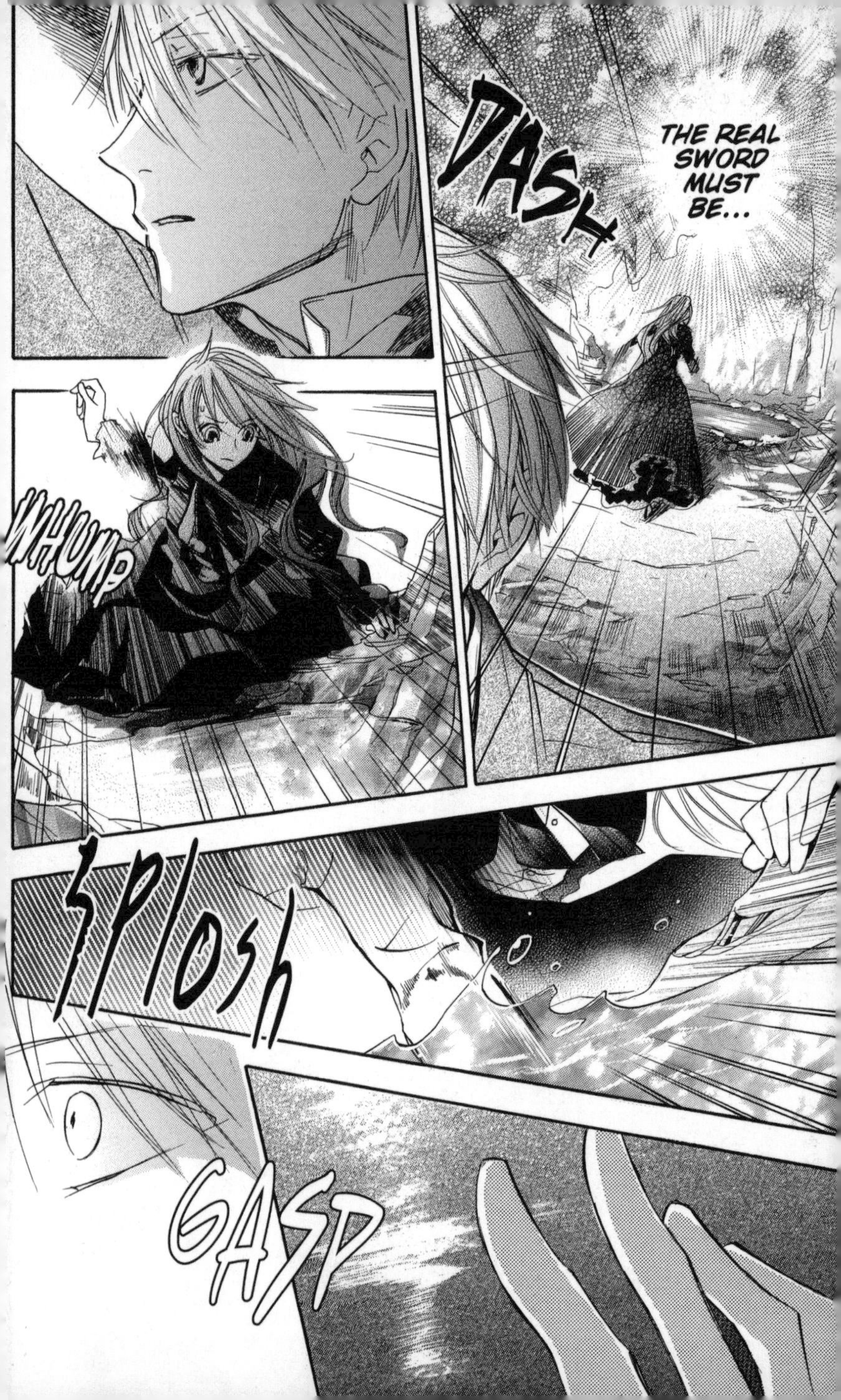
DASH
THE REAL SWORD MUST BE...
WHUMP
SPLOSH
GASP

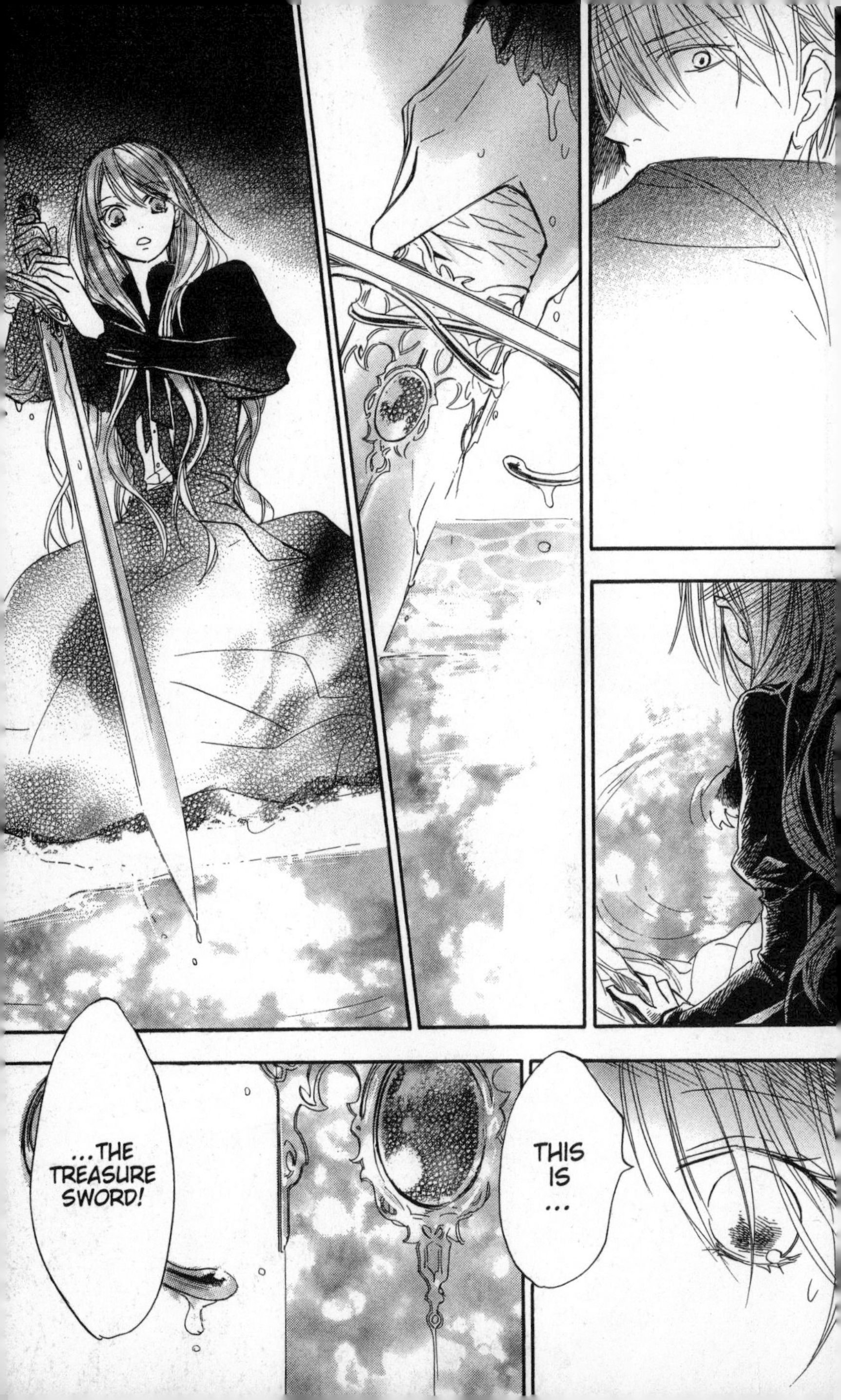
THIS IS ...
...THE TREASURE SWORD!

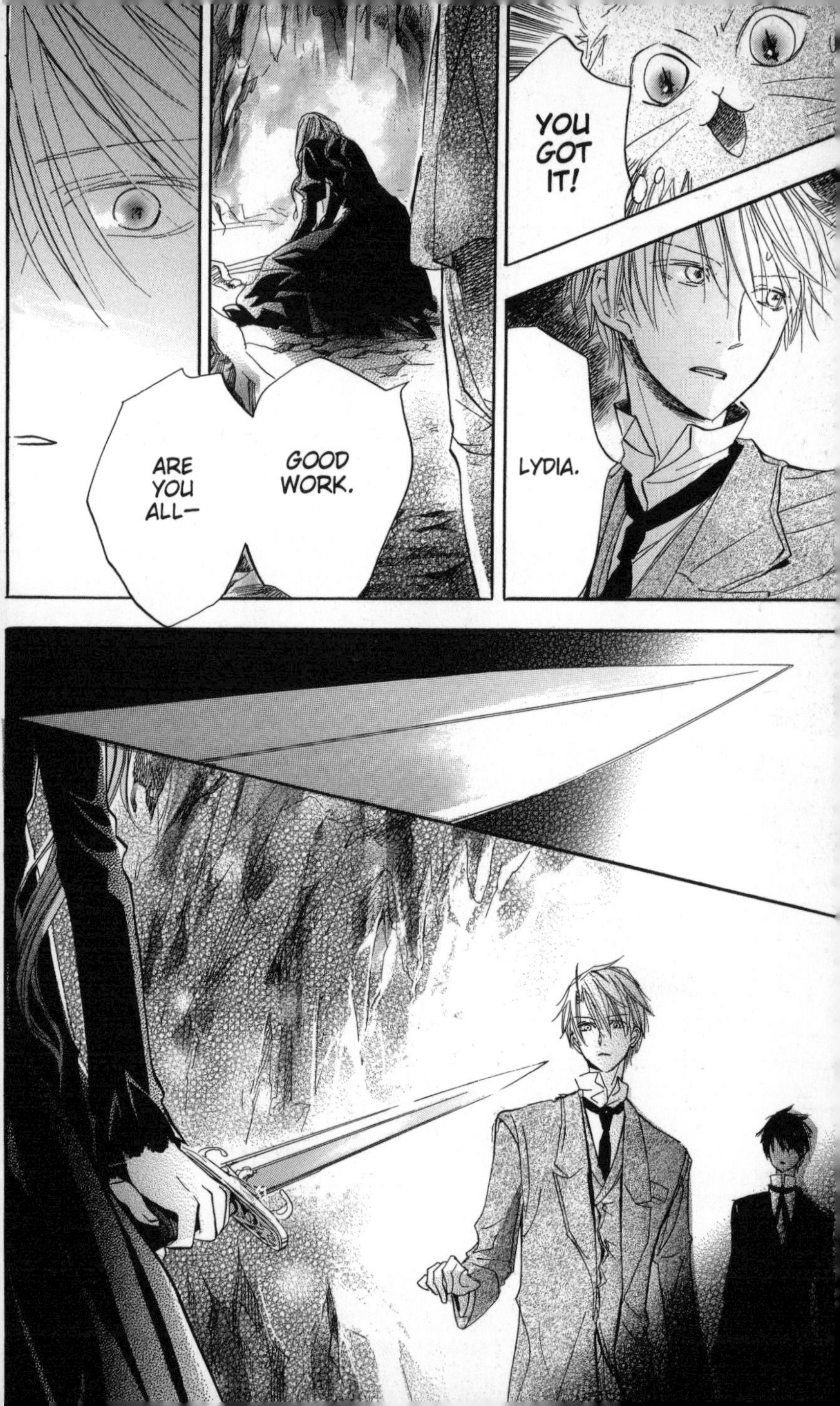
YOU GOT IT!
LYDIA.
GOOD WORK.
ARE YOU ALL—

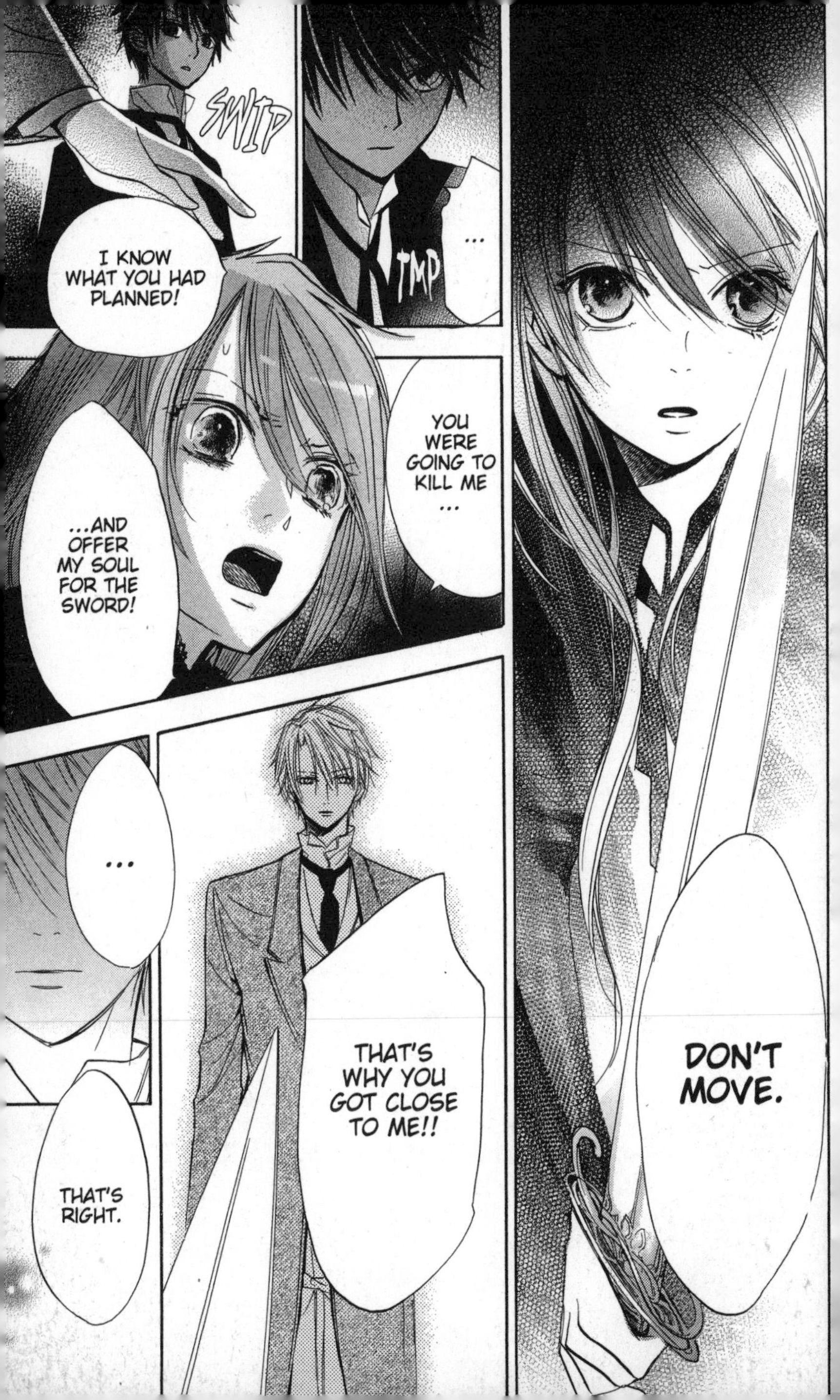
DON'T MOVE.
...
TMP
SWIP
I KNOW WHAT YOU HAD PLANNED!
YOU WERE GOING TO KILL ME ...
...AND OFFER MY SOUL FOR THE SWORD!
THAT'S WHY YOU GOT CLOSE TO ME!!
...
THAT'S RIGHT.

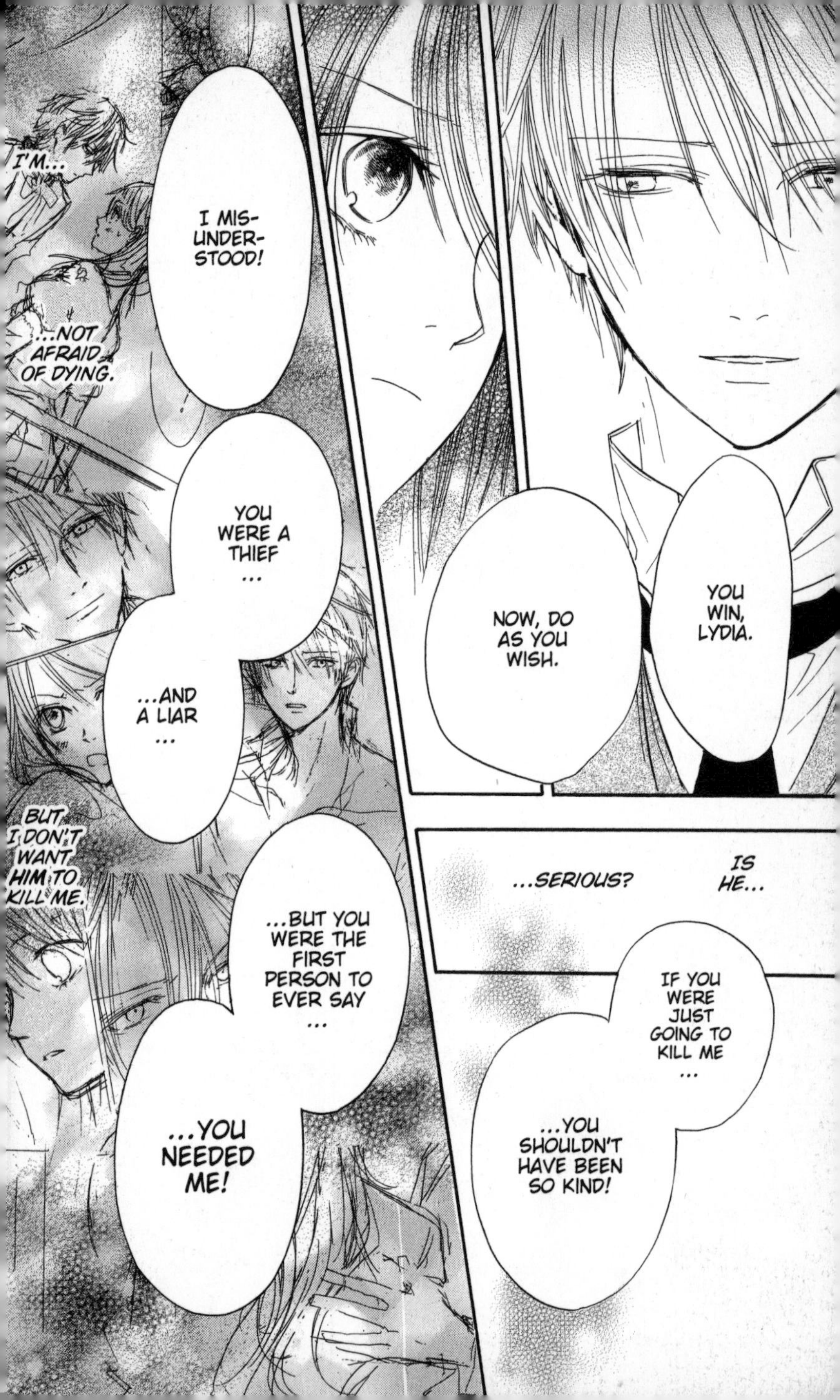
YOU WIN, LYDIA.
NOW, DO AS YOU WISH.
IS HE...
...SERIOUS?
IF YOU WERE JUST GOING TO KILL ME...
...YOU SHOULDN'T HAVE BEEN SO KIND!
I MIS-UNDER-STOOD!
YOU WERE A THIEF...
...AND A LIAR...
...BUT YOU WERE THE FIRST PERSON TO EVER SAY...
...YOU NEEDED ME!
I'M...
...NOT AFRAID OF DYING.
BUT I DON'T WANT HIM TO KILL ME.

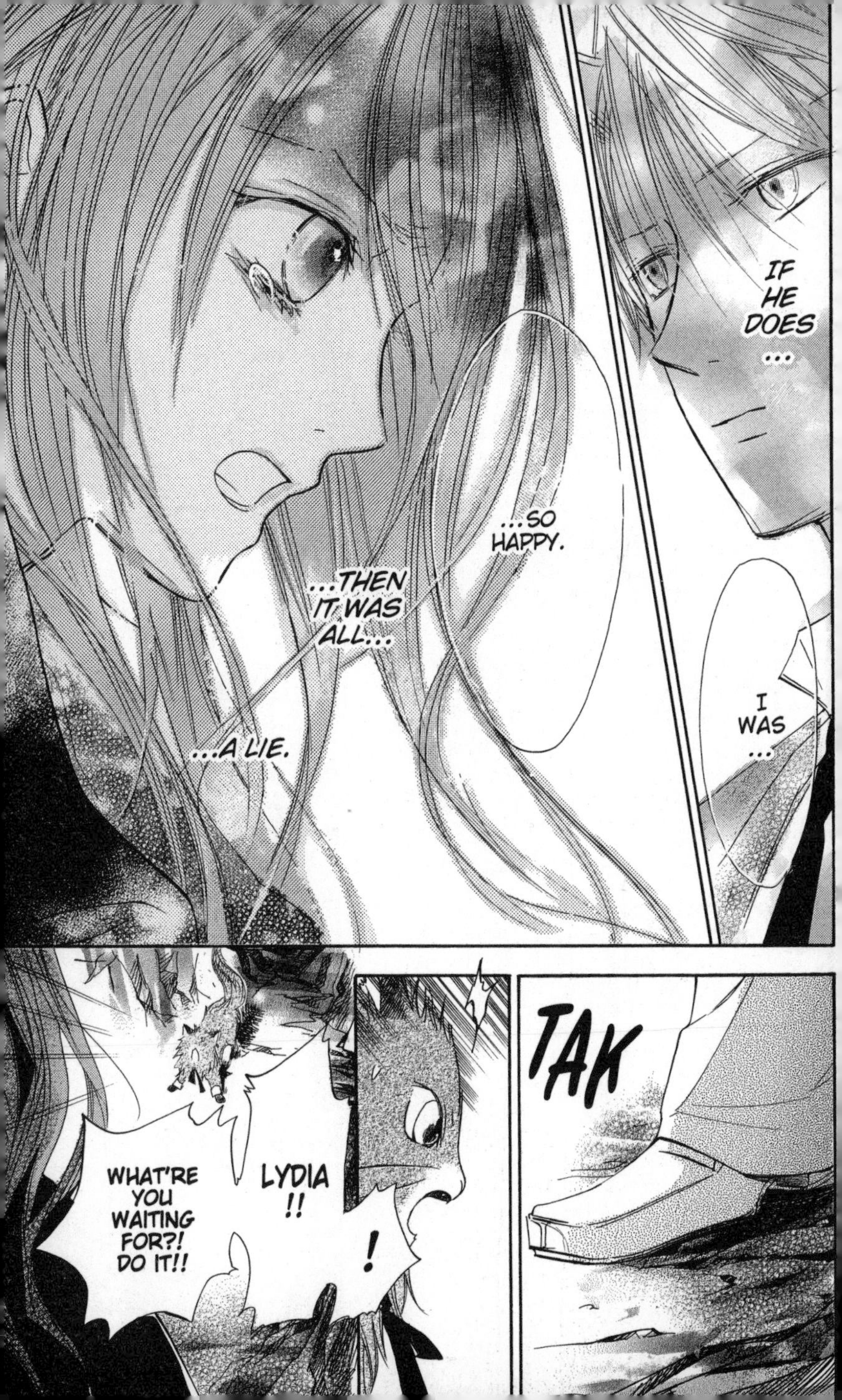
IF HE DOES...
I WAS...
...SO HAPPY.
...THEN IT WAS ALL...
...A LIE.
TAK
!
LYDIA!!
WHAT'RE YOU WAITING FOR?! DO IT!!

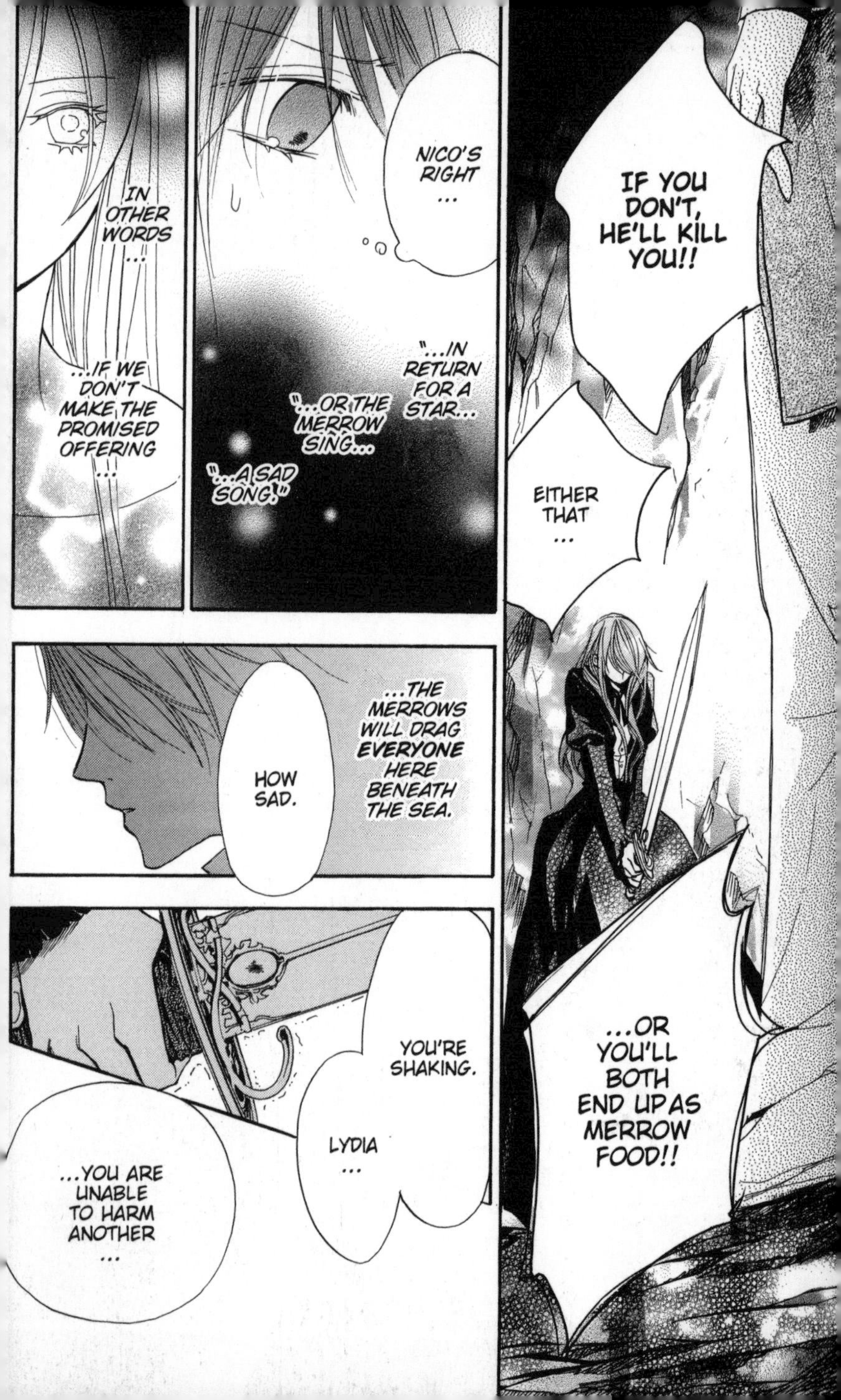

IF YOU DON'T, HE'LL KILL YOU!!
EITHER THAT...
...OR YOU'LL BOTH END UP AS MERROW FOOD!!
NICO'S RIGHT...
"...IN RETURN FOR A STAR...
"...OR THE MERROW SING...
"...A SAD SONG."
IN OTHER WORDS...
...IF WE DON'T MAKE THE PROMISED OFFERING...
...THE MERROWS WILL DRAG EVERYONE HERE BENEATH THE SEA.
HOW SAD.
YOU'RE SHAKING.
LYDIA...
...YOU ARE UNABLE TO HARM ANOTHER...

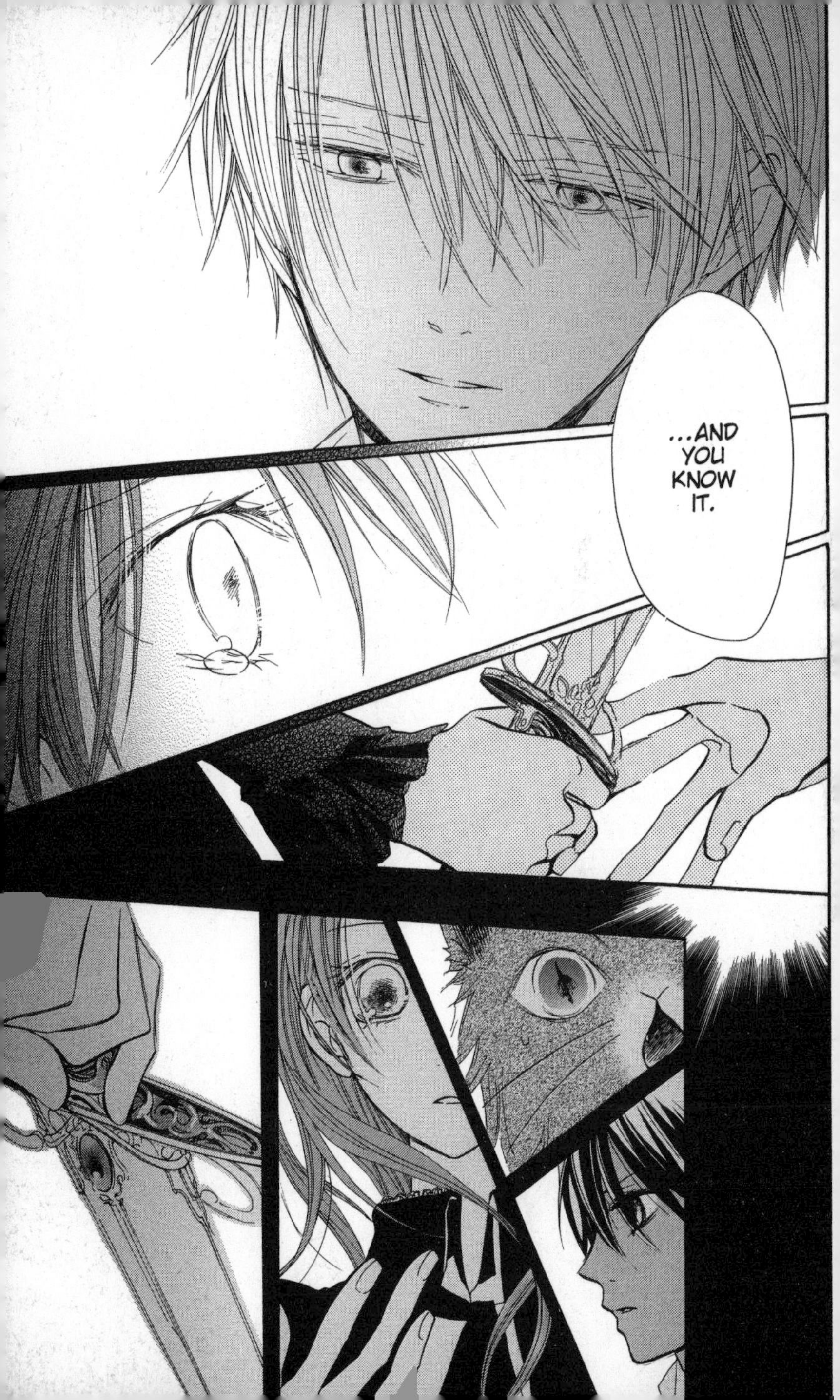
...AND YOU KNOW IT.

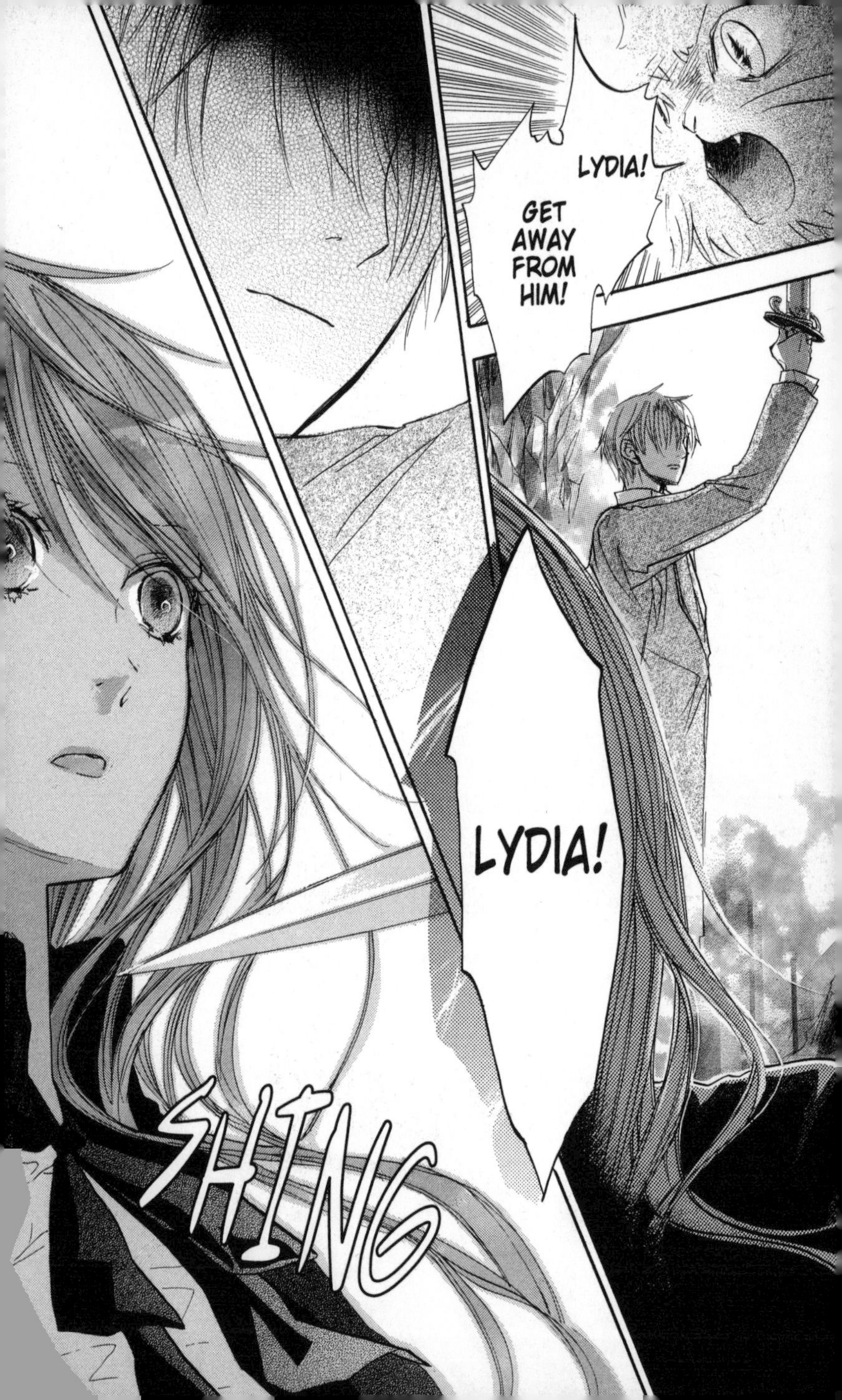
LYDIA!
GET AWAY FROM HIM!
LYDIA!
SHING

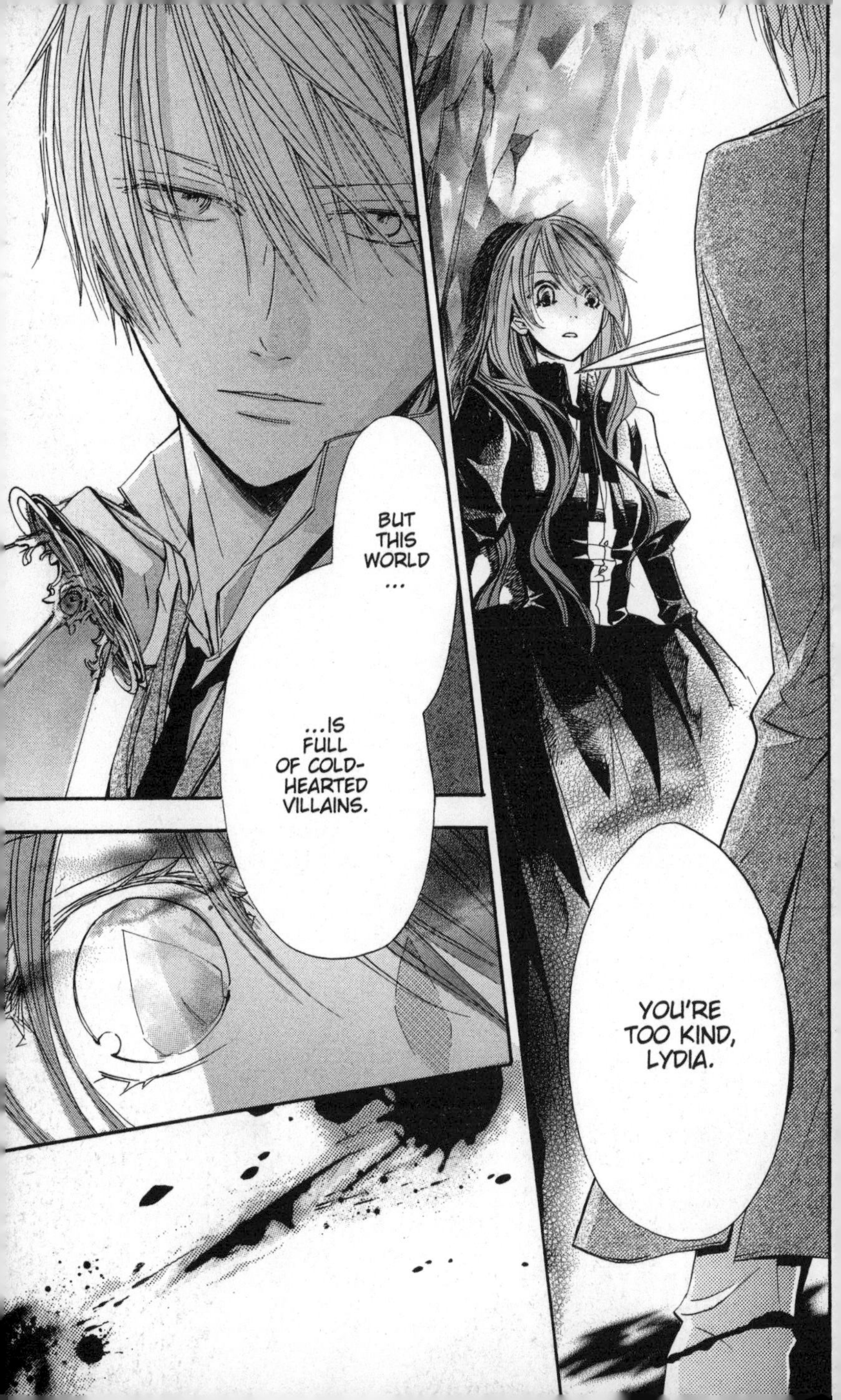
BUT THIS WORLD ...
...IS FULL OF COLD-HEARTED VILLAINS.
YOU'RE TOO KIND, LYDIA.

The Earl & the Fairy

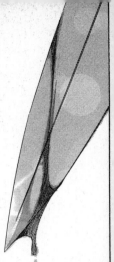

PLIP

...

EDGAR
...?

WHY
IS IT
...

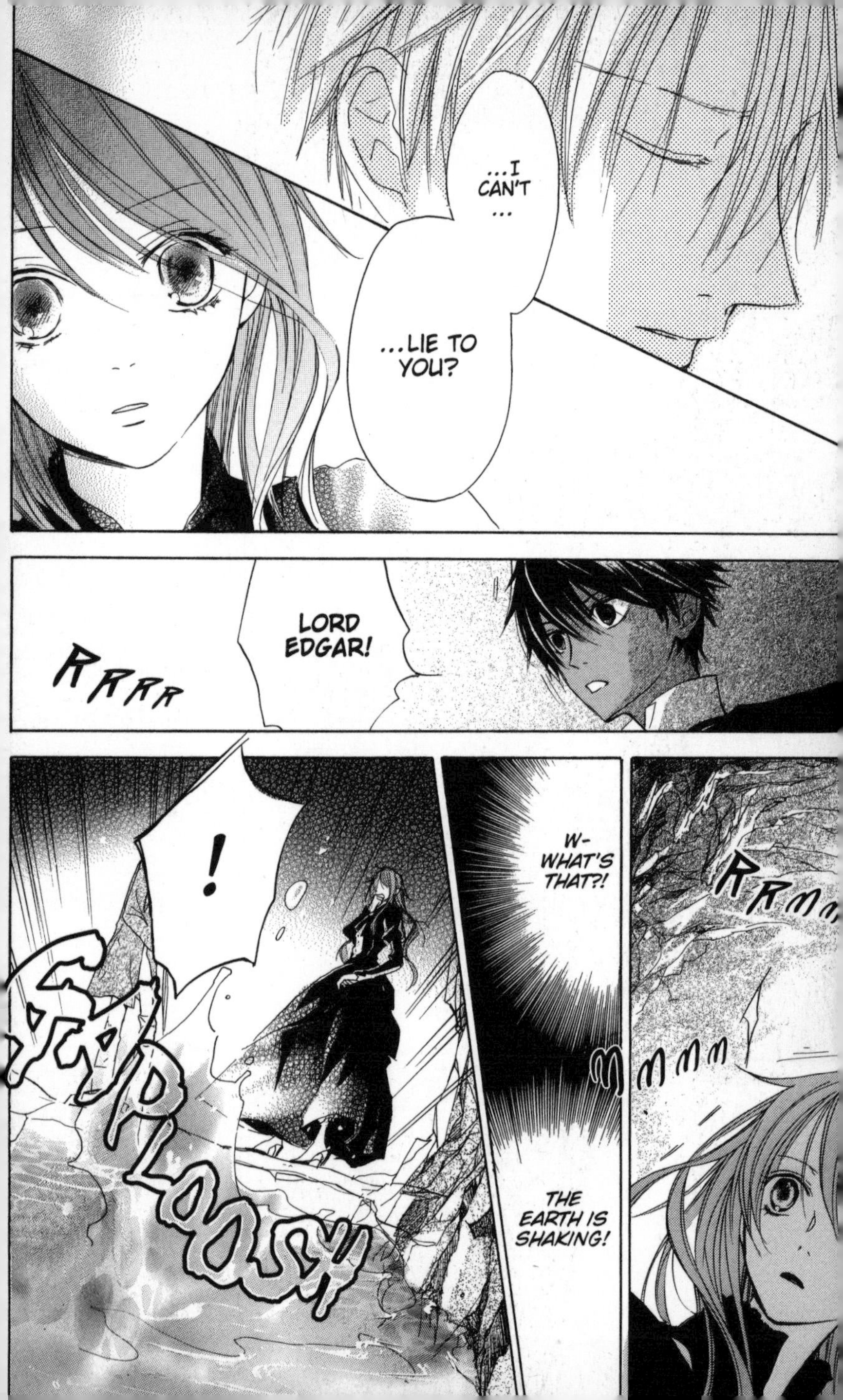
...I CAN'T ...
...LIE TO YOU?
LORD EDGAR!
RRRRR
RRmmm
mmmm
W- WHAT'S THAT?!
THE EARTH IS SHAKING!
!
SPLOOSH

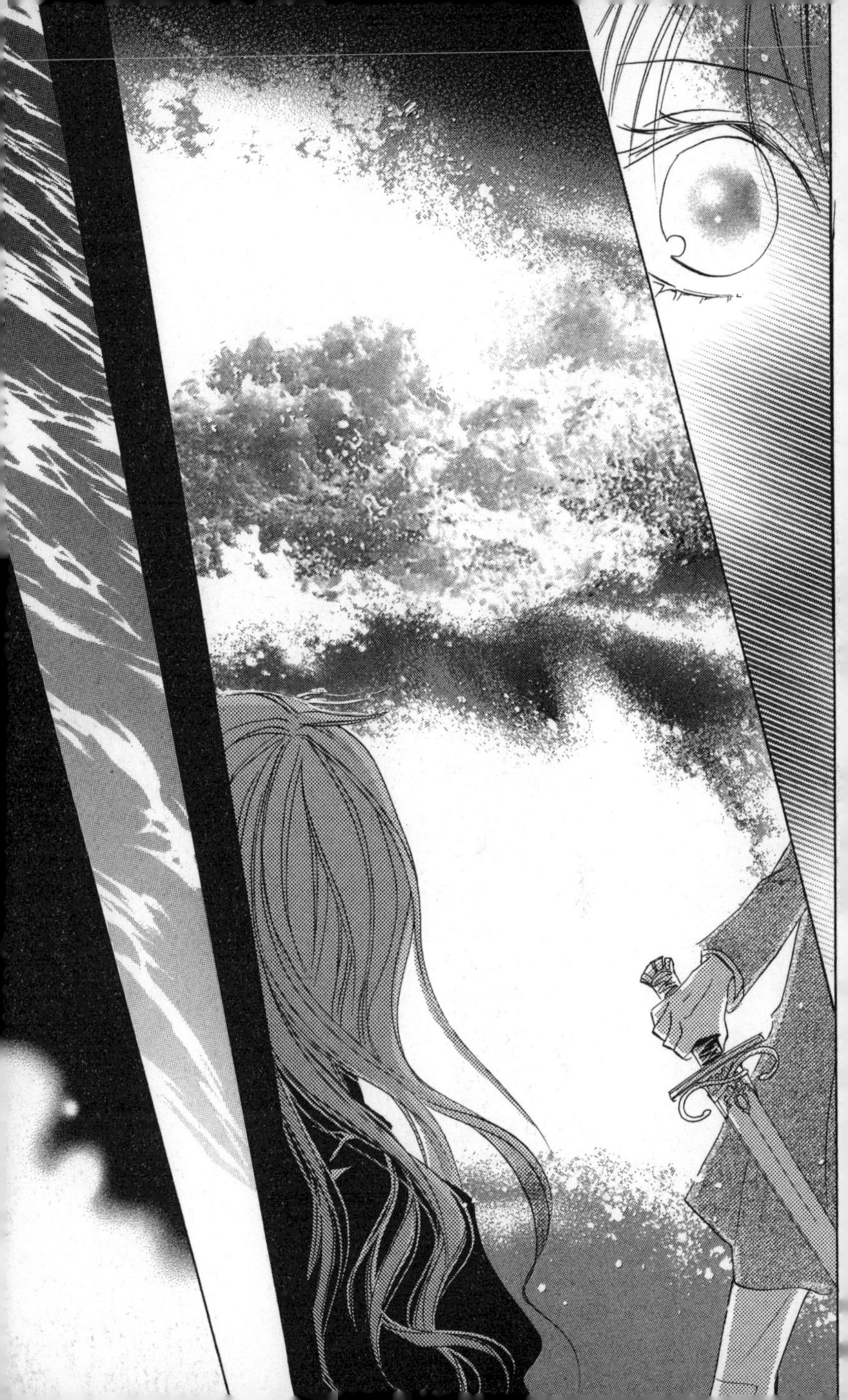

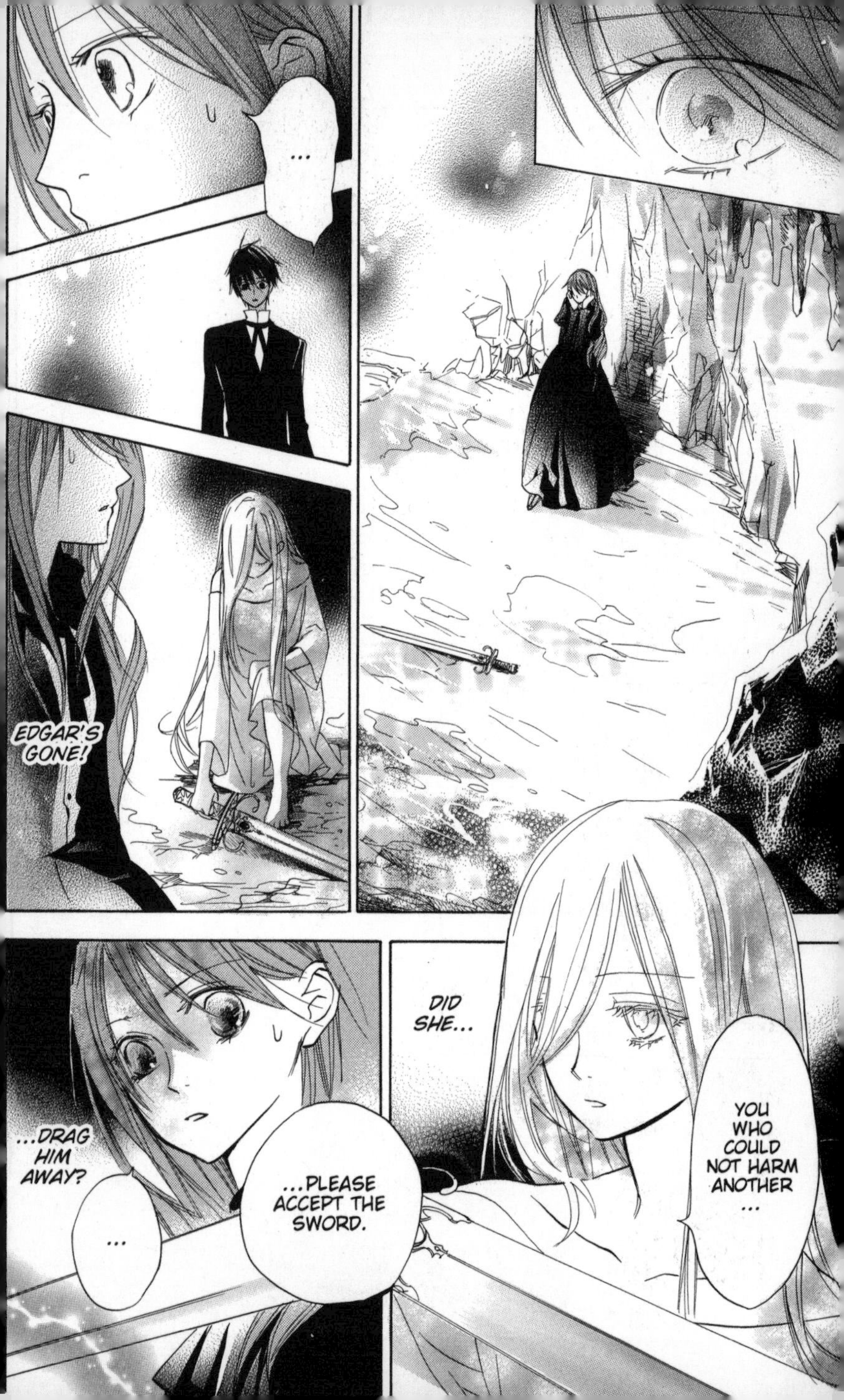
...
EDGAR'S GONE!
DID SHE...
YOU WHO COULD NOT HARM ANOTHER ...
...PLEASE ACCEPT THE SWORD.
...
...DRAG HIM AWAY?

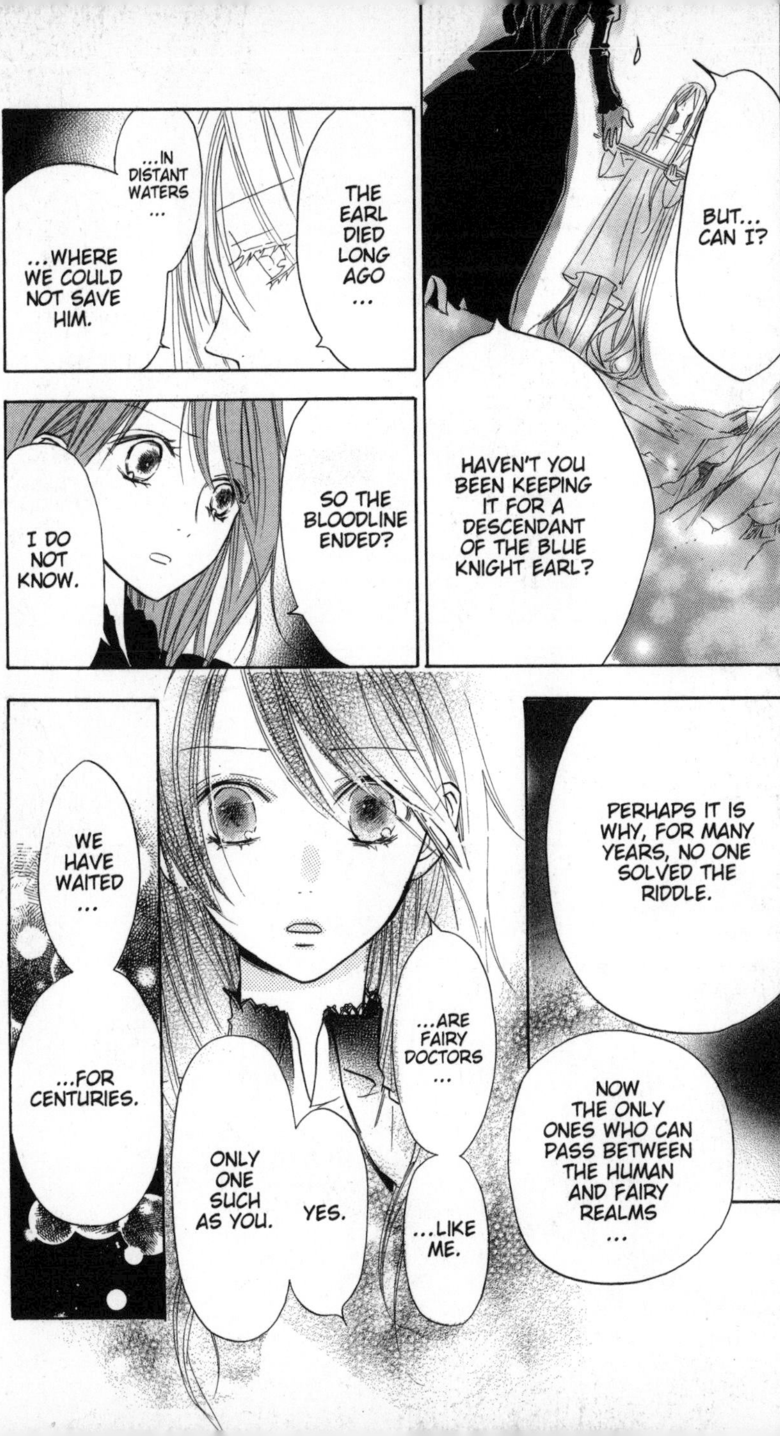
BUT... CAN I?
HAVEN'T YOU BEEN KEEPING IT FOR A DESCENDANT OF THE BLUE KNIGHT EARL?
THE EARL DIED LONG AGO...
...IN DISTANT WATERS...
...WHERE WE COULD NOT SAVE HIM.
SO THE BLOODLINE ENDED?
I DO NOT KNOW.
PERHAPS IT IS WHY, FOR MANY YEARS, NO ONE SOLVED THE RIDDLE.
NOW THE ONLY ONES WHO CAN PASS BETWEEN THE HUMAN AND FAIRY REALMS...
...ARE FAIRY DOCTORS...
...LIKE ME.
YES.
ONLY ONE SUCH AS YOU.
WE HAVE WAITED...
...FOR CENTURIES.

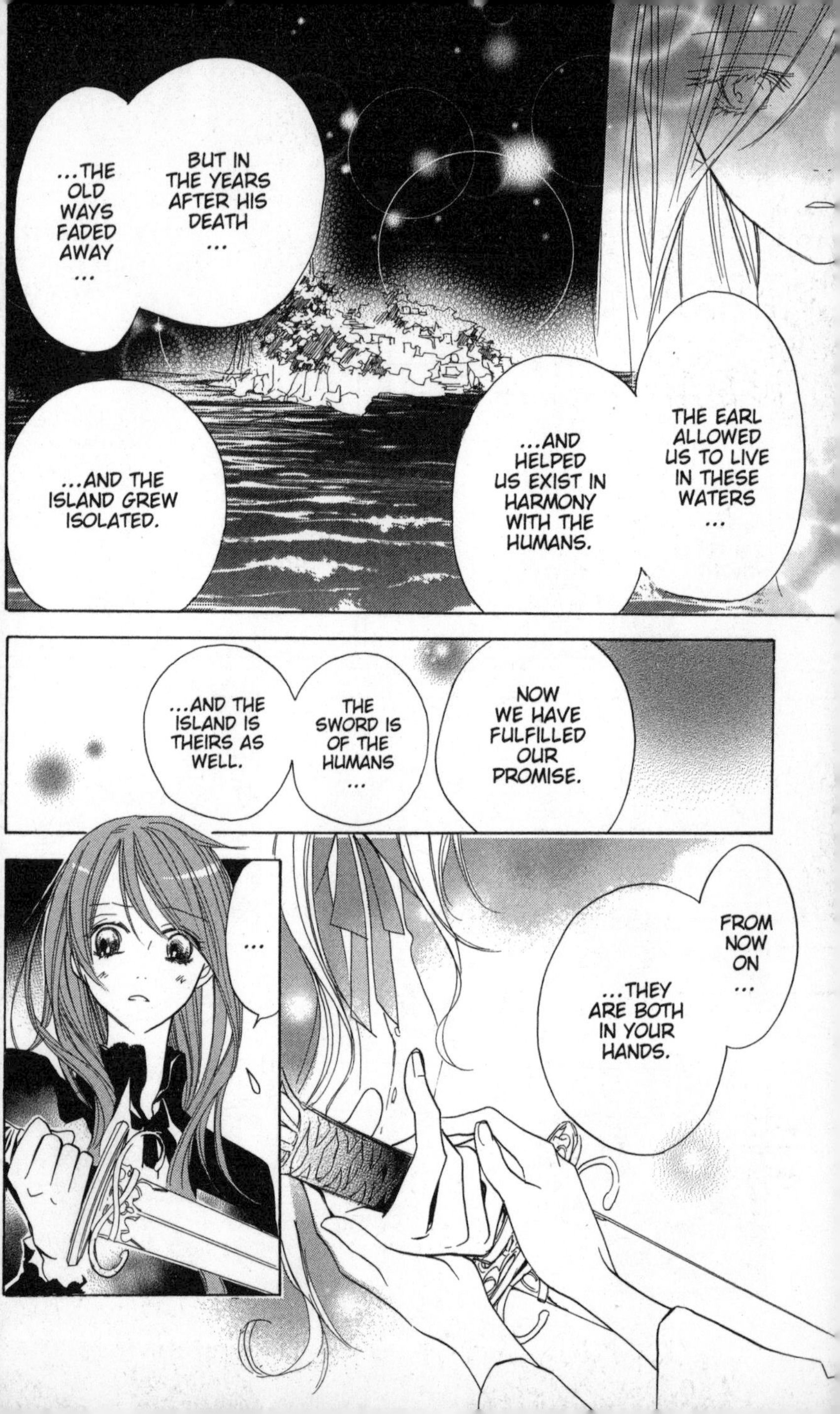
THE EARL ALLOWED US TO LIVE IN THESE WATERS...
...AND HELPED US EXIST IN HARMONY WITH THE HUMANS.
BUT IN THE YEARS AFTER HIS DEATH...
...THE OLD WAYS FADED AWAY...
...AND THE ISLAND GREW ISOLATED.
NOW WE HAVE FULFILLED OUR PROMISE.
THE SWORD IS OF THE HUMANS...
...AND THE ISLAND IS THEIRS AS WELL.
FROM NOW ON...
...THEY ARE BOTH IN YOUR HANDS.
...

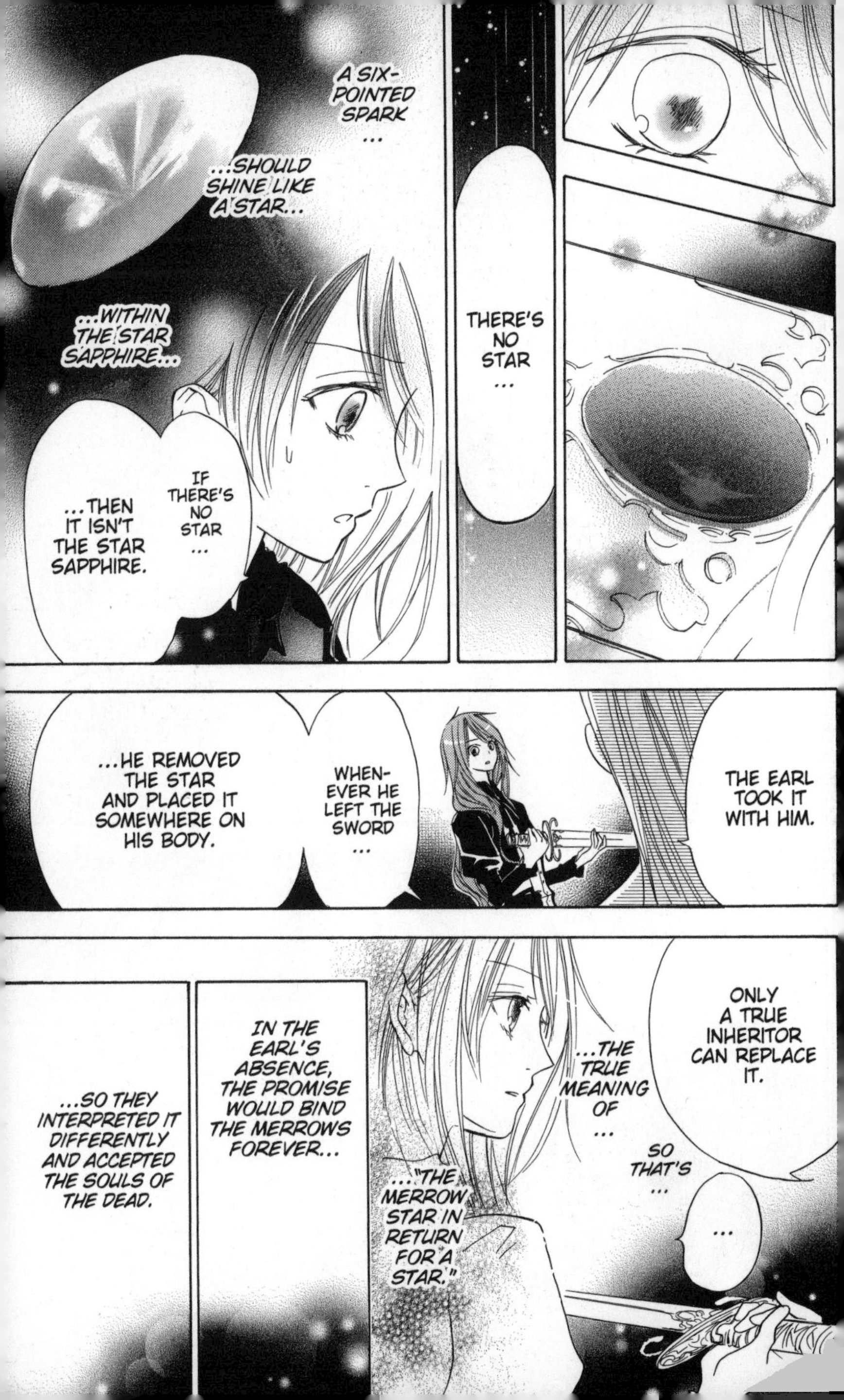
THERE'S NO STAR...
A SIX-POINTED SPARK...
...SHOULD SHINE LIKE A STAR...
...WITHIN THE STAR SAPPHIRE...
IF THERE'S NO STAR...
...THEN IT ISN'T THE STAR SAPPHIRE.
THE EARL TOOK IT WITH HIM.
WHENEVER HE LEFT THE SWORD...
...HE REMOVED THE STAR AND PLACED IT SOMEWHERE ON HIS BODY.
ONLY A TRUE INHERITOR CAN REPLACE IT.
SO THAT'S...
...
...THE TRUE MEANING OF...
..."THE MERROW STAR IN RETURN FOR A STAR."
IN THE EARL'S ABSENCE, THE PROMISE WOULD BIND THE MERROWS FOREVER...
...SO THEY INTERPRETED IT DIFFERENTLY AND ACCEPTED THE SOULS OF THE DEAD.

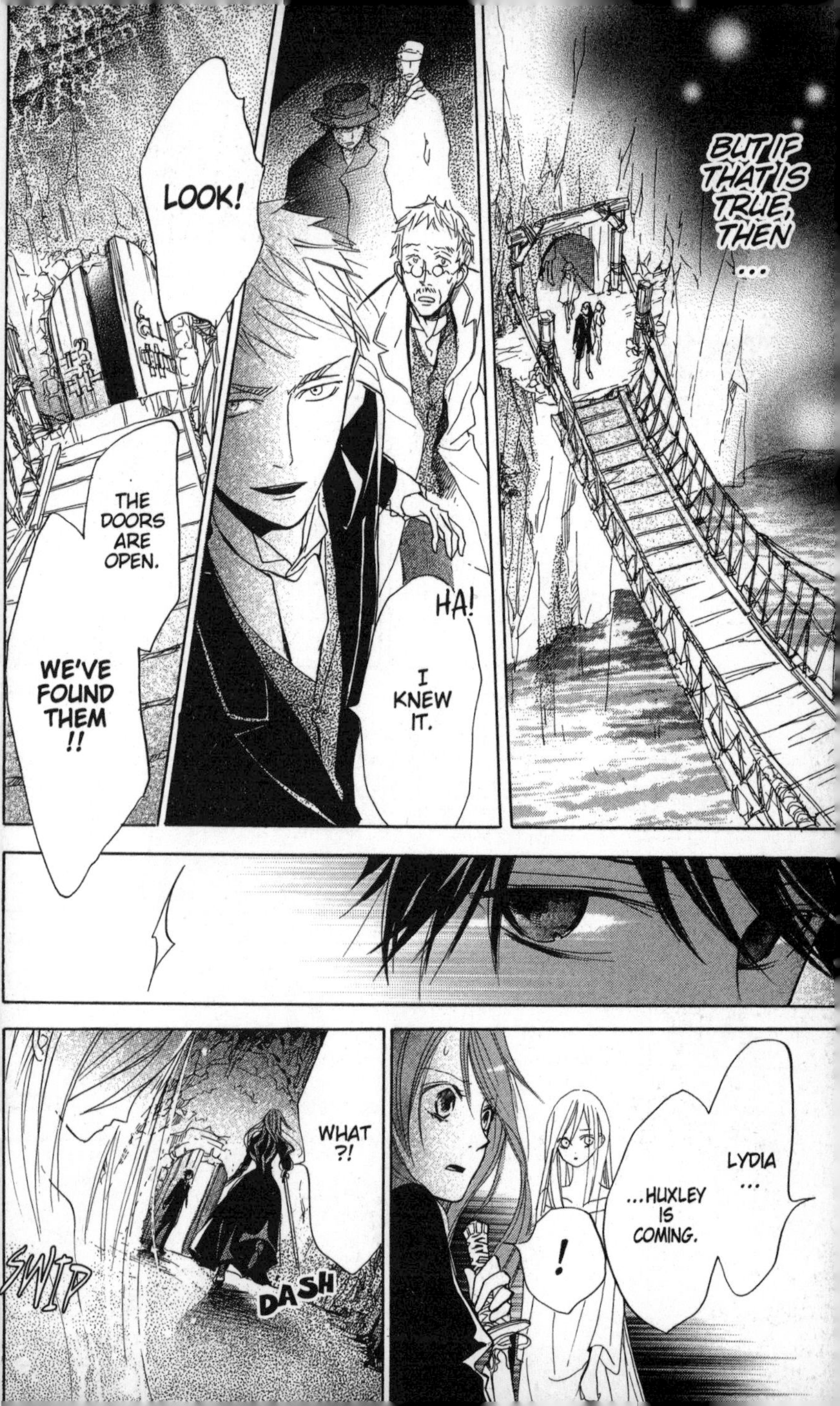
BUT IF THAT IS TRUE, THEN ...
HA!
I KNEW IT.
LOOK!
THE DOORS ARE OPEN.
WE'VE FOUND THEM !!
LYDIA ...
...HUXLEY IS COMING.
!
WHAT ?!
DASH
SWIP

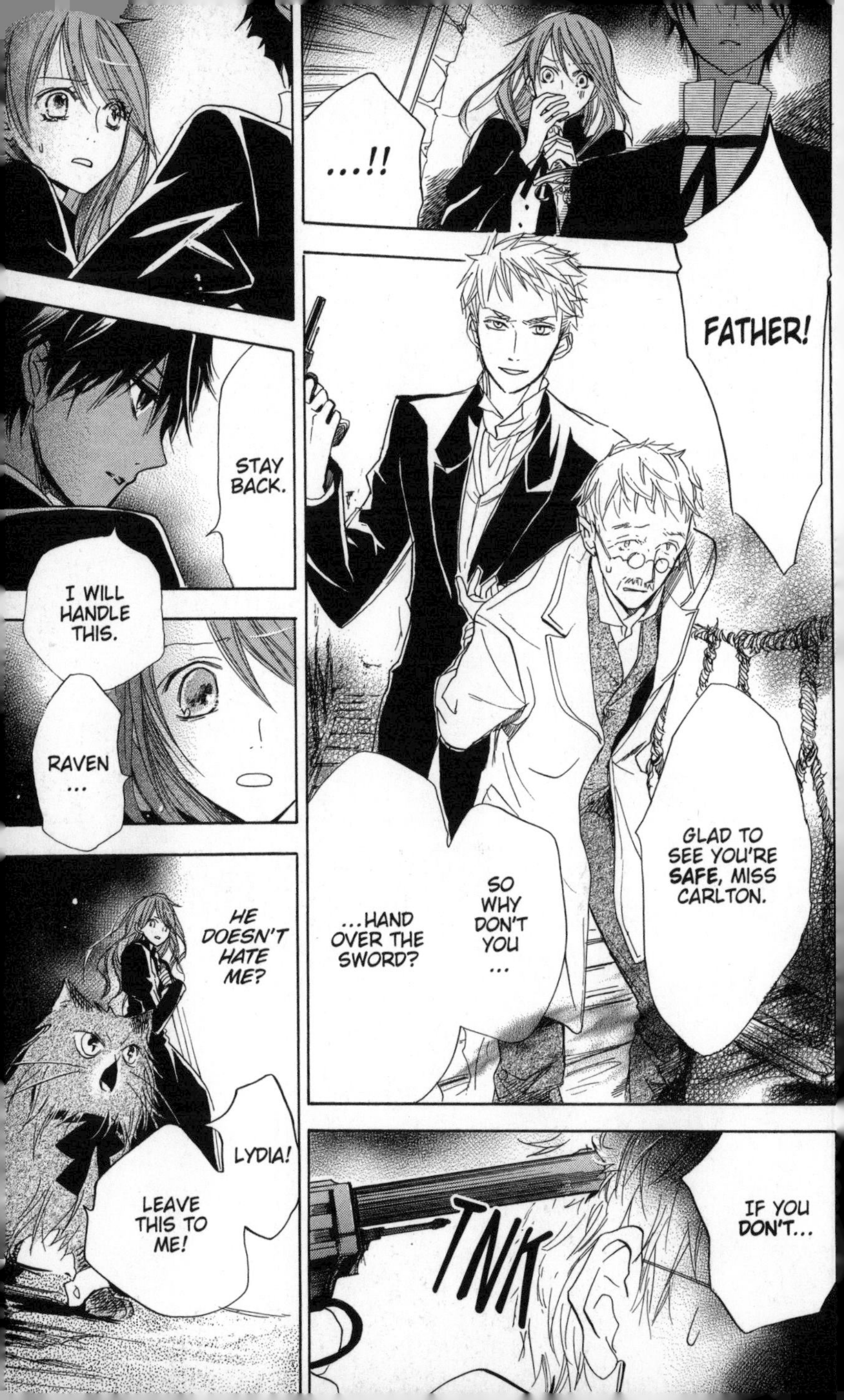
...!!
FATHER!
GLAD TO SEE YOU'RE SAFE, MISS CARLTON.
SO WHY DON'T YOU ...
...HAND OVER THE SWORD?
TNK
IF YOU DON'T...
STAY BACK.
I WILL HANDLE THIS.
RAVEN ...
HE DOESN'T HATE ME?
LYDIA!
LEAVE THIS TO ME!

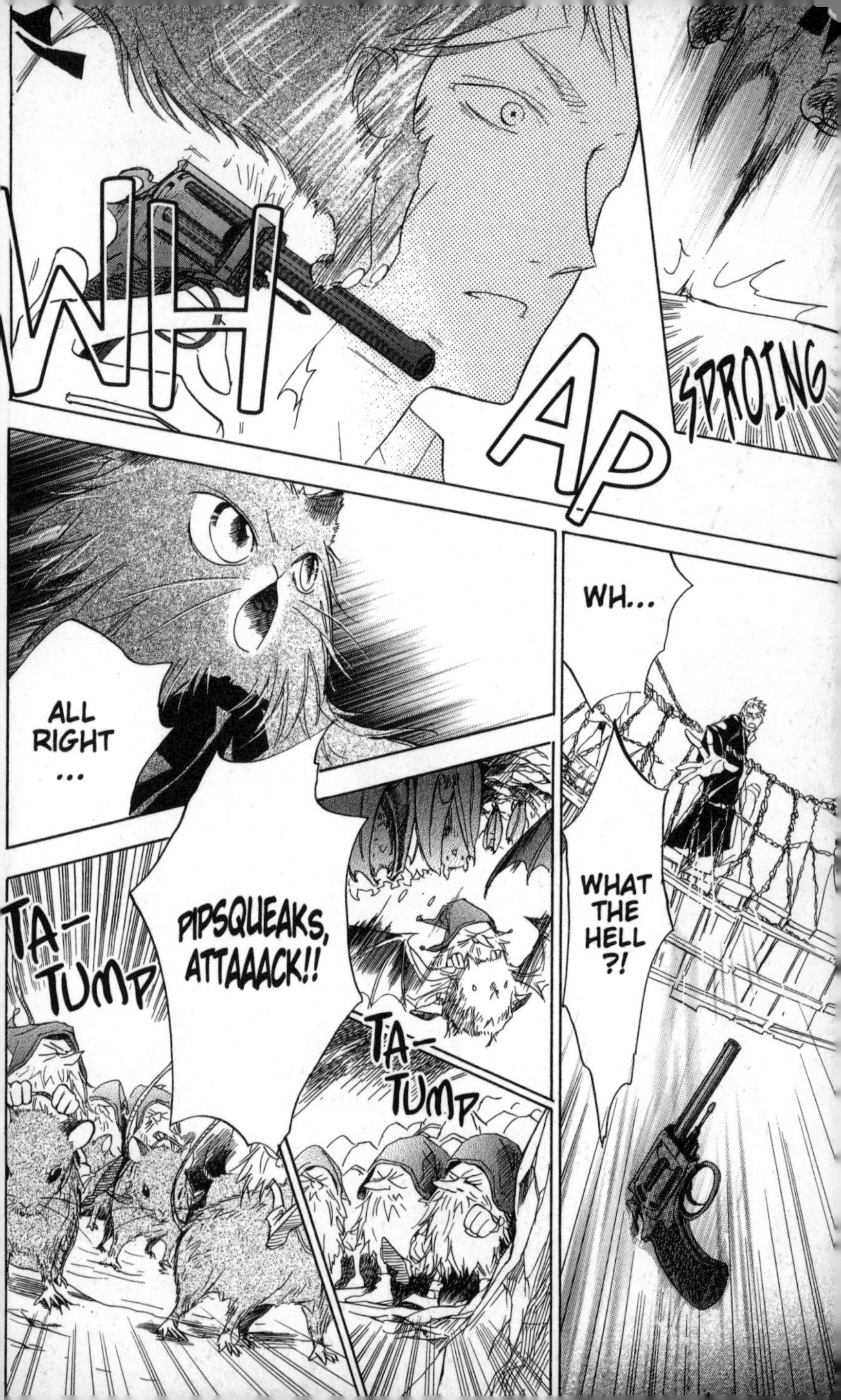
SPROING
WHAP
WH...
WHAT THE HELL ?!
ALL RIGHT ...
PIPSQUEAKS, ATTAAACK!!
TA-TUMP
TA-TUMP

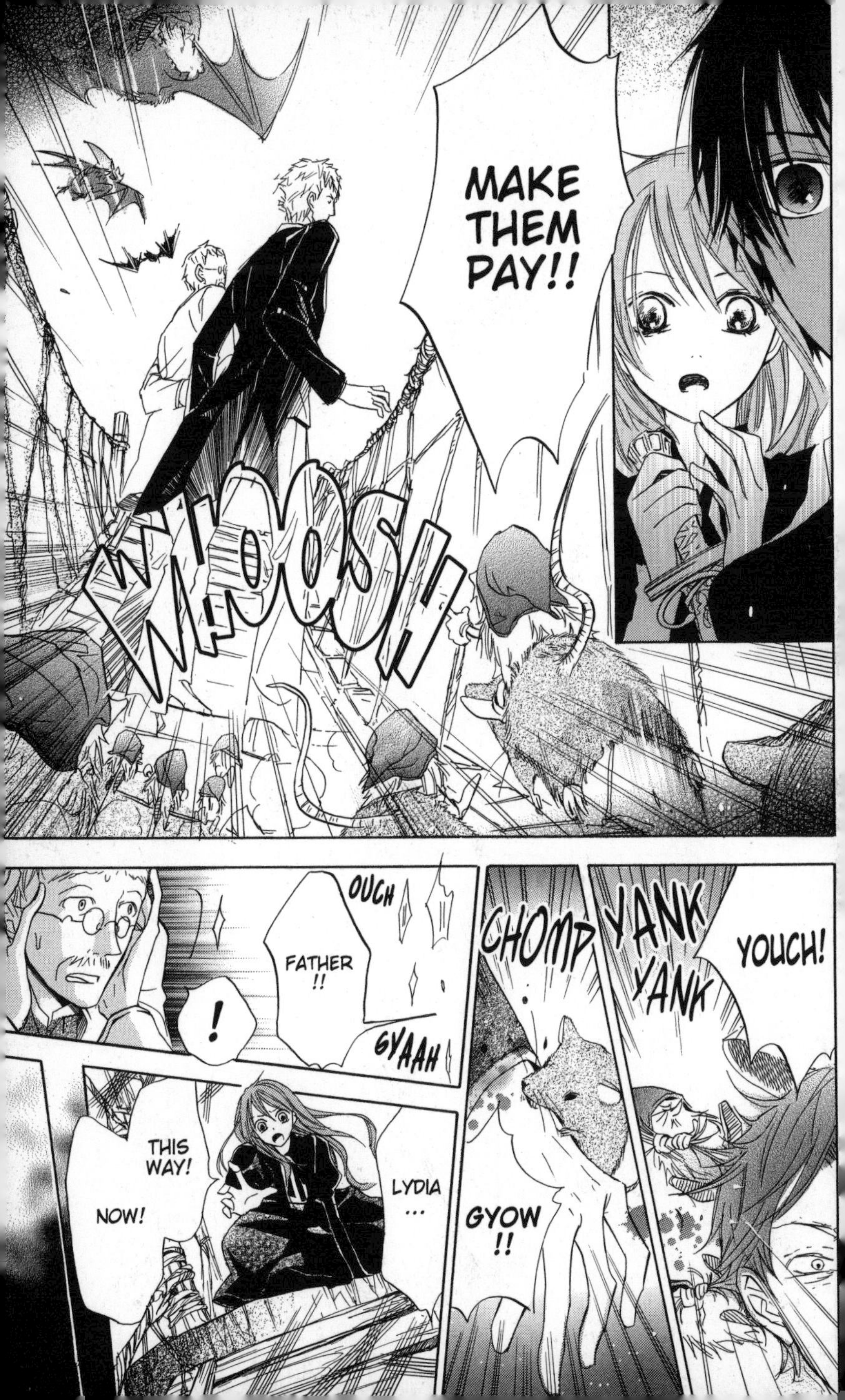
MAKE THEM PAY!!
WHOOSH
YOUCH!
YANK
YANK
CHOMP
GYOW!!
OUCH
FATHER!!
GYAAH
!
LYDIA...
THIS WAY!
NOW!

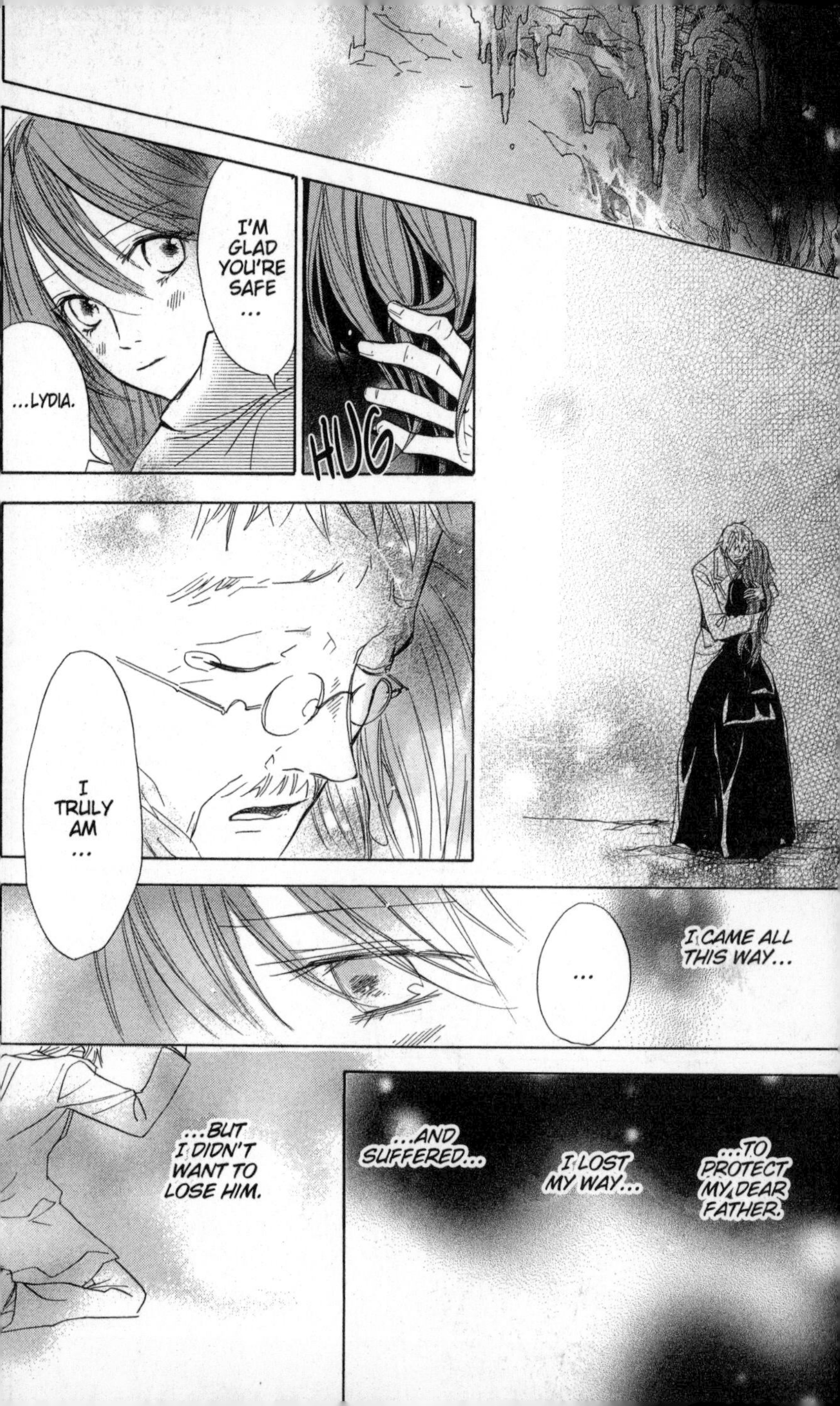
HUG
I'M GLAD YOU'RE SAFE...
...LYDIA.
I TRULY AM...
I CAME ALL THIS WAY...
...
...TO PROTECT MY DEAR FATHER.
I LOST MY WAY...
...AND SUFFERED...
...BUT I DIDN'T WANT TO LOSE HIM.

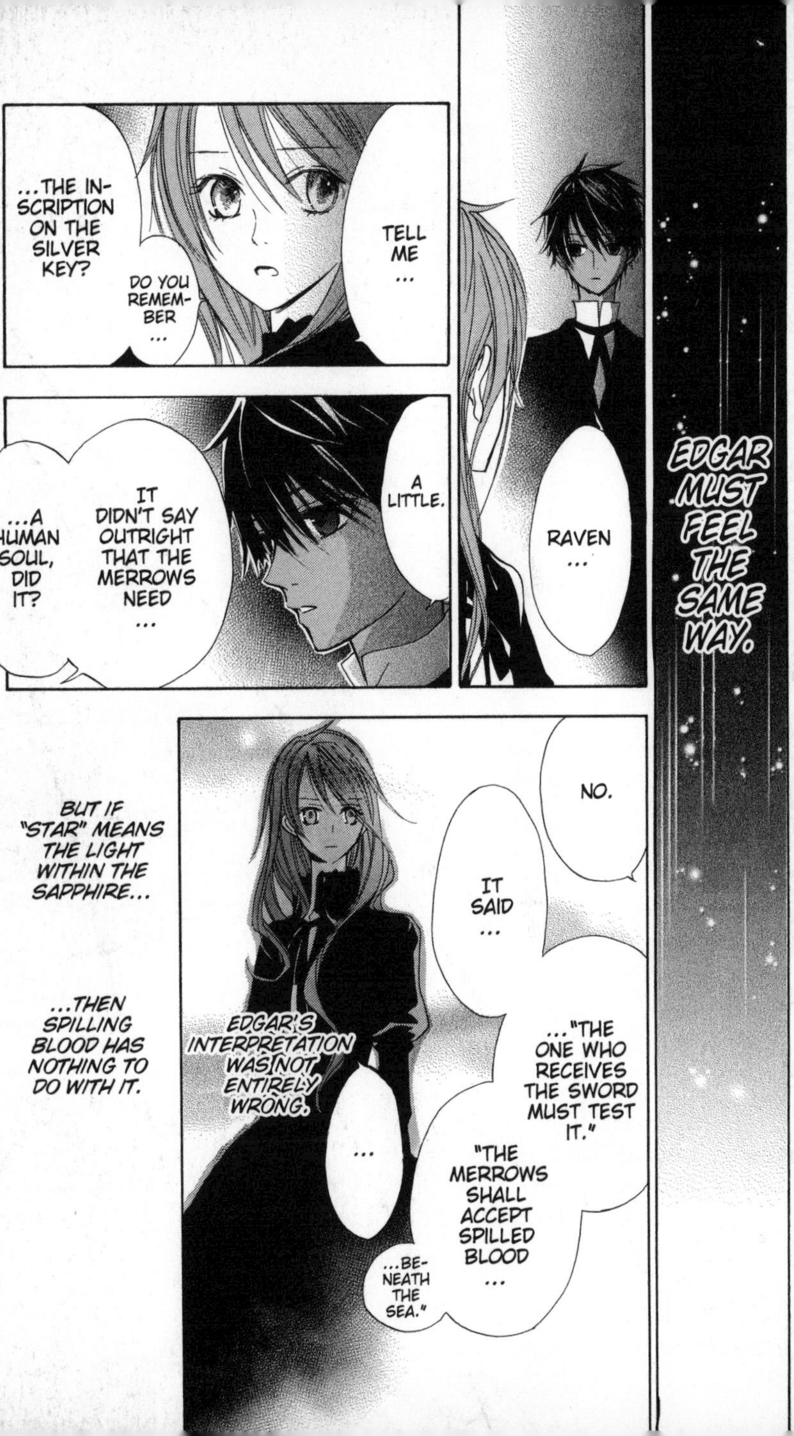
EDGAR MUST FEEL THE SAME WAY.
RAVEN ...
TELL ME ...
DO YOU REMEMBER ...
...THE INSCRIPTION ON THE SILVER KEY?
A LITTLE.
IT DIDN'T SAY OUTRIGHT THAT THE MERROWS NEED ...
...A HUMAN SOUL, DID IT?
NO.
IT SAID ...
..."THE ONE WHO RECEIVES THE SWORD MUST TEST IT."
"THE MERROWS SHALL ACCEPT SPILLED BLOOD ...
...BENEATH THE SEA."
...
EDGAR'S INTERPRETATION WAS NOT ENTIRELY WRONG.
BUT IF "STAR" MEANS THE LIGHT WITHIN THE SAPPHIRE...
...THEN SPILLING BLOOD HAS NOTHING TO DO WITH IT.

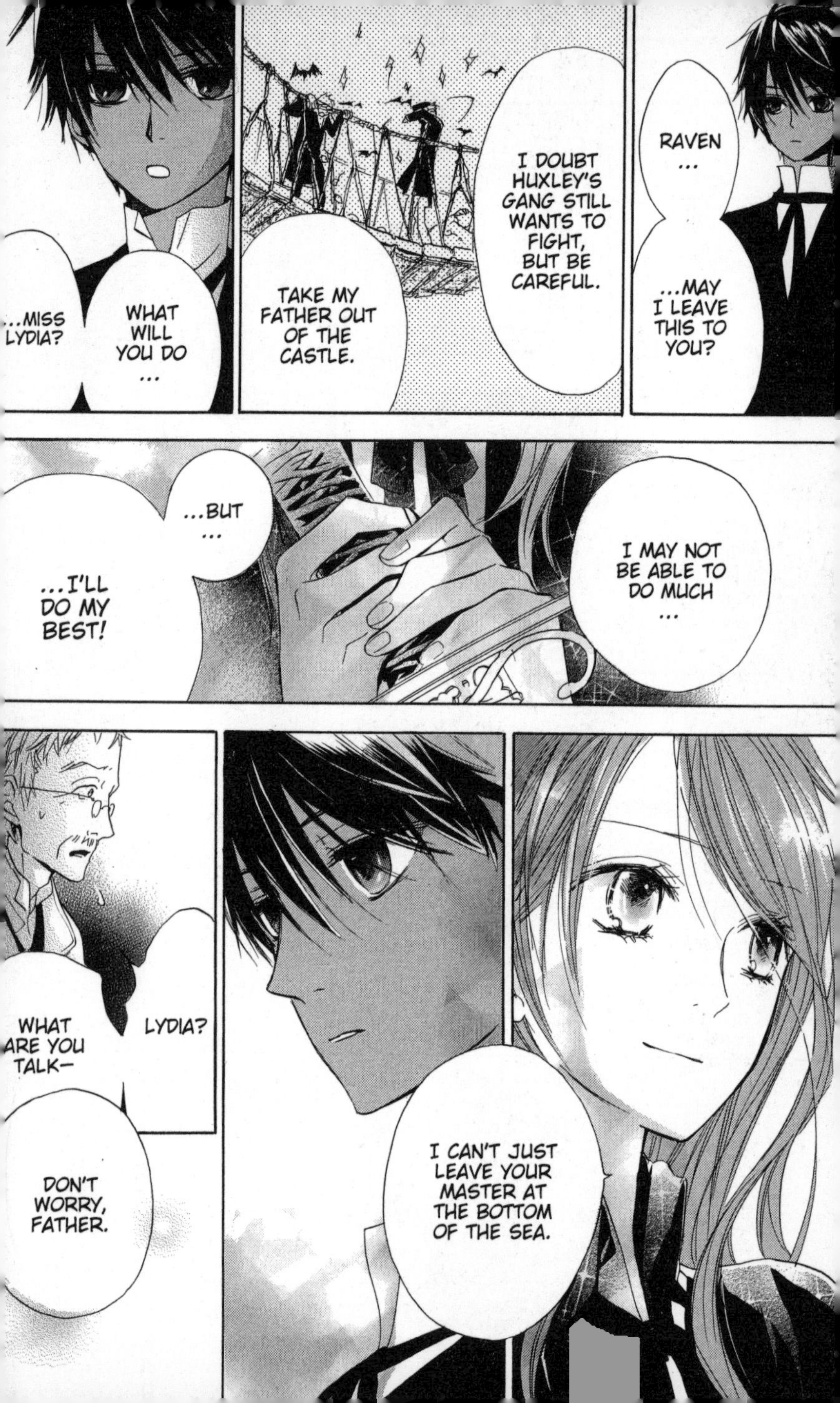
RAVEN ...
...MAY I LEAVE THIS TO YOU?
I DOUBT HUXLEY'S GANG STILL WANTS TO FIGHT, BUT BE CAREFUL.
TAKE MY FATHER OUT OF THE CASTLE.
WHAT WILL YOU DO ...
...MISS LYDIA?
I MAY NOT BE ABLE TO DO MUCH ...
...BUT ...
...I'LL DO MY BEST!
I CAN'T JUST LEAVE YOUR MASTER AT THE BOTTOM OF THE SEA.
LYDIA?
WHAT ARE YOU TALK—
DON'T WORRY, FATHER.

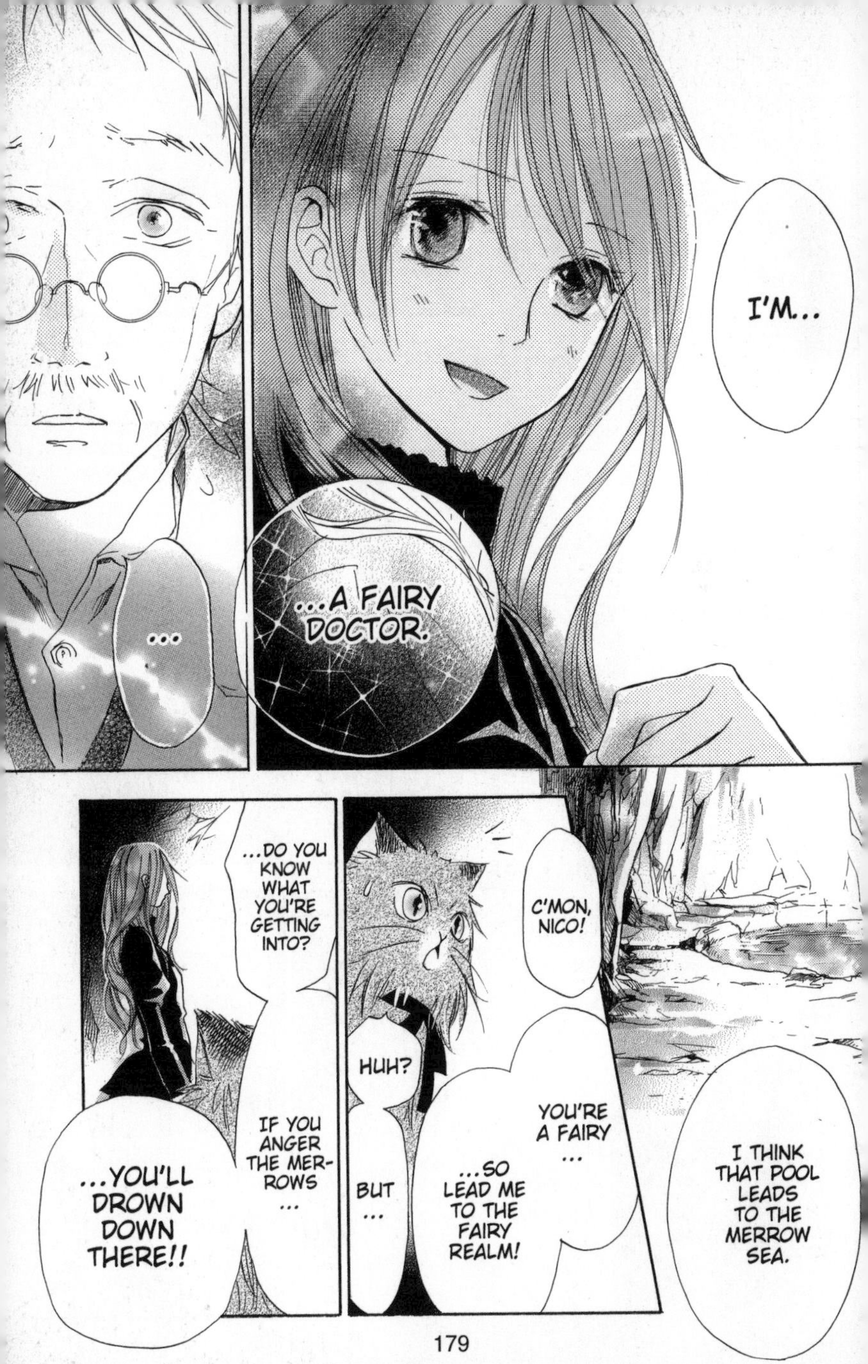
I'M...
...A FAIRY DOCTOR.
...
C'MON, NICO!
I THINK THAT POOL LEADS TO THE MERROW SEA.
YOU'RE A FAIRY ...
...SO LEAD ME TO THE FAIRY REALM!
HUH?
BUT ...
...DO YOU KNOW WHAT YOU'RE GETTING INTO?
IF YOU ANGER THE MER-ROWS ...
...YOU'LL DROWN DOWN THERE!!

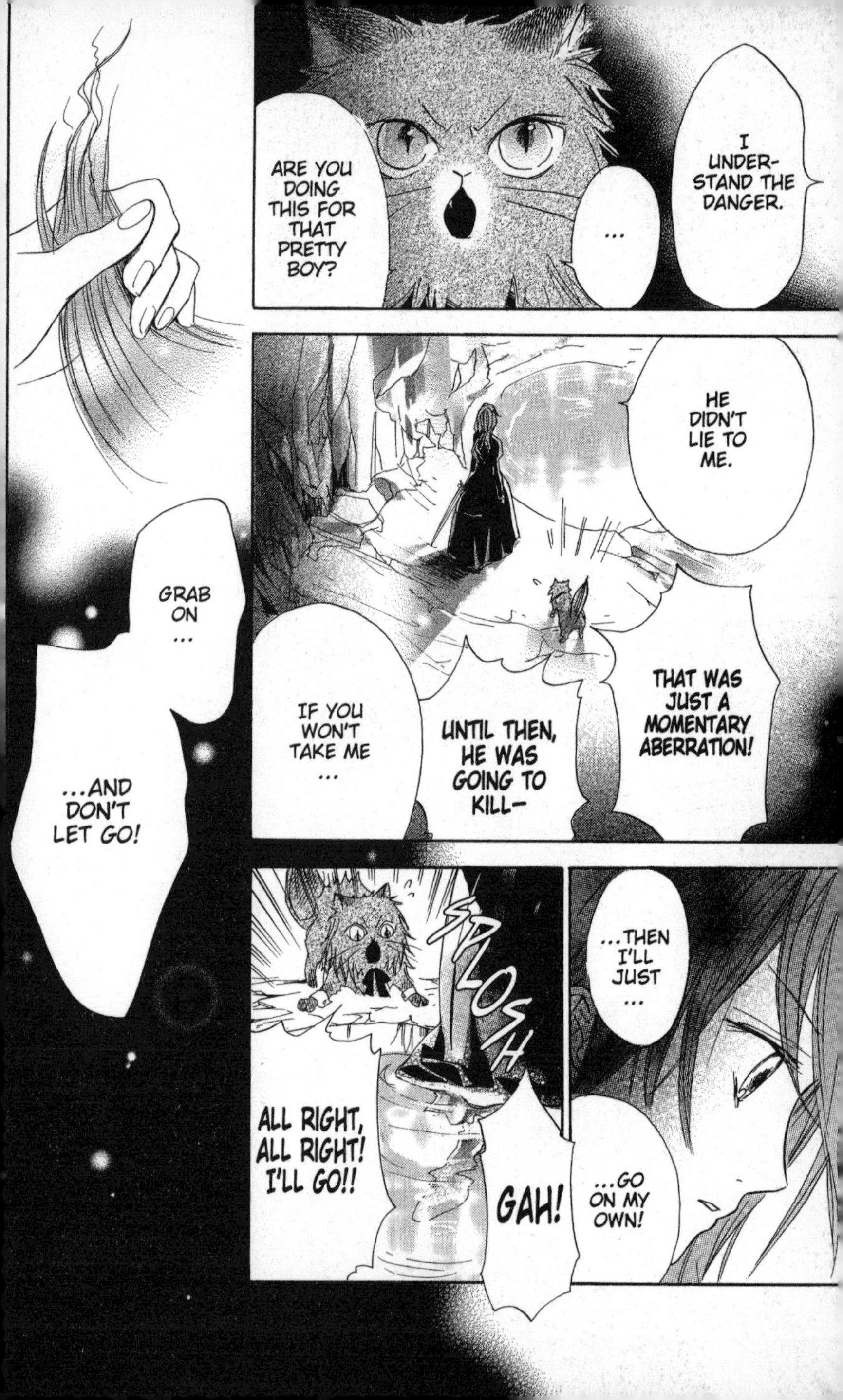
I UNDER-STAND THE DANGER.
...
ARE YOU DOING THIS FOR THAT PRETTY BOY?
HE DIDN'T LIE TO ME.
THAT WAS JUST A MOMENTARY ABERRATION!
UNTIL THEN, HE WAS GOING TO KILL–
IF YOU WON'T TAKE ME ...
...THEN I'LL JUST ...
...GO ON MY OWN!
SPLOSH
GAH!
ALL RIGHT, ALL RIGHT! I'LL GO!!
GRAB ON ...
...AND DON'T LET GO!

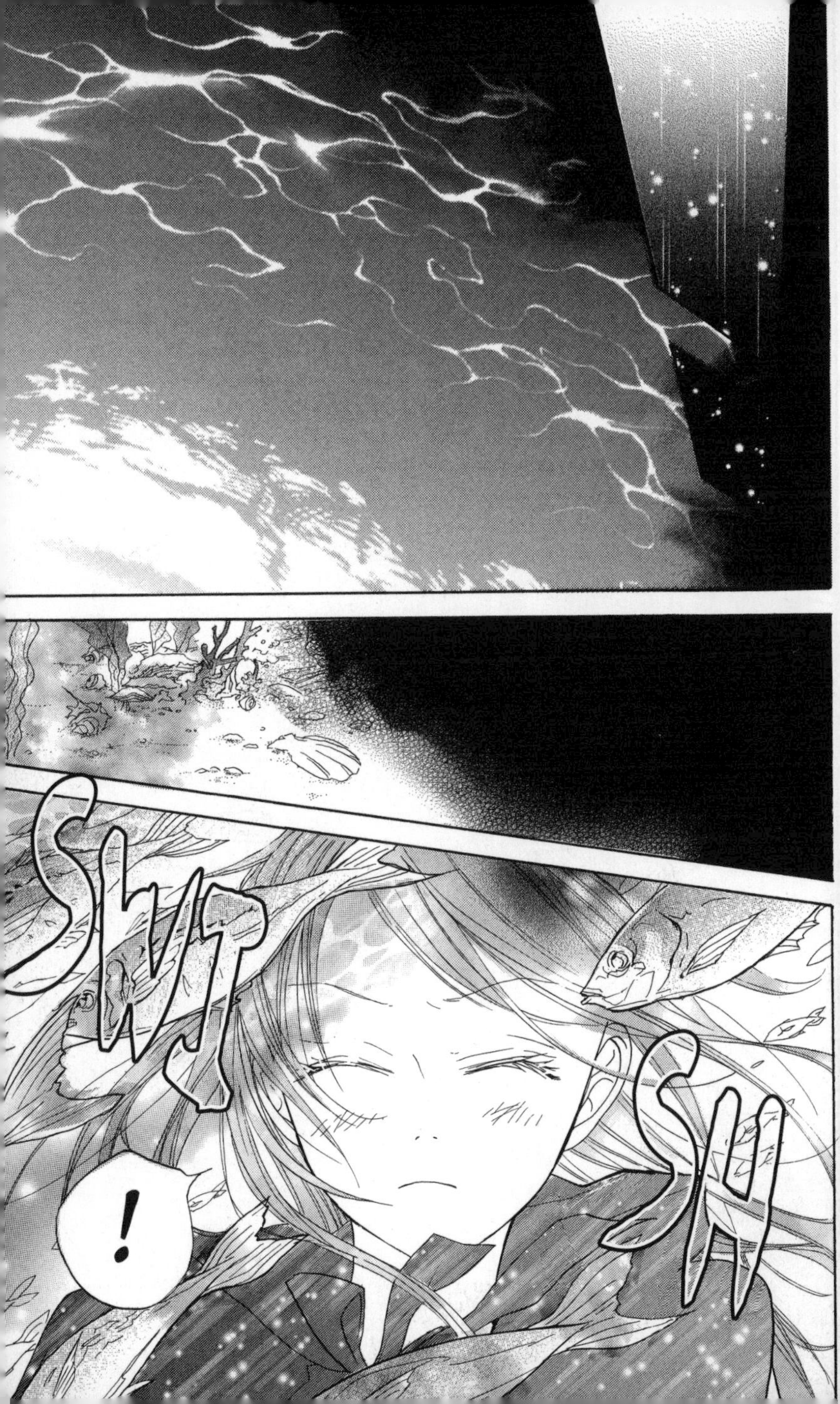
SWISH
!

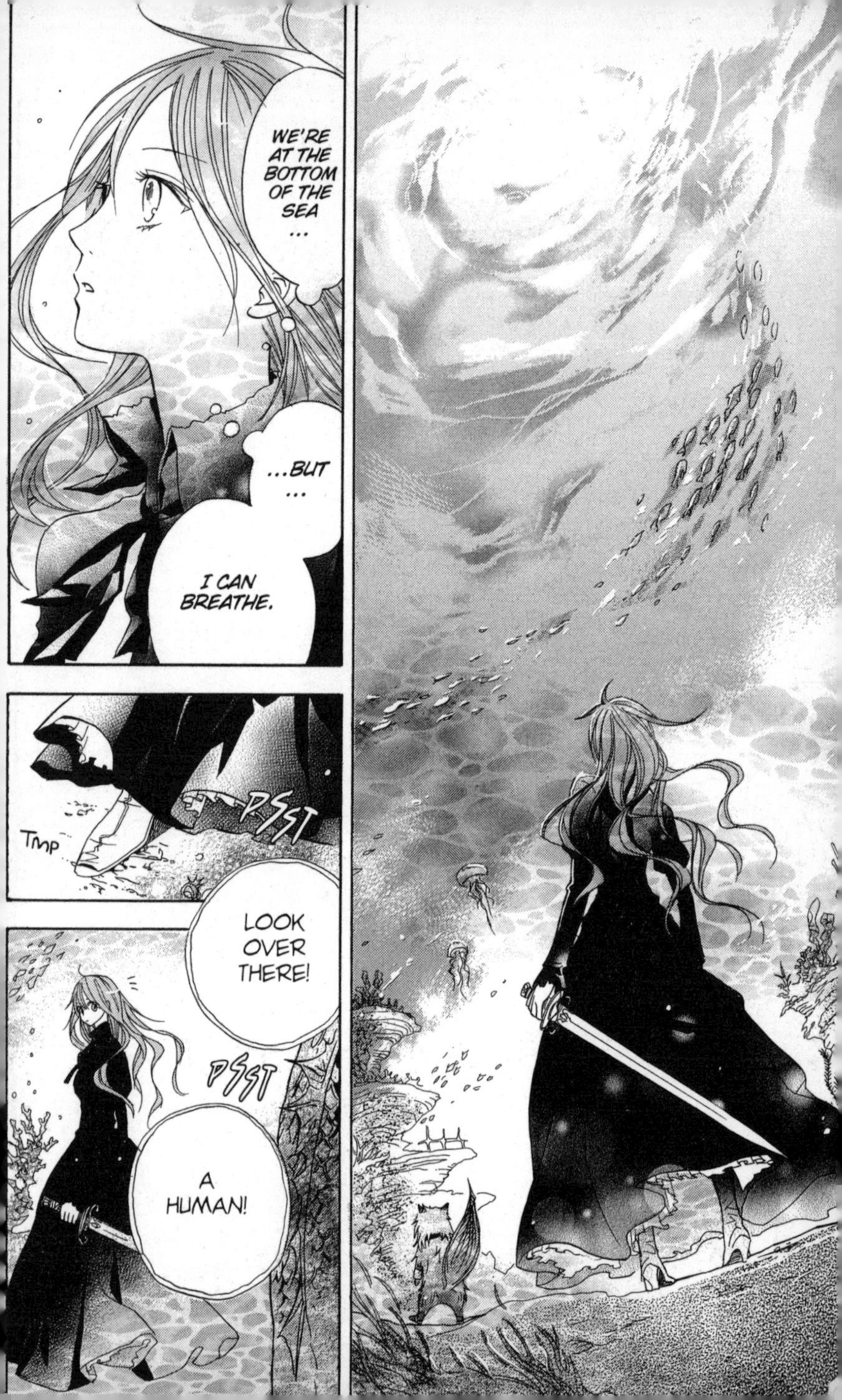
WE'RE AT THE BOTTOM OF THE SEA ...
...BUT ...
I CAN BREATHE.
PSST
Tmp
LOOK OVER THERE!
PSST
A HUMAN!

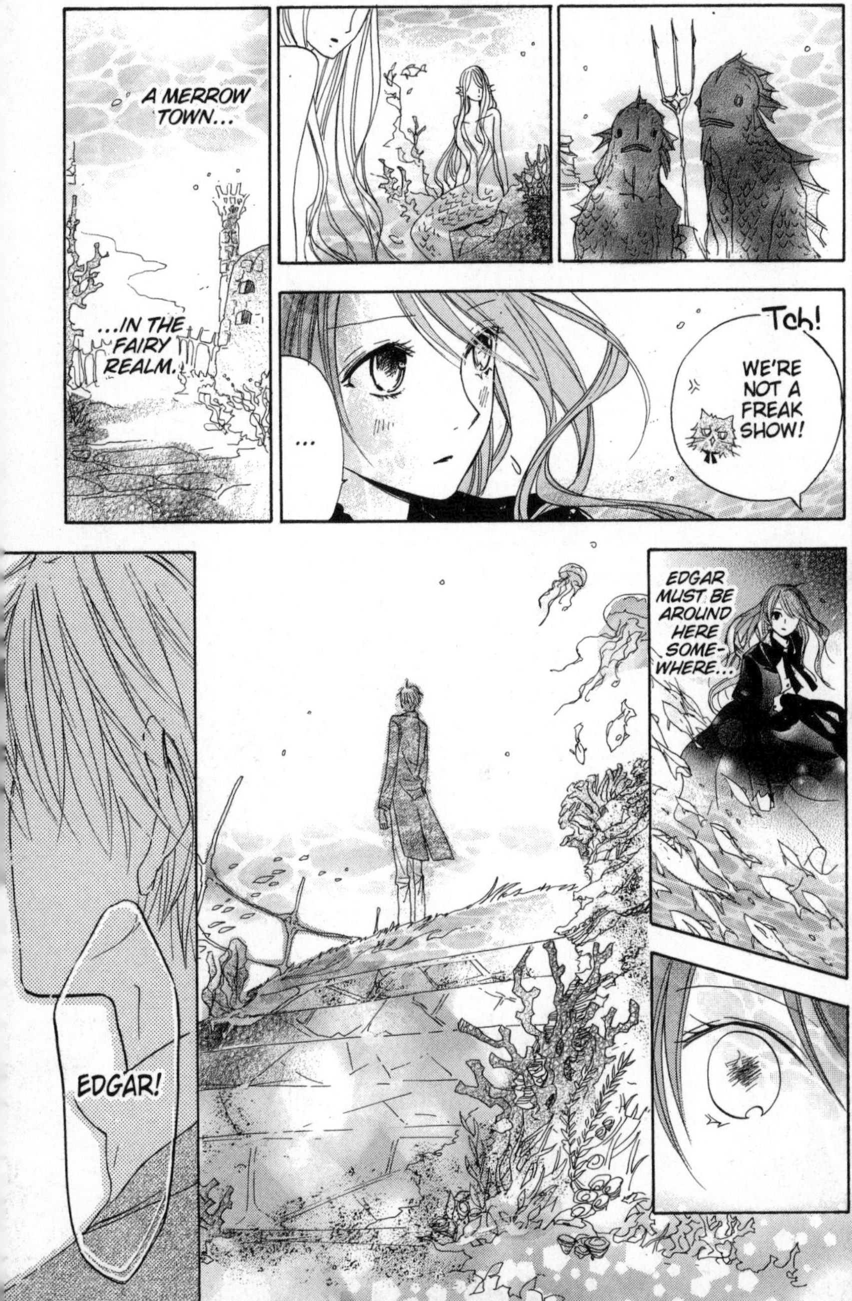
Tch!
WE'RE NOT A FREAK SHOW!
...
A MERROW TOWN...
...IN THE FAIRY REALM.
EDGAR MUST BE AROUND HERE SOME-WHERE...
EDGAR!

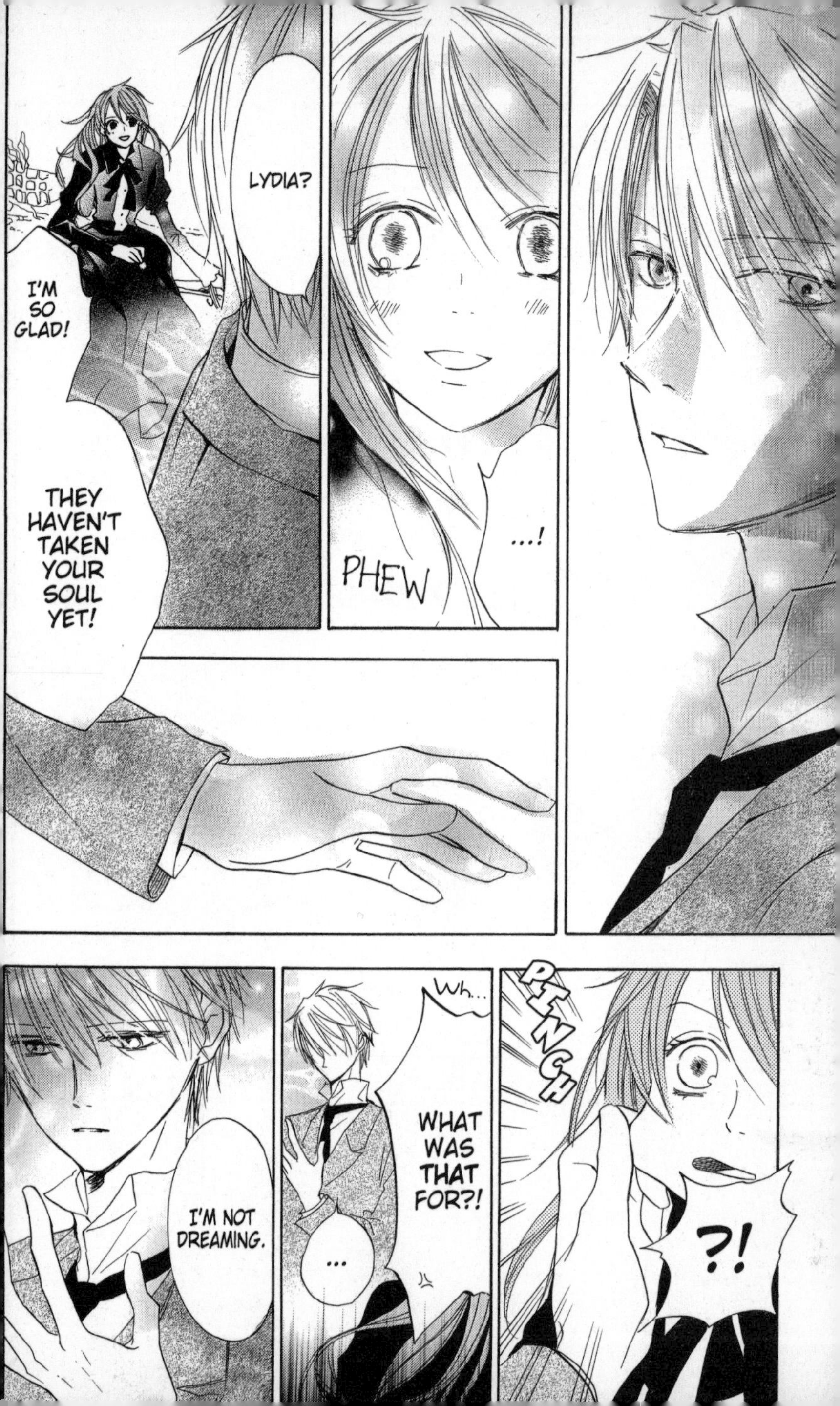
...!
PHEW
LYDIA?
I'M SO GLAD!
THEY HAVEN'T TAKEN YOUR SOUL YET!
PINCH
?!
Wh...
WHAT WAS THAT FOR?!
...
I'M NOT DREAMING.

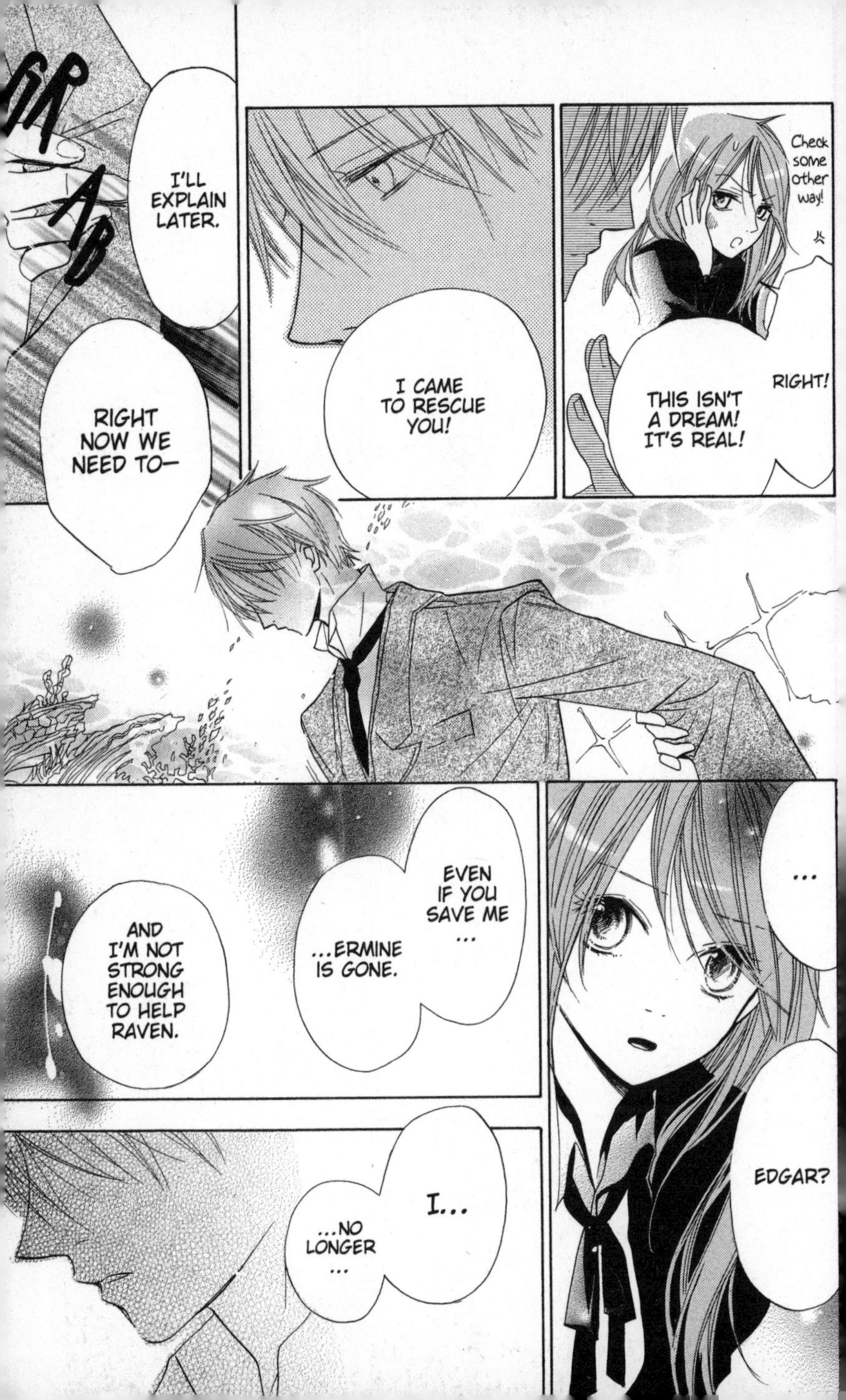
Check some other way!
RIGHT!
THIS ISN'T A DREAM! IT'S REAL!
I CAME TO RESCUE YOU!
GRAB
I'LL EXPLAIN LATER.
RIGHT NOW WE NEED TO—
...
EDGAR?
EVEN IF YOU SAVE ME...
...ERMINE IS GONE.
AND I'M NOT STRONG ENOUGH TO HELP RAVEN.
I...
...NO LONGER...

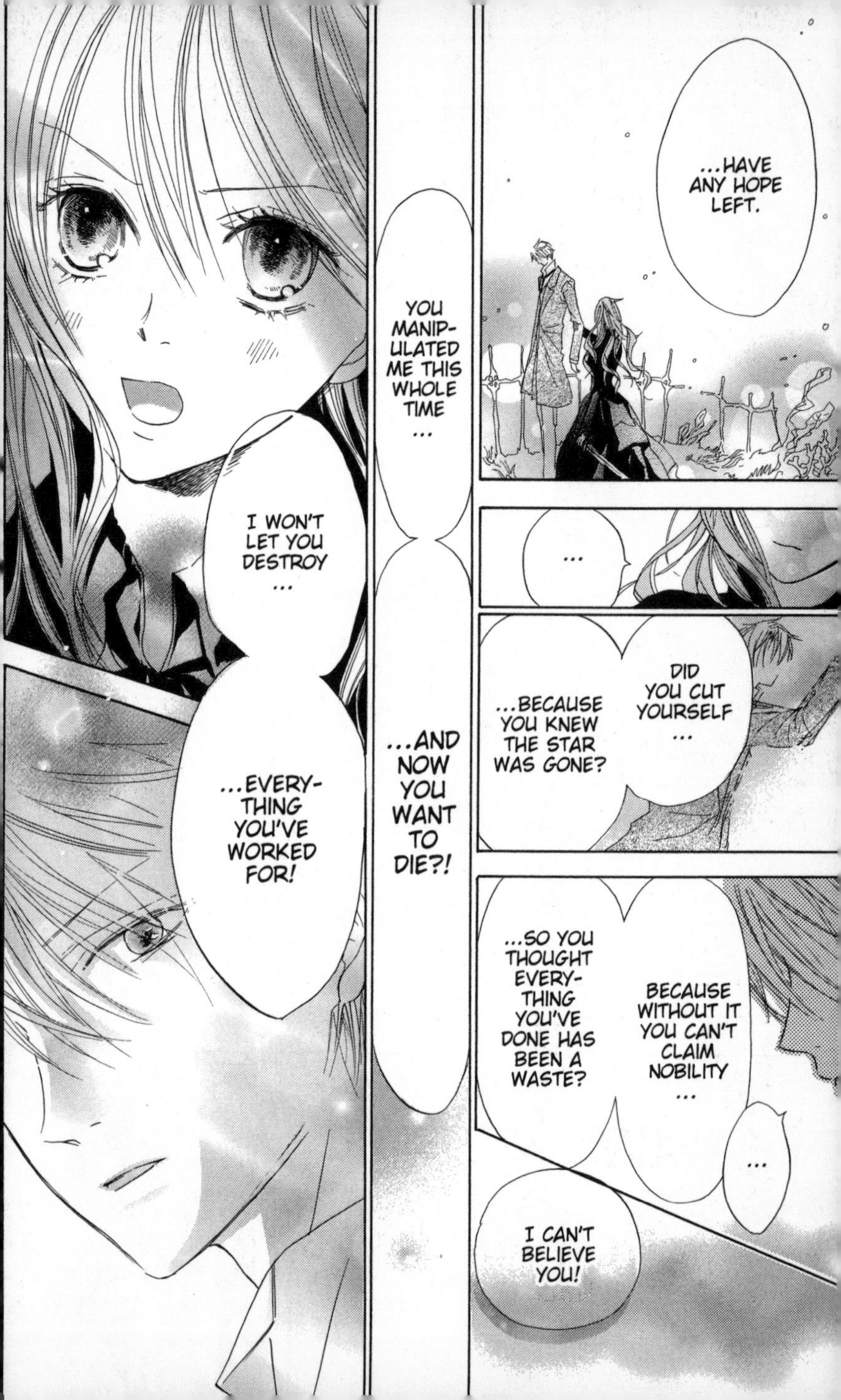
...HAVE ANY HOPE LEFT.
...
DID YOU CUT YOURSELF...
...BECAUSE YOU KNEW THE STAR WAS GONE?
BECAUSE WITHOUT IT YOU CAN'T CLAIM NOBILITY...
...SO YOU THOUGHT EVERYTHING YOU'VE DONE HAS BEEN A WASTE?
...
I CAN'T BELIEVE YOU!
YOU MANIPULATED ME THIS WHOLE TIME...
...AND NOW YOU WANT TO DIE?!
I WON'T LET YOU DESTROY...
...EVERYTHING YOU'VE WORKED FOR!

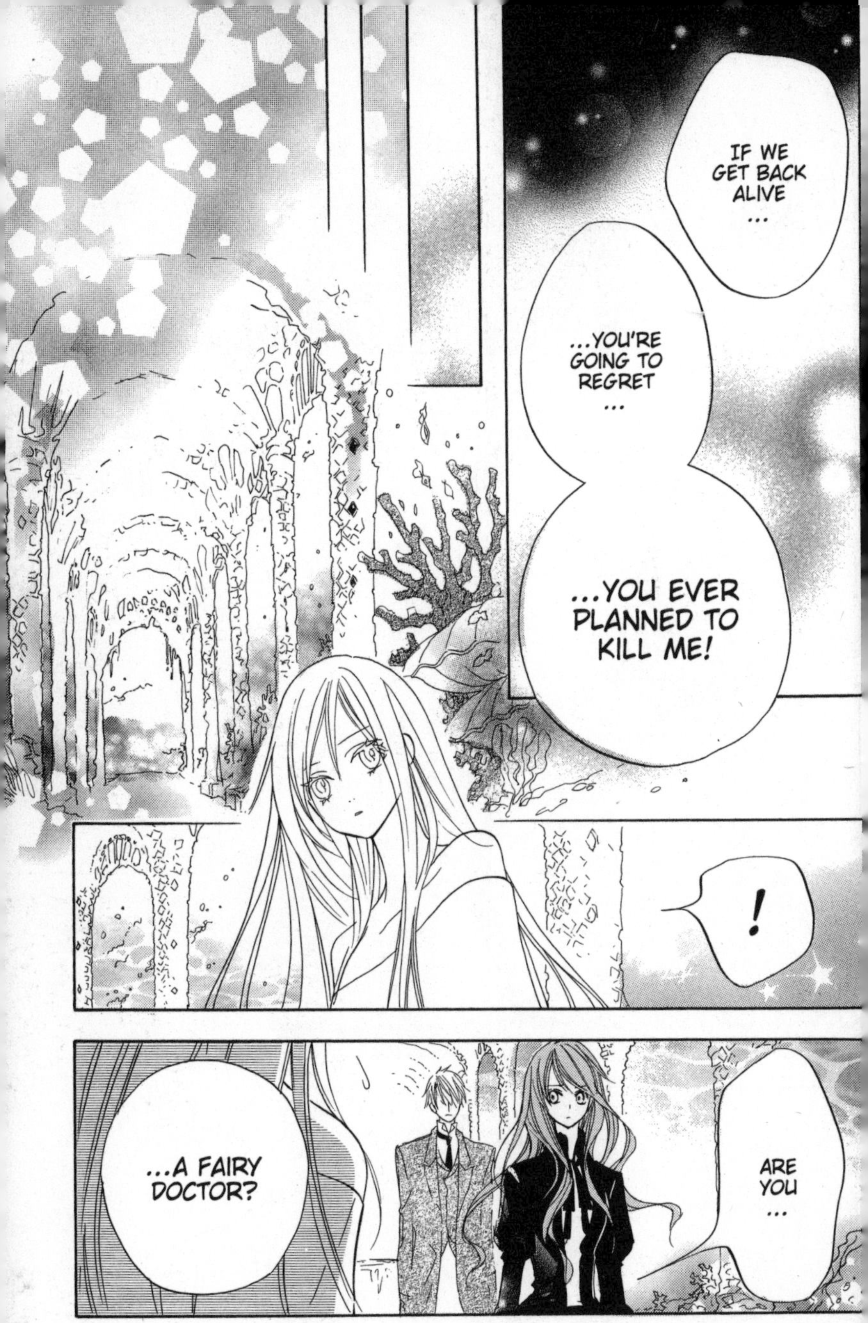
IF WE GET BACK ALIVE ...
...YOU'RE GOING TO REGRET ...
...YOU EVER PLANNED TO KILL ME!
!
ARE YOU ...
...A FAIRY DOCTOR?

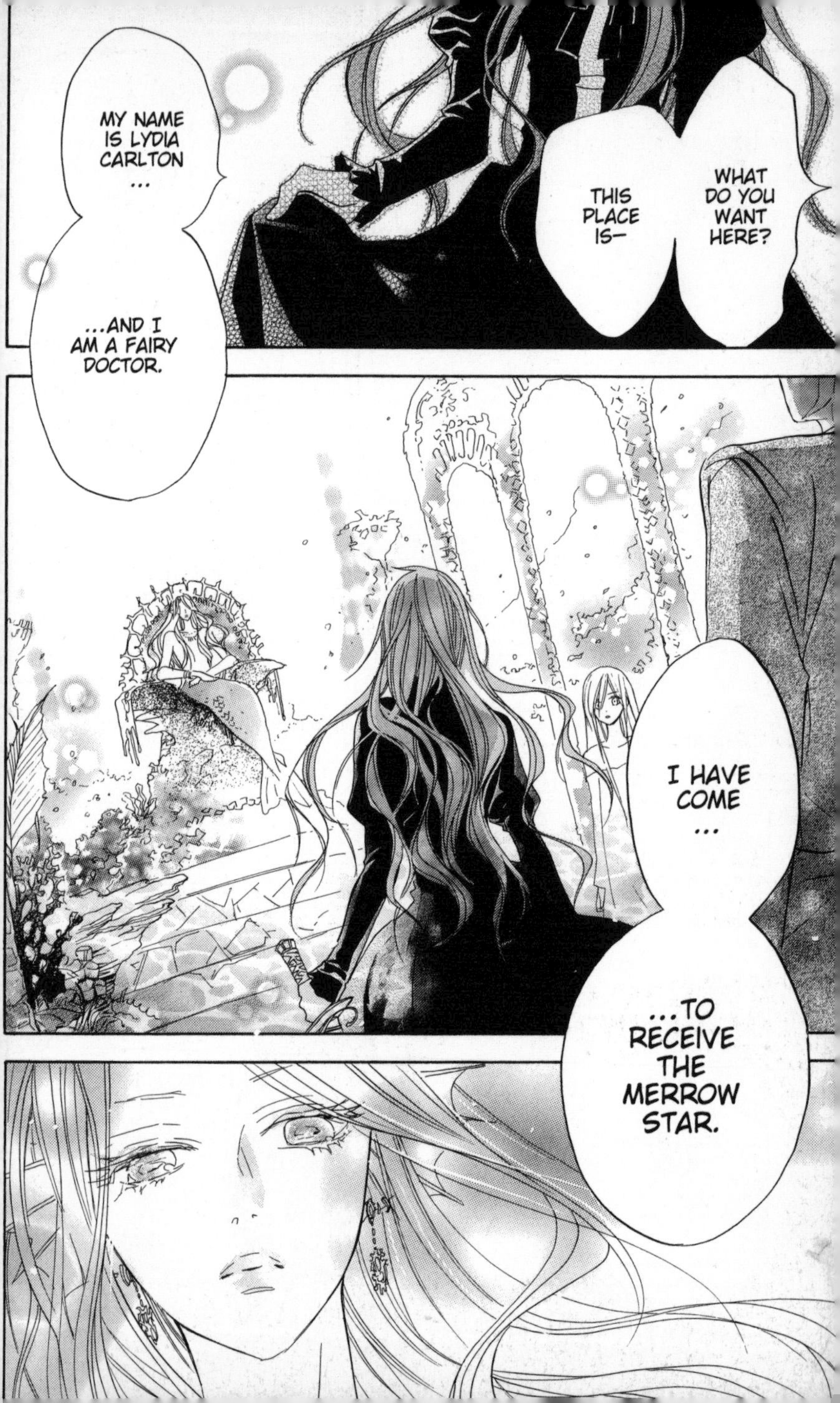
WHAT DO YOU WANT HERE?
THIS PLACE IS—
MY NAME IS LYDIA CARLTON ...
...AND I AM A FAIRY DOCTOR.
I HAVE COME ...
...TO RECEIVE THE MERROW STAR.

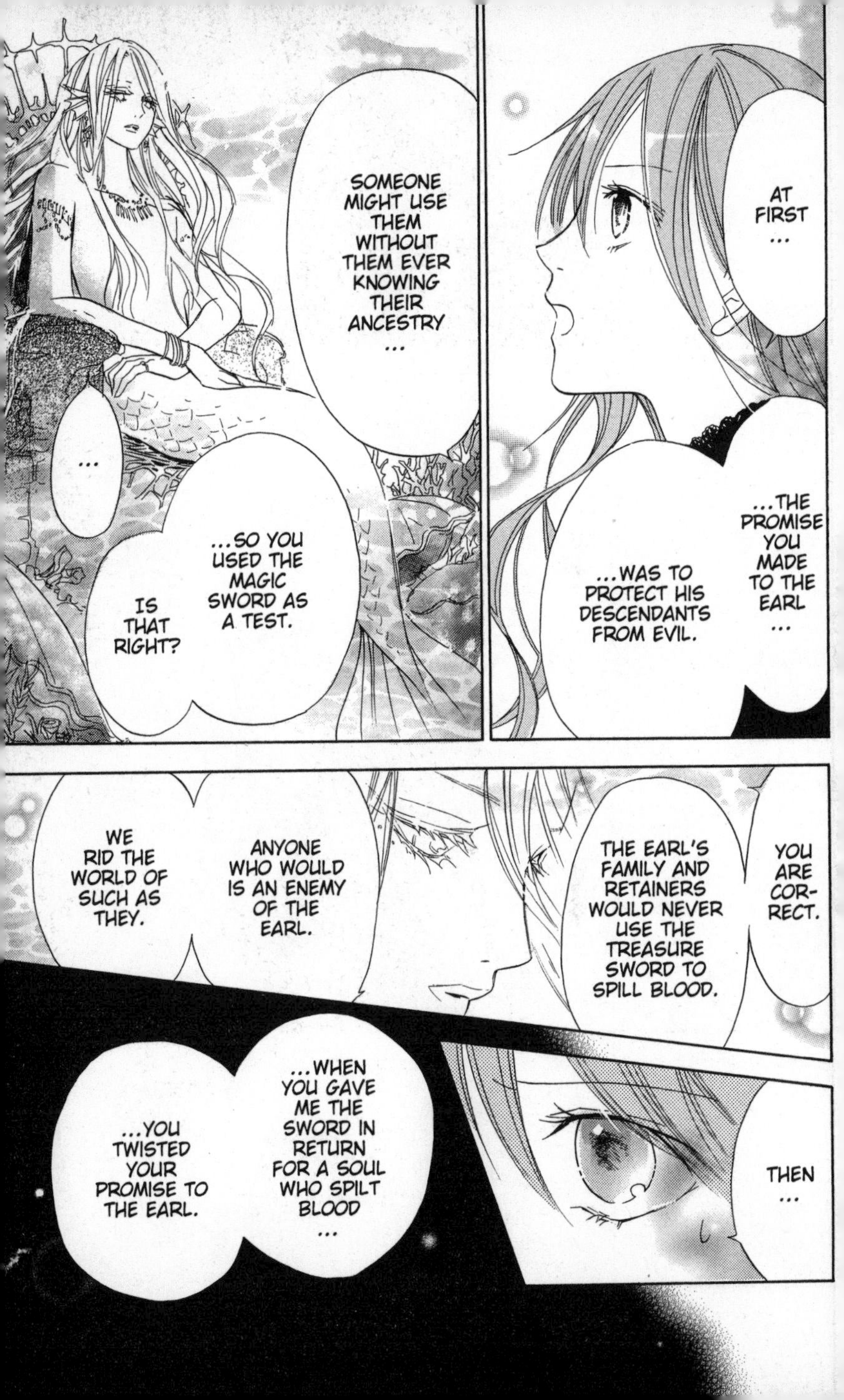
AT FIRST ...
...THE PROMISE YOU MADE TO THE EARL ...
...WAS TO PROTECT HIS DESCENDANTS FROM EVIL.
SOMEONE MIGHT USE THEM WITHOUT THEM EVER KNOWING THEIR ANCESTRY ...
...SO YOU USED THE MAGIC SWORD AS A TEST.
IS THAT RIGHT?
...
YOU ARE COR-RECT.
THE EARL'S FAMILY AND RETAINERS WOULD NEVER USE THE TREASURE SWORD TO SPILL BLOOD.
ANYONE WHO WOULD IS AN ENEMY OF THE EARL.
WE RID THE WORLD OF SUCH AS THEY.
THEN ...
...WHEN YOU GAVE ME THE SWORD IN RETURN FOR A SOUL WHO SPILT BLOOD ...
...YOU TWISTED YOUR PROMISE TO THE EARL.

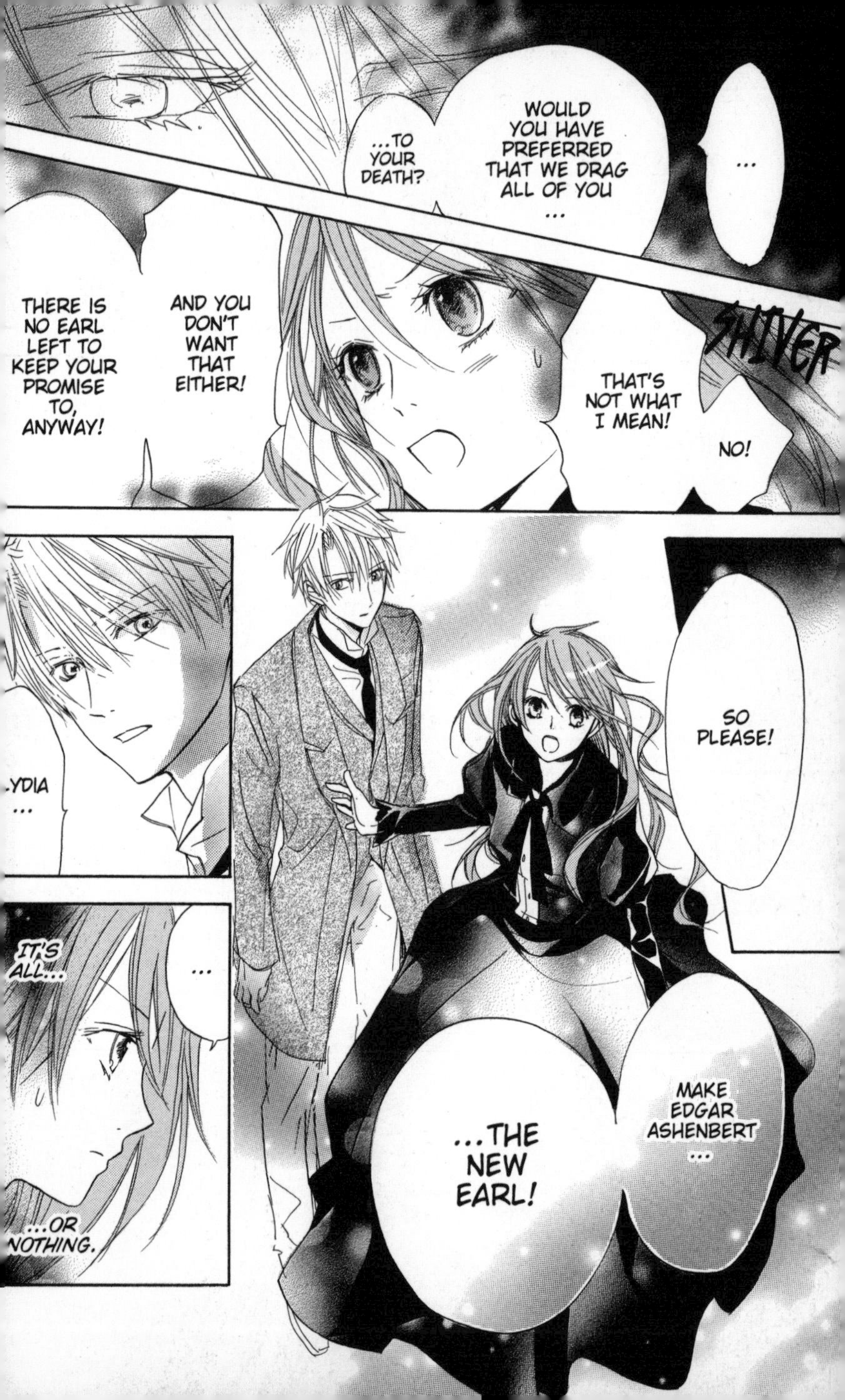
...
WOULD YOU HAVE PREFERRED THAT WE DRAG ALL OF YOU ...
...TO YOUR DEATH?
SHIVER
NO!
THAT'S NOT WHAT I MEAN!
AND YOU DON'T WANT THAT EITHER!
THERE IS NO EARL LEFT TO KEEP YOUR PROMISE TO, ANYWAY!
SO PLEASE!
MAKE EDGAR ASHENBERT ...
...THE NEW EARL!
YDIA ...
...
IT'S ALL...
...OR NOTHING.

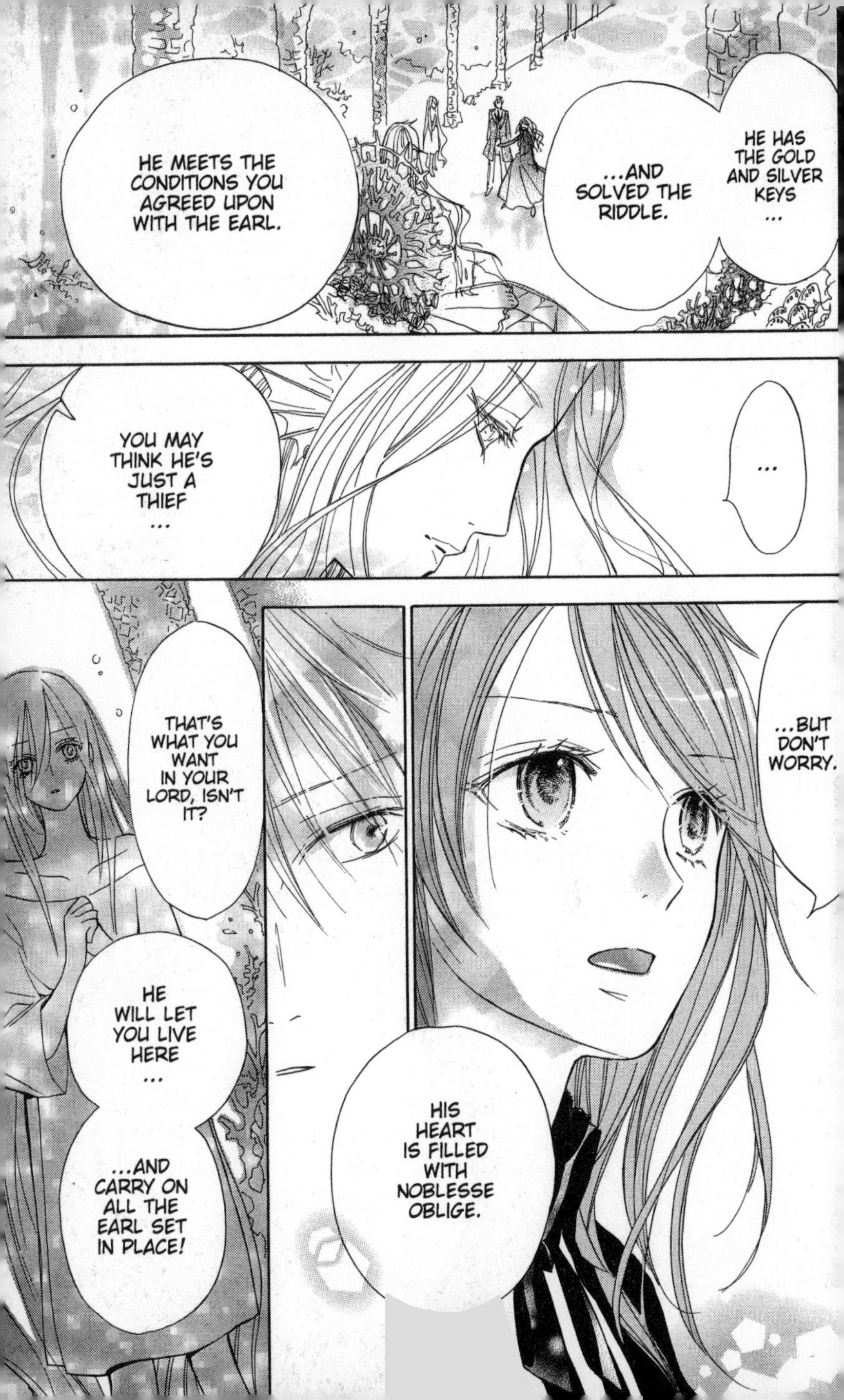
HE HAS THE GOLD AND SILVER KEYS ...
...AND SOLVED THE RIDDLE.
HE MEETS THE CONDITIONS YOU AGREED UPON WITH THE EARL.
...
YOU MAY THINK HE'S JUST A THIEF ...
...BUT DON'T WORRY.
HIS HEART IS FILLED WITH NOBLESSE OBLIGE.
THAT'S WHAT YOU WANT IN YOUR LORD, ISN'T IT?
HE WILL LET YOU LIVE HERE ...
...AND CARRY ON ALL THE EARL SET IN PLACE!

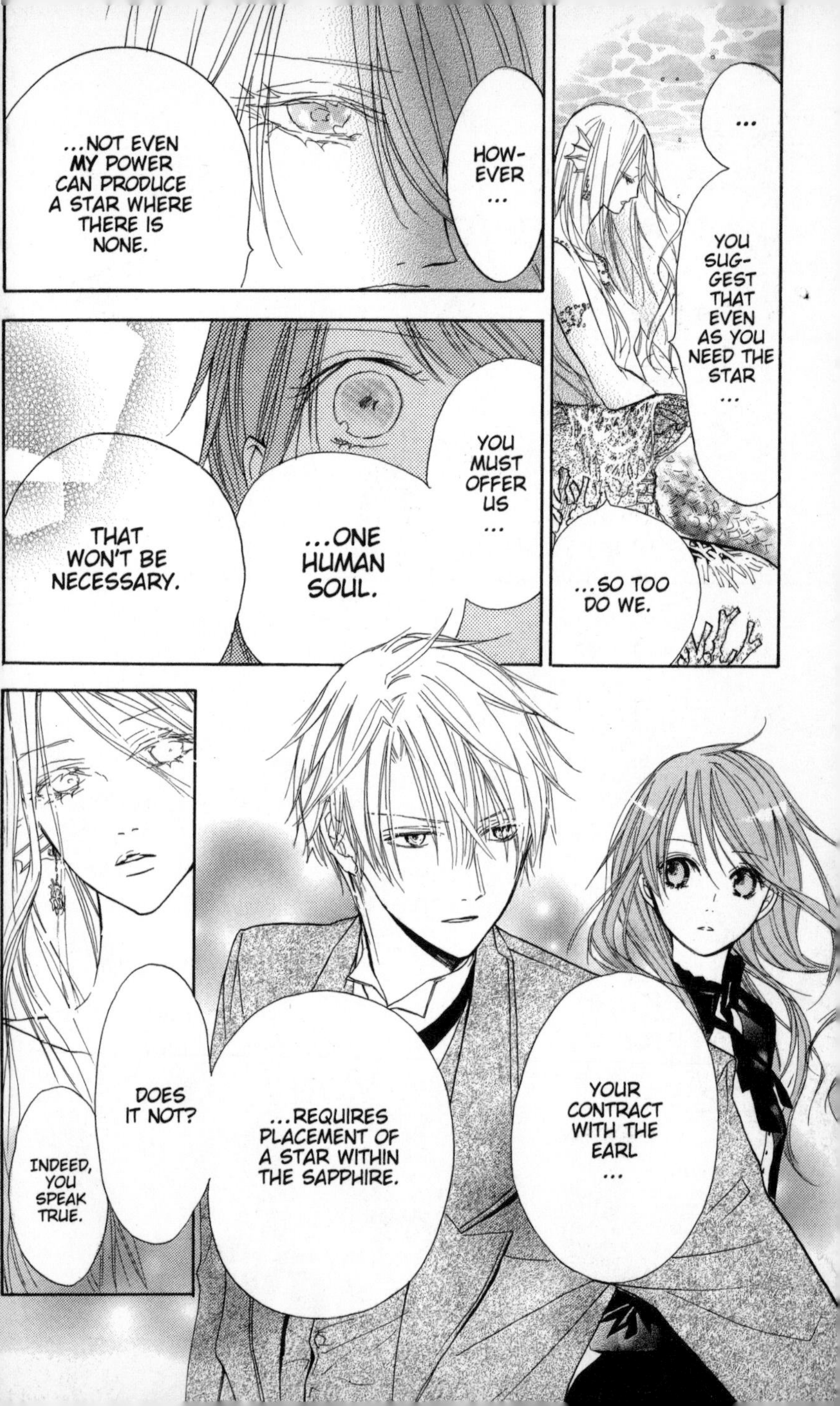
...
YOU SUG-GEST THAT EVEN AS YOU NEED THE STAR ...
...SO TOO DO WE.
HOW-EVER ...
...NOT EVEN MY POWER CAN PRODUCE A STAR WHERE THERE IS NONE.
YOU MUST OFFER US ...
...ONE HUMAN SOUL.
THAT WON'T BE NECESSARY.
YOUR CONTRACT WITH THE EARL ...
...REQUIRES PLACEMENT OF A STAR WITHIN THE SAPPHIRE.
DOES IT NOT?
INDEED, YOU SPEAK TRUE.

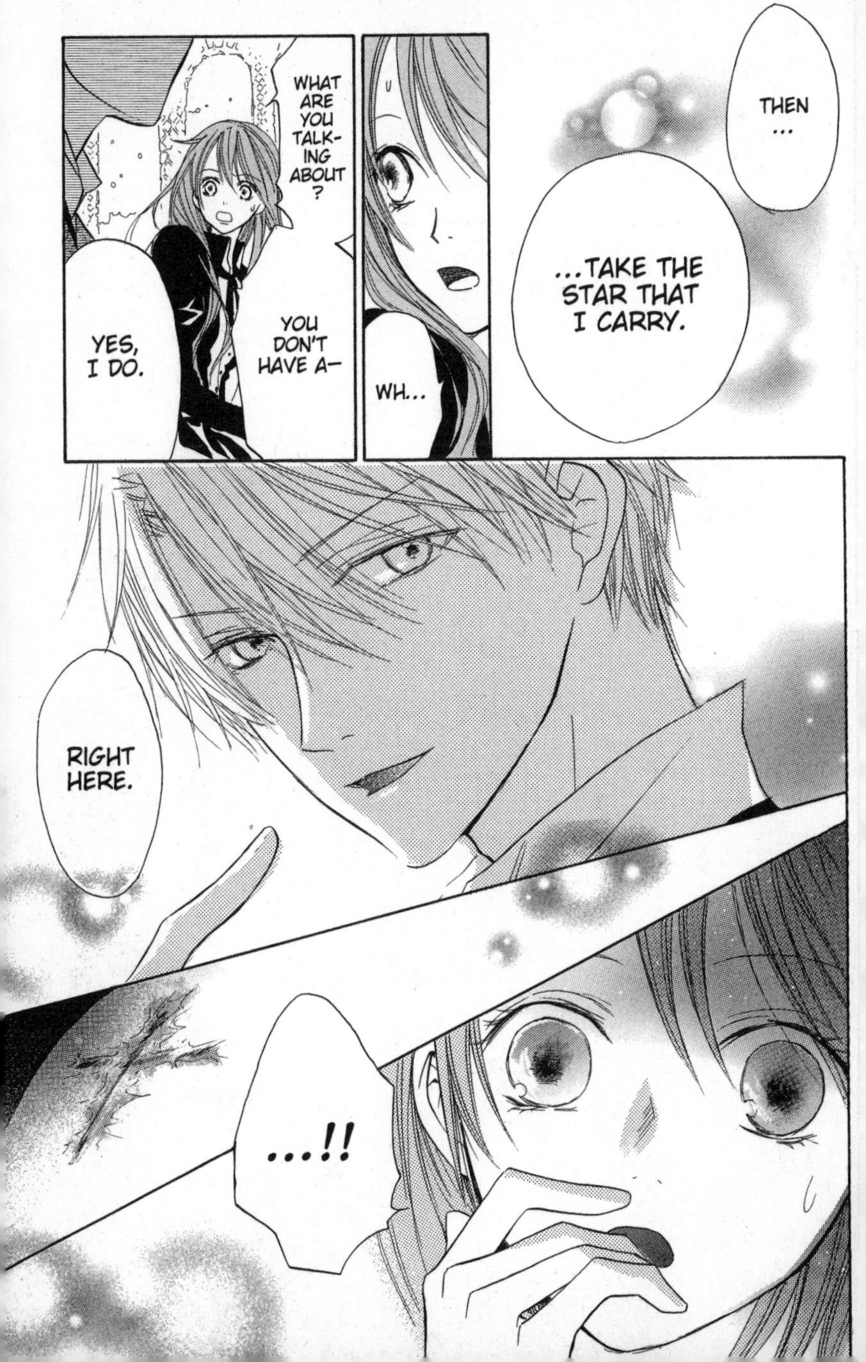
THEN...
...TAKE THE STAR THAT I CARRY.
WH...
WHAT ARE YOU TALKING ABOUT?
YOU DON'T HAVE A—
YES, I DO.
RIGHT HERE.
...!!

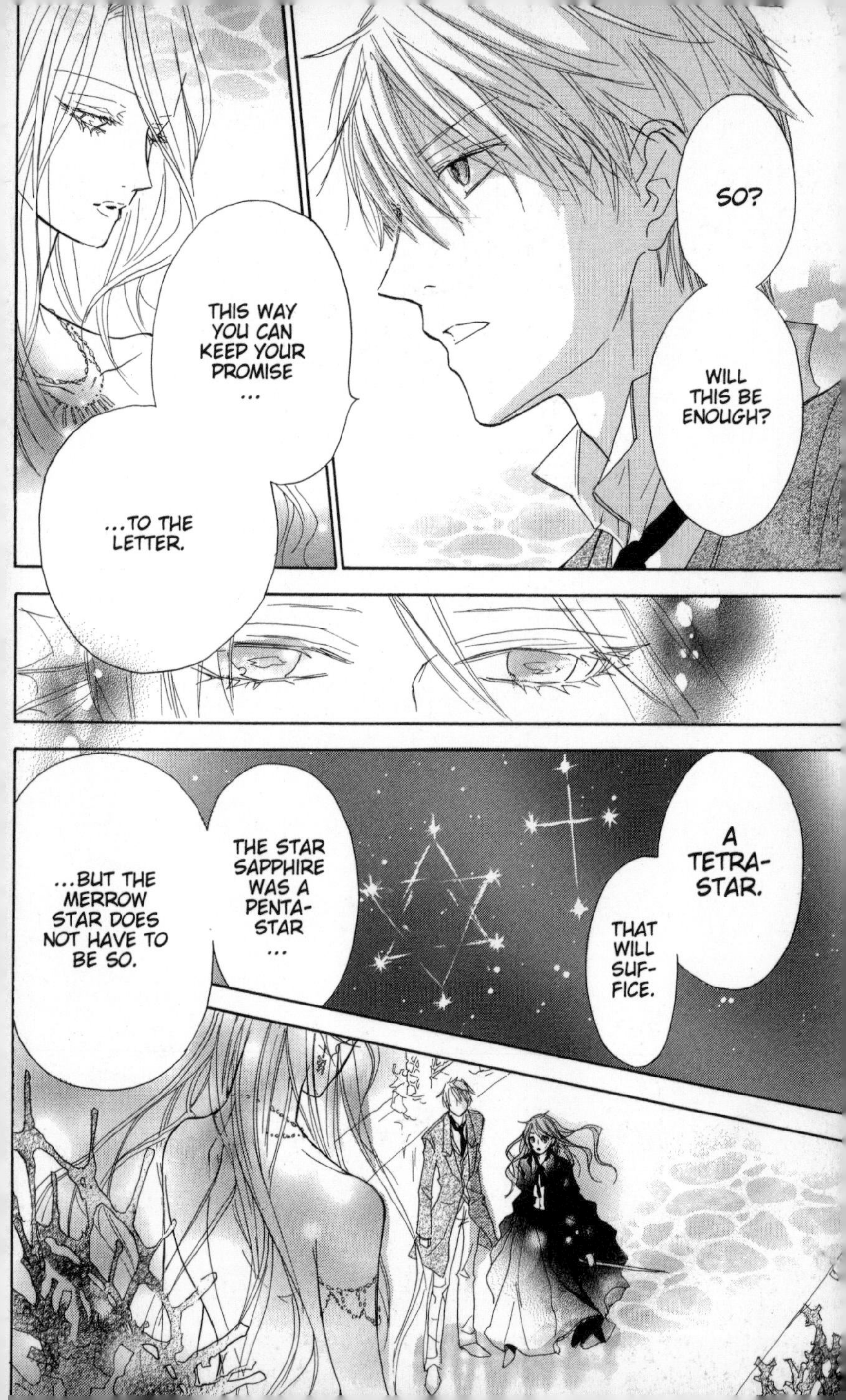
SO?
WILL THIS BE ENOUGH?
THIS WAY YOU CAN KEEP YOUR PROMISE ...
...TO THE LETTER.
A TETRA-STAR.
THAT WILL SUF-FICE.
THE STAR SAPPHIRE WAS A PENTA-STAR ...
...BUT THE MERROW STAR DOES NOT HAVE TO BE SO.

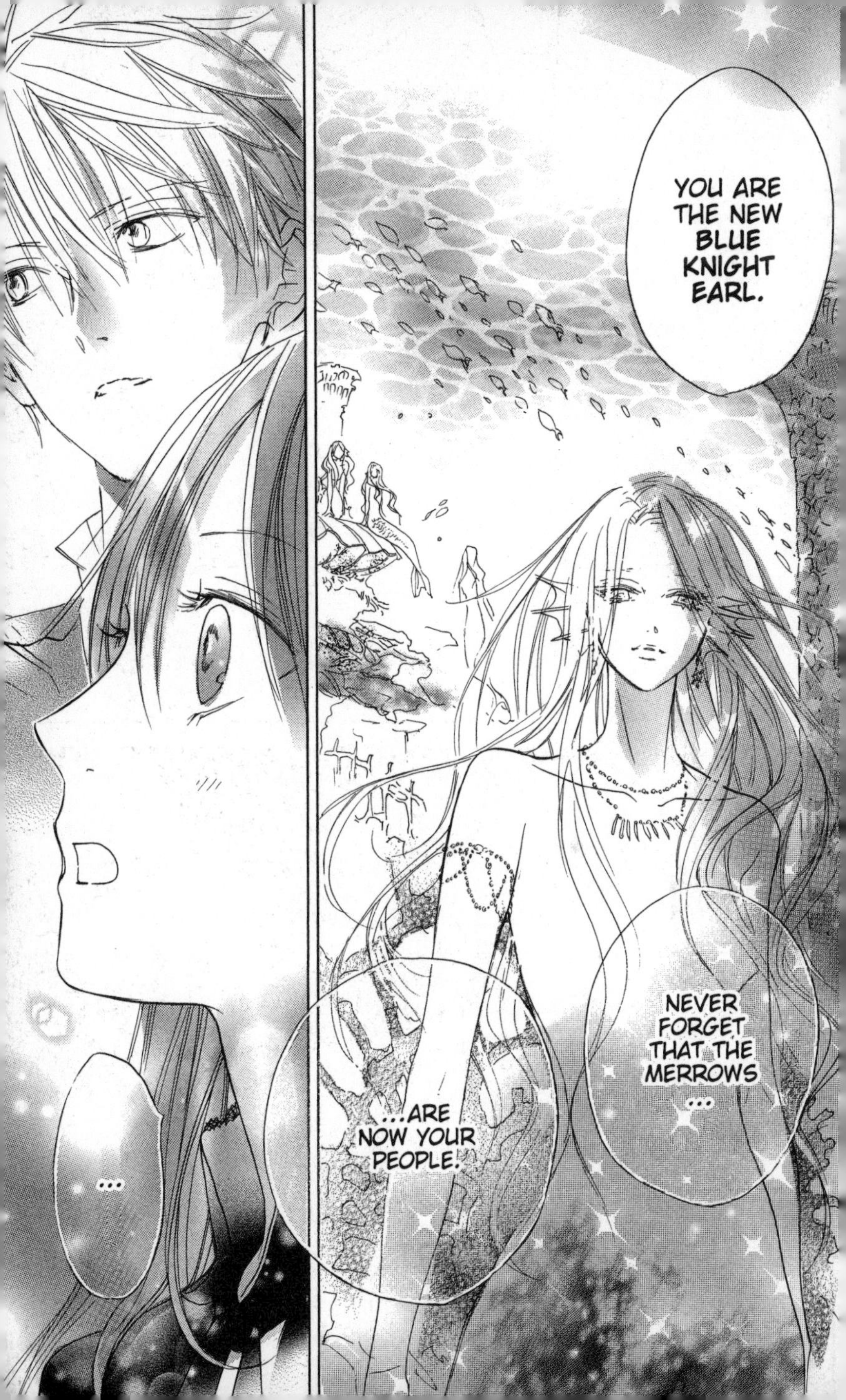
YOU ARE THE NEW BLUE KNIGHT EARL.
NEVER FORGET THAT THE MERROWS ...
...ARE NOW YOUR PEOPLE.
...

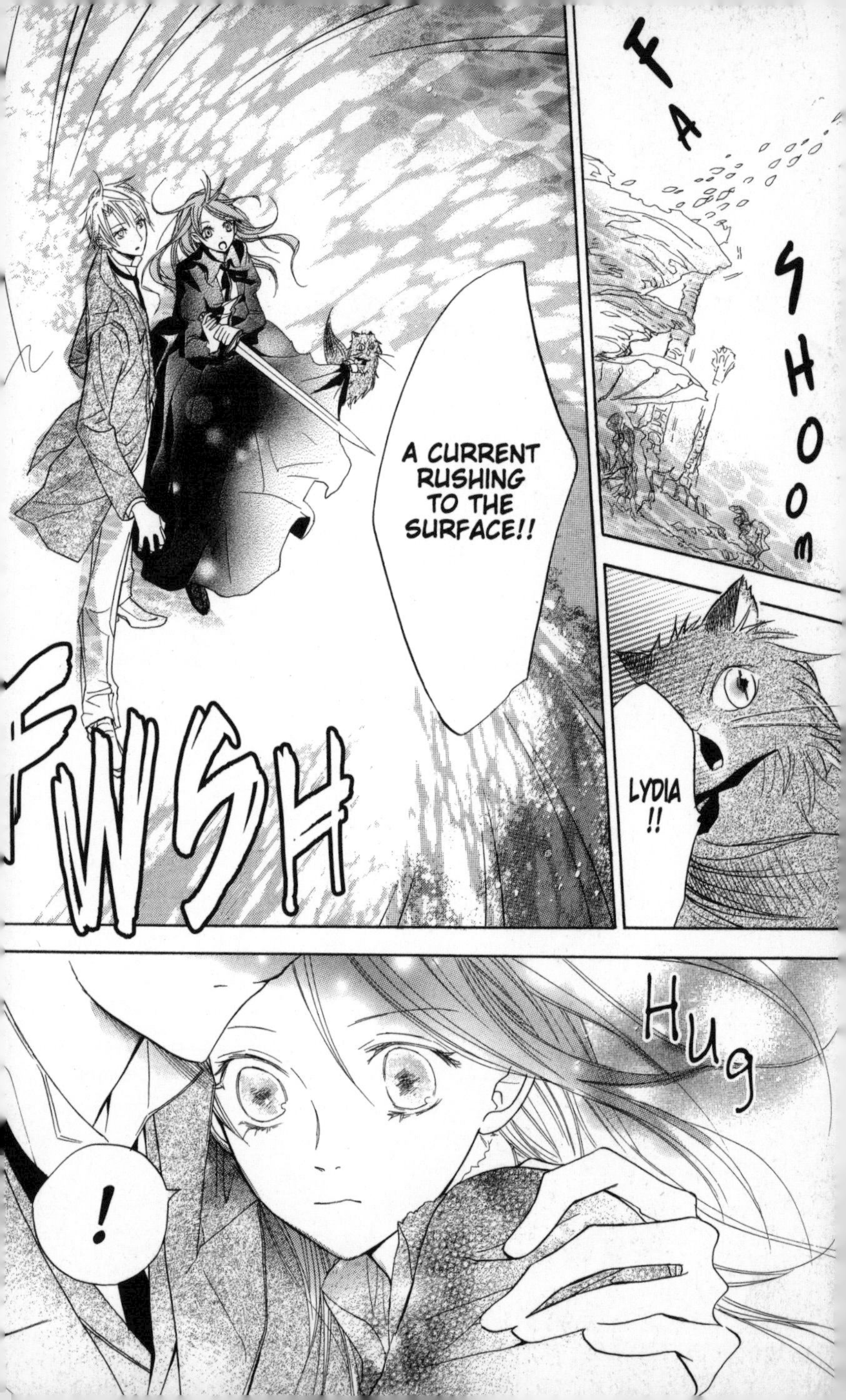
FA SHOOM
LYDIA!!
A CURRENT RUSHING TO THE SURFACE!!
FWSH
Hug
!

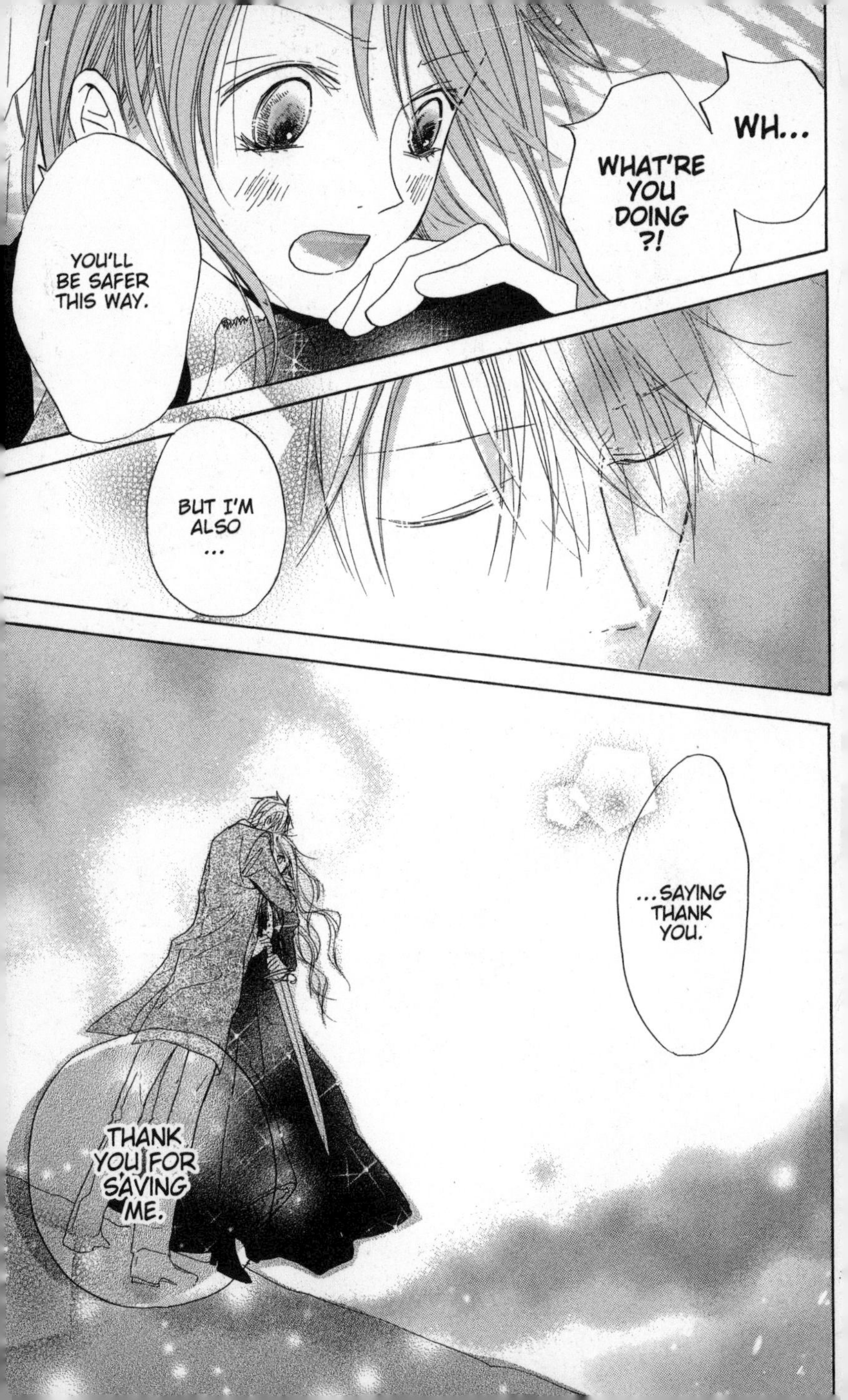
WH...
WHAT'RE YOU DOING ?!
YOU'LL BE SAFER THIS WAY.
BUT I'M ALSO ...
...SAYING THANK YOU.
THANK YOU FOR SAVING ME.

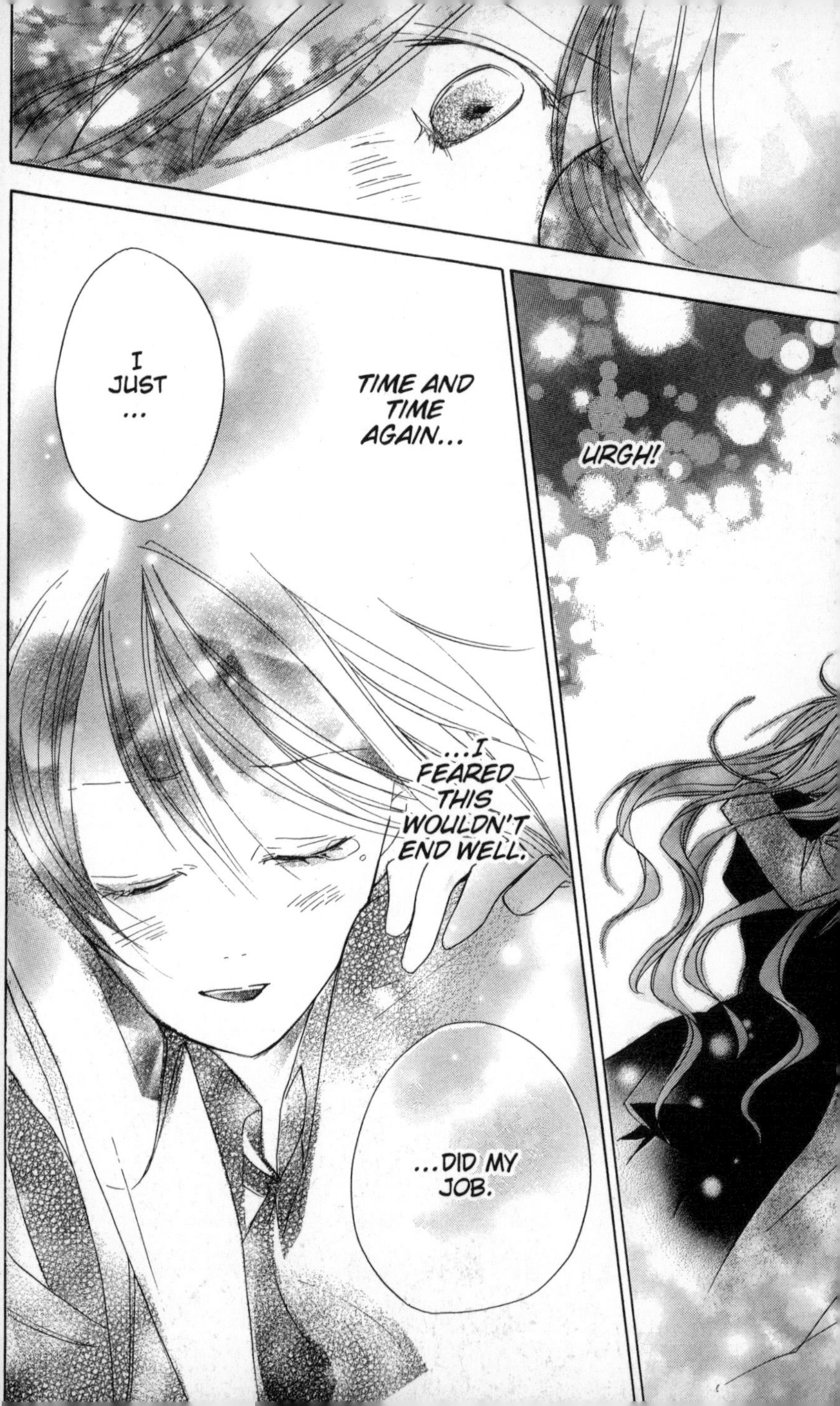
URGH!
TIME AND TIME AGAIN...
I JUST...
...I FEARED THIS WOULDN'T END WELL.
...DID MY JOB.

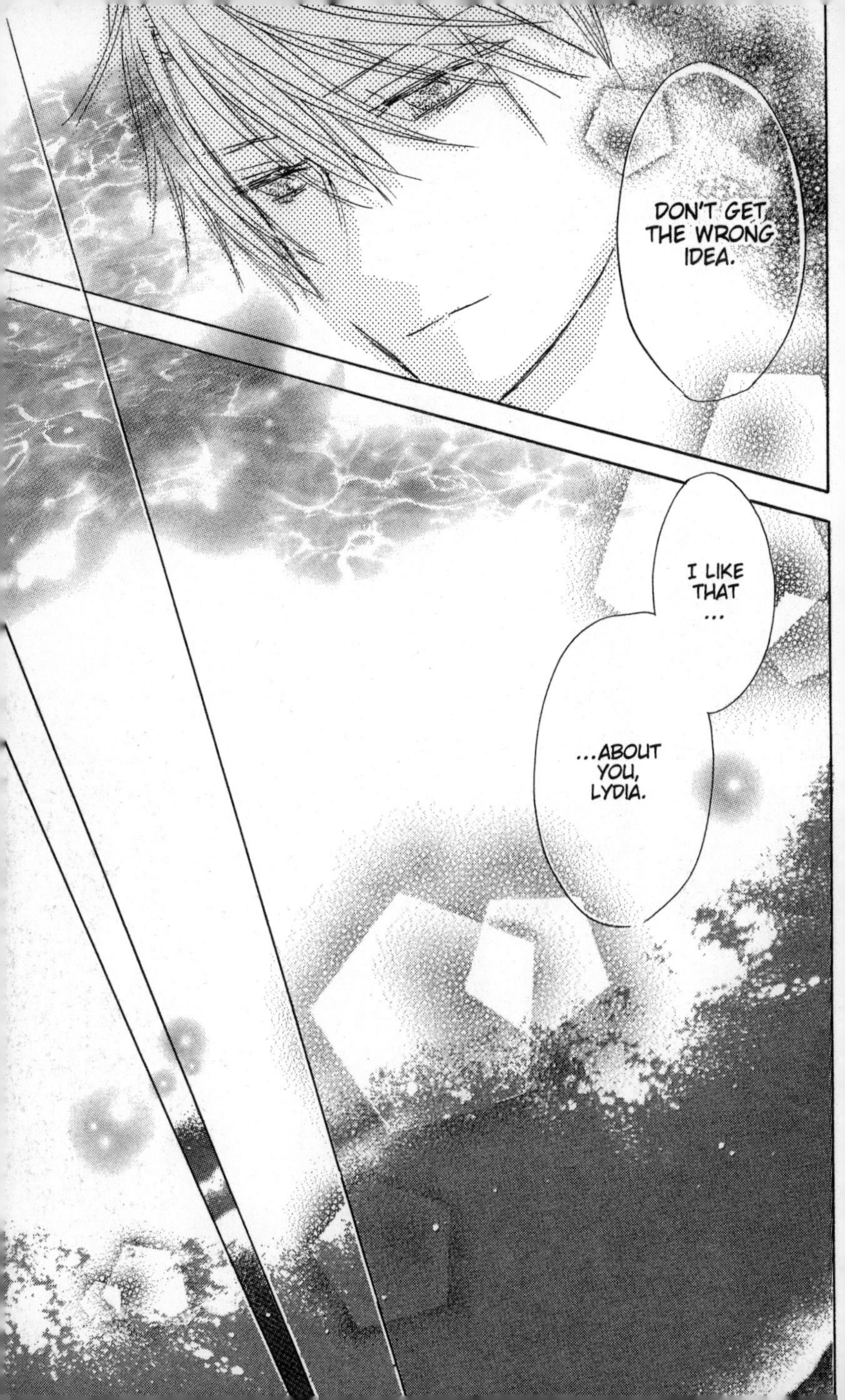
DON'T GET THE WRONG IDEA.
I LIKE THAT ...
...ABOUT YOU, LYDIA.

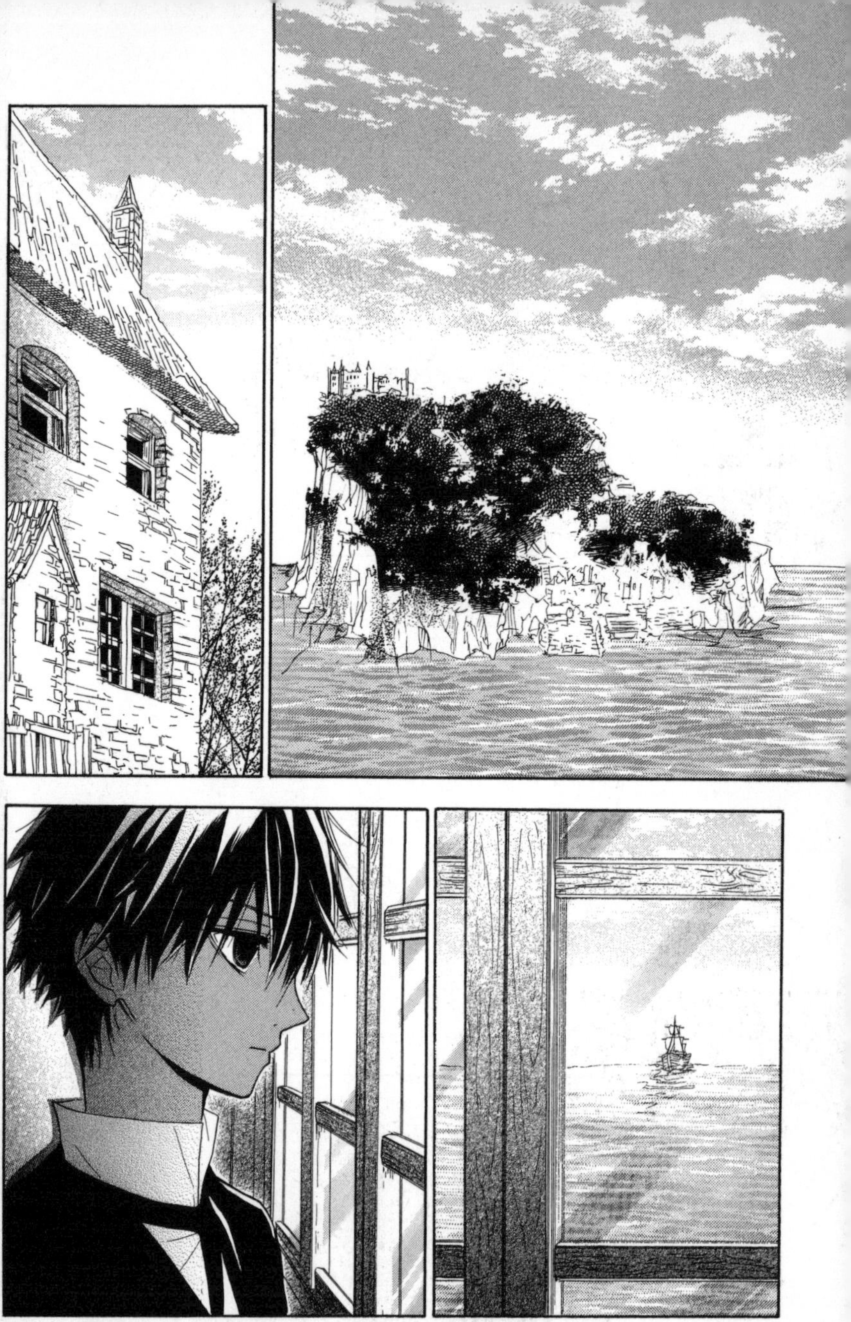

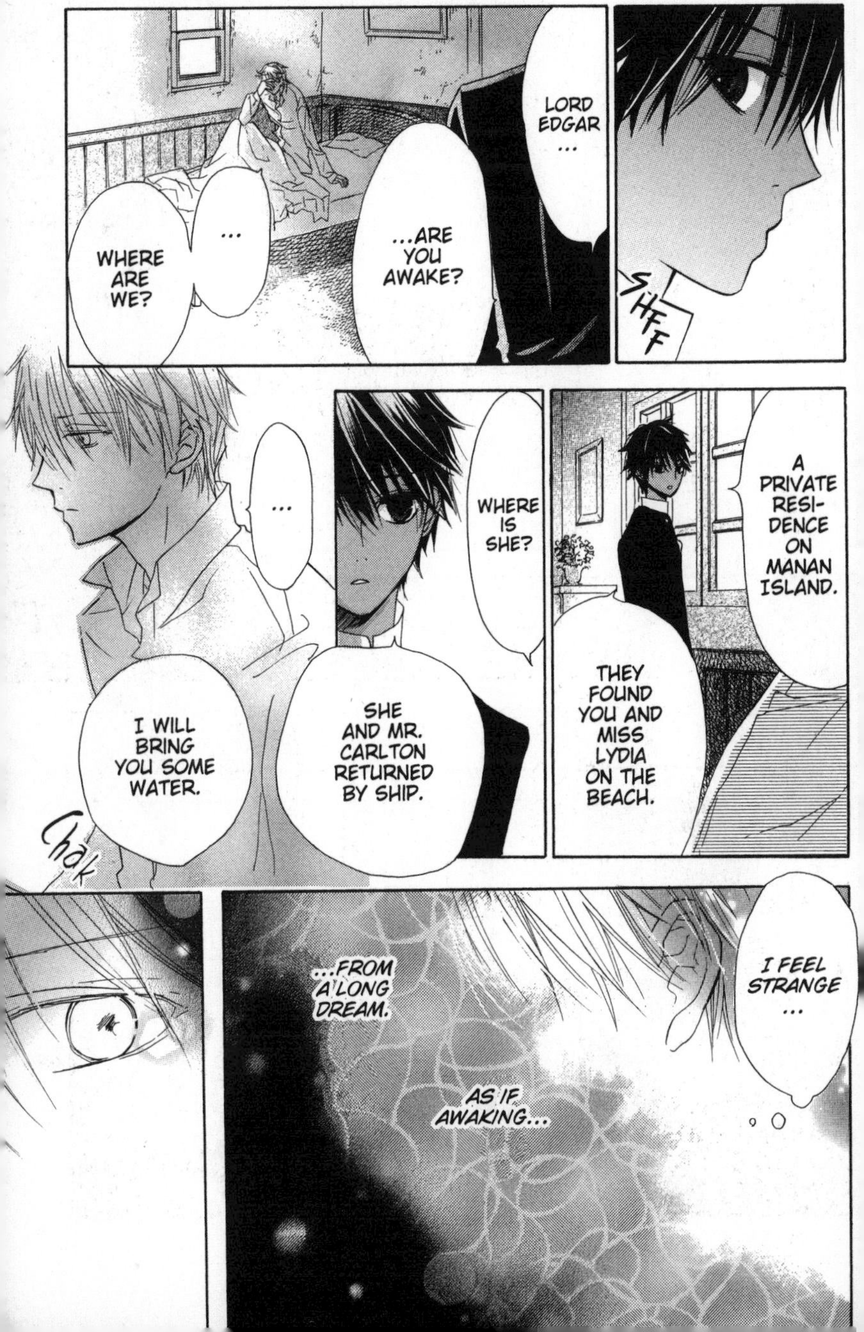
SHFF
LORD EDGAR …
…ARE YOU AWAKE?
…
WHERE ARE WE?
A PRIVATE RESI- DENCE ON MANAN ISLAND.
THEY FOUND YOU AND MISS LYDIA ON THE BEACH.
WHERE IS SHE?
SHE AND MR. CARLTON RETURNED BY SHIP.
…
I WILL BRING YOU SOME WATER.
Chak
I FEEL STRANGE …
AS IF AWAKING…
…FROM A LONG DREAM.

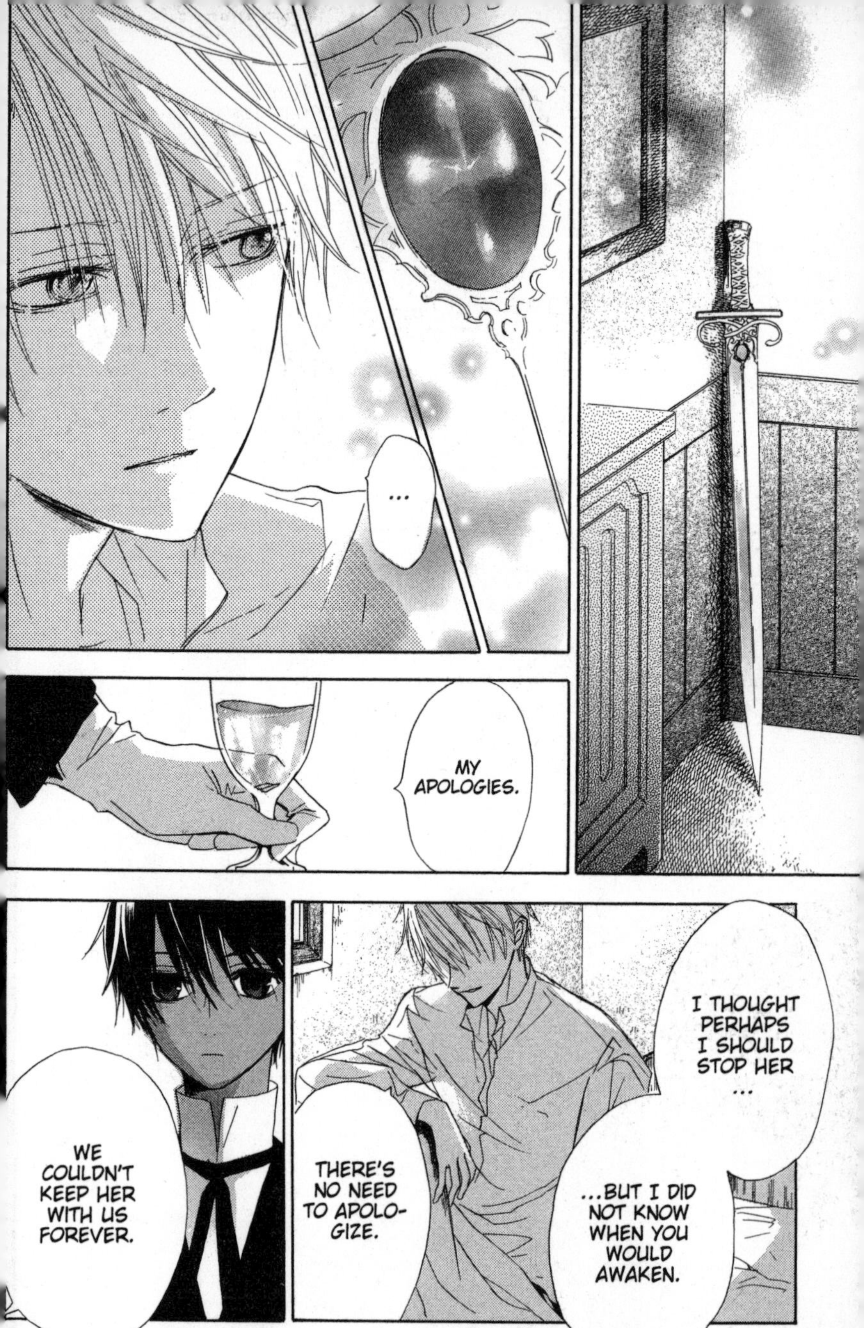
...
MY APOLOGIES.
I THOUGHT PERHAPS I SHOULD STOP HER ...
...BUT I DID NOT KNOW WHEN YOU WOULD AWAKEN.
THERE'S NO NEED TO APOLO-GIZE.
WE COULDN'T KEEP HER WITH US FOREVER.

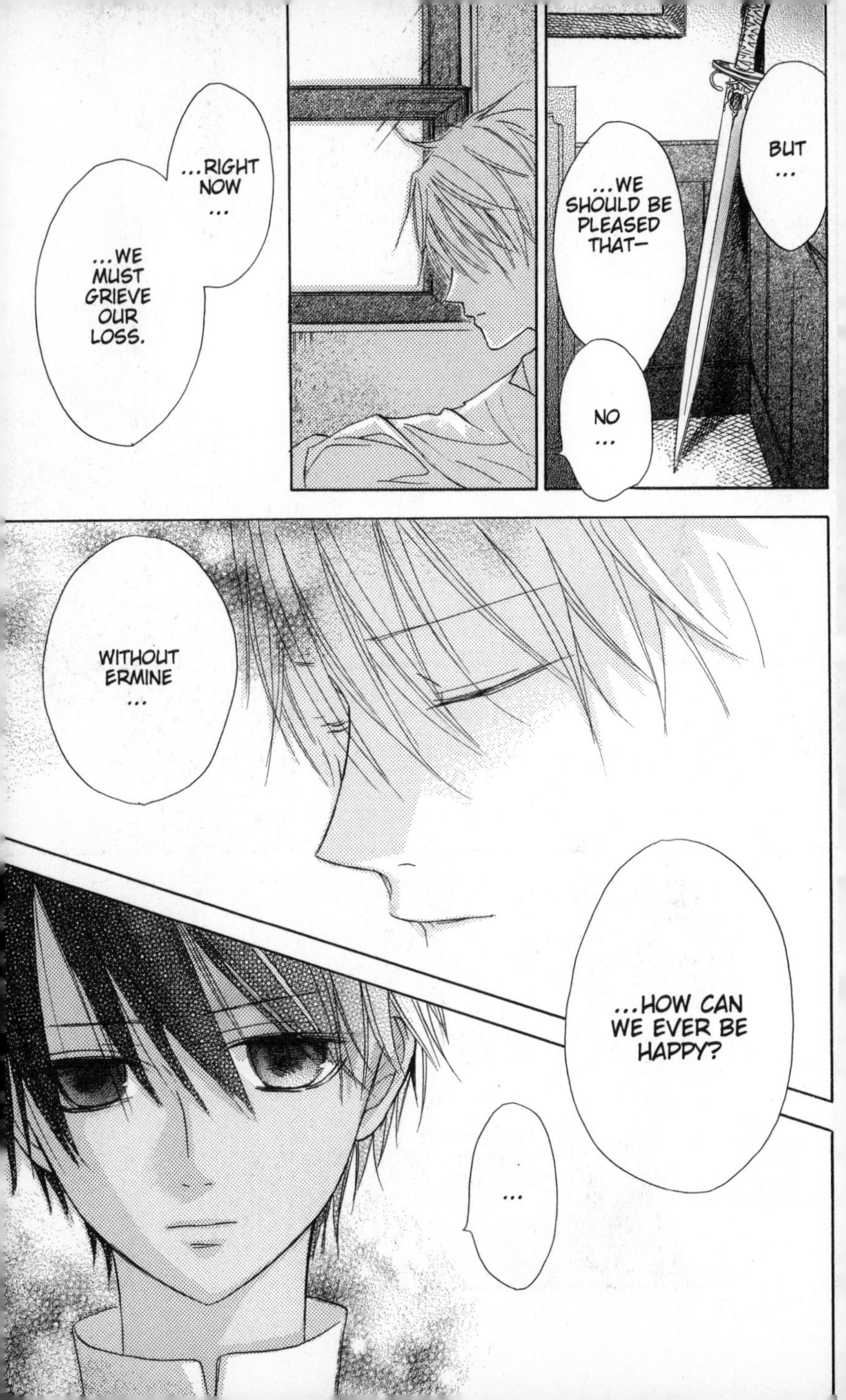
BUT ...
...WE SHOULD BE PLEASED THAT—
NO ...
...RIGHT NOW ...
...WE MUST GRIEVE OUR LOSS.
WITHOUT ERMINE ...
...HOW CAN WE EVER BE HAPPY?
...

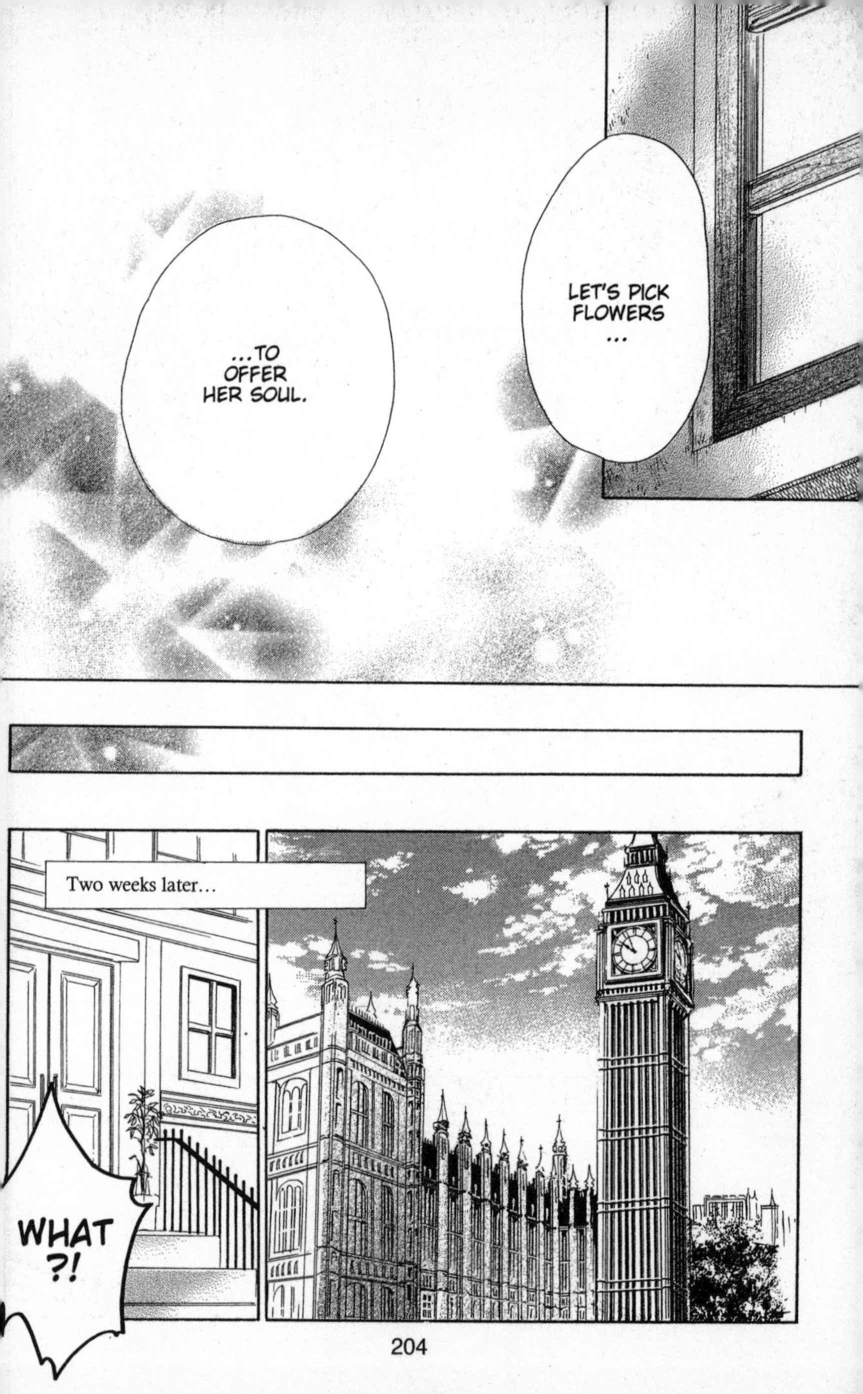
LET'S PICK FLOWERS ...
...TO OFFER HER SOUL.
Two weeks later…
WHAT ?!

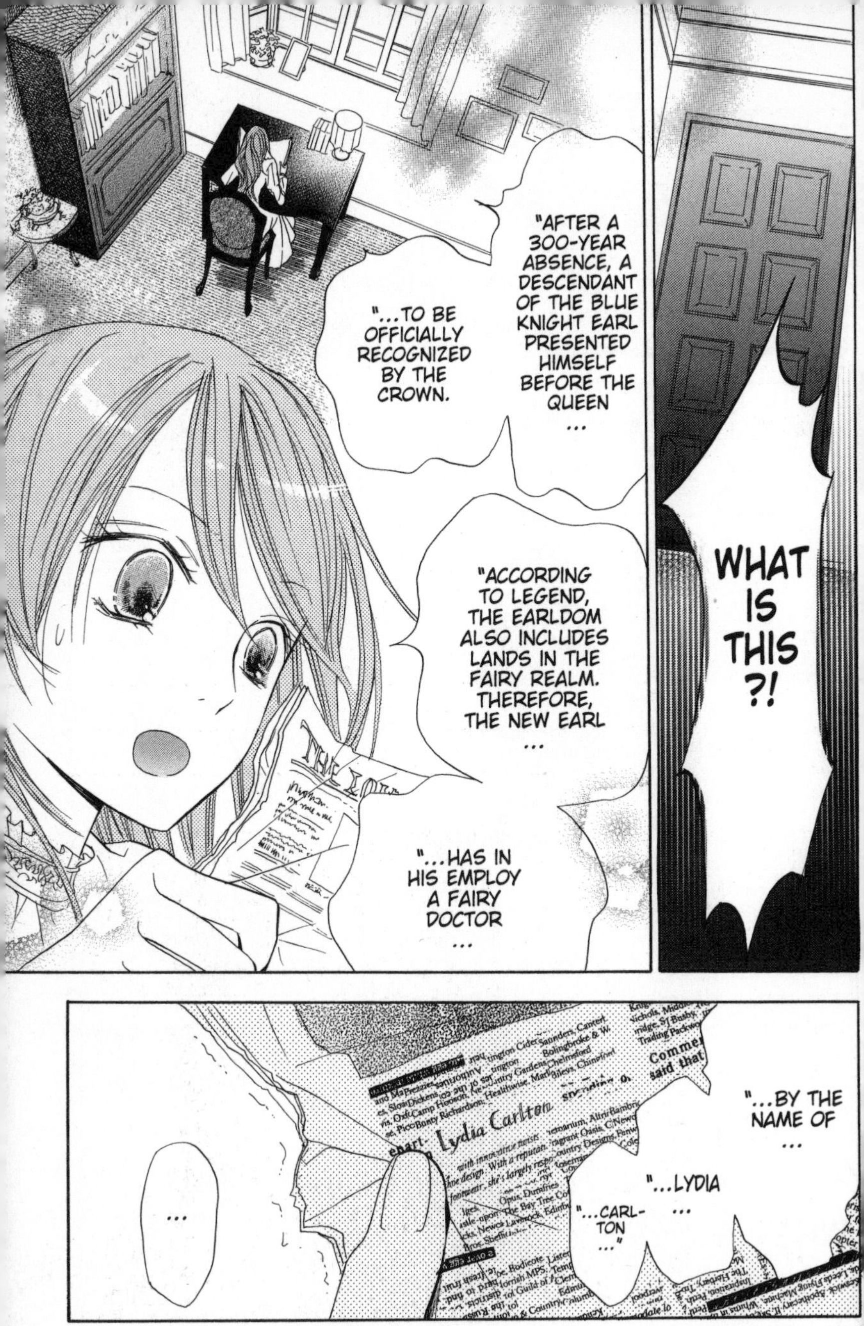
WHAT IS THIS?!
"AFTER A 300-YEAR ABSENCE, A DESCENDANT OF THE BLUE KNIGHT EARL PRESENTED HIMSELF BEFORE THE QUEEN ...
"...TO BE OFFICIALLY RECOGNIZED BY THE CROWN.
"ACCORDING TO LEGEND, THE EARLDOM ALSO INCLUDES LANDS IN THE FAIRY REALM. THEREFORE, THE NEW EARL ...
"...HAS IN HIS EMPLOY A FAIRY DOCTOR ...
"...BY THE NAME OF ...
Lydia Carlton
"...LYDIA ...
"...CARL-TON ..."
...

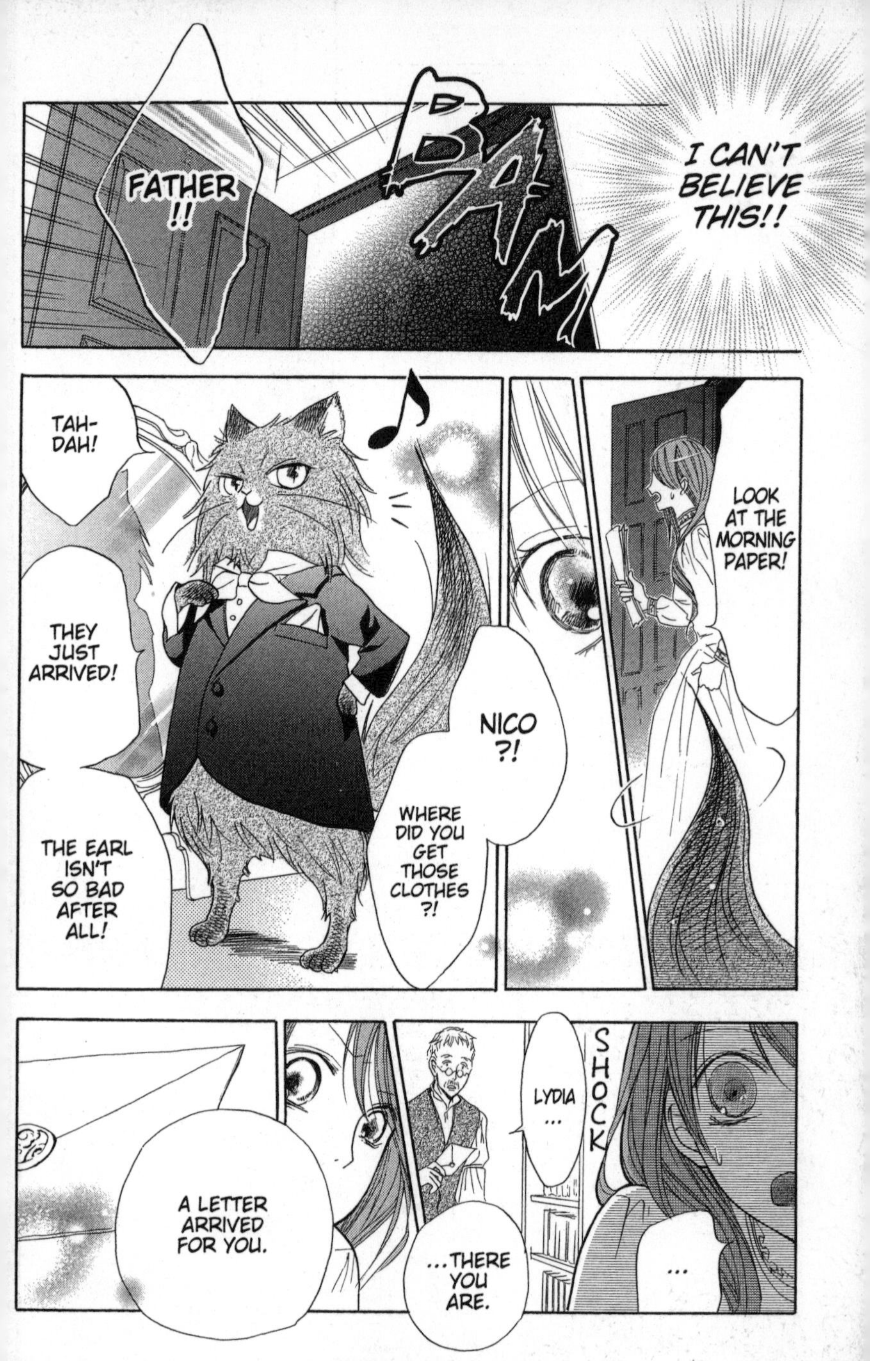
I CAN'T BELIEVE THIS!!
BAM
FATHER !!
LOOK AT THE MORNING PAPER!
NICO ?!
WHERE DID YOU GET THOSE CLOTHES ?!
TAH-DAH!
THEY JUST ARRIVED!
THE EARL ISN'T SO BAD AFTER ALL!
SHOCK
...
LYDIA ...
...THERE YOU ARE.
A LETTER ARRIVED FOR YOU.

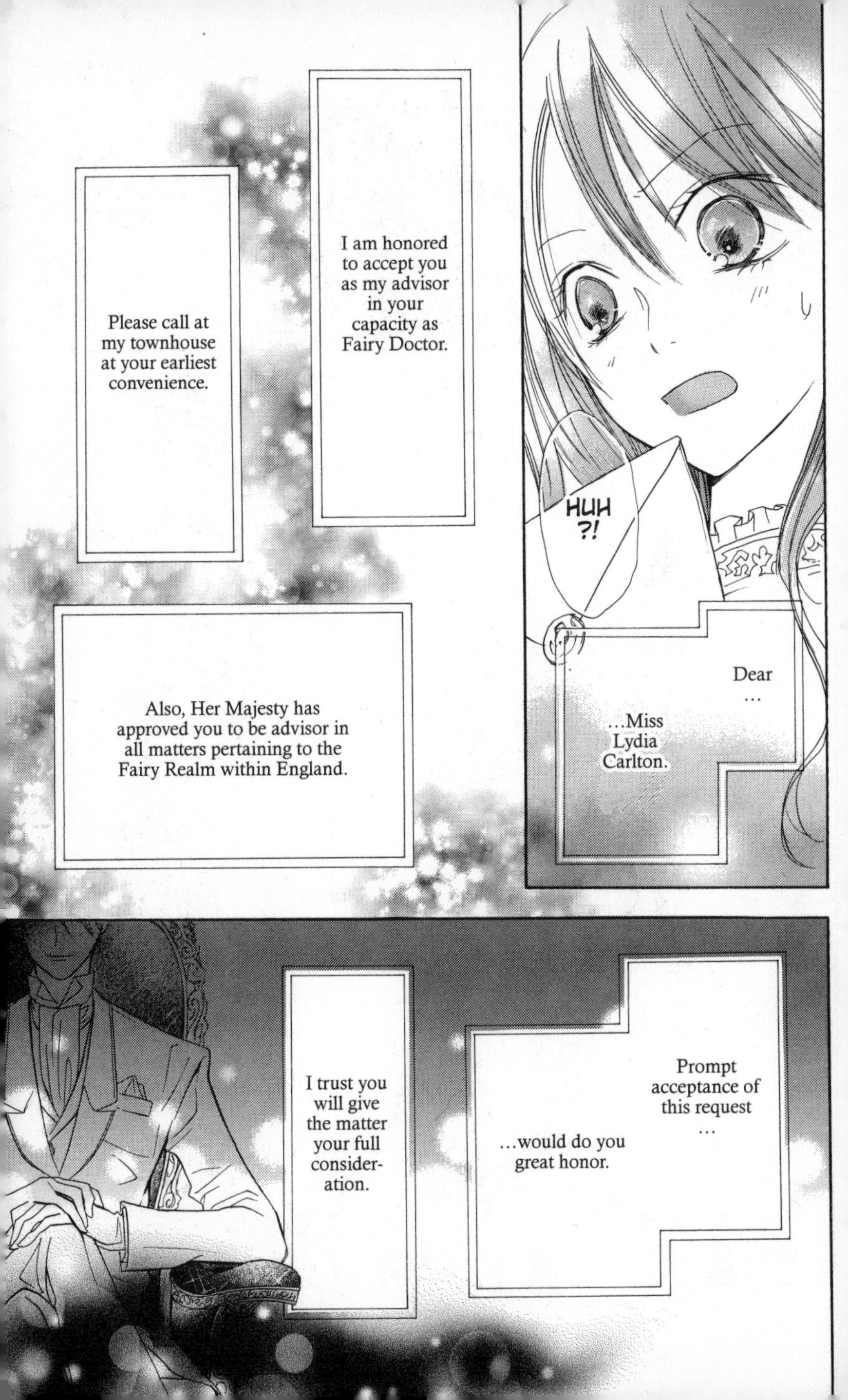
HUH ?!
Dear …
…Miss Lydia Carlton.
I am honored to accept you as my advisor in your capacity as Fairy Doctor.
Please call at my townhouse at your earliest convenience.
Also, Her Majesty has approved you to be advisor in all matters pertaining to the Fairy Realm within England.
Prompt acceptance of this request …
…would do you great honor.
I trust you will give the matter your full consider-ation.

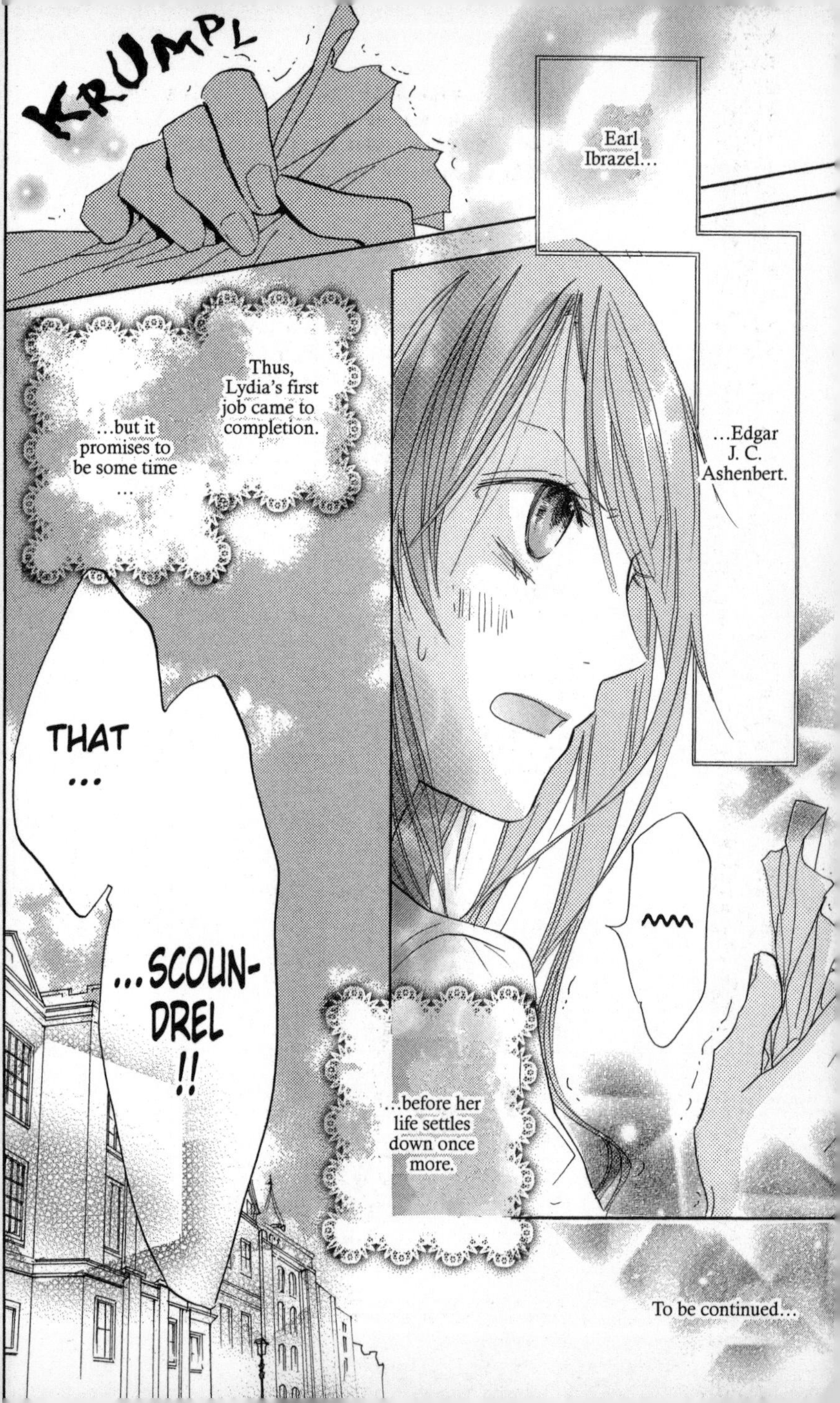
Earl Ibrazel…
…Edgar J. C. Ashenbert.
KRUMPL
Thus, Lydia's first job came to completion.
…but it promises to be some time …
THAT …
…SCOUNDREL!!
…before her life settles down once more.
To be continued…

There was a lot of the novel that I couldn't include in the manga. Please also enjoy story of *The Earl and the Fairy* through the novels, anime and drama CDs!

-Ayuko

Ayuko debuted with the story "Us, You and Me" in *Bessatsu Margaret* magazine and has gone on to publish several manga titles in addition to *The Earl and the Fairy*. Born in Kumamoto Prefecture, she's a Leo and loves drawing girl characters.

Mizue Tani is the author of several fantasy novel series and in 1997 received an honorable mention in the Shueisha Roman Taisho awards. Aside from *The Earl and the Fairy*, her other major series is *Majo no Kekkon* (The Witch's Marriage).

The Earl and the Fairy
Volume 2
Shojo Beat Edition

Story and Art by
Ayuko

Original Concept by
Mizue Tani

English Translation & Adaptation/John Werry
Touch-up Art & Lettering/Joanna Estep
Design/Izumi Evers
Editor/Pancha Diaz

HAKUSHAKU TO YOSEI-COMIC EDITION-
© 2008 by Mizue Tani, Ayuko
All rights reserved.
First published in Japan in 2008 by SHUEISHA Inc., Tokyo.
English language translation rights arranged with SHUEISHA, Inc., Tokyo.

The rights of the author(s) of the work(s) in this publication to be so
identified have been asserted in accordance with the Copyright, Designs
and Patents Act 1988. A CIP catalogue record for this book is available
from the British Library.

The stories, characters and incidents mentioned in this publication are
entirely fictional.

No portion of this book may be reproduced or transmitted in any form
or by any means without written permission from the copyright holders.

Printed in the U.S.A.

Published by VIZ Media, LLC
P.O. Box 77010
San Francisco, CA 94107

10 9 8 7 6 5 4 3 2 1
First printing, June 2012

www.viz.com   www.shojobeat.com

PARENTAL ADVISORY
THE EARL AND THE FAIRY is rated T for Teen and is
recommended for ages 13 and up. This volume contains
fantasy violence.
ratings.viz.com

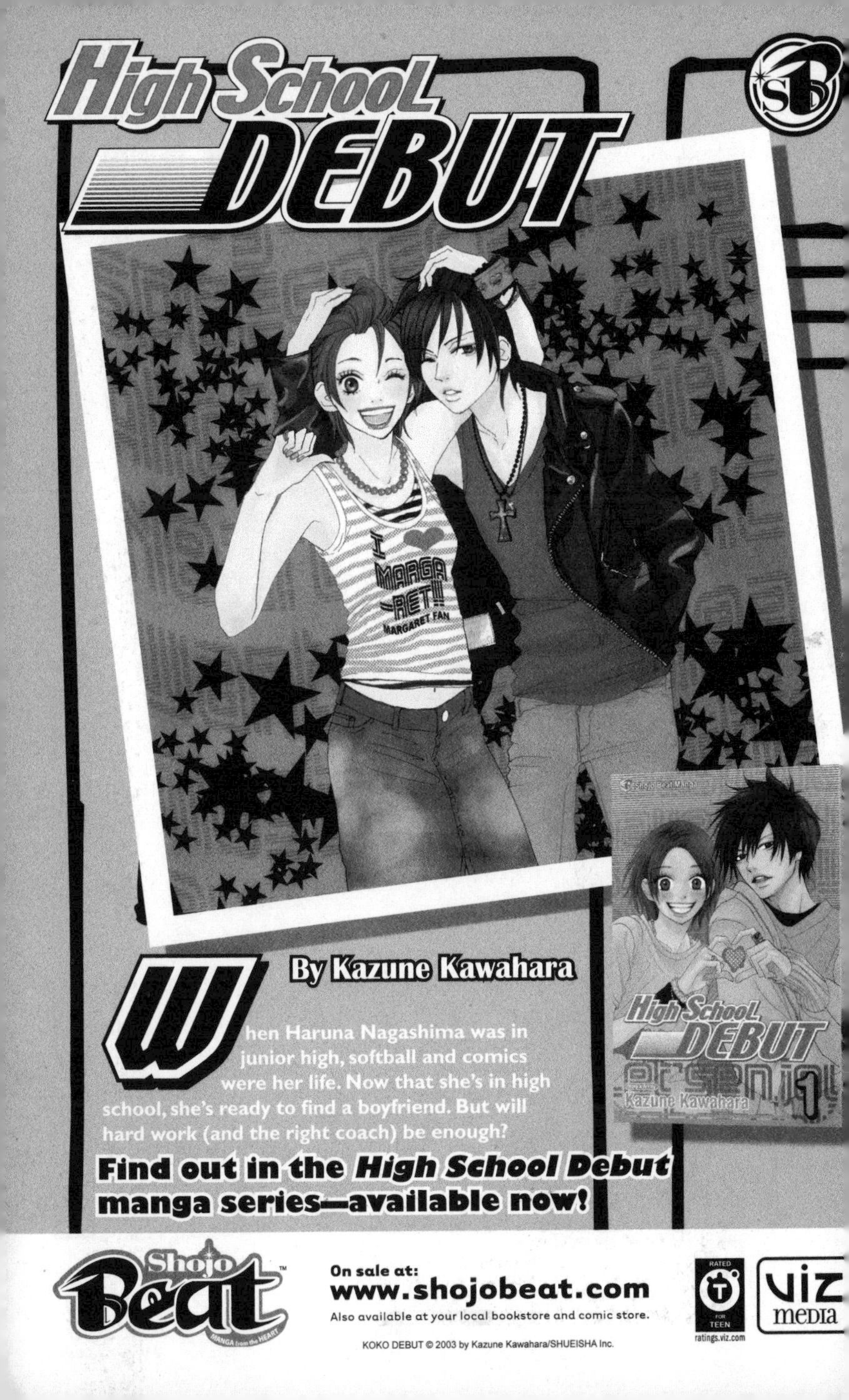
High School DEBUT
SB
By Kazune Kawahara
When Haruna Nagashima was in junior high, softball and comics were her life. Now that she's in high school, she's ready to find a boyfriend. But will hard work (and the right coach) be enough?
Find out in the High School Debut manga series—available now!
I ♥ MARGARET!! MARGARET FAN
Shojo Beat Manga
High School DEBUT
Kazune Kawahara
1
Shojo Beat MANGA from the HEART
On sale at:
www.shojobeat.com
Also available at your local bookstore and comic store.
RATED T FOR TEEN
ratings.viz.com
VIZ media
KOKO DEBUT © 2003 by Kazune Kawahara/SHUEISHA Inc.

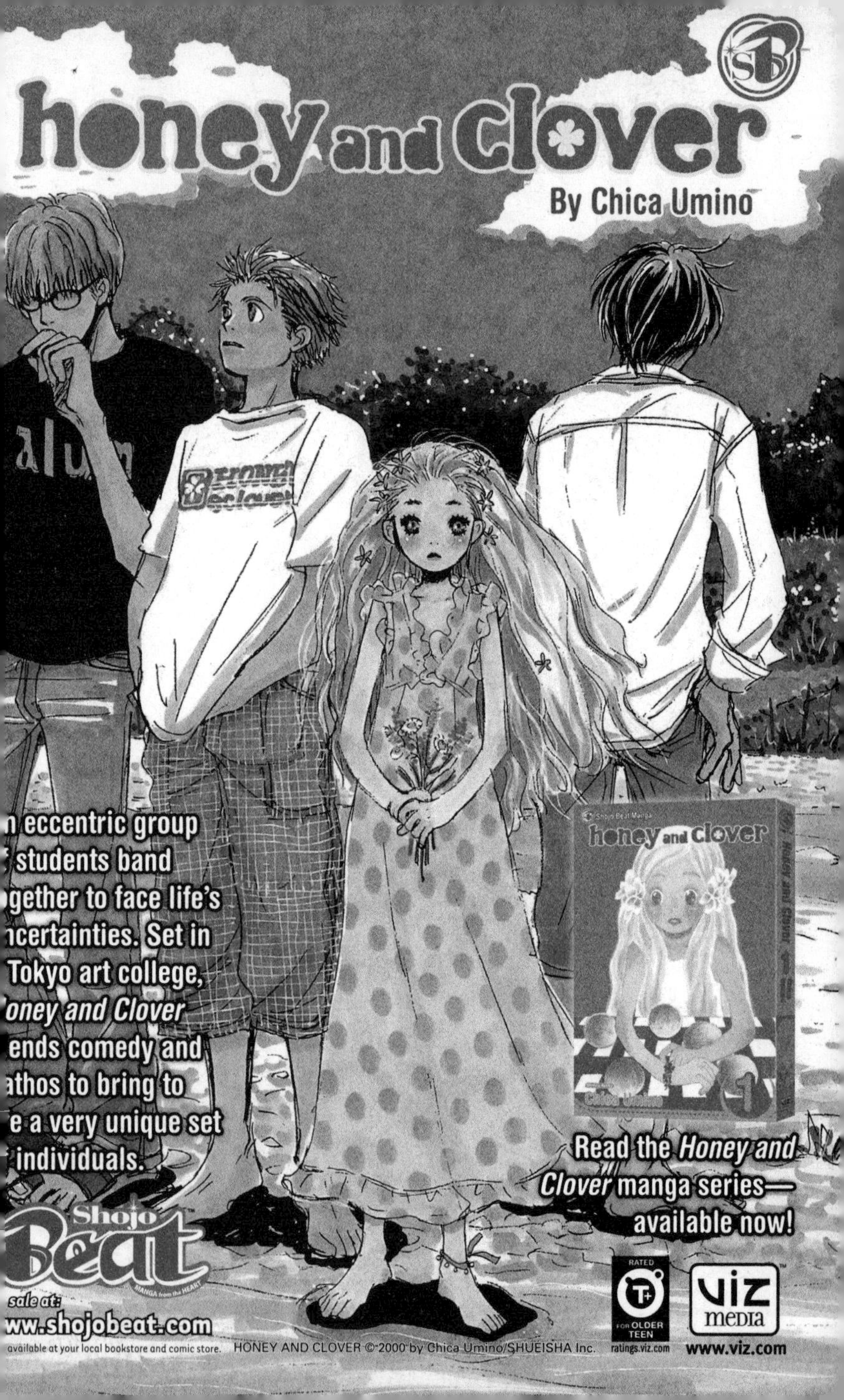

honey and clover
By Chica Umino
n eccentric group
students band
gether to face life's
ncertainties. Set in
Tokyo art college,
oney and Clover
ends comedy and
athos to bring to
e a very unique set
individuals.
Shojo Beat Manga
honey and clover
Chica Umino
1
Read the Honey and Clover manga series—available now!
Shojo Beat
MANGA from the HEART
sale at:
ww.shojobeat.com
available at your local bookstore and comic store.
HONEY AND CLOVER © 2000 by Chica Umino/SHUEISHA Inc.
RATED T+ FOR OLDER TEEN
ratings.viz.com
VIZ media
www.viz.com

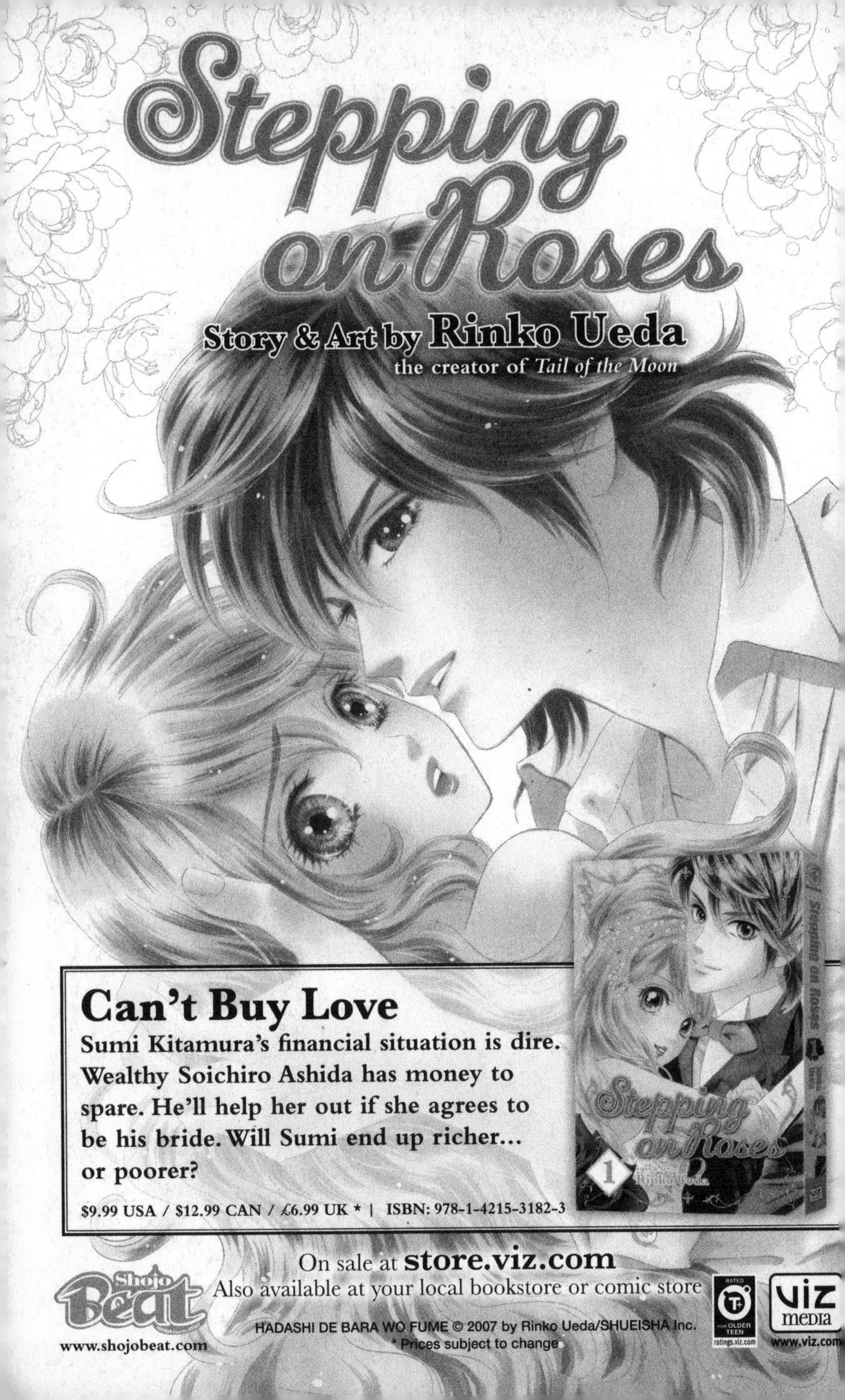
Stepping on Roses
Story & Art by Rinko Ueda
the creator of Tail of the Moon
Can't Buy Love
Sumi Kitamura's financial situation is dire. Wealthy Soichiro Ashida has money to spare. He'll help her out if she agrees to be his bride. Will Sumi end up richer... or poorer?
$9.99 USA / $12.99 CAN / £6.99 UK * | ISBN: 978-1-4215-3182-3
Stepping on Roses
1
Rinko Ueda
On sale at store.viz.com
Also available at your local bookstore or comic store
Shojo Beat
www.shojobeat.com
HADASHI DE BARA WO FUME © 2007 by Rinko Ueda/SHUEISHA Inc.
* Prices subject to change
RATED T+ FOR OLDER TEEN
ratings.viz.com
VIZ media
www.viz.com

Own the Complete **Arina Tanemura Collection!**

Mistress ★ Fortune

**Sakura Hime:
The Legend of Princess Sakura**

**The Gentlemen's
Alliance †**

**Short-Tempered
Melancholic and
Other Stories**

**The Gentlemen's Alliance †:
Arina Tanemura Illustrations**

Time Stranger Kyoko

I.O.N.

**The Arina Tanemura Collection:
The Art of Full Moon**

Full Moon

   VIZ MEDIA

Watch *Full Moon* **for FREE on VIZAnime.com**

www.shojobeat.com   www.viz.com

ALL WORKS © 1996-2008 by Arina Tanemura/SHUEISHA Inc.

Heaven's Will

by Satoru Takamiya

A Frightfully Unlikely Pair

Sudou Mikuzu has a very special talent—she can see ghosts. But when she becomes a magnet for all sorts of unwelcome monsters, she calls on her new cross-dressing exorcist friend, Seto, for help. Can the mismatched duo tackle Sudou's supernatural problems?

Find out in the *Heaven's Will* manga—available now!

On sale at www.shojobeat.com
Also available at your local bookstore and comic store.

www.viz.com

HEAVEN'S WILL © Satoru TAKAMIYA/Shogakukan Inc.

This is the last page.

In keeping with the original Japanese comic format, this book reads from right to left—so action, sound effects, and word balloons are completely reversed. This preserves the orientation of the original artwork—plus, it's fun! Check out the diagram shown here to get the hang of things, and then turn to the other side of the book to get started!